Reluctant Witness:

Robert Taylor, Hollywood, & Communism

By Linda Alexander

Reluctant Witness: Robert Taylor, Hollywood & Communism
© 2016. Linda Alexander. All rights reserved.

All illustrations are copyright of their respective owners, and are also reproduced here in the spirit of publicity. Whilst we have made every effort to acknowledge specific credits whenever possible, we apologize for any omissions, and will undertake every effort to make any appropriate changes in future editions of this book if necessary.

No part of this book may be reproduced in any form or by any means, electronic, mechanical, digital, photocopying or recording, except for the inclusion in a review, without permission in writing from the publisher.

Published in the USA by:
BearManor Media
P O Box 71426
Albany, Georgia 31708
www.bearmanormedia.com

Printed in the United States of America
ISBN   978-1-59393-968-7 (paperback)

Book & cover design and layout by Darlene Swanson • www.van-garde.com
Cover Photo: Courtesy Robert Taylor Family Private Collection

Robert Taylor, "The Man With the Perfect Profile."
Courtesy Robert Taylor Family Private Collection.

Contents

Acknowledgements and Gratitude vii

Dedication. xiii

Foreword. xv

The Last Hours xvii

Chapter One: At the Beginning 1

Chapter Two: Mother—or Wife?. 25

Chapter Three: College, Kathryn and Blanche, and Hollywood 39

Chapter Four: Being Discovered 63

Chapter Five: The Man with the Perfect Profile. 79

Chapter Six: Too Many Women, Too Little Time 117

Chapter Seven: Barbara—Wife or Mother?. 127

Chapter Eight: It's War!. 163

Chapter Nine: Hollywood vs. Washington 181

Chapter Ten: Washington Hunts Hollywood Communists. 209

Chapter Eleven: And What Are Friends For?. 257

Chapter Twelve: Lia Dileo—*The* Affair. 271

Chapter Thirteen: In Transition 283

Chapter Fourteen:	Ursula, and Bob's Exotic European Women	301
Chapter Fifteen:	Family Life … Finally	337
	Postscript	403
	Bibliography	405
	Index	411

Acknowledgements and Gratitude

This book was originally published in 2008. Well-received, it set straight a number of misconceptions about the life of actor, Robert Taylor. This version does not change the text content. However, I do want to respond to a few issues which arose after that book came out.

First, the title. I intentionally called Robert Taylor a "reluctant witness" for specific reasons. His participation in the 1947 House Un-American Activities Committee witch hunt—my commentary, not his—is the primary factor. The book will explain. However, that is not the only reason. The man himself was a reluctant witness to a whole host of historical issues—his meteoric rise to the top of a long list of Hollywood heartthrobs during the glamour days of the film industry is the first. He never asked for stardom. He forever seemed genuinely mystified over the attention he received. He was simply trying to make a living. His physical appearance, groomed personally by no less than Louis B. Mayer, propelled him forward and before he knew it, he was not only making a living but he was near the head of the pack.

Certainly not a bad thing for a young man from the Midwest, yet he was reluctant. He wanted to be known as more than just a "pretty face" and the studio wanted not much more out of him. This was the major cause of his reluctance in that arena.

He was also a reluctant front-of-the-line witness to the Second World

War. Never did he think or expect he would play such a part in this horror. Yet when he saw what was going on around him, he was determined to defend his country. His studio, however, didn't want to ruin his face, and they made his Navy work little more than a stint as a pilot trainer. His reluctance to take on nothing more than a matinee idol role became more obvious as time moved forward.

After the war, his return to civilian life, and to Hollywood, as well as to his wife, Barbara Stanwyck, brought out another reluctant period in his life. He and Barbara had changed. She was older than he, and they had married when he was still learning the ropes. Now that he had a bit of experience, in all manners of life, he felt he and Barbara were no longer moving in the same direction. He became a reluctant witness to the demise of their relationship, whereas she was determined to hold on.

Robert Taylor was a reluctant witness to many changes in Hollywood over the years, both slight and drastic. He proved to be Metro-Goldwyn-Mayer's (MGM's) longest-running contract actor. In this position, he saw the industry move from one stage of being to another, and yet to another. A lot of history went by as Robert Taylor steadfastly did his job as an actor. He became a reluctant witness to the dawn of television; initially he wanted nothing of it. When he realized he had to go along or go by the wayside, he reluctantly went along.

In his later years, he was a reluctant witness yet again to the changing winds of politics. He saw himself as a patriot. Friends and compatriots, those who shared his ultra-conservative viewpoint, wanted him to stand up publicly, in powerful ways, for their shared values. They believed he could be the perfect individual to move their state, and possibly country, forward. Yet he was reluctant to do so for many reasons, all of which you'll read about. He had good motive to decline a move into yet another bright, worldwide spotlight.

I titled the book as I did because Robert Taylor was a reluctant, yet active, witness to so much history—Hollywood's, the country's, and his own.

The other change I made for this edition is the addition of photos. The lack of photos proved to be about the only criticism I originally received with the first edition. At the time, my then-publisher wasn't able to add them. This time, I'm doing it right, including professional and intimate family photographs, most of which came through the gracious help of Robert Taylor's daughter, Tessa, and son, Terry, as well as Robert Taylor blogger, Judith Hanhisalo.

So on I go now with the rest of this book. . . .

In 1937, Robert Taylor was asked to write his life story. His answer: "I haven't lived my life yet." Still, he gave readers of the *Nebraska State Journal* an encapsulated version of the first twenty-six years. Ten years later, he appeared before the House Un-American Activities Committee in their attempt to rid Hollywood of Communism, in what became a moment on record. Now it is 2015, seventy-eight years after he made that comment. He has since lived his life. I hope the following is a fair and as-accurate-as-possible rendition of what *he* might have written.

I've put his story together using his words from letters and verifiable quotes; memories of family and closest friends; reliable press; government documents; autobiographies of other Golden Era stars; and, after more direct options were exhausted, through what I perceived to be well-researched written material.

I had "hunches" when I began which I was certain were true. Hunches, however, aren't what a biography should be based on, and I set out to find proof and came up with documentation to verify each sixth sense with which I started. There are many misconceptions out there about Robert Taylor and it's time to correct them.

I thank those who knew and loved Bob: his family—*Ursula, Terry, Tessa,* and *Manuela.* They trusted me to tell a fair, true story, and bravely allowed me to show their lives in the process. I'm grateful to *Ivy Mooring* for her love for Bob, stories she shared, letters and documents provided. We should all have such a friend. *Art Reeves* loved Bob as only a man can love another male buddy, with deep understanding and abiding loyalty. *Chad Everett* opened his heart to show a side of Bob which wouldn't have been seen otherwise. From what I've learned, Bob thought as much of Chad as Chad thought of him. *Hal Bowen* knew Bob as a good friend toward the end of Bob's life, and his vision was invaluable. *Lia DiLeo* was privy to a view of Bob different from all others.

I personally thank: *E. A. Kral*, who became my friend, and without whom this book wouldn't have been possible. A more dedicated scholar, full of knowledge and love for his home state of Nebraska, would be hard to find. *Sue Sindlar* was instrumental in the early days and I'll never forget her kindness and friendship. She lived in Robert Taylor's family home in Beatrice, Nebraska, and allowed me to stay with her when I visited town for research and events. His essence still permeated the home.

Dan Bessie, son of blacklisted writer Alvah Bessie, offered a balance of the other side of the HUAC issue without judging Bob Taylor or his choices. *Beth Naden Keller*, a schoolmate of Bob's, gave her memories and her scrapbook in order that I could have firsthand information. The Gage County Historical Society and Museum, specifically *Kent Wilson* and *Lesa Arterburn*, were always there to be of assistance. *Laureen Riedesel* of the Beatrice Public Library is a credit to her city and state. *Randy Riddle* and *Ernest Cunningham* were also helpful. *Judith Hanhisalo* offered me my pick of photographs from her vast personal collection of Robert Taylor memorabilia.

Many supported the project: Bob Taylor's fans, of which they are countless; Brugh family members; Joan Benny; Roy Brewer; Howard Eakes, Bill Martin, Bill Moore and families; Peter Ford; Larry Gates; Harry Hay; James Jolis; Janet Leigh; Joe Love; Robert Parmerter; Barbara Reeves; Robert Stack; Peggy Jackson, Freedom of Information Act Officer, United States Government; Linda Sebree, DePauw University Archives; Debra Summers, The American School of Osteopathy; Beth Weinhardt, Westerville Library, Archives of the Anti-Saloon League of America; Brittany and Barbara, St. John's Medical Center; Steve Browning, Parry Lodge; Meredith Leonard, Meredy.com; Robert Rotter, Glamour Girls of the Silver Screen; D. D., Cinemovie; Lloyd Billingsley; Stephen Cox; Joseph Farah; Jeanelle Kleveland; Robert

Acknowledgements and Gratitudes

Mayhew; Ralph Moratz; Gina Gen; John Meroney; Robert Parmerter; Rosemary Rippe; Daniel Selznick; Nancy Warnock; Jane Ellen Wayne; Jeff Wayne; Shirleen Wolfe; citizens of Jackson, Wyoming and surrounding areas. And thanks to BearManor Media for appreciating classic entertainment! If I have missed anyone, my deepest apologies. It certainly was not intentional.

Last, but never least, my husband, Tom, who realized how important this book was for me and did everything in his power to help me succeed; my parents, all of them; my great friends; and, as always, all of my children.

Linda Alexander
Montgomery, Alabama

Dedication

This book is dedicated to classic Hollywood in all its shining glory, and to all those under-appreciated actors who all those years ago gave us the best they had to give. They entertained us, took us to places we could only get to within our imaginations; their ability to make us believe allowed us to take such glorious imaginary celluloid journeys. Your kind is long gone and, sadly, it seems as if the likes of classic Hollywood may never be seen again.

Taylor Family 1995: Tessa, Terry, and Ursula.
Courtesy author's personal collection.

Foreword by Terry Taylor

On one hand, he would be embarrassed that a book of this caliber be devoted to telling his life story. On the other hand, he would be grateful that so much of the nonsense about a no-nonsense man has finally been revealed and honestly addressed by author, Linda Alexander.

Robert Taylor was my father. In my humble opinion and that of countless others, Hollywood has never seen an actor as dedicated to and respectful of his craft. As strongly as he felt about his profession, so too was his conviction and absolute belief that the spread of Communism in the United States was being fueled by the very industry of which he was a part.

He died during the prime of his family life, well before the rest of his life could be played out. He died before he could witness on earth the extraordinary accomplishments of his close friends, Ronald and Nancy Reagan. He died before he could be their guest at the White House, and proudly watch Ronnie insist, "Mr. Gorbachev, tear down this wall."

What did not die was his influence on his friend, who, as president, brought down that wall of Communism. What did not die is a distinguished body of film and television work starring "my father." What did not die is the legacy of a no-nonsense man who left his professional, patriotic and principled endowment on our world today.

My sincere thanks to Linda Alexander who dug deep and spread wide her copious research and leaps of literary faith, that reveal stunningly an untold story.

Terry Taylor, Robert Taylor's son

Introduction: The Last Hours

"Late at night,
In the dark,
When the movie house is out...
Oh, I swear
You can hear
Every hero's heartbeat.

Don't go believin'
Hollywood dreamin.'
All that you're seeing is not always true.
Characters winnin,' cowboys bleedin,'
Preacher is grinnin' –
He's grinnin' at you.

Every hero cries—sometimes.
You can see it in his eyes—sometimes,
When you bring him down to size...
Every hero cries—sometimes.
No matter how he tries—sometimes,
And the hero never dies...
But *every* hero cries.

Every Hero Cries by James Jolis
Copyright Jolisongs
Permission granted

In May of 1969, Bob and Ursula had one of those rare quiet times when they were together alone in their bedroom at their ranch. He was aware he was terminally ill. In his quiet, unassuming way, he had demanded to be taken home from the hospital. He'd always had a manner about him which, when intentionally employed, brooked no arguments and he used this technique only when necessary. This was one of those times. He never forced a confrontation. He hated confrontations.

After living most of his adult life as a vibrant public figure, he was aware the desire to go home, to be enveloped in the peace and comfort of personal surroundings one last time, would create logistical problems. Frail and unable to walk under his own steam, there was no way he could leave the hospital without being noticed.

Still, he insisted, and Ursula, his love, was always willing to work any miracle to do everything within her power to make him comfortable. She had organized the extensive preparations with the help of Art Reeves, their dear friend and ever-present ranch manager. The press, camped out nearby with vulture-like eagerness for any word on his condition, had to be outsmarted.

The plan finally worked. For the most part, reporters understood, and Bob had come home. His ranch was his heaven. He needed to be home among his acres of land, animals of every kind, furniture he and Ursula lovingly placed in each room, and the ghostly memories of the full and finally happy life he'd lived. The scene felt right to him.

As he and Ursula talked, he stoically faced the fear of that soon-to-arrive day when he would die, when he would no longer be a physical presence. As his illness had progressed, he'd had time to contemplate this sad fact. Outwardly, he ignored and talked around the obvious. Anything and everything but his mortality was discussed.

Bob had never been open with his heart. If anyone knew what was inside his soul, Ursula was the one. But the end of his life was too petrifying to put into words, even with the woman who had defined the real meaning of love

Introduction: The Last Hours

for him. He'd told her much over their years together, but had never told her all. He had never told anyone everything.

Instead, he acted as if his cancer was no more an aggravation than a fender bender on a sweaty hot day. His illness was about to take him away from everyone and everything he knew and loved, but he seemed to ignore that. Instead, he made efforts to comfort Ursula with the inanities of their life through the veil of his dry and sarcastic humor. They shared mindless chatter about their children and upcoming summer plans.

At fifty-eight, Bob had a lifetime of thoughts he wanted to impart before he died, but he didn't know how to reveal to his wife of fifteen years what was deeply buried within his soul. So much wasted time and here he was. Now, the time had grown too late to make amends.

There had been too many years of domination over his true personality. His overbearing mother had started the trend. His first wife, Barbara Stanwyck, had continued the effort, trying to mold him into a man he was not. Louis B. Mayer, MGM's authoritarian studio head, had signed his paycheck for almost all of his years in the movie business, and he made sure Bob toed the line. These people had been instrumental in helping to teach him a lesson they weren't aware they were teaching. He learned through them that he was his own best ally, and his own truest confidante. He had had many buddies over the years, but few close friends.

Now in bed, weak and barely holding on, Bob's true cronies, "men's men," all of them, tried to be a part of this final time. He knew they wanted to console him and he loved them for that. The effort cost him too much, though, and he didn't have the strength anymore. He made sure they knew he was happy to see them, but with his typical Bob Taylor attitude of light sarcasm, he successfully brushed aside their attempts to bring out his deeper concerns. He was at the end, everyone around him was aware he knew the truth, and there was no point in dwelling on that. Instead, he did what he could to make light of the last scene of his personal tragedy.

Chad Everett had wanted to be there, but Bob forbid his visit. After he and Chad met a few years earlier on the set of *Johnny Tiger*, Chad had become like a son to him. He couldn't bear to have young Chad see him as he was now.

Bob had been the mentor, the knowledgeable teacher, strong in mind and body, and Chad looked up to him. This adulation made Bob uncomfortable at times, but deep inside he was touched. They enjoyed spending time together, and socialized off the set, along with their wives. Through the friendship, Bob felt he'd learned as much about the new generation of Hollywood actor as Chad had about the old. Bob wanted Chad's memory of him to remain that of the strong advisor, in body and in mind.

Throughout this ordeal, he continued for the most part to act as if he were emotionally unaffected. Whether he was with visitors, his beloved wife, or Art, a man who became more of a family member than their onsite ranch manager, Bob's last call, his final act, was to not bring any of them down with him.

He attempted to comfort older friends with talk of their mutual love for the outdoors. He teased and cajoled the kids, encouraging their vocal opinion of him as their silly daddy. With Ursula, he was grateful for her presence, and her continuing devotion, love, and determination to do everything possible for him. He could ask for nothing more. His concerns were for their children and for her well-being. This last year had been terrible for Ursula.

He would never burden her with his deeply-imbedded fears, but he had one selfish weakness he couldn't deny himself. He never wanted Ursula out of his sight. If he reached out to her, he wanted her there to take his hand and hold tight . . . to the end.

A week or so later, the time came. Finally. Soon all the never-ending pain would stop. One week and a few days after he had come home to his ranch, Bob seemed to know in every part of his being that he could no longer continue the fight. He was tired, physically from his illness and mentally from the great acting job he'd played out for far too many years. The time *was* here.

Through the fog of his pain and drug-hazed mind, he was aware he was being taken back to the dreaded hospital. He got it into his head that this move was his stepdaughter's fault. Manuela, wearing only her pajamas, stood

Ursula and Bob. Courtesy Robert Taylor Family Private Collection.

next to her mother in the front yard as his bed was lifted into the ambulance. He focused on her and croaked, "Mani, you did this!" He saw her shudder and turn away, heard her cry, "No!" but nothing made sense to him anymore. He saw Ursula put her arm around Mani's shoulders and hug her before Ursula moved to get in the vehicle with him, and the doors were closed forever on that part of his life.

He and Manuela had had their troubles! But as Ursula took his hand in hers, and the ground underneath started to move, his wife's low and soothing words told him Mani had nothing to do with this development. He was aware the girl loved him as if he were her real father. Ursula had assured him, and made sure Mani knew he cared for her. She had nothing to do with him being returned to the hospital.

He nodded, and tried to ask Ursula to apologize for him. She made comforting noises, and rubbed his hot hand. "Everything will be okay," she told him through her tears. "Everything will be okay." She said the words over and over, all the way to the hospital, as they took him to his room, and long into the night and as the sun rose on the next day.

Later in the evening, Bob closed his eyes for the last time. As he slowly slipped away, he surely knew he had done more than his share of keeping his customers satisfied, in his professional and in his personal life. Throughout his days, he was most often tabbed as no more than a dependable, adequate actor.

All those critics over the years had been dead wrong. Robert Taylor had been a reluctant, but agreeable, witness to a world of make-believe. That world drew him in, and he had taken all that was offered to him. His entire life had been a smart, intentionally well-crafted study in acting. He had acted as others expected him to act, acted to conform, and acted as the means to an end. He had acted to become Robert Taylor, a man most often seen from the outside. Only *he* knew his performance had always been exactly that, a performance. He was born Arlington Brugh, a small-town boy from Nebraska, and he would die being that same small-town boy from Nebraska.

Those around him felt his essence ebbing away. It was as if he knew he had to make this journey. This was one situation over which he had no control. Death. His death. The Director had spoken, and the time was now for Robert Taylor to follow through with his final act. Again, as he always had, he did exactly what was required of him in that moment. . . .

CHAPTER ONE:
At The Beginning

> "Blessed be all sorrows, torments, hardships, endurances that demand courage. Blessed be these things, for of these things cometh the making of a man. Make of me a man, to be afraid of nothing, to be ready for everything—love, friendship, success. To take it if it comes—to care nothing if these things are not for me. Make me brave."
>
> – Robert Taylor's personal credo, as taken by him from Hugh S. Walpole's 1913 novel, *Fortitude*

Ruth Stanhope was a petite, frail, dark-haired eighteen-year old in 1903, and she was in love with Spangler Andrew Brugh. Andrew and his family were Ruth's neighbors, and he and Ruth had opportunity to catch sight of each other on Sundays, when families in their small town of Filley, Nebraska, came together for religious services. Ruth was considered a charmer by virtue of her small rounded build, and deep blue eyes able to look right into a person. Andrew definitely noticed her. When she tossed her dark, luxuriantly curly black hair away from her creamy face to coyly laugh at one of his comments, Andrew became tongue-tied.

Her family, particularly her father, was fiercely protective. When Ruth began courting, Andrew didn't know she was seriously ill. Doctors didn't give her much chance for life beyond the next few years. She had a weak heart, which made her short of breath and unable to stay out of bed for long stretches of time.

When he found out, Andrew still couldn't help but fall in love. Her 5 feet 2 inch frame was overshadowed by his stout farmer's build. She told him she felt protected standing next to him, tilting her head back to look up into his dark eyes. Having a woman depend on him and trust him to take care of her in all situations was a wonderful sensation.

Ruth never doubted Andrew's devotion. When they were together, she was certain he could make everything better, including her deteriorating health.

After an appropriate courtship, Andrew approached Ruth's father, a large, forbidding but kindly man, and asked for Ruth's hand in marriage. Father Stanhope sat Andrew down and patiently explained the gravity of Ruth's situation. She could never be a normal housewife. She would probably spend the rest of her years in bed. She would likely never have children. He would not have his daughter living anywhere but in the immediate call of her family, and she must continue to receive the costly medical care which had become a regular part of her existence.

Andrew was from a staunchly religious and conservative background. His family was of German heritage; his people had come to the Midwest from Pennsylvania Dutch country. Ruth's brood was Republican Methodists with solid English and Scottish roots. Their religious and social backgrounds complimented each other. They both leaned on their faith, believing God would get them through all trials which came their way.

Andrew was determined to marry and take care of Ruth, no matter how little time was left to her. He agreed without hesitation to all Father Stanhope's conditions, and he and Ruth were wed on January 21, 1904. They had a double ring ceremony with Ruth's sister, Ethel, and her betrothed, Robert Flaws.

Almost as soon as Andrew and Ruth said, "I do," Andrew was given equal partnership in Father Stanhope's local grain business, complete with a name change to Stanhope and Brugh. Filley, Nebraska, had fifty residents, two grain elevators, a depot, and a post office. Andrew and Ruth lived in

Spangler Andrew Brugh and Ruth Adela Stanhope, married in Filley, Gage County, Nebraska. Courtesy The Gage County (NE) Historical Society collection.

a home of their own, an uninsulated, one-story wood-frame structure with five rooms. They used outside hand pumps to get household water, and had an outdoor toilet.

Their lives were anything but normal, and they were soon reminded of this. Ruth loved being married but after only a year, she spent more and more time in bed. She gasped for breath over the most minor provocation. Andrew did all the housework, the shopping, and the cooking. Ruth continued to receive regular medical treatment; doctors shook their heads and threw up their hands, unable to pinpoint anything specific causing her condition to worsen.

Ruth's health fluctuated; she and her family never knew what to expect. For days she was bedridden, hardly moving, breathless, fearing each beat of her heart might be her last. She was incapable of contributing anything to her marriage. The next day, she'd be out of bed and keeping Andrew company; busy, hungry for a full meal. But as soon as she took a turn for the better, the cycle would reinvent itself, and Ruth would be back in bed, more ill than the last time. Specialists predicted Ruth would die before she was twenty-five.

The year was 1909; she and Andrew had been married five years. His devotion to Ruth never waned; despite their problems, he adored her as much as the day they wed. He was frantic and deeply frustrated over the medical community's inability to find a way to help his wife lead a prolonged, more natural life.

By now, he was well-established in the grain business but because of Ruth's need for round-the-clock medical attention, the couple's debts mounted. After careful consideration and long talks with both Ruth and his father-in-law, Andrew decided to give up his half of the business and go to medical school. Father Stanhope financially backed the idea, and Andrew and Ruth moved to Kirksville, Missouri.

The American School of Osteopathy in Kirksville was the first in its field, chartered less than twenty years earlier. Andrew found a place to live, enrolled in a four-year medical course specializing in heart diseases, and prepared to be a full-time student. He was determined to find a way to cure his wife's illness.

Ruth became intrigued with her husband's studies. She found herself lonely and inactive with long days to herself, living in a strange town, and no family or friends nearby to keep her company. She cajoled Andrew into letting her attend classes with him on the days she felt well enough, going so far as to enroll in the program.

Despite her illness, she managed to go to school several days a week. Later on in life, she told a magazine, "Arm in arm, day after day, we would go off to classes together; side by side, evening after evening, we would study from the same books – sharing a great adventure."

The Brughs were called back to the family in a rush at the end of their first year in school because the Stanhope's grain business was in need of extra hands. They expected to only be there a short time, but stayed three years. Andrew was forced to forego his formal medical schooling but he diligently continued to study.

Ruth and Andrew had been married for seven years when they learned they were going to have a baby. Ruth's delicate medical condition demanded she reconsider her pregnancy, but she had always wanted a child and wouldn't allow any discussion to the contrary. She was determined to have this baby and she went to bed for the remainder of her term. Though he'd only had a year's worth of any sort of medical training, Andrew directed her care, and he was instrumental in pulling her through the arduous nine months. She was under the official supervision of a local physician and surgeon.

At 7 a.m. on August 5, 1911, in Filley, Nebraska, on a day when the sun already promised to scorch the local cornfields, Ruth Brugh delivered a healthy baby boy. She nearly died, and the child was instantly handed over to a nurse. Ruth was still the center of attention. The birth fully invalided her and for weeks, no one could predict what would happen to her.

Her inner strength and hardy family stock once again pulled Ruth through. When she was finally well enough to be aware of what was going on around her, she didn't remember a moment of her intensive labor or the baby's delivery. She was still weak, but demanded to see the child, refusing to take no for an answer.

What should they name him? Spangler was a Brugh family name, handed down through the genera-

Infant Spangler Arlington Brugh with mother and father. Courtesy Robert Taylor Family Private Collection.

Probably the first studio picture of Arlington. Courtesy Robert Taylor Family Private Collection.

tions. Without question, Ruth decided, the boy's first name would continue this tradition. As for his middle name, again Ruth was determined. Some time ago, she had read a romantic novel and loved the hero's name: Arlington.

The baby was dubbed Spangler Arlington Brugh, and called by his middle name. Years later, Ruth admitted that family and friends had questioned her choice. She said they had asked if she'd been "trying to kill the child." Others marveled at how he ever lived to maturity under such a weighty name.

A seventeen year old girl was hired to take over Arlington's care when he was only two weeks old. She moved in with the family and became responsible for all duties relating to Baby Arlington, staying upwards of a year. With Ruth in a weak state and Andrew working full-time in the grain business, as well as holding himself accountable for his wife's well-being, the child was left in the hands of his young caretaker. His mother likely never nursed him.

Ruth and the grain business had started to strengthen by the time the baby took his first steps, and Andrew and his family left Filley for a few months in Muskogee, Oklahoma, to care for family-owned farm property. The trip was short, and they went on from there to Kirksville so Andrew could resume his studies. The nurse did not go with them.

Ruth was still sickly and unable to care for Arlington on a full-time basis, though her health slowly improved. She was known to derive a great amount of satisfaction from the frailties which accompanied her infirmities, and took advantage of the attention. She continued to demand her husband's constant care and when amidst friends and family, she played up her illness. Andrew was dutiful and never far from her side, working hard at his studies while making sure she was as comfortable and happy as possible. He lived his life for Ruth, going to school to become a doctor so he could cure her, while carrying on another round-the-clock position as her home doctor, nurse, housekeeper and never-waning emotional support. He was also now the round-the-clock baby nurse.

Arlington in a studio photo with his mother, Ruth. Courtesy Robert Taylor Family Private Collection.

Andrew packed up his son and took him along to classes as soon as Arlington was mobile, since there was no one else to take care of the boy. His thick, dark curls and big blue eyes caught everyone's attention. He never became excited over the fuss from onlookers, always sitting quietly and well-behaved at the back of the classroom, often falling asleep. No accounts ever portrayed him as reacting in any expected curious or over-excited childlike manner. He appeared either bored or politely interested in what was going on around him. From the earliest age, he seemed to intuitively understand his mother's health problems and his father's heavy burdens.

As time went on, Arlington observed everything around him. He saw things in that classroom other kids his age and far older never could have imagined. The memories stayed with him throughout his life. "I will never forget those dissection classes and the smell of dead bodies," he said in later years.

He was a tag-along, by nature of his reason for being there. He was not integral to the activities he witnessed. His father presented him with a small knife and whetstone so he would feel a part of what went on around him. Watching as cadavers were cut up and examined became commonplace for him. Medical terms heard before he was able to form words of his own, antiseptic smells of medicinal compounds, and images of death as related to life were all part of Arlington's earliest years, as normal for him as a day on the playground might be for another child.

He heard Latin words and phrases every day at school, and at home his father and mother discussed studies and medical situations. The contrast between the languages seemed to confuse the boy as he attempted to form words of his own. He tried to teach himself Latin, working on the words he heard while at school with his dad.

The formal Latin, together with the more commonplace English, jumbled and interrelated in his mind and Arlington became a stutterer. He repeated medical terms by rote when he wasn't stuttering. His mother would later remember that when he was about two-and-a-half, he came home and told her, "Dr. Ashmore was telling Daddy about neur-as-then-ia today." His stuttering grew pronounced and really alarmed his parents. He would stand in front of Ruth and take thirty seconds to say, "Mother."

Andrew was over-extended. He continued to care for Arlington, never forsaking his material needs, and making sure he was always fed and looked after properly. Yet the boy's emotional nurturing was sadly lacking. Andrew didn't have the time, and Ruth was most often self-absorbed. When she did pay attention, she often paraded him in front of others as if he were a prized pet. He never had a strand of hair out of place, or a spot of dirt on his fancy pants. His cheeks reddened each time his mother's friends made a fuss, and his extraordinary good looks became an ongoing embarrassment when he was no more than a small boy.

At the Beginning

To their credit as parents, Ruth and Andrew joined together to address Arlington's stuttering. He was discouraged from playing with kids his age, particularly by his mother. He'd had no contact with children at all; his life revolved around his parents and his father's adult, scholarly colleagues. Andrew and Ruth conferred on how to help their son learn to speak properly, and decided to take him to the country. They rented rooms in a farm outside of Kirksville in hopes the clean air and simpler life would help Arlington come out of his shell. Maybe the change would offer him the freedom to truly act like a child for the first time.

The farm's owners had a young boy near Arlington's age, and the new environment worked wonders. His mother's strict tendencies relented somewhat and he took immediately to the serenity and simplicity. He was a natural on a horse and rode every day. He learned to fish and hunt, doing well by both right from the start. Arlington Brugh seemed to have been born to the outdoors, rather than to the inside of a classroom. At first, his stuttering caused barriers with his new housemates and other local children. As he grew more comfortable in his surroundings, he learned to be less nervous and to slow down, and his speech reflected the changes.

Arlington's success was short-lived. He was five when his parents made another move to Fremont, Nebraska. His father had graduated and become a full-fledged osteopath. Ruth's health greatly recovered and she was seen as a miracle by the close-knit medical community. News of her healing spread, and Dr. Spangler Andrew Brugh, as caretaker on record, suddenly had promising opportunities ahead of him. He didn't have a practice, though, and they had moved to Freemont to decide what his next steps should be.

Their son entered another phase in his as-yet short life. Arlington and his family had already moved four times in five years, not staying in one place for any length of time, and he was never able to feel a sense of belonging. He found himself happiest on the farm amongst the animals and nature, but his happiness was fleeting.

His mother didn't approve of formal education for young children and resisted the idea of sending her son to school. Once the family settled in Fremont, she relented and allowed him to enter kindergarten. He attended one semester and was "promoted," quickly growing bored with "cutting up paper dolls," as he later called the activity. He did not attend any other school while there.

Arlington was encouraged by his mother to read, and he read constantly. Andrew was now a working physician, and this left Ruth with only her son to occupy her days. She finally went into the job of full-time mother with all her might, pouring her questionable energy into creating a cocooned life for her boy. At the same time, she continued to magnify her frailties, drawing Arlington into the "care for me" mold she required of everyone around her.

Arlington reading with his mother. Courtesy Robert Taylor Family Private Collection.

Ruth fussed extravagantly over Arlington's clothing, dressing him in immaculate, often effeminate outfits. She combed his thick, curly dark hair into a deep shine, and not a strand was ever the least bit out of place. With the country life now behind him, he was occasionally allowed outside to watch neighborhood children at play, but was instructed not to allow himself to get dirty in any way. Most days, Ruth kept Arlington to herself, filling the time with long walks, talks, lunches, and reading.

The dinner hour brought his father home for what by most accounts was a regimented mealtime. Arlington, now called Arly, was an adolescent, given to natural periods of defiance and efforts to be independent. Dad refused to put up with the slightest show of temper. If Arlington wouldn't eat what was in front of him, he was sent to bed and didn't get fed that night.

Years later, after he'd become Robert Taylor, he was quoted as saying, "... I don't ever remember being able to evade any punishments ... the notable thing about these spankings was not that there were many of them but their reliability. As sure as they were due, I collected."

Andrew and Ruth never argued, and they expected their child to live as sedately as they did. They did not discuss his upbringing in front of him. Ruth was strong-willed and opinionated but in every instance of discipline, she deferred disciplinary matters to her husband without open shows of disagreement. The few times where she thought matters might have been handled differently, she still remained quiet and allowed Andrew to hold the upper hand.

Both Andrew and Ruth emphasized a lifestyle of high, strict morals, respect for authority, ultra-conservative viewpoints about the world and what went on around them, responsibility coupled with accountability, and being rewarded only when honestly earned. They attended the local Methodist church wherever they lived, didn't smoke or drink, and were strongly opposed to the use of profanity. Theirs was the epitome of a conservative middle-American, working-class family of that era.

In September of 1917, when Arly was six, his father found a home in Beatrice, Nebraska. Time for yet another move. The town's population was slightly under ten thousand, a considerable jump from other places where the family had lived. Beatrice was the fifth largest city in the state, had a bus system, hospital, large established churches, and a railroad station serviced by daily trains. The town was located at the intersection of two graveled transcontinental highways. In the Brugh's experience, this was the "big city."

Andrew finally acquired his own medical practice. He went into partnership with an acquaintance, Dr. P. Y. Gass. Dr. Gass had an existing and sizeable clientele and the year Andrew joined him, he served as the President of the Nebraska Association of Osteopaths. Andrew was in good and prosperous company.

By all accounts, he was an excellent osteopath. His patients thought him considerate, outgoing, well-dressed, gentle, and everyone said he had a good sense of humor. He had been raised in a German household where he regularly spoke the language, and there were many Germans in the Beatrice area. Hearing his booming voice through his office door as he spoke to a patient in his mother tongue was common. He ordered first aid procedures, delivered babies, made house calls, and carefully followed state restrictions. He was law-abiding to a fault, and played strictly by the rules. He did have a soft spot, though, and offered full services whether or not his patients could pay his fee. His generosity was known throughout every corner of the community.

In addition to his nearly miraculous work with his wife, Andrew was credited with curing another patient. A neighborhood woman had fractured her larynx, and traditional doctors could find no way to bring her speech back. Andrew saw her faithfully, every day for a year, and "manipulated" her throat. Ultimately, the woman recovered her full ability to talk.

With Ruth's health vastly improved, she often worked as a receptionist in her husband's office, sometimes making rounds with him. Patients would occasionally come to their home for treatment. The Brughs were a visible and well-respected family in the Beatrice community. Arly's care while his mother was away fell to an unknown party. They knew enough people by this time to be able to procure the help, and they had the income.

Though Andrew had found his professional niche, this didn't quell his feeling that they still hadn't found the right home. They had purchased a house in Beatrice when they came to town. Still, by 1921, time for another transition arrived. They rented out that house, and moved into the first floor of another only blocks away, owned by a kindly single woman who quickly became known to Arly as Auntie Neuhauser.

The structure was a warm, two-story, wood-frame home. Inside were deep brown woods, many windows and a sweeping staircase going up to Auntie Neuhauser's quarters. A friendly open foyer opened into a living and dining area, with a kitchen in the back and two bedrooms to the right.

Arly's room was tiny, situated right off the dining area. He could smell meals being prepared in the kitchen, hear his father discussing the day's news with his mother as they sat peacefully in the living room, and always, always, sense Auntie Neuhauser's solid presence in her apartment above him. He was often invited to have breakfast with her. By his admission, she made wonderful pancakes, and he delighted in the moments they spent together.

Neighbors suspected Andrew did most of the household chores and carried the largest part of the domestic load, while he also kept up with his practice. He did the laundry and, when necessary, some of the cooking. Arly must have assisted.

Ruth did put in some time in the kitchen. She would cook large, elaborate extended family meals when her sisters or others would visit. On Christmas, cousins and sisters and husbands would spend the day with the Brughs, and one cousin recalled, "Uncle Spang [Andrew] would always have to leave to deliver a baby, but really returned as Santa. . . ."

Arly kept these special family moments deep in his heart. Over the years, his mind mixed them with the great number of memories he had of times spent at his father's side, in the elder Brugh's capacity as medical student and doctor. As Bob Taylor, he later said, "I can remember still the odors of iodoform and hot corn bread and hot chocolate which were the mixed aromas of my dad's surgery and my mother's kitchen—the smell of home to me."

Ruth continued to play on her earlier infirmities. Public perception was that she enjoyed her illness. The belief may have come from the fact that Andrew was accustomed to his caretaker role, becoming a doctor to ensure her well-being, and he never stepped out of those shoes. He was not an emotional weakling, but Ruth had the dominant personality, a fact which had been part of their marriage from the beginning. Ruth made a life out of getting her way, and Andrew had learned to live that life with her.

He continued to take Arly with him when he had medical work to which he had to attend. By this point, the child was old enough to go on house calls, and he took in all he saw and heard. Andrew never spared reality, calling his son, "Buddy," and Arly witnessed everything from childbirth to death. He learned to identify specific illnesses by their odor. He could tell one disease from the other by listening to its qualities. He began to enjoy the bonding, and wanted to do everything like his dad.

The day came for Arly to enter first grade. He would finally be able to regularly interact with kids his own age. He had to have been excited.

Ruth had her own ideas. She continued to delight in dressing him in feminine outfits. On his first day at school, she required him to wear a "Little Lord Fauntleroy" suit, consisting of short black velvet trousers and a white silk blouse, with hose, polished shoes, and a huge straw hat. His eyes were strikingly blue, his cheeks pink and soft-looking, and his head of abundant hair was nearly black, with perfectly combed waves.

Kids made terrible fun of him. That first day, a group chased Arlington home, forcing him to run hard and fast to keep them at bay. The boys were determined to see his prissy, spotless clothing messed and ruined, and his face scratched. To this end, they began chasing him home every day thereafter.

Arly became a lightning fast runner. He told himself he would enjoy this rather than be upset. He refused to let the bullies get the best of him. They would not hurt him. He was going to win. Eventually the other children realized they would never have the desired effect on the new boy, and they finally left him alone to go on to other conquests.

His mother made him wear these extravagant outfits as far as into the sixth grade, but Arly kept an even-keeled perspective. He wasn't happy with the situation, but wouldn't let anyone know, least of all his mother. He held his feelings bottled inside, never expressing an iota of displeasure. She later said, ". . . he never found fault with the way we dressed him."

Not until 1937, in a magazine interview, did Bob Taylor let on to the emotions which had brewed in his heart during those early grade school years. He openly expressed aversion for the name his mother had chosen for him, saying he'd, "... forgiven her for that and for those Lord Fauntleroy suits I once had to wear. Those suits I'll never forget, however."

His emotional softness was impossible to miss for anyone around him, including his mother, and she may have taken advantage. She called him a "high-strung child," observing that if she and her husband hadn't understood how to handle him, "he could easily have become a problem." She claimed he was "very sensitive. If anyone spoke harshly to him about some little thing he had done, he would not be able to eat or sleep."

Maybe this is why he was not quick to criticize others, and his sensitivity continued into his adult years. Both parents took these factors into serious consideration when handling their son. Ruth avowed he was, "... a thoughtful boy..." even though, "... he was apt to be blunt and outspoken, he would never come into the house that he would not kiss us...."

In grade school, Arly developed into a strong-minded, but guarded, person. "I was almost always alone," he said. "I went to school. I was a good little boy, I am afraid. I liked school. I did well in my lessons and liked them. I never played hooky. I never was sent to 'see the Principal.' I got on with the boys and girls in my classes. I was usually the room monitor and the president of the class or whatever that office is called in the grades. I played baseball on the school playground in the baseball season and football in the football season. I roller-skated and played jacks and marbles and hopscotch and all the games of the moment. I usually ate my lunches in the little town cafe or went home."

The reality of his life seemed to be in large part strikingly different from the reality he created in his head. He said he "got on with the boys and girls in his classes," while a few breaths before he said he was "almost always alone."

A female classmate gave her assessment. "People in grade school would refer to Arlington as 'little Lord Fauntleroy'... because of his immaculate dress." This was in spite of the fact that he said he "... played baseball... and football...." Another schoolmate stated that "Arlington worked out with the high school track team, and even wanted to play football, but his mother objected."

Forbidden from leaving the front porch of his old house, Arly would sit on the steps in his clean clothes, watching neighborhood children play around him. He was not allowed to join in, not even on weekends. If some of those children made an effort to come into his yard to see him, Ruth asked them to leave. One female schoolmate stated bluntly, "She didn't want them playing with Arlington."

He wrote of this period in 1937. "After school, I didn't play with the other kids. I liked to be alone and by myself. And I was alone. I never ran with a group . . . I wasn't unhappy. On the contrary, I read a lot. Not literature, I fear . . . No, I read all the boy's books there were. The Hentz books and the Alger books and books of adventure. I didn't read poetry. I wasn't at all the dreamy sort. I had my horse. I had my bike. I always had a flock of animals to care for. I just had enough to do on my own and that's how . . . I preferred to be."

A schoolmate's story told of the insular world in which Arly lived, sitting alone one day on the front steps as he hungrily watched the other kids as they playacted across the street. When he saw them holding a funeral for a bird they had killed with rocks and pellet guns, he called out, his voice shaking with emotion, "Let me do it. Let me sing now!" He begged them to be allowed to play the preacher.

As his schoolmate related, "Arlington couldn't participate because his mother wouldn't let him play with the neighbors for fear of getting injured, but he wanted to either preach or sing." The kids responded, letting him be the preacher. He loudly sang the "eulogy" for the dead bird from his spot on his porch, his voice ringing out with poignant clarity.

He told of his love for exciting male adventure stories while, in the same sentence, said he didn't mind being alone, reading quietly to himself. He was allowed a horse and a bike and animals, all physical activities which would logically include grime and sweat and exertion, but he wasn't allowed to get dirty. He said he wasn't dreamy, but he was usually left alone to dream. He pointed out that he'd had enough to do by himself, but he grabbed almost desperately at the rare chance to be a part of the kids' play going on around him.

Arly and his parents would return to nearby Filley in good weather to visit with Ruth's family. In this rural atmosphere, and because Ruth was otherwise occupied with her sisters and mother, he was left more to his own devices and not as carefully watched. He and his cousins, Earl, Charles, and Eva, would play sports in the dirt road next to the house.

There was one specific game Arly especially enjoyed. He and his cousins created the sport, called the "arrow game." After securing limber green tree twigs together in a way they felt was strong enough to spring an arrow-like creation, the children tied a cord to one end of the twig, and tied a knot to the other end. Wood roofing shingles became the arrows, complete with a shaft and a notch to hold the cord's knot. Finally, they pulled the twig back and let loose with the spring. The object of the game was to see how far the arrow would go before sticking into the ground.

Arly spent lazy afternoons with his cousins, doing nothing but hunting and fishing and playing the arrow game. He had been given "guns of all kinds" when he was only eight years old, and was aware of the responsibility which went along with such adult-like possessions. The acres of land around them were covered by trees and grass fields. The property was expansive and untouched and largely unpopulated, and their experiences were limited only by their time and imagination. Arly most often used a ten gauge shotgun for their hunting expeditions.

His love for the outdoors was given full flight when he and his parents visited friends on a farm on the outskirts of Beatrice. Andrew and Ruth first came in contact with Rose Shimerda when she fell ill in 1918 from a severe bout with influenza. Churches, schools, theaters, and several businesses were forced to close during the worldwide epidemic. A statewide Nebraska quarantine existed for a week that fall. In December alone, over twenty-one deaths were attributed to the illness. Dr. Brugh carefully nursed Rose through her illness and she made a full recovery. She and her husband, Anthony, became lifelong friends of the family.

During stays at the Shimerda farm, Arly roamed free while the adults visited and talked. The two-story whitewashed wooden home stood on 160 acres of trees on the south side of town. Arly loved to walk through the corn and wheat fields. He made friends with the horses, and played in the orchard among the apples, cherries, grapes, peaches, and plums the Shimerdas grew for profit.

They also raised hogs, cattle, and poultry. Arly acquired his lasting love and appreciation for animals of all types during his time spent on the Shimerda farm. Those animals became his closest friends, and he entertained himself by keeping company with them. Dogs and cats romped freely about, with each creature giving the other their due. As he matured, this farm became his inspiration, and he determined one day he would, ". . . have a big ranch and be a cowboy."

Mother and Dad bought Arly a pony when he was eight. He named her Gypsy and boarded her at the Shimerda farm. Sometimes he would hop on his bicycle, and, alone, make the trip from his front yard to their pasture, and spend hours riding her. He and Gypsy were close companions all the way into his high school years.

When he was about nine, he announced to his mother he was going to ride Gypsy "out to Grandpa's." Grandpa lived sixteen miles away in Filley. Ruth looked at him, gauging his intent, and decided to let him go. He'd been away about an hour when the telephone rang. Arlington was calling from a house outside of town. "Gyp keeps running up and down the banks," he told her, his voice agitated and breathless. "I can't make her obey. I'm coming home."

Mother was stern and unrelenting. "Just make the pony know you're the boss, Arlington. Cut yourself a switch, and the first time she doesn't do what you tell her, use the switch. You go on to Filley."

He did as she told him; that day seemed to be a turning point in his life. Arlington became more resourceful, more independent, and apt to figure out his own way around any problem which surfaced.

But he still appeared confused amidst these vastly different lifestyles, unsure as to which direction he should take in life. Should he be happy and comfortable in the great outdoors, hunting and riding and fishing and en-

Arly riding his pony, Gypsy. Courtesy Robert Taylor Family Private Collection.

joying the land? Or should he rein in those needs, as his mother desired of him, keeping himself prim and proper and spotless, cautious as to how he dealt with his peers?

The almost split personality foisted upon him was one of a number of early indicators that Arlington might one day make his way to the stage as a performer. His flair for the dramatic had shown up in moments such as his singing the dead bird's eulogy from his front porch. Next, only eight years old, he made his first real public appearance. He had written a piece entitled *The Sick Monkey*, and presented the work to his school assembly. By the time he was ten, he wrote another, this one on China, and he gave a recitation in front of several church and school groups. C. B. Dempster, a neighbor, and head of the Dempster Mill Manufacturing Company in town, suggested to his parents they educate him in dramatics. He was the first person to predict, "Someday that boy of yours will be a big movie star!"

But in 1922, at only eleven, Arlington had no awareness of what would become of his life. He asked his mother, "What will I be when I get to be a man?" She responded, "Opportunity will lead you. Men don't decide, as a rule, what they will be. Circumstances decide for them."

Arlington was thirteen in 1924, and he and his parents moved to the last home, still in Beatrice, the three of them would share together. This was where he was finally able to stay more than a few years, and for the rest of his life he called this house his family home.

Cousin Izetta Brugh remembered meeting Arlington around this time. She had gone with her father to visit "Uncle Spang," and Aunt Ruth cooked a meal. Izetta said they had a "delicious dinner of roast pork and candied sweet potatoes," but she was most impressed how Arlington entertained her by playing the piano. He walked her home, and she fell under his spell. Izetta and family went to Uncle Spang's and Aunt Ruth's home once a year after that, arriving about eleven-thirty. They crowded around the piano and sang before eating the traditional meal. After dinner, there would be more singing and piano-playing, usually with Aunt Ruth, Arlington, or both sitting down to play.

In this house situated on a major thoroughfare in Beatrice, an adorable brick bungalow with a garage, Arlington learned to test his masculinity, maturing and beginning to take on the responsibilities of growing up. He dreamed of what he would do with his life, where he would go and whom he would become, and he learned his first lessons about girls and dating, and life outside of his immediate family.

Arlington went to the movies with his parents almost every Saturday night. His mother said he "used to mimic Charlie Chaplin—the shuffle, the sniffle, everything. If we had ever thought that he might someday be an actor . . . we would have suspected that he would be a comedian." He also liked to pretend he was Tom Mix or Williams S. Hart. On opening night in 1926 and many years afterward, at Beatrice's downtown Rivoli Theater, Arlington sat eagerly in the front row awaiting the strains of the organ music and the excitement of the credits rolling on the screen. Eventually, he was an usher and a Master of Ceremonies for his beloved Rivoli.

In his high school junior year, Arlington hit his theatrical stride and began to earnestly test his talent. In October of 1928, he took on a role in *Aunt Lucia*, a play staged by adults in his community. He again stretched his comedic side during the play's irreverent rendition of a glee club. His father was involved in the evening's entertainment.

As a high school senior, Arlington became a member of the Dramatics Club. He snagged a major role as a hard-headed, underhanded stockbroker

Arly and dad, circa 1925. Courtesy Robert Taylor Family Private Collection.

in a three-act comedy, *Nothing But The Truth*. The local newspaper printed a glowing review of the production, but he was not singled out.

That didn't deter him from continuing in front of the bright lights. In the spring of 1929, with only months left before graduation, he took the primary male lead in the Senior High Operetta, *Captain Crossbones*. A love story was at the center of the plot, and he starred opposite one of his girlfriends, Gertrude Hamilton, giving him his first taste of being personally involved with his leading lady, on the stage and off.

Speech competitions were another of Arlington's pursuits of public recognition. A month or so after the operetta, he placed first in the oratorical category of a contest held in a neighboring town, and in another contest held in Beatrice. His talk was called, "Idealism in a School Teacher." At the twelfth annual state drama contest held the same year at Nebraska Wesleyan University in Lincoln, Arlington was the state champion in the oratorical category.

The driving factor behind the young man's ability to obtain repeated opportunities in the spotlight was always unclear to him. Was the attraction his good looks, his talent, his intellect, or the whole package? He couldn't be sure. He was an excellent student. Many told him he spoke well, had great stage presence, and was a budding comedian, but his outstanding looks seemed to always overwhelm any ability or innate talent he possessed. As Arlington matured, his physical appearance grew more handsome by the day, engulfing all legitimate efforts he would make to get noticed on his other merits. Talent or no talent, Arlington Brugh was singled out every time.

His mother said friends and relatives often remarked about this paradox. "We cared more about what went on inside of him than about the way he looked. His looks were well enough. It was his mind and his soul we were concerned with. The kind of man he would be, not look, his character, not his charm."

This reinforcement gave Arlington a sense of grounding, and a vision beyond that which greeted him when he looked in the mirror every morning. Even so, he received unending mixed messages from his mother as to what really was most important. Was that his emotional makeup and what he could do with that, or his external appearance and what he should do to capitalize on his looks?

The time came for Arlington to make his own way. His parents had a life to lead as a couple and he wanted the best for them, hoping they would have the chance to enjoy each other, really for the first time. Arlington knew that when his mother and father married, she had been too ill for them to take advantage of the joy of being in love. Then, after his birth, they had to deal with her illness, Andrew's growing practice, and him. There had been precious little time to devote to their personal happiness as a pair.

The permeating essence of his parent's love affair allowed Arlington to learn one of the most lasting lessons of his life. Theirs was a relationship where care for one another had never waned. Ruth and Andrew were known to always relate to each other in a gentle, quiet, respectful, and adoring, if understated, fashion. This model became the foundation upon which Arlington built his own interactions with women.

In an article, he said, "My parents conditioned my young idea of what marriage should be, of how a man should be with a woman. My father used to say to my mother, almost every day of his life, 'You are the most beautiful woman in the world to me. Every day we live together I love you more.'"

Though his younger years may have tended toward isolation and occasional emotional neglect brought on by his parents' exclusive relationship, Arlington nonetheless understood a great sense of genuine love between a man and a woman. He wanted this powerful emotion in his own life in the same way his parents always had.

He learned from those earliest years how love between a man and a woman should work. He was taught to respect, honor, and cherish ladies in a fashion he carried with him into adulthood. He understood from his father that women needed to be protected and always taken care of. His mother had instilled in him an instinctive high regard, almost awe, of the female sex. He came to believe that to make a relationship work, the woman must be well-treated because, if for no other reason, she was a woman. Through this fact alone, she deserved such handling.

A quote from Ruth about her marriage summed up what Arlington experienced as he watched his parents interact. "We were inseparable companions, constant inspirations to each other through the years. We had a wonderful married life. Never a quarrel, never an unhappy moment—unless we were apart. And we were seldom separated for more than a few days at a time . . . Arlington's father gave me love and happiness such as few women ever know. He even saved my life with his love."

CHAPTER TWO:

Mother—or Wife?

> "People... asked about his... romances—as if they were important...."
> – Ruth Brugh, Robert Taylor's mother

Throughout junior high and high school, Arlington kept busy with studies and music. He developed his own style, and although he slowly allowed himself to come out from under his mother's often suffocating personality, he continued to be the dutiful son. She wouldn't let go of her history of illness, and his father would not allow a single argumentative word to cross Arlington's lips, particularly while he was in his mother's presence.

He never failed to follow ritual while in his parent's household. He did a considerable amount of the housework and cooking, and took over his mother's care when his father was not home. He had a set list of chores expected of him, such as keeping furnace and fireplace wood stocked and organized, and mowing the lawn. He never openly disagreed with any of his parents' requirements. There was a no-nonsense air about how they relegated responsibility, and he followed through in like manner. "I understood that was my job and that a man does his job alone," he told a reporter years later.

Ruth was firmly ensconced in her role as matriarch and overseer. She once claimed, "Arlington told me he didn't like to see me working, that neither Dad nor he liked me to work, that he liked to find me dressed up pretty and sitting down with a book in the parlor when he came home."

With such a rigid home life, Arlington was fortunate that both parents encouraged his musical talent. Within this arena he began to discover his true persona. He could experiment with music and test his strengths and weaknesses. Andrew and Ruth approved of, and delighted in, his ability. In turn, he enjoyed the freedom of expression his talent offered him.

Arlington felt the power of music at an early age. His mother played the piano and sang, and when Arlington was ten years old, a piano teacher moved to Beatrice. The boy was signed up for lessons and he was a natural. Within two years, as he said, "The charms of the saxophone prevailed...." He studied that for awhile, but his mother didn't share his enthusiasm. She was adamant about him not playing that instrument, saying, "I did not want him to; a saxophone was so noisy and jazzy. So then he wanted to try the cello...."

His ability to make music became his personal identity, more than the stage at this point. He and Gerhart "Garry" Wiebe met in the eighth grade when they formed a quartet with two other talented class members. He called Garry his "one and only true friend." Soon, the pair became constant companions and they made their mark with music.

Under the direction of B. P. Osborn, who taught instrumental music at Beatrice Public Schools, Arlington, Garry, and other young men played for school audiences. Mr. Osborn "went to some trouble to convince Arlington that the cello was the instrument for a gentleman," his mother said. Her final approval cemented Arlington's "choice" of what instrument he would study for the long term.

From 1925 until 1929, he took lessons in nearby Lincoln once a week on Saturday mornings during school. Lincoln was where Arlington met Professor Herbert Gray, an instructor at the University School of Music. His mother was impressed from the start. "I shall never forget the day we took him to Lincoln for his first lesson with Professor Gray," she later wrote. "He told us [Arlington] did not handle the cello awkwardly, as most beginners do...."

Herbert Gray was a big, boisterous man with a domineering, persuasive personality. He was an accomplished musician long before he came to Nebraska, having studied voice and cello with private teachers in Chicago, Los Angeles, and New York. He had been a concert and operatic tenor soloist with national groups, including the French Opera in New Orleans. He was in his later years when he came to be at the University School of Music in Lincoln, performing as a cellist with the Lincoln Symphony and a tenor soloist for oratorios such as *The Messiah*.

Arly in his quartet. Courtesy Robert Taylor Family Private Collection.

In Arlington Brugh, Herbert Gray saw raw talent. He also saw large-scale promise. In Herbert Gray, Arlington saw a future beyond any he had ever before considered. He was in awe of the older man, who had great experience and seen much of the world. The opportunity to tutor with a musician of this ability and stature was not handed over to just any young man who owned a cello, and Arlington realized he was being given the highest of honors.

He also received continued support from Mr. Osborn, through special instruction the school music supervisor only offered to his most gifted musicians. In no time, Arlington was part of the Junior High Orchestra. In March of 1926, he was chosen as one of four soloists to perform in front of a school audience.

His quartet often changed members, with only him and Garry staying constant. In the eleventh grade they, along with two new members, won second place at the State Music Contest in Lincoln. Arlington did a lot of local traveling that year to contests and public performances, and each time he excelled.

His abilities were also in demand elsewhere. He sang in the church choir and the school glee club. Frank Lenhart, a local mortician, directed a community orchestra comprised of thirty-five members. The group performed wherever and whenever Lenhart secured an engagement, including church socials, town fairs, and even the Nebraska State Penitentiary. On at least three occasions, they played on local radio stations, and at the Rivoli Theater.

Though his parents were the most influential persons in Arlington's early life, Garry Wiebe and Herbert Gray were not to be discounted. Garry became his shadow, his confidante, the brother he never had. Professor Gray became his mentor. Unlike Andrew, who encouraged his son to enter the serving profession of medicine, the professor urged Arlington toward a more glamorous future in music.

Again, Arlington found himself torn between two worlds, unsure which to choose. At first, he didn't really take seriously the idea of being a professional musician. That was something he did well and most often without much effort. He enjoyed making music, and the fun of the social atmosphere when he played compelled him to want more.

He was a natural entertainer.

Yet medicine was at the heart of his family. Medicine had, through the brilliant efforts of his father, given his beloved mother a longer and more worthwhile life, and had given Arlington a chance to be born. The medical profession offered noble and fulfilling work and had the potential to matter for a lifetime, and beyond.

But could he be a doctor? He wasn't sure.

When he won a local contest playing "The Swan" on his cello, his mother said she was sure he would one day be a famous performer. He replied, "I'd rather take over Dad's practice right here in Nebraska." In the back of his mind, though, there was always a nagging call to music, and to the stage.

Professor Gray now tutored Arlington at Doane College in Crete, forty miles from Beatrice. He had become a part-time faculty member at Doane, in addition to his duties in Lincoln at the University School of Music. He seemed to have pre-planned expectations in mind for Arlington, and he encouraged his young student to move his lessons from Lincoln to Crete. Arly agreed. The location change had a lot to do with distance. Crete was closer to Beatrice. With his father's schedule always booked, and only one family car, Arlington often had to hitch a ride to get to lessons in Lincoln.

Amidst his studies, attentiveness to his parents, and his music, which always included the strong influence of Herbert Gray, Arlington still managed to find time to develop a social life. There was never a point in his maturation process where he became awkward-looking. His dark hair framed a face with refined features which complimented each other without visible flaw. One schoolmate said, "Arlington was considered effeminate until high school because the boys were jealous of his good looks and he didn't participate in sports."

The kids in school called Arlington a "clothes horse." This was more favorable than the earlier "Little Lord Fauntleroy" title, and afforded him a somewhat better chance to assimilate into less intellectual pursuits. He was still quiet and serious but by the ninth grade, he'd become accepted enough to be the first elected Student Body President of Beatrice Junior High.

Despite the opinions of his schoolmates, he didn't shy away from hard labor. He was energized by the effort and often intentionally sought out physical work. The clothes his mother made him wear, and the respectful, nearly awed way in which he always treated her, perpetuated his perceived physical softness in the mind of the community. This made him try harder to prove his manliness, and sometimes he seemed agitated by his dilemma. Pure manual labor, on his own terms and in his own time, was his salvation. He took on jobs such as shocking wheat on a farm, mowing lawns, milking cows and tending animals, and painting cars. His mother said, "Every summer, he would find a job ... [he] did not have to work; he just wanted to...."

Arlington had his first real romance in the ninth grade. He proved to be quite the average young man when it came to girls, despite his mother's attempts to keep him close to her skirts. According to his own words, he was "head over heels in love with Helen Rush," described by a female schoolmate as "short, happy, light brown hair and a big smile. The world was right with Helen."

His mother did take notice. He'd often had crushes, though he rarely spoke of them with her, and Helen was, she said, "the only girl I ever knew for sure that he was excited about." She continued, ". . . if there were any others who had the same effect on him, he was very quiet about it." Arlington called Helen "the most wonderful girl in the world."

Helen was the first in a line of many females who would come and go in his life. He never felt comfortable as an aggressor and didn't see in himself the striking young man everyone else saw. He didn't expect people to like him, taking for granted at the onset that they wouldn't, and he appeared genuinely surprised when they did. "I can't make advances," he said. "I don't mix easily."

His mother verified this in her abrupt fashion. "He is a little too backward."

Arlington's impression of himself stayed slightly off-center, and always self-challenging, while the outward picture of him as an attractive, intelligent, capable youth emerged. He didn't mix well by his own admission, but he often intentionally put himself in the public eye. During the ninth grade, his marks were excellent in every subject except Latin. He struggled to earn an average grade in the one-year course. This called to mind shades of his childhood, when the only words he seemed able to successfully utter were Latin. He appeared to unintentionally steer away from what he had gravitated toward as a child.

He studied all the normal courses given to school-age adolescents of the time, discovering to his great surprise that he didn't like science. This remained at the root of his uncertainty over pursuing a medical career.

He still did a considerable amount of oratorical work, some in classes but most was extra-curricular. As a sophomore, he was employed in his first effort as a public announcer. Ernestine Schumann-Heink, a famous German opera and concert singer, was touring the United States and made a stop in Beatrice. She was invited to perform at an evening concert at the junior high auditorium, and Arlington was chosen to make the introductions. Some schoolmates jokingly called her, "Human Shank." That evening when Arlington nervously walked to the microphone in the center of the stage, he cleared his throat and began his pre-arranged speech, announcing in a serious voice he was "happy to present . . . Madam Human Shank."

While he made a mess of his part in this public event, he didn't let the embarrassment stop him from continually seeking out the spotlight. Public speaking became an important part of his personal, social, and professional development, mostly as a challenge to himself. He later admitted, "I shall never forget the fears that overcame me every time I had to preside over a 'meeting' . . . or introduce guest speakers. Nothing since has ever frightened me as much."

Despite this, he was elected President of his Junior Class, in charge of toasts at the annual Beatrice High Junior-Senior Banquet. He was on the debate team, and did well in local competitions. A classmate stated he was "very intelligent in debate," and was able to hold his own and excel. Well into adulthood, friends said he would argue that the sky was black for the satisfaction over the ensuing discussion.

By now, he was taking everything from algebra to civics, biology to English, history to typing, and he was involved in as many social activities as he could fit into what was left of his day. He was enrolled in a high school college preparatory program, and his work was top form. His mother stated, "He never had to work to get good grades. In his freshman year, he was elected to a national honorary society. He graduated second in his class."

The most telling part of his development surprisingly came through sports. Arlington's mother had always, at least, dissuaded, and more often than not forbidden, his participation in any physical activity which would get him dirty, skewer his appearance, or risk personal injury. She didn't count on her son having a mind of his own. He thrived through physical exertion. No longer always feeling a need to obey his mother's strict edicts, he quietly and respectfully, but with firm determination, began making moves of his own choosing. He wanted to show her he had strong opinions independent of hers, and he was ready to exercise them.

A male schoolmate said Arlington "was a hurdler at Beatrice High, but the mother did not want him to continue because he might injure his face." For his last two years in high school, he participated in an informal activity known as the Junior/Senior Olympics. This late spring ritual among boys was organized for after school on the football field. They wore close-fitting turtleneck sweaters and clean, pressed pants. The juniors formed a circle around the seniors with selected opponents, and they wrestled.

Arlington gained fame throughout the town with his ability in the Olympics. A teacher was quoted in the local paper as saying, "Arlington did not pick someone his own size. Instead, he took on the biggest boy in the senior class, an all-state athlete who weighed a good fifty pounds more than he did. He not only threw him, but sat on his chest. When the afternoon was over, though his slacks were torn . . . he came out of those fights looking almost as well as he went in."

This poise, his ability to somehow always look his best emotionally as well as physically, carried him through. He had an outward image of self-confidence and assurance he didn't necessarily feel on the inside.

Despite his participation in sports, and the fact that he subjected himself to public opinion time and time again through speaking engagements, musical efforts, sports, and drama, Arlington never appeared harried, dirtied, or out-of-sorts. He dressed in spotless pressed slacks, and collegiate sweaters. This may have been a concession to his mother's wishes, a way for him to pacify her certain displeasure with some of his activities. He eventually grew to enjoy fine clothes, but his happiest moments remained times of simple relaxation, and what he wore when he was at rest was just as relaxed.

His carriage, outward self-assurance, and good looks were qualities which not only helped him rise above the crowd, but they made the general population wary of him. Arlington endured strong resentment for how he looked and carried himself. He came to hate with rare vocal intensity a title which followed him into adulthood, a title first used in these earlier years. "Pretty Boy" was a label first given to him in his mid-teens.

A female acquaintance observed, "Arlington was always well-groomed, but he was remote and didn't associate with people. He never wanted his appearance to be out of place, or to make a mistake, and never really relaxed with his peers." Another social contact stated, "He was a private person, not outgoing, not very talkative."

His schoolmates couldn't feel fully comfortable around him, and he didn't know how to feel at ease with them. Proof of popularity, indicated by the many class offices he held and contests won, and his involvement in extracurricular activities, made it obvious Arlington wasn't disliked. The dichotomy seemed to stem from his personal insecurities and how people reacted to him.

Arlington Brugh gave off an air which said, "Come close, but not too close."

A man can only be so shy, however, if he has a desire to court young ladies. And Arlington definitely had an eye for women.

In the 1920s, the nation was in a fit of public liberalism. Privately, the country's heart was built upon countless communities such as Beatrice, Nebraska, places comprised of strictly conservative, church-going, hardworking citizens who didn't care much for the future of the jazz age. Prohibition wasn't a hot topic of serious debate, for most members of these communities frowned on alcohol, and widespread contemporary dancing wasn't held in much higher regard. Theaters closed on Sundays. At one point, there was an eight o'clock curfew for all youngsters under the age of sixteen.

Paul Drew, one of Arlington's schoolmates, gave a detailed, telling account of how they learned about the mystery between the sexes in a Midwest town of the era.

"It was typical of Beatrice boys to start dating as a junior in high school. Arlington played the field." After maybe three dates, a girl might permit a boy to kiss her when they were alone in the car, which sometimes turned into a heated necking session. No matter what became of the kissing, there was an understanding that a girl had to be home no later than eleven o'clock. If a boy and girl went out together six or seven times, they were considered serious. But "a 'nice' girl had to be very discreet with the boy, and he had to make the first advance, for the girl, if she was 'nice,' would not be forward."

Some acceptable date options were church gatherings, family functions, the ice cream parlor, or the movies. Paul Drew mentioned a form of segregation in high schools. Boys entered from one side, girls went in through another entrance. Organized school social activities were limited.

A girl might want to go dancing, but only if she had open-minded parents. Some boys gave in to this, but one man said, "Boys who danced were considered sissies by many of the [other] boys." There were some young men, though, who seemed to understand how much girls enjoyed dancing, and they defied the "sissy" identification by going dancing regularly.

Arlington Brugh was one of those boys.

His mother told of how she, her husband, and Arlington vacationed together throughout his teenage years. For three summers, they had a lakeside cottage in Iowa where, among other activities, dance lessons were given to the young people. This was where Arlington mastered the art when he was only sixteen.

Many males envied his graceful surefootedness, and females openly appreciated him. He was so at ease on the dance floor that he became their favorite partner. Young ladies couldn't wait to move to the music in Arlington's arms.

His cousin remembered, "Arlington's parents let him attend dances during his school years, but they wouldn't allow him to go with the wrong crowd or drink alcohol." His mother tried to downplay his popularity. "People . . . asked about his . . . romances—as if they were important." She went on to say, "The doctor and I used to wonder if he was not too popular for his own good. . . ."

What Arlington thought of his popularity he kept to himself, but he did take advantage of the opportunities it afforded him. He enjoyed dancing with all his dates and never hid the fact. When their time together included other activities, such as the movies, a soda at local Penner's Pharmacy, or a church social, they almost always started or ended on the dance floor. His disinterest in how other boys viewed his social skills likely enhanced his already-high image in the eyes of the girls.

There were no less than eleven documented accounts of young ladies who dated Arlington while he was a student at Beatrice High. Some of the more entertaining stories tell of the era, the people, and the experience of going out with a man adored by many ladies years before he was a public figure. They also relate a composite of the type of woman that attracted him.

Catherine "Kate" Heffelfinger was his age. She was assertive, outgoing, and according to a schoolmate, "liked a good time, and had many friends." Kate was approximately five feet two inches tall, and had black hair and blue eyes. Arlington called her "a tiny, pretty girl." Her sister said, "Kate and Arlington were considered part of the '500 Group,' the more socially-prominent people in high school . . . He was a quiet fellow, on Student Council, had a creamy white face, rosy cheeks, and . . . wavy hair."

Esther Legate was a year older than he was, and she also had dark hair and blue eyes. She found herself attracted to him when they were both in the orchestra. He returned her shy glances. Finally, he called her and asked her to dinner at a cafe in a neighboring town. He and Esther drove in one car. His parents followed in another car as chaperones, and sat separate from them at the restaurant. Arlington and Esther talked for hours and had little to do with his mother and father.

More dates with Esther followed. He always picked her up at home and chatted with her parents. She said he liked "turtle-necked sweaters . . . and he wore a suit to dances." They were his, ". . . big event." She called him, ". . . the nicest boy" she ever dated. "Very much a gentleman with nice manners, he was reserved, serious, honest, intelligent, a very good musician, and a very good dancer."

One evening he took her to the Elks Club, where they did the fox trot and the waltz. On the way home, they were caught in a snowstorm. "Arlington pulled over into a farmyard and we stayed there awhile until we could move on." They talked to pass the time. "He tried to kiss me, but I wouldn't let him because there were rumors he was very interested in another girl."

After Esther, there was Helen Alexander. She was five feet four inches tall, had blonde hair and blue eyes, and was also a year older than Arlington. Then came Gertrude Hamilton, even shorter, with brown hair and blue eyes; she was a, "... nice, outgoing, lively girl." Rosana Kilpatrick followed in line and she, again, had deep, engaging blue eyes. The talkative Kathleen Mumford was petite, and had brown hair and blue eyes, and a good personality. Arlington attended her sixteenth birthday party.

In later years, he made reference to a date with Delores Harmon, a former neighbor and schoolmate, but at the time she denied having gone out with him. Bernice Grunwald was in college when she met Arlington on a blind date. He was a high school junior. She was a music student, and eventually became a concert pianist.

Arlington clearly had discovered the opposite sex. One date followed another, and then another. He admitted later his favorite date was, "... the 'All-American girl' ... I like a girl who can be a pal, who can share a fellow's interests and who is not affected and stagey. Appearance doesn't matter so much although, like every other man, I suppose I'm naturally attracted by clean-cut, good-looking girls." A male friend stated Arlington most likely, "... had his first sexual experience while in high school." No telling which of those young ladies was his initial conquest, though he had clearly tried to make the moves on Esther in the snowstorm.

He didn't like to see women smoke or drink to excess and "heartily" disliked red fingernails. They were too flamboyant for his tastes. Each young lady in whom he was interested was involved in theatrics or music.

School-aged Arly Brugh.
Courtesy Robert Taylor Family Private Collection.

Years later, when asked if the girl he would eventually marry should be an actress, he replied, "That is impossible to say for I would not marry because she happened to be an actress and neither would I decline to marry her if she were not."

All his ladies had blue eyes, as did his mother. Each stood about the same general height as she did; all were classy and attractive, well-dressed, outspoken and outgoing; most were opinionated with determined, strong personalities. Many were older. None were wallflowers. In a whole host of ways, Arlington Brugh seemed to be dating variations on the same theme. One could almost say he was dating his mother.

In school and in his social life, Arlington's striking handsomeness always overwhelmed his relationships, and his inherent talents. His appearance initially grabbed the attention and left little room for most any other focus.

His mother continued to place great importance on his appearance. She made certain he looked and played the part of the well-to-do doctor's son, though he would often have felt more comfortable in a pair of jeans and a flannel shirt.

At the age of eighteen, Arlington Brugh was living in a state of emotional confusion as to the man he would become. His talents were evident, his personality was surfacing, and his intelligence was without question. When allowed the opportunity, he had a big taste for the outdoors. Warring with this was an internal pull toward the more genteel, safer, quieter lifestyle encouraged by his parents, specifically by his mother.

Where should he go? What should he do?

CHAPTER THREE:

College, Kathryn and Blanche, and Hollywood

"Oh Doc, please don't let's park here! Oh Doc, please don't let's park...! Oh Doc, please don't let's...! Oh Doc, please don't...! Oh Doc, please... ! Oh Doc...! Oh...!!"

– Kathryn Bender to Arlington "Doc" Brugh, text from a play

Arlington graduated from Beatrice Senior High in June of 1929. Under his yearbook picture read the words: "Few things are impossible to diligence and perseverance." His extra-curricular credits were Dramatics Club, Glee Club, National Honor Society, Orchestra, Student Council, Homesteader Staff, and Senior Social Chairman. His parents gave him a 1929 beige-and-orange tinted, rumbled-seated Buick sports coupe as a graduation present. Having his own transportation was exhilarating, facilitating his movement in and around town. He continued to religiously take cello lessons with Professor Gray at Doane in Crete, and now he no longer had to bum rides.

As his father handed over the keys, he sternly instructed his son, "... one thing I must demand. Never go over thirty-five." His mother said "... he was such a good boy, and so trustworthy, that we knew we could trust him ... It was his property and his responsibility."

Around the time of Arly's graduation: mother, Ruth; grandmother, Eva Stanhope; father, Dr. Brugh, and Arly. Courtesy Robert Taylor Family Private Collection.

These words were to ring true for him from that point on. Not only the car, but the rest of his life was now his property and his responsibility. He would have to learn to handle both, cautiously and wisely. He could seek counsel, but final action would always be his alone.

Where should he go from here?

College was the only answer, but would he study medicine, music, or acting? These were three viable paths wide open for him, and the availability of choices, rather than the lack of them, became his source of frustration.

He was also in a quandary as to which college he should attend. Should he go to Doane, or to Northwestern University, in Evanston, Illinois? Garry Wiebe unwittingly made the decision for him. Garry was the son of respectable Mennonites. His family had always been well-to-do, but at some point during his early years, they suffered a setback from which they never financially recovered. Garry and his family couldn't afford college tuition.

Arlington and his father discussed options, and he spoke of his sadness over Garry's situation. Andrew told him he could go to Northwestern University alone, or consider another possibility. His father told him he could, "... go to Doane in Crete, and take Garry with me. Dad would finance him for two years. We would be together. Garry was the only pal I had. I wanted to go to Northwestern for many reasons but, after due consideration, none of those reasons seemed to weigh as much as that Garry and I should go on together."

Another factor was Professor Gray, still a constant in Arlington's life. He was at Doane, and he encouraged Arlington to follow him. And last, Mary Ellen Inglis, Doane's drama coach, had approached him after the oratorical contest he won that spring in Beatrice. She had been a judge, and she also urged him to consider studying at Doane.

The choice was made. Arlington and Garry enrolled at Doane College in the fall of 1929. The school was a co-educational, four-year liberal arts institution affiliated with the Congregational Church. Located on the bluffs overlooking Crete in the Big Blue River Valley, the property spread over three hundred and twenty acres. The campus was cozy and warm, with ten stately buildings and well-tended lawns. Streams wended their

Professor Herbert Gray. Courtesy Judith Hanhisalo personal collection.

Doane College, Crete, NE. Courtesy author's personal collection.

way around the grounds, and established trees created comfortable, attractive spots where students could study and dream.

For the two years he attended school there, Arlington was registered with the Department of Music. His grades were acceptable, but he didn't excel as he had in earlier years. There were many extra-curricular activities available and he found his place in the school's social life, though not until classmates determined he was acceptable enough to fit in. He had to overcome his clothes; most other kids wore corduroys and sweaters, while Arlington showed up for his first day in white flannels and a blue sports coat. He also had to rise above his looks, as usual.

A female classmate remarked, ". . . he was too good-looking. He was so darned handsome that he was conspicuous." One male remarked to another upon first sight of Arlington, "Hold your breath . . . you're about the meet the most handsome man in the world. Glance at the dark guy sitting in the corner over there and feast your eyes upon the latest addition to our estimable college."

One evening, as he and Garry were walking the grounds, they came upon Doane's star track man, Tom Reid. Arlington was brought up short by a public show of all the gossip going around campus about him.

"Well, well," Reid bellowed, "here comes handsome! Boys, boys," he told the others with him, "where are your manners? Don't you recognize the best dressed man on the campus when you see him? Look at him! God's gift to woman. A man who neither smokes nor drinks. An A-1 student. A plutocrat of plutocrats. Gentlemen, I say *bow* to the King of the Campus!" Tom executed an exaggerated sweep and the boys with him obediently followed his lead.

Arlington's cheeks tinged a light pink, but he recovered fast enough from the embarrassment to act as if Tom's rudeness didn't bother him. Still, he was hurt; the remark had cut deeply. That night in his room, he stood in front of the mirror and tried to see himself as others did. He walked toward the mirror, and then backed up. He walked to the mirror again, scrutinizing his every movement.

He recognized how he carried himself with his shoulders up and back, and ramrod straight; this worked against him. His mother had taught him to walk like a soldier on parade. And his clothes... His clothes had always been a source of public aggravation, and now more so. His sweaters were made from fine wools. His pants were carefully creased. His shoes were new, and polished a sleek black. He looked like money.

Garry was also frustrated. He felt guilty because his friend had been treated badly. He convinced himself that by accepting Dr. Brugh's generous offer, he was the reason Arlington had decided against Northwestern, choosing instead the less prestigious, more rural Doane. This decision pushed Arlington into an unnecessary class struggle.

"Cut it, will you?" Arlington heatedly demanded the next morning as they discussed the problem. "If you try to fix me with the boys . . . I'll never forgive you. I'll work it out myself." And he set out to do exactly that. By toning down his wardrobe, relaxing his movements, forcing himself to join into discussions he might otherwise feel too shy to become a part of, and in general working hard to step out of his shell, Arlington won over most of the boys who had originally made fun of him.

He was successful enough to be elected President of his freshman class, Doane's largest freshman class ever. He was accepted as a member of Iota Delta Chi, a local fraternity, and joined the Doane Symphony and the Doane Players.

He continued to test his skill as a sportsman, and while he didn't make a long-standing name for himself, he overachieved in each physical activity of which he became a part. His favorite was track. A classmate noted ". . . he went out for track and ran the hurdles faster than anyone else. Then he retired. . . ." Whether or not this had anything to do with Tom Reid is uncertain, but he likely remembered how Tom had treated him early on, and he didn't want to compete.

His cello, public speaking efforts, and drama took up most of his time. The school did not have on-campus housing for men that year. Arly rented a room with a local couple in their two-story home. His neatness became a source of amazement to his landlords and neighbors. Another local said, "[he was] a 'realist,' a man raised with religious principles and high morals who always conducted himself in a manner which reflected his upbringing."

That winter he was encouraged by Miss Inglis to enter a local oratorical contest sponsored by the Anti-Saloon League of Nebraska. The topic was "Ten Years of Prohibition." According to his mother, this was "the biggest ever held in that section of the country," and she also wanted him to enter. Both she and Miss Inglis were certain he could win. He was not.

"Mother," he told her, "I can't win that . . . There are three ordained ministers entered in it—and every one of them knew how to win an audience before I was born."

But Ruth knew her son, and she knew how to tempt him. She believed this particular competition would be important to his future. She thought a minute, and came up with a brainstorm.

"He was begging for a coonskin coat. Not that he needed one; but he wanted one badly." She changed tactics. "I'll tell you what," she cajoled him. "If you enter the contest and win, I'll get you the fur coat."

Arlington entered the contest and worked harder over that speech than any other. When the big night arrived, he insisted his parents not be in the audience. He wanted them to stay away because they made him nervous.

Andrew and Ruth dutifully remained at home and waited. About ten o'clock, the phone rang. "Well, Mom," there was excitement in Arlington's voice, "you'd better get to Lincoln and get that coat!"

Not only did he receive a coat from his parents for doing well, but as the overall winner, he was sent to Detroit for a week in January of 1930 to attend the national convention of the Anti-Saloon League of America. He was an honored guest; all expenses were paid and all materials required to participate were supplied. At least one hundred high school and college students attended, and convention meetings were held at the Hotel Statler. Harry Houdini had stayed at this hotel only four years earlier. The event offered much excitement for a young man not yet twenty years old.

Though not intended as such, this was his first tentative foray into politics. The Anti-Saloon League was a well-formed group dedicated to solving "the liquor problem," doing so through "the two-party system with a nonpartisan approach." They worked to elect individual politicians who supported their cause, believing if saloons were closed, the public would have fewer places to buy alcohol and consumption would decrease. Arlington wasn't a drinker, but he wasn't known as a crusader, either. The contest was a means to an end for him. While he never grew to love public oration, this particular contest proved to him he could do this well when something important was at stake.

He was back at Doane the next month. Garry, he, and a young man named Russ Gibson, who played the piano, trumpet, and French horn, had formed a trio. They received attention within the Doane community, and that winter they went on the road to perform in a neighboring town. On Valentine's Day, they were featured at the college dance. Arlington gave a speech that night entitled, "Hearts

The Harmony Boys: Arlington Brugh, Russ Gibson, Garry Wiebe. Courtesy Robert Taylor Family Private Collection.

Resound to Cupid's Tread." The newspaper said, "His theme was of romance not only among the students but of the alumni and students for Doane...."

He auditioned for a place in the school drama troupe the first month of his freshman year, and traveled extensively with the Doane Players. By December, he had a minor role in the school production of *Helena's Boys*. When the play was selected as the performance for the college's annual spring trip, he had the leading role. The troupe visited at least ten different towns.

Arlington was paired to room with his Doane adversary, Tom Reid. He quietly had asked officials to allow him to be Tom's roommate. When they reached their room the first night to unpack, Arlington opened his suitcase and his track shoes fell out.

"What are you doing with my track shoes?" Tom demanded.

"These aren't yours. They're mine."

"Oh, so you think you're a track man, too! I guess you think you can be just about anything you want to be around here, don't you?"

Arlington still wasn't immune to Tom's brand of biting sarcasm, but he saw an opportunity to finally break down the wall between them. "I thought you might help me," he responded quietly. "I've got good legs. I can run. Not like you, of course. But if you'd help me."

"*Me* help *you*?" Tom was incredulous. "That's a good one. Why, I wouldn't help you on a bet."

Arlington dropped the subject. The next morning as they awoke and got ready for the day, without explanation Tom took his roommate up on his request. They ran through the streets of town, and Tom coached Arlington on the finer points of track. Track never became one of his major interests, but he and Tom had finally made peace.

By the close of the year, Arlington was leading the cast in a three-act comedy/drama written by one of the Doane Players. He continued to receive plumb parts, sometimes as the lead, but as often as a supporting cast member. One such role in a play entitled *Holiday* required him to play a young man who drank to suppress his feelings. He did well, despite his in-

Doane Players, Doane College Yearbook. Courtesy author's personal collection.

experience with the ravages of alcohol. He understood the character's need to mask emotion. The way they were masked was the vehicle, not the issue.

Soon the Doane Players traveled as far away as eastern Colorado. Arlington worked not only as an actor, but also as the advance publicity man. He was learning the minutest facets of the theatrical world, and found himself falling deeper under its spell. His acting gave him membership, first in the dramatic fraternity of Delta Omicron, which in turn qualified him to belong to Alpha Psi Omega, a national dramatic fraternity. He accepted and embraced the benefits these prestigious organizations offered him.

Often during these road trips, his musical trio would go ahead of the troupe. During the day, they sang and played in local high schools where the drama group was scheduled to appear that evening. On one of these trips, Russ Gibson suggested they advertise the upcoming drama production on KMMJ, a radio station in Clay Center, Nebraska. Gibson said the effort was a resounding success. Not only were they allowed to play on the radio that day, but they were invited to audition at the station manager's home, and he hired them on the spot to perform every week that summer. They took on the name, "The Harmony Boys," and were paid one hundred dollars for each performance, the sum covering the three members.

The station was sixty-five miles west of Crete, and the boys made the trip through the summers of 1930 and 1931. On the station property was a building housing the station office and the store, which sold almost everything, from blankets to incubators, fly sprayers to candy. The listening audience spanned one hundred miles in all directions. Radio stations of the time were usually without national affiliation and had their own announcing and entertainment staffs. KMMJ had at least twelve announcers, about fifty entertainers, and programming was live from eight in the morning until seven in the evening. Entertainment consisted of "hillbilly singers, old-time fiddlers, orchestras, bands, and gospel singers." Each act was used to sell a specific product.

The Harmony Boys were given a fifteen-minute program, three-to-four times a day. They had every other Sunday off. Their spots sold "Old Trusty

Fly Spray." Gibson said when they weren't on the air, they stayed at the studio "rehearsing for anything from the Polka Band to the Symphony." They sang, in addition to playing their instruments.

Their job paid well, a respectable use of time for young college students. Those summers, while living in Clay Center, the boys stayed together in one rented room. According to Gibson, Arlington's preference for nice clothes followed him on the tour. "He had ten suits there, and took all the closet space . . . We were never extremely popular with the radio audience, and our fan mail was practically nil, but we did have lots of fun."

One day while they were not on air but in the studio, an announcer decided to jazz up his presentation. He pretended there were farm animals in the room, then started to moo like a cow, yelling at Arlington to run to the store and fetch an Old Trusty Sprayer to keep the flies off "old Bessie."

The studio brimmed with people. Arlington did as he was told, rushing out to find the stack of sprayers. He grabbed one and flew back. Unfortunately, he didn't remember the crucial last three steps leading from the main room into the studio. He staggered over the first two and tripped over the third, finally sliding into the crowd while gleefully waving the spray can high above his head. The announcer was hollering at him to move faster and faster, continuing to make moo sounds.

"We could not continue," Gibson concluded. "We went off the air. The audience out front was dying at the silly antics. . . ." But, "Brugh recovered, came running to the microphone," and squirted the fly spray into the air. "He gave us all a good shot, including the announcer. I could not breathe for five minutes. . . ."

Arlington casually dated quite a few females during his days at Doane, but there were only two over whom he was ever serious. His longest relationship was with Kathryn Bender. She followed in the mold of every other woman in his life to that point, being of mid-height, dark hair, and blue eyes. They met when both were formally accepted as members of the Doane Players. Kathryn was struck by Arlington's appearance and quiet manner.

To get him to notice her, she made sure she congratulated him in each of his roles. By December, she had a part in *Helena's Boys*, and a growing place in Arlington's dating life. She played romantically opposite him on stage, as well as in real life.

Kathryn called him "Doc," and was sure he didn't realize how attractive he was. "He was a perfect gentleman," she asserted, "very attentive, very handsome, a 'ladies' man, prompt, reliable, very honest, very intelligent, not a storyteller, did not gossip, was well-groomed, meticulous and had a bass voice. He also had a wonderful widow's peak."

He phoned her regularly, and even let her drive his car, a sure sign of his trust. Dinner with his parents was a frequent outing. He and Kathryn saw each other after classes, went together to school functions, attended movies and dances, and had picnics at the park. At the close of their freshman year, after dating regularly two times a month or more, he gave her a photograph signed, "Best regards, Doc."

But the relationship was not as casual as his inscription sounded. He wrote in her 1931 yearbook, "We've had a lot of good times together these past two years… Remember the 1930 spring Players trip—remember the night going to Sutton from Fairmont—remember our croquet games and those nights last summer? I surely do."

KATHRYN BENDER
Crete, Nebr.
Phi Sigma Tau
Choir; Doane Players; Vice-President, Sophomore Class.

**Kathryn Bender, Doane College Yearbook.
Courtesy author's personal collection.**

In addition to formal dates, they traveled together with the college drama troupe. They shared close quarters on the road, as well as on the boards.

He kept in regular touch with her while she was at summer school after their sophomore year, and things got a bit rocky between them for a time. One of his letters read, "You asked if I remembered the night of the third of July last year? I certainly do. I had a good time, did you? In fact, I enjoyed every one of those nights last summer. Remember how we used to sit out on the porch swing or else on the steps of the back porch, and talk? We were wonderful friends and I don't know why we ever broke up, so to speak, as we did. I guess that is just one of those unexplainable things... Love, Arlington."

Their college yearbook, *The Tiger*, was known for its gently sarcastic humor and happily-disrespectful spoofs on school life. The relationship between Arlington Brugh and Kathryn Bender did not escape notice.

The 1931 issue featured text from a mock play entitled, *Act IV—A Soliloquy*. The setting was a highway in Lincoln after a school football game. The skit starred Kathryn and Arlington, and featured the lines: "Oh Doc, please don't let's park here! Oh Doc, please don't let's park...! Oh Doc, please don't let's...! Oh Doc, please don't...! Oh Doc, please...! Oh Doc...! Oh...!!" The ending read, "Cur-

ACT IV—A SOLILOQUY
(On the Lincoln highway after the Cotner football game)

Kathryn Bender: Oh Doc, please don't let's park here!
Oh Doc, please don't let's park . . .!
Oh Doc, please don't let's . . .!
Oh Doc, please don't . . .!
Oh Doc, please . . .!
Oh Doc . . .!
Oh . . .!
!

CURTAIN!!

(That curtain is getting to be a nuisance)

Editor's Note: The next seventeen acts have been censored by the Board of Publications. We continue with the twenty-third act.

Above text from Doane College Yearbook.
Courtesy author's personal collection.

tain!! (That curtain is getting to be a nuisance)." A postscript teased, "Editor's Note: The next seventeen acts have been censored by the Board of Publications. We continue with the twenty-third act."

Kathryn remained closemouthed about the intensity of their relationship. She avowed, "... it was a matter of dating, not a serious love relationship or affair." Arlington also refused comment and forever stayed loyal to their privacy.

During the school year, Arlington may have been seriously courting Kathryn Bender but in the summer of 1930, after becoming known as an entertainer in Clay Center, he wasted no time in also dating the locals. He was familiar to townspeople because he came into their homes through their radio every week, and this undoubtedly gave him clout.

He met Blanche Gilsdorf at a dance one night while he was staying in Clay Center. She was a secretary from a neighboring town. Rumor was she had a boyfriend but Arlington continued to pursue her. Blanche followed in his favored-girl mold. Beth Naden Keller, a good friend of Arlington's from Doane Players days, confided he was "crazy over Blanche. He was the type who never let on to his feelings, but with Blanche, people knew how much he cared."

She came from a strict Catholic working family and did not attend college. Arlington continued a relationship with her throughout the next year. His schoolmates saw a difference in him each time he was with her. His demeanor changed; he was happier, more serene and introspective. Arlington Brugh was seriously "in love." Blanche kept him at bay, while also keeping him on the line.

As their acquaintance progressed, she decided the time had come for him to meet her parents. He agreed, and he asked her to dinner, informing her his parents would accompany him. She took painstaking efforts to sew a beautiful dress to wear for the occasion. After she ensured her hair looked perfect, she awaited him while animatedly discussing the upcoming evening with her sister.

Arlington and his parents arrived. Blanche introduced the three of them to her folks, and they had a short, civil conversation. The Gilsdorfs knew the Brughs were strict Methodists, and this seemed to dampen their enthusiasm over having Arlington date their Catholic daughter. Her mother was put off by his startling looks.

"Be careful!" she warned Blanche.

"Oh, Mother! He's not like that."

Again, as he had done on his date with Esther Legate a few years earlier, Arlington drove Blanche to the restaurant in one car, and his parents followed in another. They sat separately, and the couples had nothing obvious to do with each other as they dined. The date was pleasant, but likely not the exciting evening Blanche had envisioned. Whether a result of her parent's lukewarm response to Arlington, or the fact that his parents sat not far away, keeping tabs on their every move, Blanche went home feeling less than satisfied.

Not only had Kathryn Bender called Arlington, "Doc," his classmates did, as well. Everyone knew his father was a doctor and despite his rising dramatic and musical success, he still stated that he would probably follow in Dad's footsteps.

Arlington's few close friends understood he carried a serious torch for Blanche, but general school acquaintants were oblivious. They knew about Kathryn but were never quite sure how involved that relationship was, and Arlington didn't tell. Most everyone knew he kept in contact with both women. He was one of the few Doane students to have his own car, and he had a bit more spending money than most, thanks to his job. He and Garry often double-dated. Arlington gave an outward appearance of playing the field, casually going out with many girls.

A female friend of a fraternity brother said "some of the Doane boys got jealous . . . because he had a car and dated all the best women. The boys tried to boycott [him] because he was having too good a time."

His mother said, "Once in a while . . . he would mention some girl. Doane was co-ed, and he liked several girls there. But as for his getting serious about any of them, I do not think so. He was always very sensible about girls, not one to fall for flattery." It's likely she didn't know much about the frequency, or volume of his dating habits. Arlington kept certain things from his mother, things he felt she would frown upon. While she had never openly discouraged his interaction with the female sex, he was aware that if she could have her way, he would stay home and live with her for the rest of his life.

But that wasn't what he wanted. During his second year at Doane, Arlington kept up his studies and busied himself with continuing participation in the Doane Symphony. He also joined with three other instrumentalists, one of them a school professor, and formed the Doane String Quartet. They began public performances in the fall of 1930, with a heavy schedule throughout the school year, playing local high schools, rotary clubs, and college functions. Soon their public dates had them going out-of-town, and they were heard on KMMJ and other radio stations, at churches in northern Nebraska, and made a short tour of towns in Iowa.

Professor Gray was always working behind the scenes with Arlington. He was there when his student needed counsel, both professional and personal. He encouraged him and applauded him. When the professor played with the Lincoln Symphony he would occasionally ask Arlington to join him. This was something of which both were proud. The student had become more than capable enough to accompany the teacher.

The only thing which marred the relationship between Arlington and Professor Gray was Arlington's theater work. As he explained, "In my freshman year, I played the leading role in the campus performance of *Helena's Boys*, greatly to the disgust of Professor Gray, who wanted to know why I 'fiddled about with such nonsense.' He said that I should concentrate on the cello, that I had the makings of a concert artist, what had I to do with 'play-acting?' I couldn't tell him. I didn't know myself . . . I only knew that there was something in the musty smell of backstage that I liked."

Mary Ellen Inglis created the Doane Players. Within each school year they staged three major plays, performed in several communities in a spring college promotional trip, and held a winter or spring banquet. Her curriculum included such courses as Voice and Characterization, Play Production, and Repertoire. In addition, she sponsored six one-act plays. She was well-liked by students and seen as gentle, outgoing, and loving. Her expectations were high, but she was not harsh in her demands for excellence. Miss Inglis sensed talent and then set out to nurture his talent. From the beginning, she saw talent in Arlington Brugh. She liked him, thought he was a nice, thoughtful young man, and she was determined to set him on a course toward the stage.

His mother wanted Arlington to forever stay close at her side. His father encouraged him early on to seek a future in medicine, but never pushed. Herbert Gray saw him as a concert cellist. Mary Ellen Inglis knew he was destined to be an actor. Everyone seemed to want something different out of him.

Mary Ellen Englis, first professional to recognize
Arly's potential as an actor, Doane College
Yearbook. Courtesy author's personal collection.

Arlington felt he could probably make a decent living at any one of these professions. This wasn't a cocky assertion, but a careful and detailed observation of his background and abilities. The question wasn't at which one he might be best; the mystery was hidden in the confusion around which path he most wanted to take.

By the close of his second year at Doane, Arlington was out of sorts. "I liked dramatics better than anything else, but still thought of them as a hobby, something to play about with until the real business of life should begin."

He continued a close relationship with his parents, and talked over all major decisions with them. There was a strong obligation inside him to eventually take over his father's practice and as a result, he seriously considered attending medical school. He wrote them a letter, saying "he would miss terribly not becoming the sort of man that his father was." He felt he should drop out of Doane and go to medical school in Kirksville. Schooling would probably take about eight years for him to become a doctor, and he thought he should begin right away. His plan was to become a general practitioner, and take up orthopedic surgery as a sideline.

This idea wasn't foisted upon him by either his mother or father. The idea was Arlington's alone, not necessarily out of any real desire, but as a means to give back to his father for the many opportunities that had been afforded him. His parents were touched by his dedication, but told him he was too young to be certain he wanted to devote his life to medicine. He would be wisest to finish college before making a final decision.

In May of 1931, Herbert Gray announced he was moving to Pomona College in Claremont, California. He would fill a vacancy as instructor of voice, orchestral instruments, and ensemble work. He openly encouraged Arlington to make the move with him. Gray had spoken to Andrew and Ruth at great length about the expansive opportunities available to a musician with Arlington's talent, and he urged them to see that their son took advantage.

His mother, surprisingly, wasn't against the idea, even though her son would have to move a great distance away. She saw upward mobility for him and urged him to go, stating emphatically that Pomona "had a high scholastic rating and was a much larger school than Doane" where "... he had everything his way—in oratory, music, acting, singing ... he was not getting the right preparation for life." She went on to say she and his father believed a larger college would benefit him more. "... Professor Gray would be there ... and nearby, in San Bernardino, was my husband's former partner, Dr. Gass...."

Arlington still had not made a choice when summer rolled around. Through his own admission, he was "becoming very restless," but he couldn't pinpoint exactly what was behind his unease. Doane offered him Professor Gray's position, even though he was still a student. This spoke highly of his skills and maturity. The honor was a great one, but he wasn't excited over the prospect. He outlined his concerns to Kathryn Bender in a letter he wrote in July. "I really like Doane and would hate to leave all the friends I have there. Then, too, I would be close to home and the folks. That means a lot to them and more to me than I can realize now."

His final pick was made, but only after he did what he usually did when he needed to make an important decision. He talked everything over in great detail with his parents. Professor Gray's counsel, and his enthusiasm for the California college, as well as the professor's resolve that he was destined to become a professional cellist, were final qualifiers. Gray's opinion was so well-regarded by all three Brughs that they felt he knew what was best. Ruth and Andrew pushed for their son to transfer to Pomona College. He finally agreed.

Arlington felt a need to visit his "farmer friends" before his departure from Nebraska. He instinctively knew he would probably never again sit companionably with them in the same offhand way, gossiping in the evening as they gathered after a well-cooked meal, and "chewing" over local news. He loved those times in his community, feeling cocooned inside an intense, intimate sense of belonging. He didn't want to lose that sensation, though he knew that once he left Beatrice this time around, those moments would be gone.

Arlington's mother "mended and packed and didn't shed a tear" when he went off to Pomona, driving his graduation present and making the trek alone. Though he was leaving his comfortable, well-known home state, neither his mother, his father, nor he showed much outward emotion. Of his mother in particular, he said, "She never has been demonstrative." He stressed, "Nor am I."

As he left, his parents stood on the front porch waving. The memory of his dad's admonishment to drive no more than thirty-five miles per hour remained foremost in his mind, while the urge to race down the road was a great temptation. Soon, the trip itself proved to be an adventure for which he hadn't bargained. When he reached Laramie, Wyoming, he met a race car driver and his wife hitchhiking to California. He was naive and lonely, and offered them a ride if they'd help with the driving. They agreed.

Pomona College front gateway.

He had given the wheel to his race car-driving passenger, and was in the backseat trying to take a nap when he had a sense something was wrong. He looked up and saw his driver drinking from an indiscreet liquor bottle. The other man's steadiness didn't seem to alter, though, and Arlington relaxed. He was soon back to sleep.

He awoke later in a ditch. There was a deep, bleeding gash in his forehead. His car was on the side of the road, and resembled an accordion. The hitchhikers were gone. "I wasn't killed because it just wasn't my time to go," he observed fatalistically. Locating a garage to repair his car delayed his trip a few days. As he waited, he had the cut on his forehead taken care of, and he found a cheap place to spend the night.

His car had been, fortunately, salvageable. Despite the hard-earned lesson to not trust just anybody, he eventually arrived in Pomona in one piece. He spent the afternoon of his arrival aimlessly wandering tree-shaded streets. The California landscape was different than any he'd ever seen, and he was in awe of the purple hills and the big, healthy-looking oranges growing on the heavy fruit trees.

After Arlington settled into classes, he changed his major to business. He and Kathryn completely severed their relationship. He kept a close association with Professor Gray, while developing another student/teacher friendship with psychology professor Robert Ross. According to his mother, ". . . because he was good-looking and well-dressed," he was immediately dubbed with another label. "The Sheik" was seen as aloof and conceited and ". . . other boys did not give him credit for having any brains."

He lamented, "I was so utterly lonesome at first that the problem of starting to make friends had me baffled. . . ." Arlington turned to his only local confidante, Professor Ross, and they had their first serious talk. The teacher asked him, "Not quitting, are you?"

"I hadn't thought of that," Arlington replied. He said he was the type that had to see things through.

Professor Ross was pleased. "Right. Stick it out, my boy."

Classmates slowly discovered Arlington Brugh was not actually conceited, but he was extremely tentative around new people. His natural inclination was to keep to himself. In the beginning, he felt like "an intruder." He was in a place where he had no family or intimate friends, and it wasn't long before he realized that being alone wasn't always comfortable.

Arly Brugh, college age.
Courtesy Robert Taylor Family
Private Collection.

"I didn't have any outlet, any means of casual contact," he lamented. "I couldn't pour my agony out in my letters home. I knew better. I knew that my mother would write the words she had spoken long ago, 'You just cut yourself a switch, young man, and make her go.'" He was sure his mother would tell him, "Buck up, Arlington."

In the summer, between junior and senior years, he enrolled in Professor Ross' six-week lecture course on psychiatry. This teacher, like Professor Gray a few years earlier, saw a standout quality in Arlington, and the two men often shared lively discussions. After those six weeks of summer school, he returned home, and Doane College again tried to persuade him to work for them. This concerned his mother. She wanted him to stay at Pomona. She said Doane "urged him so strongly, and made him such attractive offers, that he intended to drive out to Pomona, pick up his belongings and credits, and go back to Doane for his last year. It did look to me as if he was a little too easily influenced. . . ."

Eventually she, Professor Gray, and Pomona won again. Arlington finished out his college years there, participating in plays and making efforts to adapt to California life. He got a job as a "smudger," working with smudge pots burned by the local citrus growers to keep frost from nipping the fruit trees.

"I forget whether we used to get thirty-five or fifty cents an hour...." he related in a later interview. "When the cold was severe... they paid as high as a dollar an hour. We used to pray for cold and go to bed hoping we'd be wakened before daylight... we'd climb into old clothes and ride up that baseline road, where the wind came right down off snow-capped Baldy... We'd go around with a torch made out of a piece of burlap sacking, dipped in oil, and light up the pots... it wasn't long before our eyes and lungs were full of smoke and our ears, nostrils, lips and the corners of our eyes were filled with that sticky, greasy soot that is almost impossible to wash out. Then we'd go home and try to grab an hour's sleep before showing up for a seven-thirty class...."

California was confusingly different from the Midwest, and he was, at heart, a small-town boy adrift in a big world. His mother said he "went through a torment of loneliness." He received a bit of comfort through his few familiar associations, Professor Gray, Professor Ross, and Dr. Gass, and wrote home regularly. He'd had little sustained contact with Blanche since he left, but he thought about her constantly, dreaming about how life would've been if he could have married her. When they did have brief exchanges in letters and notes, he was never quite sure how she felt. She didn't let on either way, and the relationship was at a standstill.

His first serious theatrical review came during his senior year at Pomona. "Arlington Brugh gave an intense and finely drawn performance as Captain Stanhope, the harassed commanding officer whose nerves were near the breaking point."

He wrote to tell his parents of the success. "I think Dad heard the bells of the future, my future, ringing," he said. He found out his father commented afterwards, "It doesn't seem to make much difference where that boy goes, he always lands on the stage."

There were many almost-fatalistic elements present. This was his last, and best, performance in Pomona. The play was titled *Journey's End*. His character shared a last name with his mother's family, and the character, Stanhope, was a tormented man whose emotions were being pulled in opposite directions. These realizations made Arlington seriously think about taking to the stage as a career, if only through the process of elimination. He'd already decided against law, or the ministry, or even the concert stage. None held his attention well enough to consider making his living at them. He also realized medicine and surgery weren't for him. He didn't see himself as one who would, for the rest of his life, "probe the secrets of the human body."

Journey's End had been a part he "hadn't wanted to play," he said. "On the same night there was an oratorical contest in Oregon and I was slated for both. I had chosen the contest because I had not been in Oregon. But the school chose the play. I wasn't too happy in the part...."

That this unwanted role brought about his first review was almost prophetic. He settled the indecision in his mind. The play was "not a journey's end, but a beginning." He "felt the part . . . felt it in every fiber. . . ." Acting pulled out of him emotion he wasn't naturally able to relate in day-to-day life. "I must have put it over, for there was considerable applause and, the next day, there was a call from M-G-M studio. Would I come to Culver City and have a personal conference with Mr. Louis B. Mayer?" Ben Piazza, a studio Casting Director, had reportedly been in the audience during the play, and he felt young Brugh deserved a MGM screen test.

Arlington was stunned. Could he do an admirable job? "I just plumb didn't think I'd heard right. I thought some of the fellows were horsing me . . . but . . . I sent an excited airmail, special delivery letter home," before he attempted to make any sense of the opportunity.

His mother's response, "Whatever you do, finish your education before you decide. Your father and I agree that this is a matter for you to determine...."

Hollywood. Moving pictures. His chance to "make it big." Did he want this enough to agree to a nerve-wracking film test in front of critical strangers? So far, he'd gone on stage because he enjoyed the audience feedback, because acting seemed to come easy, and he found the experience to be an amusing pastime. This would turn a pastime into a job. This would undoubtedly prove his mettle one way or the other. He had a monumental decision to make, more important than any other he'd ever made.

Could this truly be his *Journey's End*, or an exciting, challenging new beginning?

CHAPTER FOUR:

Being Discovered

> "Robert Taylor is the only person who
> has never heard of Robert Taylor."
> – Old friend

The handsome young man from Nebraska didn't find instant success in Hollywood. Arlington informed his parents he would "try acting for a year—and then, if it did not pan out, he would make use of his business degree." He took on the challenge on the strength of the talent agent's recommendation and went through with the screen test. There are a few interrelated stories of how he worked his way into the movie industry. Though unverified, one which deviates from the traditionally-told tale is interesting enough, and possible enough, to relate.

Ray Bourbon was a vaudeville performer and female impersonator, and he toured the country from theater to theater. On one such stop in Beatrice on March 30, 1929, Ray claimed he "met Robert Taylor." He and his theatrical partner, Bert Sherry, were on their way to Hollywood via Lincoln, from Kansas City. Billed as "Bourbon and Sherry," they were on after three other performers. A movie for kids was playing when they got there. Other acts there were singers, contortionists, dancers, and as Ray related, one was worse than the next. "I actually think we were as bad. . . ."

When the evening was over, as Ray and Bert sat in their dressing room, there was a knock. Bert opened the door to Arlington Brugh, part of the four-piece house band which had been playing upon their arrival. The young Arlington, who would've been eighteen, was the cellist. He'd heard Ray and Bert were on their way to Hollywood, and he wanted to talk to them. They invited him in to sit, and in barely-contained excitement, Arlington proceeded to explain how he, too, wanted to go to Hollywood. He thought he might be able to get work in pictures. He told them his father was a doctor who wanted him to follow in his footsteps, but he wasn't interested in medicine.

Ray suggested he get his parents to let him go to college in California. This would be the best way to get into movies, he said, rather than blindly making rounds at casting offices. He gave Arlington his agent's address and phone number in Los Angeles, and told him to look him up. The agent, a personal friend, always knew how to get hold of Ray. That evening, when he wasn't playing his cello in the orchestra pit, Arlington spent all his time chatting with Ray and Bert. This chance meeting ultimately helped to change his destiny.

"Two or three years later," Ray recalled that he got a call from his agent. A young man attending college in Pomona phoned that afternoon and left his number for Ray, and he knew who it was before he even read the name on the note.

"I called Arlington," he said. "They were doing a play at the college, *Death Takes A Holiday*. He was playing the lead and would I come out and see it? I explained that I was not sure I could get away [from a club engagement] but I would have a friend . . . catch it."

Ray called George McCall. George was an on-air radio personality with a fifteen-minute, twice-a-day semi-news and motion picture gossip segment. Ray told George all about Arlington Brugh. He explained how they'd met, how talented he was with the cello, and what he saw in him as a performer. His friend agreed to go to Pomona in his place to see Arlington on stage.

The next night, George showed up at the club where Ray was soon finishing his last show. "All right," Ray asked, "what happened?"

George produced a contract, signed in ink and witnessed. The only thing he said was, "That is one of the most handsome people I have ever seen in my life."

Ray replied that Arlington also had talent. George agreed, and thought if he had coaching and "a little experience," he would become "one of the BIG ones." George wanted to go to the studios the next day and "do a little selling."

Ray asked him to visit MGM first. "Put out the word," he said, about "the great find in Pomona. Above all, don't let Arlington know that anyone is seeing him from the studio's [sic]. That way he won't be self-conscious."

The next day, Ray received a call from George. He'd sold Arlington's contract to MGM. In his unpublished memoirs, Ray Bourbon finished his story about the soon-to-become Robert Taylor with the words, "From the day Arlington walked on the MGM lot, he was a STAR."

This vignette varies from the traditionally-told story of Robert Taylor's discovery. Bourbon's tale could have been nothing more than an entertainer's fantasy, written at the end of his career for his own edification; there is also the possibility he related the truth, that Ray Bourbon had something to do with the MGM talent scout being in the audience during Arlington Brugh's performance that fateful night. Since Ray Bourbon's telling didn't necessarily fit in with what MGM considered the most respectable explanation, they may have added their own tweak, or left parts out.

The actor himself had a bit of a different spin when he wrote of his recollections in 1937. He was in Pomona during the same showing of the same play. As he explained, "Before the play opened, we heard rumors that Metro-Goldwyn-Mayer was sending a scout to look for possible motion picture talent. Everyone was excited about it." He said a half hour before curtain time, the cast took turns at plastering their eye to the curtain's peephole. An audience seat reserved for the talent scout remained empty. Afterwards, the crew went out to eat together as they usually did.

The next evening after the show, as they were having their late night meal, the restaurant boss came to their table. He was grinning and said to Arlington, "Well, I guess you did yourself proud tonight, Clark Gable."

"Where do you get that Clark Gable stuff?" he demanded.

The other man told him someone from MGM had been at the restaurant earlier, asking about him. He caught the show and thought the "Arlington Brugh" guy was a standout, but Arlington didn't believe him. He was sure he was being ribbed, as often happened between these friends. True to the story, though, two days later he received a telegram from MGM, inviting him to report to the studio for a screen test.

The Ray Bourbon story could fit in, considering how Arlington Brugh was not signed to a contract as soon as he showed up on the lot. All three versions may have been variations on the one truth.

The young man's first trip to MGM was successful enough for the studio to give him advice and string him along. Oliver Hinsdell, MGM's dramatic coach, gave him six pieces of statuary: The Winged Victory, The Sower, Greek friezes from the Temple of Minerva, Solitude of the Soul, Diana of the Chase, and Diana of Gabii. He told Arlington to take them home and study them. "If you can't understand what these statues can teach you of correct posture and movement," he said, "there is very little hope for you."

Arlington thought Hinsdell a "kindly, inspirational man," and he read a few scenes for him. "He handed me a short side of lines and business which was excessively dramatic and which wound up with the line, 'He shot me. I'm dying.'" Arlington was later philosophical. "I suppose the bit was as much a personality test as anything. I'm sure I couldn't have crowded a great deal of technique into the action, but I did read the concluding lines softly and with an awestricken manner."

Hinsdell only grunted, "Okay," and walked away. Bob thought he was hopeless, and that would be the end of his chances. He found out later the drama coach had been impressed. Hinsdell started all new pupils with the same lines to see how they handled the propensity to become hammy. Ar-

Spangler Arlington Brugh official screen test. Courtesy author's personal collection.

lington mostly resisted the urge and, in reward, he was given a chance to have a talk with Louis B. Mayer, or as he related, ". . . he had one with me. He advised me to finish my college course, get my diploma. I didn't get a test. They didn't want me that badly. Mr. Hinsdell suggested that I report to the studio each Saturday morning for dramatic coaching."

Arlington took the advice all to heart. He came back again and again, learning from Mr. Hinsdell and the other students. He did his homework, going to the library to figure out what the statues portrayed and what they could teach him. He discovered: The Winged Victory showed physical grace; The Sower represented perfect rhythm in man; Diana of the Chase, perfect rhythm in woman; Diana of Gabii told of how people used their hands. Solitude of the Soul, he decided, was the most important, and the most complex. In that statue, the body was in perfect repose. Relaxation was the hardest skill for an actor to learn.

He was flustered by all he saw in those early days. "I . . . was awed by the vast sound stages, the deserted villages and city streets and store fronts and churches which, they said, were 'sets' . . . eighty-two acres of ground for one studio . . . huge squares of solid concrete rising like giant's blocks in every direction . . . mammoth doors, guarded by a single, small red electric light— blinking on and off from early morning until late in the night . . . I caught my first glimpse of cameras on dollies, of sound tracks, cutting rooms, gigantic prop rooms . . . I got a kick out of passing Clark Gable and Jean Harlow on the lot. I felt a powerful tug at my imagination. The same appeal music had always had for me, only stronger . . . I only knew that I felt sort of at home."

He returned to Pomona, reeling from the experience, close but not close enough. "They had been kind to me, but not too flattering. But they had planted the seed. I was advised to get an agent and see what he could do for me." He did secure an agent on the strength of the MGM meeting, and with that, he was first taken to the Samuel Goldwyn Studio where he tested for a part in *Roman Scandals*. He was passed over.

At that point he thought, "They didn't want me, either . . . but it hadn't been my idea in the first place. So what the heck?"

His schoolwork had been piling up, and Arlington decided to dig into his studies, determined to leave college with decent honors. His mother came to California the month before graduation, and his father joined them before the ceremony on June 19, 1933. Arlington felt proud and happy his family was together once again. "It was good to be finishing a part of the race and good to have my people around me."

His mother took ill during the trip, and her condition fluctuated. She made his commencement but they decided to get her home to Nebraska as soon as possible, and Arlington wanted to go along on the trip. He was aware that, technically, his period in California could be over. He needed to make a decision, a decision to which he must stick. Once they were back in Beatrice, he and his parents sat down to some serious discussions. "I told them I should like to try my hand at acting for a year." He felt the studio people had been somewhat encouraging. "They seemed to think I might make good."

His father replied, "If you want it, that's the thing to do." He added that if acting turned out to not be right for him, Arlington could return home and find some sort of "general business occupation."

With no guarantees, Arlington went back to Hollywood. For an introverted young man from the Midwest, a man who possessed a college degree, but no job, he was making a bold move. He found a room to rent, signed up for acting classes, and let MGM know he was finished with school and free to work.

The studio put him back in contact with Oliver Hinsdell for coaching every week. MGM "took an option" on his services and gave him a small salary, and Arlington added income by working with the Pasadena Playhouse. Still, week after week after week, there was no contract, though he was regularly given screen tests.

His old nemesis, isolation, again became his shadow. He did his best to keep his spirits up, repeatedly telling himself to be happy with his lessons. He must be doing well. After all, MGM hadn't told him to go home, had they?

By August, Arlington had been back in California barely two months when his world crashed in on him. He received word his father was gravely ill and in the hospital for an emergency operation. Arlington jumped into his car. He needed to talk with someone who really cared about him, someone who knew him well. He drove directly from Hollywood to Pomona to see Professor Gray, looking for reassurance that everything would be okay. He was going home to take care of his parents, but first, he needed the comfort of a strong shoulder.

The professor noticed the shock on Arlington's face as soon as he showed up at his door. The emotional upheaval in his charge's troubled blue eyes was etched into his every move. After Arlington explained what had happened, Professor Gray made a split decision. "I'll go with you." The older man threw some things together and climbed into the passenger side of Arlington's car. With Arlington already packed, they hit the road.

Knowing he was breaking his father's cardinal rule, he put his foot to the pedal and raced at speeds he'd never known he could drive. Professor Gray would occasionally take the wheel and give him a short break. The older man spoke gentle words to try and allay the boy's concerns, attempting to calm his nerves, if even for a short time.

Now and then Arlington would give voice to memories of his father, fears which at the time, he let slide because he could tell his dad didn't want to hear. He told the professor, "Last summer he said to me, when I remarked that he didn't look so well, 'I'm all right, son. You go back to Hollywood.

Work hard. Maybe you won't ever be president, but you might be another Tom Mix!'"

Professor Gray listened; that was what Arlington needed. "I'm glad I said to him," the young man continued, in a voice muffled with an emotion he didn't want to show, "I'm glad my last words to him were, 'Whatever I do I want to make good at it—for you and Mother.'"

Arlington was unable to still the memories, no matter how hard he tried. He recalled the horrified, defeated looks on children's faces back home when he'd gone on house calls with his dad, when the kids had known they were about to lose a loved one. A phrase long forgotten surfaced suddenly. "Others he saved. Himself he could not save." He couldn't quell the urge to cry out in his emotional pain. What would happen if his father left them?

Most stories say he and Professor Gray drove straight to Dr. Brugh's hospital bed. Arlington stayed a month, with his dad alternately seeming to rally, and then slip again. Dr. Brugh was able to finally collect himself enough to have a heart-to-heart talk with his son, and encourage him toward his future, telling him he was getting better and needed to return to his life in Hollywood. He reiterated his hopes that his son might become "another Tom Mix."

"I let Father convince me he was sure to recover," Arlington said at the end of their visit, with a bit of guilt deepening his voice, and he did go back to California, though not before he asked for his father's blessing and a wish of good luck. He still wanted nothing more than to make his parents proud. He thanked his dad for teaching him how to handle difficult situations. He knew his father had "met life and death and all of the exigencies of both with firm sympathy, with matter-of-fact common sense. I tried to follow in his footsteps."

Arlington sensed deep inside his dad was not going to be okay. He allowed himself to be fooled, but he knew the truth. "I don't know how he hid the pain he must have been suffering . . . he couldn't really have thought himself out of danger."

His father died the following month. Arlington returned to Beatrice once more, this time alone and by plane. Andrew Brugh's life was over, and his son was a changed man. Arlington was glad the suffering had ended, and he was certain his dad had gone on to a better place. He had to do the same, and he allowed himself no overt emotion. After the funeral, he gathered his strength to himself and supported his mother at the usual gathering of family and friends.

"Everyone gave me advice," he said. "Some said that I should remain in Beatrice, go into business, stay with Mother in her familiar surroundings. Others said I should go back to California and try to make good. Mother... thought it best for me to go back to Hollywood, to give it a year's [sic] trial and if, at the end of that time, I felt that I would be successful, I could send for her."

He put his foot down, absolutely refusing to leave her alone. "I told her that either she would go back with me then and there or I would never go back at all." He seriously considered saying the heck with MGM to stay in Beatrice, get work there, and utilize his business degree to feed his household. He went so far as to secure a job with an area oil station.

His mother continued to vacillate. A man who had been her entire life, a man she fondly called "Dear Doctor," was gone. Gone! And now her son, suddenly stoic and a bit like his father, was making the decisions. As life was with Dear Doctor, life would be with Arlington. Ruth had been totally dependent on her husband, and now the job of being the man of the family fell fully and completely on the shoulders of her twenty two-year old son. This time was difficult for both of them.

They settled Dr. Brugh's affairs together, and went on to make the final decision as to how to proceed. Arlington didn't have only his mother to take care of. He suddenly found himself as the sole breadwinner of a small family of people who depended on each other. His grandmother lived most of the year with his mother. Arlington had to figure out how to take care of his mother, and grandmother, while he continued acting classes and followed through with studio obligations. His mother adamantly told him not to throw away the amazing opportunity in Hollywood. He needed to return. Once more, she urged him to leave without her.

Again Arlington flatly refused. This burden was almost more than he could handle, and he did something he rarely did. He snapped at his mother. She and his grandmother were going to California with him, he told her, or he'd stay in Beatrice. End of discussion. This was an early show of backbone. He played this card only when stakes were important enough to make him stand up against her. He rarely argued unless he was certain an argument was in the best interest of all.

The altered family unit finally left Beatrice for Los Angeles on November 25, 1933. Arlington settled his mother and grandmother in his small apartment, and went directly to see Mr. Hinsdell. He had enough money left over from his father's estate to keep them going for a short time and find them a real place to live, but the days of experimenting, of wondering what he would do with the rest of his life, were over. Finished.

The time had come to get serious.

He was offered a more intense screen test this time around. The set was a drawing-room scene, and Evalyn Knapp was cast to play opposite him. Evalyn was three years older than Arlington, and when she walked on the set that day, she already had an active film career, with her first title out in 1929. The Director, Harry Bucquet, was working his way up in MGM. He was an assistant who did mostly shorts and screen tests; he had directed Greta Garbo in hers.

Arlington wore evening clothes. The scene called for him to be a drama coach, instructing Evalyn's character in the best stage love-making techniques. He said the, ". . . punch of the scene . . ." came when they made it clear neither character was play-acting anymore. This was serious business.

Being in the studio was a thrill for him. Onlookers watched with interest, remarking on his "grave restraint," and his "rich-toned voice and his self-possession." They were struck in particular with how he moved. He was graceful, strong, and lithe. Those eyeing him felt he might have potential. Still, the only person whose opinion ultimately mattered was Louis B. Mayer, and he wasn't in the studio.

No one said anything when Arlington finished the scene. He was thanked and sent on his way. Nothing as much as a, "Don't call us, we'll call you." As he left the studio lot, he didn't think he had a prayer. When he saw a poster stuck on a telephone pole which read, "Suppose nobody cared?" he felt it was appropriate. He didn't have to suppose. He knew.

Later that day, Louis B. Mayer was alone in a projection room watching a test of the latest young hopeful, a lad from Nebraska named Arlington Brugh. He leaned in toward the screen as he analyzed Brugh's money-making possibilities, the same way an investor would assess a potential venture. He made notes on what needed to be changed, what worked as presented, and how he could possibly shape this new acquisition into a star. He considered taking the chance; this one could be a winner.

Two days after Arlington made the MGM screen test, he was called into Louis B. Mayer's office. Mayer told him his progress was "promising." On the other hand, Arlington's appearance needed improvement. He didn't comb his hair right. "And an actor should dress well," Mayer continued. "A great deal depends on that."

Arlington wasn't sure what he meant since he had for so long been seen as a snappy dresser. He wasn't going to question Mr. Mayer, though. He nodded and continued to listen to the older man's criticism.

He wanted Arlington to change his name to one the public could easily pronounce, read, and write. Next he ordered him to his personal tailor for a new wardrobe. That was definitely out of the boy from Beatrice's budget, and Arlington respectfully told him so.

"Charge it to my account," Mayer brusquely ordered, "and do it now."

Soon-to-be Robert Taylor with Louis B. Mayer.

He gave Arlington specific rules to remember as a representative of MGM. He was in the movie business now, in the public eye, and Mayer told him that part of his job was, "... to dress decently and to keep up appearances. Every salesman has the same problem, but not many of them are as fortunate..." as Arlington was that day. His new boss made sure he was aware he had to sell himself like any other peddler had to sell a product, but Arlington's territory was the whole country. Mayer then dismissed the bewildered young man.

The studio grapevine went wild. Buzz went around that a new discovery had been made. Arlington did exactly as Mayer instructed as soon as he walked out of the boss' office. He not only went to Mayer's tailor, he also visited his barber who "changed the part" in his hair and added a different trim. Arlington was amazed; he said the change was "immense."

His looks were noticed at that early date, much more than any acting talent he may have possessed. What he might have at first lacked in strong ability was more than made up for with the start of the camera's love affair with him. His persona was a natural in front of the lens. A friend in the movie business once said about him, "... while he was a good physical man, he was very much a love statement . . . He was phenomenal in close-ups! . . . His face didn't hide anything. When you got in there on him, you saw it, you saw a lot. I don't think that he held back. I think that he just knew; it excited him." The friend was sure that the whole process motivated the young actor. "The camera moving in close . . . was playing to his strength, and I think the adrenaline went and stuff happened. He knew it."

As Arlington slowly became accustomed to life under Hollywood's intense spotlight, he never forgot he was responsible for the well-being of others. This was an indicator of what would drive him for the rest of his days in everything he did. He had a heavy sense of duty toward those who depended on him. There was a love factor in his sense of responsibility, one involving affection and familiarity, but as much imbedded in his psyche was the hard reality that he couldn't shirk the obligation to his family. For those who leaned on him, he would make sure they got what they needed. No matter how much, or how little, money he had in his pocket, no matter how much success he ultimately achieved, the Arlington Brugh in the man becoming Robert Taylor never forgot that second when he fully understood how his father's death would forever after dictate the direction of his existence.

That was how Arlington Brugh, his mother, his grandmother, and at some point, quite likely on the same trip, Garry Wiebe, set up house together as a family in California. Arlington was the primary breadwinner and caretaker.

There is little verifiable knowledge as to Garry's part in this, except for a letter written in 1940 by Ruth from Beverly Hills to a Beatrice minister and his wife. Right after Bob married Barbara Stanwyck, Ruth related, "I bought me a home and I am much happier . . . I had to have something to be interested in. It is more like living and makes a nice place for the children to come home. I want Larry to feel this is just like he use[d] to when he lived here. I had to give [up] Arlington and Larry both in one year. . . ."

Documents prove Ruth and Andrew Brugh had only one son, and there is nothing to suggest any other family member lived with them in California. The official supposition was that the "Larry" of Ruth's note was actually "Garry," who did go to college with Arlington at Doane due to Andrew and Ruth Brugh's generosity. Arlington called him his "only true friend," and with his parents treating Garry then as if he were their son, Garry was the only logical person to have gone to California to live with the family.

CHAPTER FIVE:

The Man With the Perfect Profile

"What Queen Elizabeth is to the British government,
Gable and Taylor and Shearer were to MGM. . . ."
– Howard Strickling, the MGM "Fixer"

Arlington Brugh would have never become Robert Taylor if the situation hadn't been just right. Though Hollywood was no longer in its infancy, the country's fascination with the town was still in adolescence. The business of making movies was learning, making mistakes, and when all went well, Hollywood was getting abundantly wealthy. Star-building was the not-so-secret weapon used to create profit, mainly for studio executives.

If not for the studios, Hollywood wouldn't have been Hollywood. They became mother, father, sibling, accountant, business manager, lover, hand-holder, angel and devil, and the final authority on all that was moral and true and right for their stars, in their opinion, anyway. And after all, they held the contracts and the purse strings, and their opinion was ultimately what mattered.

Countless young men and women wanted to go to Hollywood from all parts of the country, and the world, to become a "star." That was their dream. There was no shortage of candidates, and in comparison to the droves coming into town and begging for the chance, few actually made their way into the system. Why?

Money. Hollywood was always about money. If an individual was selected to be recreated and reborn into a star, and the selection was a wise one, that person became a studio property. Property equaled assets. Assets equaled profits. And profits equaled the perpetuation of the dream. Then the process started all over again.

Bottom line, money was the desired, the required end result.

Were the stars, those properties, the ones getting wealthy? Not in the early days. Not really. They had a job, albeit a glamorous one, but in many ways things for them were not unlike going to work for a corporation. The individual auditioned, and his or her resume was reviewed. Pros and cons were discussed behind closed doors. If the ingénue was selected to work for a specific studio, he or she received, and signed, a contract for a certain amount of money per month, per year. The now-employee took assignments, in this case, movies, as they were doled out. If the actor/employee didn't like a job, he or she could negotiate with the studio head. Occasionally that yielded results to their liking, but more often, the employee was sent back out to do the job as originally scheduled.

Such was the atmosphere when Arlington was signed to his MGM contract in early 1934. Talkies were a somewhat new delight. Routinely converting films to sound had only really started less than six years earlier. American movie attendance equaled about ninety million dollars in paid admissions from 1926 to 1930, barely a handful of years before Arlington Brugh became Robert Taylor.

The studios generally owned most of the country's theaters. In those early years, the five major studios owned about 2600 first-run theaters in the United States. They created a monopoly, generating three quarters of the revenue's total bottom line. Again, the game belonged to the studios, and to the men who ran them.

Arlington Brugh became Robert Taylor at the suggestion of Ida Koverman, Louis B. Mayer's "close friend" and right-hand assistant. In various documents she was also called his secretary, his aide, or his second-in-command. Whatever her official title, Ida was a powerhouse all unto herself. She had come to MGM from the offices of Herbert Hoover, where she served him well and faithfully as a publicity assistant during his campaign for president, and then as his secretary once he was in office. From Hoover, she went on to be hired by Mayer, who had campaigned heavily for, and who had considerable private influence with, Hoover.

Ida Koverman, Louis B. Mayer's "secretary," renamed Spangler Arlington Brugh and created Robert Taylor.

Ida made suggestions to Hoover in support of issues which could promote Mayer's interests, and she made suggestions to Mayer which could benefit Hoover's administration. Mayer would suggest political appointees. In one case, a friend of his was selected to become an ambassador; in another instance, someone he could faithfully rely on became the head of California's internal revenue system. Louis B. Mayer ultimately played a part in the appointment of Herbert Hoover, Jr. as head of the radio department of Western Air Express. This was a win-win situation for both Hoover and Mayer. And for Ida, she got her dream job. She was well placed within the Republican Party, and that figured greatly into how quickly she climbed the MGM ladder as an insider, and Mayer's closest confidante.

She was a solid bridge between Herbert Hoover and Louis B. Mayer. In turn for Hoover's favors, Mayer opened access to Hollywood for Hoover's administration. Ida was respected throughout the studio as Mayer's assistant, and her place in the middle of these powerful men gave her considerable influence and her own real sense of power. She was called a "mother figure" by some contract players, as well as "the only woman executive whose advice was respected by the male stars."

This proved to be true with Arlington when Ida selected the name he would become forever known by on the silver screen, and for the rest of his life. He and a member of MGM's publicity department, Kay Mulvey, originally petitioned to have his name changed to Ramsey Taylor, an idea which never went anywhere. Ida's direction won out.

※

New MGM contract players were assigned to different department heads to be re-worked as needed. One such person was Don Loomis. Sometimes called "MGM's muscleman," Loomis' job was to bulk up actors who had potential, but who needed greater physical stature. James Stewart had also been put under Loomis' direction. He said Loomis was ". . . a great, enormous muscleman with a gym shirt on and his neck just came right down. And every time he talked, muscles seemed to come out. He was a weight lifter. . . ."

Loomis determined Bob's "shoulders were too narrow," and his "neck was too thin." Through the use of bar bells and extensive physical exercise, the new actor was re-sculpted. Bob's weight went from 148 pounds to 168 pounds under Loomis' skilled attention. His chest gained five inches and his neck went from over fourteen inches to sixteen inches.

With ongoing workouts, lessons on everything from physical deportment to how to talk to the press, and a myriad of other types of personal attention, the now-named Robert Taylor was indoctrinated into the MGM star-making process, and he was a fast and intuitive learner.

Bob had not forgotten the assignment given to him by Oliver Hinsdell to figure out the mysteries of the statues. The one that stuck in his mind, Solitude of the Soul, continued to frustrate him as he worked to get good enough for his first real role in front of the cameras. He had to sit for fifteen minutes each day and engage in the art of relaxation, and Sundays were not excluded.

After six months of such study, he walked into Oliver Hinsdell's office, dropped into a chair and, without a single word, as Bob said, he "demanded that he look at me." His arms hung limp, all tension drained from his face. He must have done something right because soon after, he was cast in his first picture.

Newly-sculpted young actor now named Robert Taylor.

Bob got full credit for his part in *Handy Andy* (1934), a light comedy starring Will Rogers, and officially released in July. Rogers died the following year, becoming best known as a "humorist" despite the over fifty films officially listed to him. On the *Handy Andy* shoot, Bob saw him as a kindly older man who ". . . showed such considerate patience with me when I first acted before a camera."

The movie came to Los Angeles' first drive-in theater in September, a place named, simply, Drive-In Theater. When the film made its debut in Nebraska, Bob's adoring cousin, Izetta, was giddy with excitement, and she and a roommate made a twenty-two mile trip to Nebraska City. The picture show was jammed and the pair "waited outside for what seemed hours" before they were allowed in to find their seats.

The drive was worth the long time on the road. Having known him before he was Robert Taylor, Izetta was entranced as she watched him on the screen. That was her cousin! She said he looked natural, and she gleefully noted when he "put his right hand in his pocket as he started to walk." This was, she said, "an old gesture of his." He had advanced into the big league in Hollywood, but those who knew him from childhood were still able to clearly see the boy, Arlington Brugh, in the movie star he now was.

Bob, Chester Morris, and Virginia Bruce in *Society Doctor*. Courtesy Judith Hanhisalo personal collection.

In November of 1934, Bob was selected to play second lead in *Society Doctor* (1935), and he was grateful MGM had "the courage" to give him that responsibility. He hadn't to this point attracted any large-scale attention, but this experience brought him his first real fan letter. "The first note I had... tickled me silly," he remembered many years later. "I had the paper framed and hung it next to my bed. I was afraid I might never get another."

He did, though. After having taken on a handful of small roles, a few uncredited, in both short and feature-length films, the young actor was delighted with his part in this movie. His first heavy-handed review in a New York paper came in as a result of *Society Doctor*. He was starting a new year with a bang.

One line in particular of the review, and of him, had him gloating. "A young unknown named Robert Taylor gives a good account of himself in spite of his matinee idol looks." Bob laughed. "The writer said, 'in spite of,' see? Now looks are good or bad, according to taste. My appearance doesn't fascinate me, but I'm not the one who has to be pleased, either. It's a big help to an actor if people like to look at him, but it has nothing to do with acting."

Bob with cast of *Broadway Melody* of 1936.
Courtesy Robert Taylor Family Private Collection.

That year, after *Society Doctor*, he made six more movies, all taking little time to produce and put out in rapid succession. He played the lead in two of them—*Times Square Lady* (1935), and *Murder In The Fleet* (1935). He supported the stars in two more—*West Point of the Air* (1935) and *Broadway Melody of 1936* (1935).

But it was *Magnificent Obsession* (1935) which made serious waves with the movie-going public when it was released on the 30th of December. Bob's portrayal of a playboy-turned doctor was all-around considered to be his first major hit for ticket sales, and his stock as a moneymaker increased.

The ever-adoring Izetta said he reminded her of his father. In a scene where Bob's character sat outside the operating room, waiting for results of what had been a serious medical procedure, he wore a somber expression, with his hands clasped between his knees and his head leaning forward.

**Bob with Irene Dunne in *Magnificent Obsession*.
Courtesy Robert Taylor Family Private Collection.**

Izetta saw his dad in this posture, recalling many conversations she'd had with her uncle as she sat with him in his office. Uncle Spang would always sit that same way when discussing something of import, or when chatting with children.

Bob was amazed at all the commotion surrounding him, though he had too much self-presence to let that show. "... I pinch that actor, Robert Taylor," he said, "and find that it hurts the fellow from Nebraska, Arlington Brugh." There were special connotations for him in playing a doctor. The spirit of his father in him which Izetta recognized was not accidental. "I tried to get into the character some of the reverence I had for the memory of my father, who brought such compassion to the practice of medicine...."

Howard Strickling, an important person in Hollywood, was called a "fixer." He owned all matters of publicity for MGM, particularly anything affecting its "assets," otherwise known as the actors under contract. Only those considered to be big-ticket moneymakers, and a few potential big-ticket moneymakers, were put into his hands. He was a genius at what he did.

"What Queen Elizabeth is to the British government, Gable and Taylor and Shearer were to MGM. . . ." Howard Strickling was quoted as saying. "But it's the only business in the world where all the assets walked out the gate every night. In other businesses it's different, like if an editor gets drunk too often you hire another one . . . Okay, you've got Gable and Taylor and Garbo, but there's only one of each so you work things out. . . ."

He explained how he "worked things out."

"When I started out I discovered that everybody needs help and particularly actors. . . . I was a company man. I found if I could help Gable or Taylor or Harlow, I became important to them. And in that way I could get them to do things. But, well, my relationship with Clark, and Bob Taylor—maybe Jean Harlow and Norma Shearer—was different, because I was closer to them than to some of the others."

The publicity campaign launched to introduce Robert Taylor to the world was considered the most extensive and expensive public relations effort ever put in place to debut a new actor, at that point and for years to come. MGM executives clearly saw something in the lad from the Midwest.

Keeping Bob as a part of the MGM stable was a logical plan of action for Louis B. Mayer for this reason alone. He fully intended to make good on his investment; a lot of money was devoted to each signed actor contract put on the fast track. He was being paired with the most visible actresses in town. Whatever needed to be done was done to ensure Bob was firmly in place as the next star attributed to MGM, the studio with the slogan, "More Stars Than In The Sky."

Franchot Tone, Joan Crawford, Barbara, and Bob out to dinner the night Bob left for a New York trip. Courtesy Robert Taylor Family Private Collection.

During the filming of *His Brother's Wife* (1936) with Barbara Stanwyck, Bob was sent to New York City on a publicity junket. He had created a stir with this one, and MGM wanted to capitalize on the hoopla. He was flown to New York, arranging the concurrent filming in Los Angeles to ensure that the scenes in which he didn't appear were scheduled first.

Bob had never been to what he called, "the big city." The morning after he arrived, he was hardly able to contain his excitement and he got up at 5 o'clock to take a brisk walk around town. He found the streets surprisingly empty. A few hours later, he realized while the early morning hours might not be hectic, the city grew busy in quick time.

He was there for five days. The frenzy may have been in part thanks to Bob Strickling, but Bob Taylor was the one who was stampeded and mauled. "I lost my necktie," he explained, "all the buttons on my coat and my pockets were torn off." One day he was forced to run down the hall of the seventeenth floor of Radio City to get out of an overzealous crowd. He stopped for a moment, trying to catch his breath. He thought he was safe, but the door to the stairwell popped open and a horde of people came at him, almost all of them women.

He ducked inside the studio office right in front of him and slammed the door as the crowd started pushing from the other side. They managed to break in, and Bob got out of their line of attack barely in time.

Bob and Barbara in first official photo shoot together, for *His Brother's Wife*. Courtesy Robert Taylor Family Private Collection.

Life magazine debuted as a weekly spread on November 23, 1936. Publisher Henry Luce paid $92,000 for the name, an outrageous sum of money at the time. He was convinced the public would go for the new format, fifty pages of pictures and text condensed into small paragraphs to compliment the photos. He was right; the newly-redesigned *Life* magazine became an almost instant success. An indicator of Bob's skyrocketing popularity was a photo layout featured in the first *Life* magazine weekly. The piece was called, "Mr. Brugh = Robert Taylor."

Also in 1936, Bob had his portrait taken by "Hollywood's premier portrait photographer," George Edward Hurrell. Hurrell's first star photograph was of Ramon Navarro in 1929. In October, he photographed Norma Shearer. Shearer's husband was studio executive Irving Thalberg, and he was so enthralled with the end product he offered Hurrell a job as MGM's Head Photographer. Bob's portrait was shot during the same period as those of Joan Crawford, Joan and Constance Bennett, and Madeleine Carroll. Bob said later in life, "Everything in those days was aimed at glamour."

MGM seemed to intentionally cultivate the long-lasting persona of Robert Taylor as a simple man, an easy-going, uncomplicated man who did what he was told, when he was told. Somewhere during the time surrounding the debut of *Magnificent Obsession*, he was approached by a reporter and asked about his performance... what was the driving force behind his work?

"A screen metamorphosis," he replied thoughtfully, "is more psychology than histrionics. The thing is to analyze the character you are playing and then the various stages of self-development become a logical outgrowth of that individual finding himself."

The reporter was floored. He stuttered in response, unsure as to how to respond. Bob's words were high-brow, intellectual, off the top of his head, and his honest response to the question asked of him. The reporter managed to accurately quote him, and Mayer called him into his office after the interview showed up in the press. He wanted to know what the hell Bob thought he'd been doing to answer in such a way. Bob re-read the quote, shrugged, nodded, and said his words had printed correctly. Exactly what he had said.

"You sounded like your jockstrap was on too tight!" Mayer exploded. He told Bob to not talk to any more reporters for awhile.

The collegiate wasn't the public image Mayer wanted for his new gold mine, though that's exactly what Bob was. Mayer was looking for something out of Bob more subdued, with quiet strength. He wanted Bob to offer fewer words to the public, ensuring his male beauty would be the focus, not his brain.

Bob had received a "happy surprise" in the form of a letter from an old girlfriend in March of 1936, before he finished shooting *Small Town Girl* (1936) with Janet Gaynor. Dolores Harmon had years earlier stated publicly she and Bob never dated. Her "nice letter" to him "brought back... many happy memories of when we used to live across the street from each [other] on Sixth Street. Remember?" He told her there was "nothing like having an old girl friend bob upon the scene when you feel 'down in the mouth,'" a reference to his fatigue. He explained his hectic six-week schedule working on *Small Town Girl* and said he was looking for a rest. Bob was pleased to hear

Bob in early promotional head shot.
Courtesy Robert Taylor Family Private Collection.

from her, though he made no attempt to continue the correspondence, and he signed his letter with a saucy, "Best wishes to you and the rest of the Colorado co-eds... Sincerely, Arlington Brugh." His pseudo-formality seemed to be a gentle jab at her for denying they had ever dated.

A male reporter sent to spend a "regular day with Robert Taylor" around this time said many folks believed he couldn't possibly be as good-looking in person as he was on screen. "Yet he is," the reporter avowed. "The cameras picture Bob exactly... He's what every male ought to look like, and the virility and character so evident on the screen are not assumed." This served to reinforce what Mayer wanted out of him.

Bob was on his way, and soon to be shoved on the set with Hollywood heavyweights. He was scheduled to star with Greta Garbo in a film which could take him over the top. A bit of physical tweaking—an actor could never be too good-looking—wasn't beyond studio bigwigs to ensure he stood up alongside an actress established as a top box office draw.

Some articles tell of Bob's nose being worked on prior to the shooting of *Camille* (1936). "Robert Taylor, who seems to have been born with the almost perfect face, actually had a small operation to straighten his nose before shooting began," one report said. Other stories mentioned some well-placed putty, rather than an operation.

Bob's character, Armand, could be no less perfect than that of Garbo's portrayal of Camille. She was a bona fide star; he wasn't. In some ways, MGM was working a gamble to play him against such an actress.

Years later, Bob said Garbo was, ". . . always arriving alone in her chauffeured Packard. Everyone was impressed, not by this peculiarly lonely dispo-

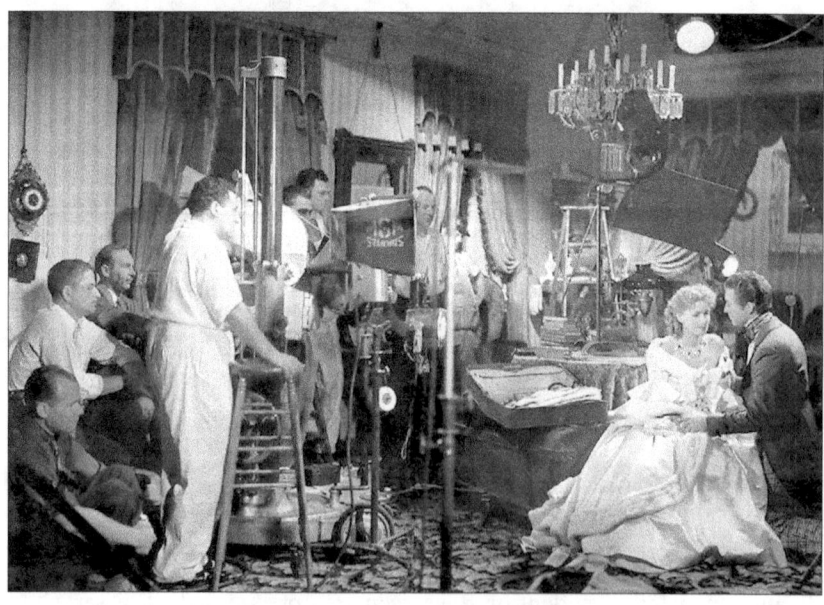

**Bob with Greta Garbo on set of *Camille*.
Courtesy Robert Taylor Family Private Collection.**

sition, but by her talent. She was one of the finest and most professional actresses I have ever worked with and it was a pleasure. On the set she wanted to work—and worked hard—but the warmth which audiences felt, and which attracted them to her, was likewise felt and appreciated by everyone near her. The crews who worked her pictures were, to a man, fanatics in her service."

The film premiered in New York City on January 22, 1937. Audiences flocked to see Garbo as well as Robert Taylor, the newest star on the MGM horizon. Women clutched at their friend's sleeves, ran one in front of the other, and struggled every-which-way to get a glimpse of the real-life movie stars.

Much gossip circulated during the filming, and directly after. Some was the result of MGM's well-oiled publicity machine a la Strickling, put out for the express purpose of making Robert Taylor more visible. Other stories came from the growing number of women absolutely smitten with the latest film sensation, and this was exactly what MGM wanted. The studio dubbed him, "The Man With The Perfect Profile," and all available media outlets ran with the new tagline.

One story dramatically had Bob dropping Garbo to the floor during a re-shoot of the death scene. ". . . He didn't," Garbo stated. She seemed determined to clarify how Robert Taylor was nothing but a gentleman. "He was a very well brought up young man, a bit shy perhaps. He did everything to make me feel better. I was often actually rather ill during filming. He used to have a gramophone with him that he would play because he knew I like music. It helped distract me. . . ."

Bob would have used his love of music to soothe the nerves of his co-star. As Garbo had stated, he was raised well, and he loved music. The interviewer who spent time with him to discover what his "regular day" was like said music ". . . always is around Bob . . . music while he's driving, wherever he goes to eat, and Joe [his 'houseboy'] has orders to turn on the living-room radio the minute Bob's awake. Melodies flood the house and Joe flicks on the music when Bob's car rolls into the driveway after a day at the studio." Bob drove a Cadillac coupe.

Music also figured into an out-of-character bit of mischief with Garbo, Bob and Jessie Ralph, the actress who played Camille's maid. Between scenes, they decided to play a joke on George Cukor, and started singing a three-part harmony version of "Home, Home on the Range." Bob said the song was, "... as discordant a mess as three voices could make it." Cukor corralled them, set them back on track, and they returned to work.

The next day, Garbo had a difficult scene to accomplish and asked the Director to have someone "start a spiritual on the amplifier." Music always got her in the right mood; whatever the scene, corresponding music was played. As she waited for the soothing tune she asked for, "... there burst from the device the most horrible medley of screeching imaginable," Bob related with a hearty laugh. Cukor secretly had the sound engineer record their silly singing from the day before. He had figured them out and couldn't resist the urge to have the loop played when the cast was otherwise occupied.

Bob and George Cukor. Courtesy author's personal collection.

How much time Bob and Garbo spent together alone during the filming of *Camille*, away from the cameras or the stresses of the set, isn't certain. Reports indicate they had enough private time to get to know each other with some familiarity, and even talk about their personal lives.

Garbo said, "Robert Taylor... told me that his best friend during his youth in Nebraska had been a Swede [Garry Wiebe]...." She spoke of their differences. "I have never liked sitting in the sun... But Robert Taylor was the exact opposite. He worshipped the sun and then he was forced to abstain from the outdoor life for the weeks we were filming since we both had to be equally pale...."

There were reports of a romantic entanglement, possibly nothing more than fuel for the press, another Strickling masterpiece. One telling had Bob going home with Garbo, and spending the night, after an especially intense day of love scenes. Bob refused to speak about the rumors, ever... at the time of the movie, and forever afterward.

Years later, Garbo made at least one comment to revive the curiosity. "Robert Taylor was most attentive, trying without success to make me respond to his love. I noticed his ardor, and I became especially patient with him in explaining how he must act, since he was young and inexperienced." This referenced their work, but then she switched gears. "But I never spent any time with him in the evening after work... The energy I needed for this role drained me of any social or sexual desires...."

Did this mean he had tried to make a move on her? Bob was shy, especially during his earlier years, and Garbo was a bit older, and she was experienced. At one point he said about her, "I don't know whether it was because it was Garbo or my first assignment, but something made me nervous. With the aura that had built up about Miss Garbo... for a young fellow of twenty-five to walk on the set and be thrown into a love scene without having met her before, was a pretty big order."

Did she make a move on him? Garbo was aloof even then, but she was a method actress long before that was popular. A leading lady often would get lost in her role and engage in a dalliance with her leading man. This could have all been nothing more than another point in favor of the studios running the lives of their "assets." Droves of swooning women wondering if the beautiful people, Robert Taylor and Greta Garbo, were acting out in private what they showed to the world on screen was exactly what MGM wanted.

With a moniker like "The Man With The Perfect Profile," Bob had to deliver. Not long after his face hit the screen, women started mobbing him everywhere. He ignored them as much as he could. A good friend once said, "Robert Taylor is the only person who has never heard of Robert Taylor."

During this period, he had a chance to return to Beatrice for the first time since he hit the big screen. The official occasion was a party for his grandmother's eightieth birthday. His mother and grandmother had been traveling back and forth between Nebraska and California since their official move, and they accompanied Bob on this trip.

The town went mad. Seven bands turned out as well as glee clubs, a drum corps and the National Guard. All the stores, their fronts draped with bunting, were closed, as were the local schools.

The sound of the steam whistle at the box factory filled the air. Bob hadn't heard that since the armistice. He said, "The sound symbolized so much good will from all the folks I liked so well that I almost cried." He was swooped away from the local airport, put in an open touring car, and ridden through the streets in a parade in his honor. "I got plumped on top of the back seat so everybody could wave better and off we started in a tumult."

And of course the local newspaper wanted time with him. The reporter met him at his old home where he had grown up, and Bob acted as if he were a young kid. Sitting on the dresser in what had been his bedroom, his legs dangling, he engaged the newspaperman in excited chatter, clearly happy in his natural environment. He looked out the window and marveled at the mild October landscape. He laughed, saying he had wanted to leave the

Bob, aka Arlington Brugh, returns home to a hero's welcome in Beatrice, Nebraska. Courtesy Robert Taylor Family Private Collection.

plane that morning to wade in the snow at Cheyenne as they made their way to Nebraska.

But when questions turned to his personal life in Hollywood, his tone changed. He wouldn't give up any details. He smiled politely, he was still friendly, but if he was asked something he felt was too personal, he said he couldn't answer.

He was learning how to be a star. Bob had taken discreet advantage of the female attention coming his way as a marquee name. The reporter asked if he liked blondes. His reply was, "Certainly—and redheads and brunettes and brownettes." Since his adolescence, he had often been the center of feminine interest. This may have been why he was able to matter-of-factly handle the invasive questions into his personal life, growing more intense by the day.

Both prior to his work with Garbo in *Camille* and after, Bob had an acquaintance with actress Eleanor Powell. Eleanor was born in 1912, and they got along well. She had been discovered in 1922 for Vaudeville Kiddie Review. This took her on to a Broadway career, and by the time she met Bob when she was twenty-five, she was a seasoned entertainer. Coming to Hollywood in 1935, she soon became known as the "Queen of Tap Dancing" for her amazing ability to make music with her dance steps.

Bob had worked with Eleanor on his tenth film, *A Broadway Melody of 1936*, and again a few years later in *A Broadway Melody of 1938* (1937). According to Peter Ford, her son with Glenn Ford, "Bob and my mother worked together and he was in love with her . . . they had talked of marriage but it never happened."

Bob's life started moving fast, and he had to do his best to keep pace. His next film was *A Yank At Oxford* (1938), the first movie filmed overseas by a major United States studio. To get from the United States to Europe in those days was quite an ordeal, taking a train to Chicago, another to New York, and then an ocean liner to England. The publicity machine worked overtime through all facets. This was a first-time trip for Bob. As the ship prepared to sail, the hoopla over his presence died down and he went to his cabin looking for a few moments of downtime.

Bob had no sooner closed the door, when two heads poked out from under his bed.

"What the . . . ?!"

Squeals could be heard down the hall as Bob threw open his cabin door and stomped down the hall to locate the steward. The teen-aged girls were shepherded out of the room, giggling the entire time, and they were unceremoniously dumped on the dock as the ship readied to sail.

Newspapers got wind of the antics and went crazy, and that was as planned. Bob's anger turned to lopsided amusement when he learned the story behind their appearance. Not until an interview many years later did he confess the young ladies were studio plants, paid to be there to create a ruckus. As Bob said, "It was good copy—and the boys [the studio] milked it."

Seven writers worked on *A Yank at Oxford*, including F. Scott Fitzgerald, who received no credit. Fitzgerald wrote to his mother-in-law about a line in the script with his trademark. Bob had spoken that line to his co-star, Maureen O'Sullivan, "Don't rub the sleep out of your eyes. It's beautiful sleep." Fitzgerald was then on the decline; Bob's star was rising.

A scene in a rowboat really put him in the gossip columns. He was shirtless, wearing only a pair of shorts, and the ensuing result was bedlam. In response to a few disparaging comments in the press from men about his near-nakedness, and his masculine "beauty," Bob said the first thing that came to mind in a fit of aggravation, "... I've got hair on my chest!"

Bob and Maureen O'Sullivan in *A Yank At Oxford*.

He lived to regret his outburst, though ultimately the incident offered him a quirky place in history. That six-word phrase was repeated over and over in every media outlet available. While the scene continued to irk men, female delight was fueled to distraction, and the wardrobe choice endeared Bob to his female fans in a way nothing else up to then had been able to achieve. Ladies started requiring of their men, in any way they could get it, what Robert Taylor adamantly proclaimed he had naturally. They wanted men with hair on their chest. A "chest toupee" craze began, and men bought them in large numbers to make their women happy. This invention worked the same as a dickey; it showed underneath the shirt only enough to add a hint of virility. Though he could have never known this at the time, Robert Taylor became a pioneer in the "fashion" of hairy chests.

Louis B. Mayer was quoted as saying there was "an inseparable and common bond between radio and television." He added Bob as one of the regular hosts of a MGM-sponsored radio show called "Good News." The vehicle showcased upcoming talent and promoted the "good taste" of Maxwell House Coffee as the sponsor.

In the late afternoon of March 31, 1938, Bob became part of one of the earliest incidences of simulcast media between the United States and Europe. The major guest was Mayer himself, who from the studio in California sent a welcome message to an English movie audience. The clock had barely reached 1 AM the next day in Britain. Viewers had finished watching their premiere of *A Yank At Oxford*. Mayer's message told them this movie was "an important step of development of the motion picture in England," and he hoped MGM "contributed vastly" to the burgeoning industry.

Denham Studios was the brainchild of Alex Korda, an influential European moviemaker, and his London Film Productions. On the western edge of London, the complex consisted of a commissary, dressing rooms, stables, a film laboratory and production offices. Korda had made a big splash in the burgeoning movie industry in England in the early 1930s, but by later in the decade, he had financial difficulties. What was originally created as his film kingdom had to be farmed out to United States-owned studios.

Big American stars were shipped overseas, and casting was supplemented by British talent, technical as well as onscreen. The effort, called MGM-British, was an example of international marketplace on a grand scale, and became a production effort to promote American and British cooperation. The timing was intentional; the world was in desperate need of global unity. Louis B. Mayer had family members on the payroll; his son-in-law's brother worked as the studio manager.

Mayer's message to the "Good News" radio audience that afternoon included a quick "ad-lib" from the movie's Director and major cast members.

Bob kidded with the Director, saying he remembered during filming when "the boys . . . threw me in the river, and I landed on my head in the mud." Mayer pretended anger at such antics done on company time, and Bob replied, "Oh, Mr. Mayer, we were just playing around." They all had a good laugh, and Bob said he would always remember the "steaks at the Lord Belgrave." The Director wholeheartedly agreed, and everyone laughed at what was an inane but important, and ingenious, production.

Christmas offered a glimpse of how Bob would relate to children for the rest of his life. A young cousin from Colorado came to visit. Harold Moore was eight, the son of Bob's aunt. His grandmother spent her days moving from spot to spot to visit her daughters. When time came for her to leave Colorado to be with Ruth, Ruth decided her mother shouldn't travel by train alone. The job of keeping her company fell to young Harold. Aunt Ruth sent tickets for the best sleeping arrangements in the Pullman car. Harold was told to take care of Grandmother. Once situated, the conductor came by and asked for tickets.

Ruth Brugh, second from right, her mother next to her, and other family members. Courtesy Robert Taylor Family Private Collection.

Their tickets didn't match arrangements made by Aunt Ruth, and Harold and Grandmother were sent to the "seated" car. Upon arrival in Los Angeles, young Harold wasted no time in explaining what happened; Aunt Ruth, in turn, gave the railroad's Complaint Department an earful. After the hoopla died down, Harold, Grandmother, Ruth, and George, the butler, drove to Aunt Ruth's house. George took Harold to his room, complete with a bath with a white porcelain bathtub almost large enough to swim in. And with running water!

Harold was told his cousin, Robert Taylor, would spend Christmas with them. While he waited for the special day to arrive, Harold enjoyed time with George. They window-shopped around town, and talked about what he wanted for Christmas. George took him to toy and bicycle shops, and repeatedly asked Harold what sort of bicycle he liked. Thinking this was a game, Harold noted one in a window. Red and white, with whitewall tires, chrome, and battery-operated horn, the bike was complete with a red light and a carrying basket.

This country boy from Nebraska wasn't sure what was real anymore, and when George repeated the question, "What do you want for Christmas?" Harold said something about a pair of leather gloves with rabbit fur. The subject was dropped, days continued to tick towards Christmas, and Harold delighted in every minute of his vacation.

Finally, Christmas day! Bob arrived about noon, and he had Barbara Stanwyck with him. Harold was sent to put on his best clothes. He was in awe at mealtime, gazing constantly at his cousin and Barbara as they chatted with Grandmother and Aunt Ruth. Afterward, he was told to change clothes again, and go outside to play. Harold was disappointed because he didn't want to leave his cousin. But he did as he was told, and as he changed his outfit, Aunt Ruth called up the stairs. Cousin Robert wanted Harold in the living room. He scampered down and stopped short at the door. Aunt Ruth and Grandmother sat on one side of the room, and Cousin Bob sat in the middle of the floor, surrounded by packages.

Harold still didn't know what was happening. He was told to sit with Bob, who proceeded to help him open the gifts, all of which were for him. There was a sheepskin-lined rainproof sports coat with hood; knife and hatchet in leather case; complete set of encyclopedias; automatic rifle; double-barrel twenty gauge shotgun; and an all wool suit.

Barbara also gave him a gift. He fumbled with the wrapping and when he finally was able to open the box, he found a watch with her name engraved on the back. Harold buried his face in Aunt Ruth's lap and cried for awhile before trying to dry his tears and look up at his cousin.

Bob didn't give him the chance to dry his tears. Smiling, he jumped up and walked toward his den, motioning Harold to join him. Harold slowly took the few steps to stand behind Bob. He stared, mouth open, into his cousin's study, where everything seemed to be done in leather. Only one item in the room seemed to be different and that was the same red bicycle he had told George he liked a few days earlier. George hadn't been toying with him! The bike stood in the middle of the room in full glory. His cousin had bought all these things for him.

Bob took Harold and the bicycle outside, sat him on the leather seat, and said, "Ride!" The overwhelmed child tried. Bob was patient, but determined his young relative would learn how to ride before he left California to go home. Harold sat on the bike, rode a bit, fell off. Then he got back on and again fell off. Over and over, he tried to ride the bike.

By the time they were finished, Harold had learned to take the bike a few feet on his own. Before he left Los Angeles, he was riding up and down the tree-lined street. Bob made arrangements for the boy's gifts to be safely transported to Colorado, and made sure he and Grandmother had the best train accommodations available. He employed a male companion to see to their safety and "play games" with his young cousin to keep him occupied on the trip.

"Butler George" took Harold to the train station. On the drive there, Harold received one last surprise. George handed him a package and said, "Open." Inside was a pair of black leather, fur-lined gloves.

Bob had taken center stage a few years earlier, in a film which would become of much note in his life. *Personal Property* (1937) was originally called *The Man In Possession*, and he was cast in the lead, along with Jean Harlow. As a dry-run for their movie pairing, Bob and Jean were handed a radio script for a production called *Madame Sans-Gene*. On December 14, 1936, they appeared on Cecil B. DeMille's *Lux Radio Theatre of the Air* in a shortened version of the comedy, the story of a feisty laundress in Revolutionary France. Jean played Catherine Hubscher, the "Madame" of the title, and Bob played her soldier-lover, LeFebvre.

The script was silly and the plot dated, but they did an admirable job, with no attempt to use foreign accents. What the public didn't know was how actors were trained to "speak words so they sound natural," as Bob later explained. They were taught to "not use the English, New York or Southern pronunciation, but an international one . . . The secret of a talking picture voice is in its naturalness, its native personality."

Jean Harlow, like Garbo before her in the succession of Bob's so-far short list of leading ladies, was experienced in life as well as in movies. She was more worldly than he, though she was not six months his senior. By the time they came together, both only in their mid-twenties, she had been married three times; Paul Bern, her last husband, had died under suspicious circumstances. She'd had at least one publicized romance with a married man, boxer Max Baer, and was in a steady relationship at the time with William Powell.

She and Bob became friends, but never lovers. They had a lot in common and could commiserate with each other. Her original name was Harlean Carpenter. Though that wasn't as cumbersome as Arlington Brugh, she was turned into Jean Harlow on her way to becoming a star. She was a Midwesterner born in Kansas City, Missouri. She was also the offspring of a doctor; her natural father was a dentist, and as a child she lived in an upper middle class environment. She was an only child.

**Bob with Jean Harlow in *Personal Property*.
Courtesy Robert Taylor Family Private Collection.**

Jean began in films with many bit parts, quite a few un-credited, and her start was a handful of years prior to Robert Taylor's birth as an actor. *Personal Property* turned out to be the last full film she ever did. She had poor health throughout her life, beginning at the age of five when she contracted meningitis. *Saratoga* started filming right after *Personal Property*, and was finished with long angle shots and using a double. Jean had died during the shooting.

After her death, Bob said, "I don't think anybody, including Jean, would say that she was a great actress. She made no pretense of being a great actress ... I think Miss Harlow would be a great personality on the screen, today or any day. She was a wonderful person, and I think that would be almost the unanimous opinion of anyone who knew or worked with her."

Whereas Jean Harlow was unknowingly at the end of her short but illustrious career when she and Bob came together, Bob was only beginning. He had been part of sixteen productions and was already feeling the pressure. *Personal Property* was a physically grueling shoot, and illness plagued the entire cast. Jean had recently been badly sunburned, on which she blamed her overwhelming fatigue. She had neglected her swimming and tennis exercise, and was certain that also had something to do with her lack of energy. Bob was exhausted after a number of film productions shot back-to-back with no breaks between them. He was also courting a case of influenza.

No one would've known of the stars' illnesses, though, to watch them onscreen. "Jean was as strong as an ox," recalled a co-worker. "She climbed over boats and sets like a cat. . . ." Sheilah Graham wrote of Bob, "It used to be the girls who stuck the flower between their teeth. However, this was before Robert Taylor, before the advent of a manly beauty so overwhelming, all the old traditions tottered before its might."

She continued with her salacious commentary. "In *Personal Property*, one may have Mr. Taylor in a lather or rinsed. I may quiver to the way he wraps his robe close to his splendid chest and beautifully modeled loins, I may sigh as he ties the belt snug to his waist with such dashing disregard of the buckle. I may learn how he achieves his magnificent coiffure, how he coaxes with his own two hands his lustrous black hair into that proud, clean-swept line. I may even watch him clean his nails . . . it is a stirring performance that Mr. Taylor gives in this sequence—natural, confident, and yet deeply hygienic—and it provides the flaps with a high standard for comparison. Nor . . . do Mr. Taylor and *Personal Property* forget the matrons. They can always be a mother to him."

Was there a female star in this production? Insofar as Sheilah Graham was concerned, the movie belonged solely to Bob. She finished, ". . . *Personal Property* executes so conscientiously its mission of pandering for Robert Taylor, it can hardly be expected to take full care of Ms. Jean Harlow. . . ." Which seemed to say the film was made almost exclusively as a vehicle to showcase The Man With the Perfect Profile.

Other reviews were less positive for both actors. "Both Mr. Taylor and

Miss Harlow have enjoyed roles better suited to their talent," said Regina Crewe in the *New York American*.

Bob gave an interview at this time which offered a look into his life beyond the make-believe. During a brief moment of rest, he had a terrible headache and sat in a corner with a MGM nurse rubbing his forehead. The wardrobe department head waited obediently off to the side to speak with him about clothing for his next film.

After Woody Van Dyke, the Director, "... mockingly asked if 'Mr. Taylor' would mind stepping on the set for a scene," and he had fulfilled his request, Bob retired back to his corner. "Sometimes," he wearily told the reporter, "I pinch myself and wonder if this is really I." He was in a retrospective mood. "I think back to ... Pomona when I was 'smudging' ... it was the worst job I've ever had but, at the time, it seemed to me I was one of the luckiest boys in the country to even be working."

Bob was aware he had a good life. "Often when I go home, after the day's work at the studio is finished, to my comfortable house with an open fire burning, to a good dinner, I think of those nights when I was likely to be called out of bed at any hour."

He paused. "It's funny—always having everything you want, never thinking about where it came from or wondering if you *could* have it. It's just there for you and you take it without thinking anything about it ... You sit down to dinner at night and there it is. And after dinner you go to bed and there *that* is. It never occurs to you that the dinner and bed won't be there. It's only when you're broke and don't know where your next meal is coming from or where you're going to lay the body that night that you realize everyone doesn't have those things...."

He was asked if he had worked at hard labor throughout his growing-up years. In his earlier days in Nebraska, physical work was his choice, not a need, and he explained, "When my father was alive there was always plenty. I don't mean," he added hastily, "that we were rich, because we weren't. But there was always more than enough for our wants."

Well, then, what happened?

"Dad died," he said. "He had a good practice . . . When he passed on the income stopped. I went home to settle up the estate . . . He had about $25,000 owing to him . . . He left us a lot of land on which we had to pay taxes . . . It was during the depression and we couldn't have sold it if we'd wanted to. He left some insurance. Not a lot, but some. By the time we'd settled his bills, paid the expenses of his illness and funeral there wasn't much left. A few hundred dollars.

"Mother and my grandmother came back West with me. We were trying to make that money last as long as possible, but a few hundred dollars won't last forever . . . I had to find a job . . . right away. I never intended to be an actor . . . MGM had been after me intermittently to sign a stock contract and it seemed to be the thing to do."

This comment lends credence to Ray Bourbon's story about his helping to "discover" Robert Taylor. If MGM had "been after" Bob "intermittently," the truth likely wasn't as cut-and-dried as was officially and neatly reported. Howard Strickling and his bunch were known to create pat answers to the more often asked questions.

In this interview, Bob was more on his own with his responses. He didn't seem to care if he were monitored. Dreams were fine. Plans were good, too. But clearly, from what he had experienced, life was something of a crap shoot, and the real stuff came about after the plan had stepped to the side for a break.

The reporter persisted. Why did Bob take on a job he didn't necessarily want?

The actor smiled. "I just told you I had to find a job quick. And we can't always do the things we want. When I was in college we once put on one of Philip Barry's plays . . . called *You and I*. There was a line in it I've never forgotten: 'Expediency's heel on the neck of inclination.' It was about a man who had wanted passionately to be an artist. His aspirations were dashed when he married, and there was never time or money enough to enable him to study painting. He had his family to look out for. Instead, he became a successful advertising man. Years later, when his son was grown, a boyhood pal of the man's came to visit them. He *had* done what he wanted, and had been successful at it. They were talking and the friend was commiserating with the would-be artist. The latter said, 'Most men lead lives of quiet desperation.'"

Robert Taylor's moments of deep introspection weren't often made public. Louis B. Mayer had made sure to hide that side of him. He was climbing popularity charts with leaps and bounds, and people hung on his every word. This was sad commentary from a censored man.

"And as soon as you signed your contract you lived happily ever after, eh?" The reporter laughed.

"No! That was when things got *really* tough . . . I got $35 a week and my mother, grandmother and I had to live on it. Don't tell me," he added hastily, "that lots of men raise families on less. I know it. But you live according to the scale you're used to."

Bob's grandmother had written a note to minister friends in Beatrice. She said her daughter had been ill and in and out of the hospital. Eva continued how Ruth had "been without a maid," but they had "all pitched in" and the experience "wasn't so bad."

Ruth Brugh hadn't had a maid in Beatrice, to anyone's knowledge. From all accounts, housework and cooking was done by Andrew and Arlington. After Andrew passed away and her son was her sole supporter, he had to figure out how to work full-time, keep up the social life now a part of his every day, as much for the studio as for himself; and not let his mother and grandmother down in any way. Having a maid was obviously part of a bargain which fit the living "according to the scale you're used to" scenario . . . a scale to which Ruth had become accustomed in a few short years.

Bob continued with his interview, verifying that a friend from home had lived with them in California. "A chum of mine came to live with us. The four of us had three rooms. My mother and grandmother were used to certain comforts. Regardless of how willing they were to make sacrifices, I *couldn't* let them make any more than were absolutely necessary. I was the breadwinner... If there were any sacrifices to be made, it was *my* place to make them."

Bob, his mother, and grandmother separated into two different houses in this transition. Ruth's larger home sat right behind Bob's bungalow on a quiet Beverly Hills street. Grandmother lived with Ruth. His "chum" probably found his own living arrangements.

"I was twenty-two then and trying to be the head of the family. What did I know about managing?"

He was discouraged, trying to do his best to take care of everyone. In his discourse with the reporter, he highlighted the moment when he understood what he had to do to make this life work for him and his family. "There was that awful night when I realized we had one thin dime in the world. I had been studying hard at the studio, trying to do everything they told me. But I seemed to be getting nowhere, and getting there fast. . . ." He breathed deeply, then continued.

". . . I had to figure things out. I went for a walk . . . By the time I got through analyzing things it seemed to me . . . I had nothing and no prospects of ever getting anywhere . . . I walked most of the night. When I finally returned home my mind was made up. I hadn't any chance of being a success in this business but I had confidence in myself. I knew I could land *something*—maybe a salesman's job—and make more money than I had been getting. We would be all right, then.

"In the morning I went to Mr. Louis B. Mayer and asked him to release me from my contract. I told him why and how I had things figured out. If I live to be a thousand I'll never forget his kindness. He delegated himself my personal counselor. He showed me how to revise my budget so I could save money on what I was making . . . Above all, he showed me how to cultivate patience. It wasn't long after that I got the part in *Society Doctor*. It's been smooth sailing since then. Too smooth, I'm afraid. I keep telling myself it can't last."

The interview ended when Bob was called back on set. One of the most insightful tidbits of this interplay came in the part about Louis B. Mayer.

An often-told story, recounted in almost every little bit ever written about Robert Taylor, has told of him going into Mayer's office to ask for a raise. Mayer talked him down, in such a way that when he left, Bob felt as if he'd "gained a father."

The meeting where Bob requested a raise was likely the same as he discussed at length in this interview. He desperately needed a father figure. He was looking for the paternal guidance recently taken from him when his dad died. His affinity for, and loyalty to, Louis B. Mayer, not only in the early years but throughout

Bob in a clinch with Jean Harlow as a "friend" looks over his shoulder, in *Personal Property*.

his career, was rooted in his post-adolescent period when he evolved into his mother's, and his grandmother's, keeper. Mayer became what Bob greatly needed at that time in his life.

Director Woody Van Dyke was nicknamed "One Take" Van Dyke, and *Personal Property* was completed in all of two weeks. At one point, Jean lapsed into a coughing spasm, possibly a precursor to the graver illness to overtake her later. Van Dyke refused to re-shoot the scene. The cast worked late into the night and over weekends; nerves were put to the test. The script was considered mediocre, and the stars had to do the best they could. Jean didn't believe herself in top form with English comedy, and Bob was still relatively inexperienced.

There were other reasons behind the rush. The crew had been invited to Washington to celebrate President Roosevelt's birthday, an event that by this time was annual. The extravagant party was first held on his fifty-second birthday, January 30, 1934, in New York, Washington, Chicago and dozens of other cities. A brainchild of Carl Byoir, a New York public relations expert, the event was a way to raise money for the polio foundation. The 1936 party was the first Washington political event to involve Hollywood personalities as publicity tools, and proved to be the cornerstone of the marriage of Tinseltown, Washington, and Louis B. Mayer. He accepted the invitation for his actors based on the condition that the film was wrapped prior to departure.

The picture was accomplished in time. Despite the idiosyncrasies of a mediocre picture and less-than-topnotch performances, the show turned out to be a pleasant, good-natured comedy. Barely had Van Dyke yelled, "Cut!" on January twenty-first, before Bob and Jean were on an eastbound train with separate rooms in a sleeper car. With them were twenty-one pieces of luggage, many full of evening wear from the film, gallon bottles of spring water to wash Jean's famous platinum hair, Jean's mother, a studio hairdresser, and a publicity man. Attendance at the President's party was only one piece of the *Personal Property* press junket. MGM wanted every last bit of face-time squeezed out of the trip and as they stepped onto the train, Jean and Bob were handed a list of appearances they were expected to make in the Capitol City.

The troupe had been required to do pre-arranged stops along the trail to Washington. When they finally alighted in D.C., with cameras flashing at every angle around them and print media salivating over the least detail, the couple was whisked to their first official event. They danced the night away as if they were fresh and thrilled to be there. All total, they showed up at twenty-two events; they greeted the March of Dimes Chairman, attended a press conference at the Naval Academy in Annapolis, made short visits to Alexandria and Mount Vernon in Virginia, and stopped at parties scheduled all over Washington.

The hectic atmosphere took a toll on Bob almost as much as Jean. His grandmother wrote a letter to a friend where she said he was ". . . pretty well tired out. He does not enjoy these trips to the larger cities. They wear him out. He was sick . . . though not in the hospital as the paper stated. . . ." Newspapers did run a piece which had him in the hospital, but those reports were an exaggeration. As bad as he felt, he plodded on through his case of influenza. He could have used the break a hospital stay would have afforded him, but he wasn't even allowed a few extra days in his hotel room. The down-to-the-minute schedule had to be followed.

Keeping up with appearances was a full-time job, not to mention the task of dodging eager females who did almost anything to try and get his attention. He would find messages at his hotel, bold invitations such as, "Came to see you, but you weren't in," or "If you would like to see me, which I am sure you would, insert an ad in the paper. Love, Adele." There were also those who hid in the lobby all day, hoping for the slightest chance he would make his way to his room through the most public route. And these weren't plants. They were bold females wanting a piece of the glamorous Robert Taylor.

On the evening of January 30, 1936, the stars appeared at seven hotels hosting Presidential Birthday Balls, going from one, to the next, to the next. Prior to the main event in which the week of activities culminated, they were taken into Roosevelt's "fireside chat" room, and introduced to the President and First Lady. This in particular was a trial for Bob, who could not stand Roosevelt or his politics. He employed his best acting skills as he smilingly moved amongst the crowd, most of whom he normally wouldn't have stood with in the same room.

Bob and Jean hobnobbed with not only the President and Mrs. Roosevelt, but an influential group made up of members of the United States House and Senate. One senator was from Bob's home state. While camera bulbs flashed, they came together for a photo opportunity, the likes of which would be admired decades later. Caption declared, "Film stars on a Washington merry-go-round!" and Bob and Jean stood with Senator Nathan L. Bachman, Tennessee; Senator Alben W. Barkley, Kentucky; Col. Edward

Bob, Jean Harlow, and others with Mrs. Roosevelt in Washington, D.C. during *Personal Property* road tour. Courtesy Robert Taylor Family Private Collection.

Halsey, Secretary of the Senate; Senator Robert R. Reynolds, North Carolina; Senator Edward R. Burke, Nebraska; and Senator George L. Radcliffe, Maryland.

According to record, all were Democrats, another jab in Bob's side. Some were already involved in aligning the forces to direct the activities of Hollywood's more liberal hand. That hand was finding a way into the pocket of those with beliefs starkly at odds with Bob's core ideals.

Senator Reynolds from North Carolina, Chair of the Senate Foreign Relations Committee in 1940, fielded a letter from a constituent who had a beef when Charlie Chaplin was "permitted to use the US film industry to air his personal antagonism towards a foreign government."

In the summer of 1940, Senator Burke from Nebraska, whose inclusion in the press event was likely not a coincidence, introduced a bill considered "the most controversial step taken to that date toward war-readiness."

This trip planted a seed of social awareness in Bob. He was able to test the waters as a political animal, as well as a full-fledged screen star. Being a part of the activities he was expected to attend helped him solidify what he truly believed in, and why. He now had a personal platform. He saw how he could publicly, as well as personally, make his stand against a government currently taking his country in a direction in which he didn't approve.

Bob was under the tutelage of Louis B. Mayer in many ways, and he allowed himself to be strongly guided by his boss's opinions and interests, of which an important factor was political power. Mayer could easily throw his weight around by doing favors for others of influence, and through favors owed to him that he called in from friends in high places. Louis B. Mayer was publicly considered a conservative, but in this scenario he appeared to be selling ideals for movie profits, with no consideration of his personal beliefs. Bob must have questioned the direction of Mayer's allegiance. This is the period when he began wondering how to balance the certainty of his next paycheck with the clearly-disagreeing politics showing up between him and the man who signed that paycheck.

The day after the command performance with President and Mrs. Roosevelt and all the Washington politicos, Jean and Bob and everyone involved with the film climbed wearily on the train and headed back to Hollywood. The entire party had now come down with varying degrees of influenza, and they suffered through a quiet, painful trip.

Jean seemed to get more ill with each mile traveled. By the time the train reached Pennsylvania, her mother had hired a private nurse. Bob periodically looked in on her to offer help and sympathy. She continued to fail, and by the time they reached home, she took to her bed. She never rallied back to full health and after a number of ups and downs, and a case of blood poisoning and liver failure, Jean Harlow died on June 7, 1937.

CHAPTER SIX:

Too Many Women, Too Little Time

> "You can't ask a girl for a date and expect
> her to just sit home and look at you."
> – Robert Taylor

That Bob created hysteria in female members of the audiences flocking to see his movies certainly wasn't unexpected. That was intentional. Even before MGM tweaked his appearance, he had stopped ladies in their tracks for years. In Hollywood, the city of forever make-believe, living up to what movie magic might make of an actor or actress was hard for any mere mortal. In Bob's case, he came close, often even hitting the mark.

Joan Crawford said, "You have to know Bob to fully appreciate him." While looking at him and watching him act was one thing, observing him as he went about real life sealed his appeal. Joan said visitors to the set of *The Gorgeous Hussy* (1936), a film they did together, would see his "easy, graceful naturalness" and realize he was as good-looking in real life as on the screen. They also saw he had more than his appearance to stand on.

As Joan got to know him better, she realized Bob didn't feel comfortable all gussied up. The man was more at ease in casual, simple clothes. Neither of them had ever done a costume piece before *The Gorgeous Hussy*. The plot outline, which had President Andrew Jackson striking up a friendship with an innkeeper's daughter, immediately identified the period and the ward-

Bob and Joan Crawford in *The Gorgeous Hussy*.
Courtesy Robert Taylor Family Private Collection.

robe. Joan played the daughter, and Bob was cast as her husband, a naval lieutenant. He made it clear he didn't like the costume part of the job. "I feel too fussed up, too dressed up, too showy . . ." he told her, "as though I were on parade. I don't like being on parade."

Bob started smoking as a youngster, although his mother was probably unaware. Certainly as early *The Gorgeous Hussy*, cigarettes were a regular part of his life. His stand-in walked into his dressing room one day to find Bob vigorously spraying mouthwash down his throat. He explained he had a love scene with Joan Crawford. "She doesn't smoke very much and I do." In 1937, he was an active and open puffer. Eager to tell the world about his favorite cigarette, he became an advertising spokesperson for Lucky Strikes. But smoking was the thing to do then. The norm, not the exception. More often than not, a star did smoke; females as well as males.

Cigarettes didn't appear to make a difference either way in his private

**Bob and Irene Hervey at the Trocadero.
Courtesy Robert Taylor Family Private Collection.**

life. He had a smorgasbord of female opportunity from which to choose. Whatever Bob wanted, whether blondes, brunettes, redheads, older, or younger, he could usually have the ladies for the asking. He was more than able to pick and choose. According to him, though, he didn't have much of a social life.

When he was asked if he dated all the best-looking actresses he appeared with on screen, he replied, "We might, if thrown together . . . have a drink or a snack between scenes, but I didn't like the idea of talking shop. . . ."

In another interview, "That first year I hardly had a date. There was no money for that sort of thing. You can't ask a girl for a date and expect her to just sit home and look at you." The reporter scoffed. Bob laughed. " . . . I'm not kidding . . . I happen to have been lucky in this business. Lots of girls would be glad to sit home with a movie star—any star—not just me. But it's the romance and glamour that hypnotize them. . . ."

In his words, the studio "offered me every opportunity in the world if I made good...." In turn, he was required to pay his dues. MGM made sure, in his earliest days, he was available to them at a moment's notice for all sorts of publicity events. He was regularly called on to squire wives of visiting dignitaries around town. And most of those ladies wouldn't have been in his personal line-up.

More often than not, he'd have already planned a quiet night at home with his steady, actress Irene Hervey. This romance was said to have started in the publicity office. They had become sincerely friendly, and their personal plans were regularly derailed by the studio's needs. A call would come in to tell him he was on for a night on the town. As one article explained, the studio voice on the other end would say something like, "Bunch of salmon canners here from Seattle and the boss says show their wives the town. Give 'em the business and everything. Would you call for Mrs. Doodleflicket at the Ambassador at seven-thirty?"

And he would do as he was told, first contacting Irene to explain. She would respond, "Sure, Bob. I know how it is. Call me tomorrow."

In those days, when asked about love and marriage, he responded, "I hope to marry before I am thirty."

His mother, a continuing influence in his life, stated emphatically, "Marriage with an actress would be too complicated."

When he was grilled about his ideal girl, he became embarrassed. "Oh, I don't know what kind of girl I want! I'm... very fickle. I have a lot to learn yet about women. I suppose people think girls throw themselves at the feet of young leading men like myself. Nonsense!"

His protest was weak. Women *were* throwing themselves at him, pulling at his hair, grabbing for pieces of his clothing... getting their hands on him in any way possible. The adulation baffled him. He didn't see in himself what others saw, and he couldn't grasp the intensity of emotion which would draw someone to a stranger in the way women followed after him.

Magazines of the day focused in on his relationship with Irene Hervey, and

Bob, Irene Hervey, Carole Lombard, Cesar Romero, posing for photographers. Courtesy Robert Taylor Family Private Collection.

whether or not their romance was real. A few years older than Bob, she signed on in 1933 with MGM as a contract player. Bob came on the scene in a small way in 1934. Gossip columns screamed how she came startlingly close to becoming Mrs. Robert Taylor. A photo of Bob and Irene in December of 1935 was captioned, "They were all set for matrimony but now Irene Hervey and Bob Taylor just go out together occasionally." Rumors dogged their every footstep. Everyone with a microphone and a pad and pen tried to gauge the truth of the stories swirling around the couple. When asked by a cagey reporter if he was in love with Irene, the question caught Bob off guard. He blushed, visibly agitated, and flippantly replied, "Maybe I am, and maybe I am not."

As late as May of 1936, the questions persisted. "It has been reported that you were all set to marry Irene Hervey," one newspaperman asked, "but the studio wouldn't let you, for fear you might suffer at the box office. Is that true?"

Bob went with the party line. "No, it isn't. The studio hasn't interfered at all. I am perfectly free to marry any girl any time I want to."

By June of 1936, all supposition was put to rest. Irene married Allan Jones, and a year and a half later she was the mother of his son, Jack.

Without a doubt, the studio had control over the lives of, as Howard Strickling had called them, its "assets." The studio world was foreign and confusing for a new green actor coming into the fold. Someone like Bob, who relied on a regular paycheck, wasn't likely to make waves. He would do what was expected of him.

He spoke of his MGM working environment. ". . . when I first came to the studio I was greatly excited. It had an air of immense power, magic and mystery about it. Uniformed policemen stood at the gates, and in the front office quiet-voiced, athletic young men handled a battery of telephones. . . ."

What happened if he didn't do as he was told? After all, he was under contract. That was how the system operated, and each working actor had signed up to follow the system's rules. If Bob hadn't taken roles as assigned, or done the publicity required, or gone along with the plan of growth created specifically for him, he would've likely been dropped.

In Hollywood, being dropped didn't mean only forfeiting a contract or losing a job. Studio heads controlled everything. They owned the town. They had every last ounce of the power. The saying, "You'll never work in Hollywood again," wasn't an idle threat. These words were fact. If an actor lost favor with their studio, he might be picked up by one of the others, but that was unlikely.

So if a young, impressionable individual like Arlington Brugh, turned into the dashing Robert Taylor by Louis B. Mayer and his people, was one of the fortunate ones hand-picked to be sculpted into the image of a silver screen asset, the game belonged solely to the studio. While Bob would certainly benefit, he'd benefit only at the pleasure of his studio. The plan was one of carefully orchestrated deception. Reality could become illusion in a matter of seconds.

The young Bob Taylor felt fortunate to come to the direct, personal attention of Louis B. Mayer. Mayer was one of the original Hollywood moguls, to include Sam Goldwyn, the Warner brothers, and Harry Cohn. Of them, Mayer was arguably the most well-known for taking a personal interest in his assets. If he gave his time and spent the money to make someone a star, he in essence became their father in ways the asset, that new actor, had probably never before considered. The actor's every move was under the microscope and nothing in his life was too small for Mayer to consider.

And he did take a close interest in many of his assets. James Stewart said of these movie-making giants, "They loved the business, and they had a tremendous capacity of knowing what would be right for the audience at a particular time." He added, "You hear so much about the old movie moguls and the impersonal factories where there was no freedom. MGM was a wonderful place where decisions were made in my behalf by my superiors."

Tony Martin summed up the system as, ". . . being an actor at MGM was the movie equivalent of being a pitcher on the New York Yankees—you were first-class, everybody knew you were first-class, and there was no reason not to be grateful for having the privilege."

Mickey Rooney said what was seen on screen was often "the invention of our scriptwriters, who had combined what they knew of us to produce ever more exaggerated versions of ourselves." The system was clearly a system. There were good points, but above all else was the impenetrable wall surrounding the all-important palace of make-believe. Actors lived behind these walls every day. Success depended on the public believing everything put up on that silver screen.

For whatever deep-seated reason on Mayer's side, he honed in on Bob, certain he could be molded into the world of the movie star. History indicates there was something more than dollar signs he saw every time he looked at his latest acquisition to stardom. He genuinely seemed to care about the young man.

Mayer offered Bob a contract which, along with his timing, signified stability, something Bob needed after the loss of his father. Louis B. Mayer was gentle with him, kind-hearted. Like a father. How genuine was he? The system created an all-encompassing world, one which required allegiance as well as a professional work ethic. To have new talent believe without question Mayer and his staff would take care of him was crucially important to the success of studio operations.

Did Mayer have anything to do with the end of the Taylor/Hervey romance? Considering the date of the magazine photo caption, Taylor's answers in the interview as published in March of 1936, and Irene's soon-thereafter marriage to Allen Jones, Bob might have been unwise to respond as candidly as he did, but as he said at the end of the same interview, "I am very impulsive. I say and do a lot of things impulsively."

At least he did then. He learned fast, though.

There was a significant romance with Virginia Bruce. One year older than Bob, she came to Hollywood in 1929. A marriage in 1932 to John Gilbert ended in divorce a few years after the birth of their daughter. Virginia was once again single, and before her next marriage to J. Walter Rubin in 1937, she and Bob hooked up on the set of *Society Doctor*. This was the film where he started to feel comfortable about his acting. He still didn't see himself as a real star, but he was confident he could hold his own in front of the camera.

When asked in an interview what he thought of himself onscreen, he replied, "... somewhere during the making of *Society Doctor* something happened to me. I had been playing in a number of MGM pictures before that, but I was still camera shy, still nervous, held myself so taut I thought I'd cleave in two if anybody looked at me crooked. Then, suddenly, one day I said to myself, 'What's the sense of all this tension? Where's it getting you? There's nothing to be afraid of.' And then—bingo—like a flash I relaxed. I wasn't afraid of the camera anymore. And when I saw the rushes I realized that at last I was getting somewhere. I looked natural on the screen for the first time. Not tense. And after that I started getting my first mention in critical reviews."

Bob with Virginia Bruce, talking with actor, Ross Alexander. Courtesy Robert Taylor Family Private Collection.

Bob became comfortable with his leading lady, as well. The fact he and Virginia dated wasn't well-publicized and the rumors, quiet though they were, gave strength to the studio system's involvement. The story claimed MGM didn't approve. Did that disapproval have anything to do with the fact Virginia was going through a divorce, a point which could reflect negatively on Robert Taylor, their shining new box-office draw? She also received kidnap threats against her young daughter. She needed to stick close to her child, the studio kept an eye on Bob, and the bottom-line result was that the relationship between Bob and Virginia started, suffered, and ended with little public fanfare. They did as well as they could for as long as they could before the system and circumstances again took a toll.

CHAPTER SEVEN:

Barbara—Wife or Mother?

> "All I had to say about the whole thing was 'I do.'"
> – Robert Taylor

In a telling 1942 interview, Zeppo Marx's wife, Marion, explained how she met Barbara Stanwyck in 1935. Zeppo, Barbara's agent, had a business appointment at her house. He suggested Marion come along, saying, "I think you and Barbara would like each other."

She and Barbara not only liked each other, they became fast friends and business partners. Marion said of Barbara, "Meeting her for the first time is a baffling experience. She looks just as she does on the screen—so you expect her to be just as dramatic and demonstrative . . . You don't know how to take her at first encounter. At least, I didn't."

On the way home from that get-together, Marion said to her husband, "She certainly doesn't make up to people on first meeting, does she?"

Zeppo proceeded to give his wife a short lesson on the life of Barbara Stanwyck. He told her Barbara had been pushed around a lot, and this put her on guard with people. She made sure she could trust before she'd be "anything but matter-of-fact" with someone new. He then explained, "Barbara had been orphaned when she was four—brought up by strangers, who never gave her anything more than bed and board, because that was all they were paid to give her—entire childhood was spent in a crowded tenement district, where no one cared whether she lived or died—she had to go to work when she was 13, and soon learned not to expect anything from anybody unless she earned it."

As an adult, Barbara spoke of that period, saying, "I just wanted to survive and eat, and have a nice coat." She rarely discussed her childhood, showing that hard outer shell as early as her first days in Hollywood, when people began nosing into her background. She made the subject taboo right then, only finally saying much later in life, ". . . let's just say I had a terrible childhood. Let's say that 'poor' is something I understand."

Zeppo's explanation put solid history behind Barbara's hard-to-crack exterior. Marion made regular visits to her house with Zeppo and slowly, Barbara began to trust Marion. When her relationship soured with her husband, actor Frank Fay, she and her son went to live with Marion and Zeppo. Barbara and Fay had adopted a baby boy in an attempt to save their marriage. When that didn't work, they divorced and she got custody of the boy, whom they called Dion.

Marion explained, "Barbara was desperately unhappy, hardly interested in living. Her whole world seemed to have gone to pieces. She had no faith in the future, no confidence in herself. She had gone through so much, and had so little self-confidence left. . . ."

Marion tried to help Barbara with her self-image. There were times Barbara couldn't believe she was attractive. She didn't cater to fancy diet regimens, and swore the best way to take care of her weight was with swimming and horseback riding, and lots of sunshine. Finding clothing to flatter her figure was always an issue, not because of her figure, but because of how she saw herself. She would beg Marion to shop for her, which Marion did. A long time passed before any headway was made. Marion said about Barbara, "She's the only pretty woman I've ever heard of who had to be told about it. And she not only had to be told, and shown, but re-told and re-shown."

During the time Barbara stayed with Zeppo and Marion, they had to coerce her to stick around if anyone new came to the house. More difficult was

Young Barbara Stanwyck. Courtesy author's personal collection.

getting her to agree to go out to a night club with them. "When we finally did talk her into going along one night," Marion explained, "one of the first people she met was Robert Taylor. He was sitting at the next table. Zeppo introduced Barbara, and Bob asked her for a dance."

Whether or not there was studio intervention in this ultimately-historic meeting is in question. A 1937 article focused on the great many love affairs started for publicity reasons, only to ultimately become the real thing. The relationship between Bob and Barbara was one listed as originally a "press agent arrangement."

Bob may or may not have been there that night on purpose to be seen meeting *the* Barbara Stanwyck; either way, he could not have known at the time how much their first dance would mean to her. Marion knew, though. "Even if she had never seen him again, that dance still would be one of the big memories of Barbara's life. It did that much for her."

Years later, Barbara confessed to Bob how their twirl around the floor had affected her. He responded, "You weren't the only one who got a mental life from that dance...."

According to Marion, Bob and Barbara didn't fall immediately in love. Months went by before they were willing to tentatively trust each other as friends. Once they were at that point, they slowed their relationship down more, and took great pains to make sure their attraction went beyond the flashing camera bulbs. The romance between them blossomed only over time.

At first, they were socially involved as much, if not more than they were romantically involved. As of September, 1936, Bob was bringing home $2,300 a week. Hollywood fan magazines screamed they hadn't seen the likes of such a sex symbol since Valentino. When he made a promotional appearance at the Dallas Exposition, a beauty contest runner-up took his hand, offered to her in a firm, warm gesture of introduction, and promptly fainted in his arms. He received about eight thousand fan letters each week, which his mother and grandmother helped him catalog and answer.

He was asked, "What do you think has made you click so heavily with the public?"

Bob blushed. "Oh, honestly, I don't know," he responded, a bit of frustration in his voice. "Sure, I've wondered about it. I don't think it's any intangible or mysterious thing...."

The reporter pushed on. "I've been talking to your friends, your agent, and a lot of studio people, and what they say boils down to this: 'People like

A young Bob and Barbara driving away after a night on the town.

him because he's so doggoned sincere. Women feel that when he says, 'I love you' on the screen, he really means it.'"

Bob gave a few minutes to serious thought. "I guess I am sincere, all right. I have to be. I'm no actor—mean no technical actor . . . The parts I have I must feel. And maybe people like me because they know I'm a pretty normal kind of pretty ordinary American."

He still wasn't totally comfortable in such a magnified light. He wasn't at ease being put on a pedestal as a man, or as an actor. Many things were expected from a new face in Hollywood. He was required to dress a certain way, live a certain lifestyle, and project a certain persona. All of this, however, was a façade. "I've tried to do what was expected of me," he said. "I've met the 'right' people and have been—at least once—to all the 'right' places."

He needed people around him that would treat him as the normal guy he knew he really was. He lamented over the fact there were restrictions on his activities because of his fame. He could no longer "drive down to an amusement pier and ride the rolly-coaster." Much of this was why he became comfortable with Barbara. She intimately knew the world in which they both lived. She understood the pressure. They were seen together at the best clubs, the racetrack, parties of the rich and famous. They were publicly considered an "item" before they allowed themselves to realize they really were.

They went dancing, something he still loved to do, to "really dance, not just mill around on the jammed, postage-stamp floor of a smoky night club." He and Barbara would pop into the Palomar, a Los Angeles ballroom. Sometimes they would meet friends for the evening and the bunch of them would create a stir. Eventually the patrons became used to seeing them, and gave them space. They understood the more well-known among them were there to enjoy themselves, not be on stage for that evening.

One night in 1936, Bob and Barbara dropped in at Billy Gray's Band Box, a well-known spot at which to be seen; a location where stars went to watch great acts, specifically comedians. On this particular evening, Bob and Barbara were enjoying the show when someone became angry with the owner and started a slugging match. Some celebrities couldn't handle the

Bob and Joan Blondell clown around during an evening out with Barbara and others. Courtesy Robert Taylor Family Private Collection.

fracas, such as Broadway-turned-Hollywood actress, Eleanor Whitney. Bob and Barbara were safely tucked into a corner, and went home with quite the story to tell.

Their second movie together was *This Is My Affair* (1937), made in 1936. Bob played a lieutenant in the Navy, and Barbara was his love interest. Their dating may have initially been a studio-created coupling, but they found they genuinely enjoyed each other's company. Soon after filming wrapped, they were still seen having fun on their own time, beyond the soundstage or the glare of the nightlife.

One day, they went on a shopping trip to find a top-notch leather craftsman. Bob wanted a specially-made car horn, with a sound mimicking the Mississippi fur-trading steamboats which had floated down the river a cen-

Bob and Barbara in their second appearance together on screen in *This Is My Affair*.

tury or so earlier. The sound was one he'd been enamored of since childhood and now that he could afford to indulge himself, he was determined to recreate the sound... with his own car horn. He got what he was looking for, and Barbara became the girl beside the guy driving a car as infamous as the owner. The instrument was rumored to be almost four feet long, and fastened onto the left side of the hood. Folks knew when Bob Taylor was coming down the street because of the horn's unique sound, and his was known to be the only automobile horn with such a presence.

This was the sort of frivolity Barbara had known little of before she met Bob. She had grown up fast and hard, and had a scarred memory of love placed in trust, and lost, over and over. Bob was reserved in his emotional sharing, but he had an innate sense of fun, sometimes downright childlike, qualities which attracted her. She was falling for him. Bob enjoyed being with her, but wasn't convinced she was his type of woman for a long-term relationship.

When asked, he repeated that he was attracted to "the 'All-American' girl." He had said he liked, "... a girl who can be a pal, who can share a fellow's interests." He'd become accustomed to how Hollywood operated, but the fact that some behaviors, such as smoking and drinking to excess, was the norm in the community didn't do anything to alleviate his distaste for seeing women partaking in those activities.

From the get-go, Barbara presented something of a sense of unease in him. She was his paradox. She could present that "pal" sort of persona, but he wasn't sure she could be one to share his more masculine interests. She was attractive, though not extraordinarily feminine, a trait important to him. Her naturalness was what really appealed to him, how she was exactly as advertised. She wasn't the Hollywood starlet type, the sort he had most often been seen with and introduced to since settling in Tinseltown. Barbara was Barbara. Honest. Often blunt.

But she had been around, and he was still somewhat inexperienced. He was well-educated. Her smarts were from the streets. She had been her own boss since she was barely a teenager. He had been, and was still being, carefully groomed by his mother, and he listened to Louis B. Mayer as an obedient son would follow along behind his father.

Bob easily forgave others, and was well-versed in tact and drawing room etiquette. He'd had many opportunities come his way in his short life. Though he selected acting and his star rose fast, he wasn't always certain he had chosen the right career path. Barbara was determined, brash, and for many years, had known exactly what road she must walk to get where she needed to go.

The relationship between any man and his mother is usually complicated, and Bob's was all that, and more. Unfortunately, something nagged at him about Barbara; in some ways, she reminded him of his mother. That was always an uncomfortable sense in the back of his mind.

He was raised to never speak against his mother, to do exactly as she told, and to stick close to her. She made sure he understood on an emotional level she always knew what was best for him. Since he was responsible for her well-being, in addition to his grandmother, this added to his burden of female dominance. Their relationship developed an aspect which intrinsically made him not only her son, but her protector and her provider. In some ways, this nearly turned him into his father.

Many people said he was a "Mama's Boy," but in the years leading up to his departure from Nebraska, he had bit-by-bit weaned himself from her, always with respect for her place as his mother, and bit-by-bit, the emotional distance between them began to show. The Robert Taylor he would become blossomed, and he was destined to be a man far different from the Arlington Brugh he had been.

He resented having to feel subservience in relation to his mother's domineering will, and that translated into his relationship with Barbara. Bob didn't have a problem being with a strong woman. He was comfortable with a woman who could demonstrate how she knew her own mind. He was a rather shy, quiet sort when his star began to rise, and a steely woman knew how to get the most out of his sedate demeanor. Such a woman knew what worked with him, and what didn't work.

Over the years, many reports have suggested he was gay, and his marriage to Barbara was a "lavender" union to mask the fact they both enjoyed the company of their own sex more than the opposite sex. The accusation has never been justified. History has repeatedly shown Bob was decidedly heterosexual. Every interview conducted with people who had attempted to "out" him in print boiled down to a rumor of a rumor of something which might have, and as possibly might not have, happened.

Harry Hay was one of the most deliberate propagators of these rumors. Considered an early leader of the gay rights movement in America, as well as a closeted-gay member of the Communist Party of America, Hay was asked directly if he had proof of Bob's homosexuality. He sheepishly admitted he did not have an iota of corroboration. In discussing previous commentaries about Gilmor Brown's Pasadena Playhouse, of which Bob was a part in the 1933 to 1934 season, Hay was unable to verify the haziest rumors based on nothing more than Brown calling the then-Arlington one of his "favorites." All Hay could offer, with a bit of embarrassment in his voice, was the repetition of tales that had gone around for so long they had become "the" rumors to repeat in the gay community. He acknowledged there was nothing but gossip involved; none of the oft-repeated fantasy was based on the slightest bit of fact.

All the years thereafter repeatedly proved Bob's heterosexual lifestyle. Mickey Rooney recounted a story in 1938 when he was making *Stablemates* with Wallace Beery, one of Bob's hunting buddies. Rooney and Beery became friendly, and they often went out on the town. One evening Beery invited the young Rooney to a party at Errol Flynn's house. Beery picked him up at home and the two drove to Flynn's place on Mulholland Drive. Rooney was new in the business as a leading man figure, and he wasn't certain about what awaited him at the hands of the worldly Beery and Flynn.

"I had my biggest surprise. . . " he said, "when we got to Errol Flynn's house. When we knocked on Flynn's door, it was opened by a pair of exquisitely beautiful twins." Rooney was floored and couldn't resist staring at the nubile young ladies. "They were absolutely nude," he gushed. Flynn told him he was welcome to look and look again, and again. It was Flynn's joke for the evening, a "gift" to his guests who included not only Beery and Rooney, but Clark Gable, Spencer Tracy, and Bob.

Men of that era liked being together, they intimately understood each other, and male stars were part of an exclusive club, making a big thing of their ultra-manliness. Gable or Taylor or Beery or any of the elite, top-of-the-heap stars of the day would often host a party and invite only other men as the partygoers, with women as the entertainment. A few years later, when Rooney married Ava Gardner, Louis B. Mayer held a bachelor party, as much a publicity affair as anything else. Any male star of any import was invited and was expected to attend. Bob was part of that group.

The party was done in classic roast format, and Bob told Rooney he'd "be using some new muscles." He advised, "Take it easy at first. A sprained back will be hard to explain to Louella [Parsons]."

Clark Gable told him, "Nibble her ear but not too much. It ain't like it was a steak sandwich, kid."

As time went on, all who knew them well understood Bob and Barbara's relationship was not one of convenience. The attraction was real. Despite attempts to write away the complications of their life together, they were a pair that worked for a time because of their differences, because they each fed needs the other desperately wanted filled.

Bob was first drawn to Barbara through the intrinsic similarities in her understanding of life, while the same traits seemed to later push him away. The more-than-passing parallels between her and his mother showed each to be a strong, dominating woman. Both spoke their mind, and intended on most occasions to get their way. What's more, each woman expected to get her way with Bob. There was also a side to both paradoxically vulnerable and soft, a side begging to be taken care of. Bob wanted that "pal," a woman

Bob and Barbara at the horse races.
Courtesy Robert Taylor Family Private Collection.

who would be with him whenever he needed a companion; he also wanted a woman to look to him as her provider and protector. Though Barbara wasn't traditionally seen that way, at her core she was an emotionally helpless creature in many ways.

From her early days, Barbara had recorded accounts of many physical accidents. She always ended up with some sort of injury, no matter the activity. A 1933 press report called her the "Hard Luck Girl of Films." She herself said, ". . . in every single picture I've made so far I have been burned, or trampled, or thrown from a horse, or hurt in some way . . . I sprained my ankle and had to stay away from the set...." At one point she ended up in the hospital, burned during the filming of *The Purchase Price* with George Brent.

While she was married to Frank Fay, there were reports on more than one occasion he was physically abusive. At five feet five inches, she weighed one hundred and twenty pounds, not exactly a heavyweight. She repeatedly and pitifully apologized to him. She told him she knew all their troubles were her fault, and she understood she was the reason behind his bursts of anger. Only after there was a child in their home, a child for whom Barbara felt responsible, did she finally pick herself up, dust herself off, and tell Fay he would never again raise his hand or voice to her. Those days were over. She was finished with him.

This all had a hand in how she related to Bob. What may have seemed to others on the outside like indifference or asexuality was a studied, painfully-learned carefulness between them. According to Marion, they felt the need to test every aspect of who they were, individually and as a couple. "They made sure of their understanding of each other and the permanence of their emotions," she said, "before they became husband and wife."

An instance in 1937 gave insight into their relationship. Barbara had recently completed *Stella Dallas*. The role of the same name was meaty, and a part she had really wanted. Stella was a mother, a woman who married beyond her social status, and when her husband lost interest and divorced her, she raised their daughter alone. She gave up all for the sake of the child who, as she matured, became ashamed of her socially-unacceptable mother. The film called for an actress with a complete register of emotional depth.

This version was a remake. The title role was coveted, and nearly every A-list actress in Hollywood tested to play Stella. William Wyler was the Director, and to him went the job of casting. Zeppo enlisted friend, Joel McCrea, to help get the part for Barbara. He and Barbara had made a number of films together and he had pull with Sam Goldwyn, who had resurrected the script from the mid-1920s.

McCrea and Goldwyn had a meeting and conversation turned to who would play the lead. McCrea suggested Barbara.

"She's just got no sex appeal!" Sam Goldwyn blurted.

"Well, you better not let Bob Taylor know that." McCrea laughed uproariously. "He's nuts about her, and he thinks she has sex appeal."

That got Barbara a screen test. She hated to do them, but wanted this part so much she relented. During a brief chat with Goldwyn prior to going before the camera, he still obviously wasn't sold on her, and she knew that. He told her she was too young, a bit of flattery to get her to back down. She didn't. He then suggested that since she'd never given birth to a child, she wouldn't know how to best portray a desperate mother. After a convincing argument otherwise on her part, Goldwyn finally relented and gave her the screen test, and after that, the role.

Stella was rough, out of shape, a bleached blonde with a vulgar sex appeal. She was the sort of woman Barbara might have become if she hadn't found a place in Hollywood. She may have recognized this in herself, and put her all into her portrayal of the sad, forlorn woman. About the opportunity to play Stella, Barbara said, "... there was unusual stimulation in the dual nature of the part; it was like playing two different women simultaneously. Always Stella has to be shown both in her surface commonness and in her basic fineness." Being Stella required Barbara to dig deep into any knowledge she had of a woman who wanted just about everything. She sashayed rather than walked. Her jewelry was loud, garish, and cheap. Her clothes were from a bargain-basement store.

The meat of this role was ironically in the richness and depth of Stella's ability to emit a sense of wealth, not in her lifestyle, but in her dedication to being a mother. She was willing to give up not only all material items for her child, but also selflessly give up her child to a better life. There was something in Barbara's interpretation of motherhood that went beyond acting.

Bob accompanied her to a Hollywood preview of the film on July 23, 1937. Sam Goldwyn had hired police officers to protect the stars in attendance who included, in addition to Bob and Barbara, Claudette Colbert, Ginger Rogers, Harpo Marx, and Anne Shirley, another of the film's headliners. Barbara had created a final screen portrait so poignant her depth of understanding of the character surprised everyone, including herself, and she was thrilled to share the opening with her contemporaries.

She was getting over a wrenched ankle. She and Bob and Marion and Zeppo had gone riding not long before *Stella Dallas* wrapped, when her horse stumbled into a gopher hole and threw her to the ground. A few days of recuperation would've been a good idea, but the cost to the film would've been considerable; instead, she struggled through the scenes and finished the last day on the set, only then taking the time to nurse the injury.

Her ankle was still tender when she entered the theater for the preview. Amidst a throng of stars and autograph-seekers, she held strong to Bob's coattails while he forged on to create a path for them to get to their seats. He was immediately recognizable in spotless dress clothes. His famous profile couldn't be mistaken for any other. Barbara, on the other hand, had on an old hat pulled down over her face, and her collar was turned up. She blindly held on to Bob and shuffled along behind him, never letting go of his jacket.

"Oh, no you don't!" yelled Officer Glenn Abney as he grabbed Barbara from behind. Abney was well over six feet and weighed about two hundred and ten pounds. He yanked her away from Bob, and held onto her as she struggled and kicked to break free. A tussle ensued, with the big man giving no quarter to the small woman he believed to be a hapless autograph-seeker hanging onto America's film idol, Robert Taylor. Abney was intent on doing his job, and he tried to force the squirming female outside the theater and back onto the street.

The whole incident took only seconds, but when Bob finally made his way through the crowd and turned to wrap his arm around Barbara and get her seated, he realized she was no longer there. Instead, there was a strange woman hanging on to the back of his coat, and she rudely demanded an autograph. Bob paid her no mind and rushed back to where he could hear Barbara noisily trying to get away from the policeman.

Bob went right for Abney with a raised fist. The crowd had seen him lunge, and they delightedly thought they were going to get a show before the show.

"Sock that cop!"

"Hit him!"

People crowded around the three people. Gary Cooper had come in with his wife. Other stars had also entered the theater and witnessed the fracas, but none realized the woman held by the policeman, the woman with the cap still down over her eyes and sobbing to be let go, was the star of the film they were there to see. None of them noticed the woman was Barbara Stanwyck.

Only Bob knew, and he was livid. His usual restraint was lost when he saw Barbara helpless and pinned in the arms of a burly cop. He grabbed Officer Abney and shoved him around the lobby, threatening to whip him. The policeman had since loosened his hold on Barbara, but studio officials still had to cut in to keep the 170-ish pound, six feet tall Bob Taylor at bay. He glared at the bigger man, struggling against those holding him back as he bellowed, "I'll punch you in the jaw!"

The policeman stammered, "Gosh, I didn't know who she was."

Bob and Barbara were rushed away to a private space. She refused to leave the preview, and tried to calm Bob, but he wasn't easily mollified. He was determined to see Officer Abney arrested by the Hollywood police precinct. Sam Goldwyn and, surprisingly, Barbara, would have nothing of that. "The man did what he was hired to do," Goldwyn stated.

Bob and Barbara at *Stella Dallas* premiere. Confused and frightened, she was mistaken for a zealous Taylor fan. Bob is livid and disarrayed. Courtesy Judith Hanhisalo personal collection.

Barbara, having been put in the position of a fan for the first time, seemed to gain a new appreciation. "Nothing doing, Bob," she told her Prince Charming. Looking down at him as he rubbed her feet, she wiped away the tears still on her face and tried to straighten the disheveled sleeves of her gown. "I don't blame the officer, but I certainly wish something could be done for the autograph fans who get in the same predicament that I did." Barbara reached for Bob's hand and he enveloped her fingers in his, moving next to her, their bodies touching and soaking in the comfort of closeness.

After the show, she was escorted to the offices of the studio physician, Dr. Geoffrey Grace. Barbara had received multiple bruises on her arms, but otherwise was physically unhurt. Headlines the next day screamed, "Star Roughed By Policeman At Own Show!" and "Taylor Rescues Barbara Stanwyck From Officer!"

She was nominated for an Academy Award for her portrayal of Stella Dallas, but didn't go home with the coveted statue.

The ultimate rumblings of war between Robert Taylor and Communism may have started as early as 1938. In March, Massachusetts Representative Francis X. Coyne decided movie actors were using "phoney names" to "deceive the public" and they should be "banned from stage and screen" in his state. Coyne argued to have a bill created to force all public performers to appear under their actual names. He asked J. Edgar Hoover to "investigate Reds and Communists" among Hollywood's elite. Bob was ironically included in a publicly-distributed list of ten actors and actresses considered to be of questionable patriotic nature.

In December, he participated in a "Rededication Day Observance." This was a star-studded show on Hollywood's part to show how the world of moving pictures stood firmly behind the strength of the American people. Citizen loyalty was becoming front and center, and anyone who was anyone was pegged to stand up and be heard. "With every American heart beating thankfully that we're living in the good old U.S.A. instead of in one of Europe's powder kegs," official press for the event read, "it is fitting that Hollywood and the motion picture industry should offer its services toward the nationwide commemoration of Rededication Day."

The fifteenth of December was the anniversary of the ratification of the Bill of Rights. Hollywood was "eager to lend its voice to the celebration of our freedom and the right to pursue happiness as it is given to few peoples of the world today." A nationwide radio hookup was arranged to connect such movie luminaries as Bob, Clark Gable, Edward G. Robinson, Edward Arnold, Paul Muni, Jeanette MacDonald, Bing Crosby, James Cagney, Lionel Barrymore, Pat O'Brien, Deanna Durbin and Shirley Temple, to the likes of Archbishop J. J. Cantwell, first archbishop of the Roman Catholic Archdiocese of Los Angeles, Dr. Robert Millikan, Nobel-prize winning and renowned physicist, and Joseph Scott, an enigmatic and zealous Catholic lawyer in Los Angeles.

The event centered on *Ships Sail Forever*, a patriotic play directed by Frank Capra. Sam Briskin chaired the participation of the motion picture industry, and the production was a handy way to showcase a broad range of stars in a palatable arena. Politics and patriotism were carefully and intentionally mixed to become top draw for Hollywood.

One of the considerations in the Taylor/Stanwyck relationship, a big consideration, was her son. Bob was four years younger than Barbara. He had never been married, and had little contact with children. Fatherhood didn't seem right for him at this point in his hectic, cosmopolitan life, and he wasn't sure he wanted a ready-made family. He was kind to Dion and always treated him well, and Dion seemed to like him; the boy called him "Gentleman Bob" . . . but there would be a big change between being the gentleman friend of

Bob on the phone. Courtesy Robert Taylor Family Private Collection.

Dion's mother, and being Dion's father figure. That was an important role, as Bob well knew.

Whether getting married was Bob's idea, or Barbara's, is a question which may never be answered. There is more than a fifty-fifty chance the action behind legalizing their union was Louis B. Mayer's brainchild. The fact they were a couple was not in question, but the timing of their bond becoming legal may have been the studio's coercion. Age, background, education, and experience all came together to make them something of a mismatched pair. Despite the conflicts, their union worked, in the beginning, at least. When they were apart, they communicated regularly via telephone and cable. "We cable each other every day," Barbara said in the fall of 1937.

In early 1938 she was still amidst troubles from the end of her marriage to Frank Fay. Their son was at the core of the battle, and Bob wasn't spared the fall-out. Barbara was in court in January fighting Fay for full custody. Since Bob was her regular companion, he was the perfect foil for Fay's side of the argument, and his name became the game point as to whether Barbara or her ex-husband was the better parent.

Under cross-examination from Fay's attorney, Barbara was forced to admit Bob was a frequent visitor at her home, and he "gave the child gifts and frequently played with the boy." Fay's attorney insinuated that Barbara orchestrated these activities to make sure Dion would become used to Bob as his father figure . . . replacing Fay in the role, and paving the way to move Fay out of Dion's life forever. She vehemently denied this. The court ultimately gave the boy to Barbara, but allowed Fay visitation rights, with little interest in the relationship between her and Bob.

Later that year, an article in *Photoplay* titled "Hollywood's Unmarried Husbands and Wives" officially exposed their intimate romance, as well as those of other Hollywood pairs considered to be "living in sin." This was an embarrassment for MGM since the official studio line said they were simply friends. The entire piece was nothing but innuendo, but it was seen as the most blatant copy written to that point about the private relationships of the stars.

"Barbara Stanwyck is not Mrs. Robert Taylor," blazed the headline. "But she and Bob have built ranch homes next to each other. Regularly, once a week, they visit Bob's mother, Mrs. Brugh, for dinner. Regularly, once a week, too, Barbara freezes homemade ice cream for Bob from a recipe his mother gave her. . . ."

Louis B. Mayer was not happy.

He forced a retraction from *Photoplay*. Before that could appear in print, MGM had announced a formal Taylor-Stanwyck engagement. With all future access to MGM stars in danger because Mayer had threatened to cut off press connections, the magazine published a full-page apology the next month, admitting their quotes had made "friendships" between certain stars appear in a "light far from our original intention."

But the damage, considered as such by Bob, though not yet by Barbara, had already been done. Bob commented years later, "All I had to say about the whole thing was 'I do.'"

Amidst the fanfare created by the magazine article, but before the ceremony took place, Bob and Barbara became parts of baseball history. On May 2, 1939, Gilmore Field opened on Beverly Boulevard. The Hollywood Stars were a minor league team with a checkered past, a few different names and, in early days, a group of ballplayers in need of a regular place to play.

The team borrowed Wrigley Field from the Los Angeles Angels during the Depression, but they couldn't hold together. After the end of their 1935 season, they were in debt and could no longer afford the cost of renting. They seemed to slowly become lost to history.

Three years later, the team slowly revived. The Hollywood Stars found themselves under the direction of new owners, Victor Ford Collins and restaurateur Bob Cobb, of now-famous Cobb Salad fame. In those days, though, Cobb was a locally well-known man who desperately wanted to see baseball played in Hollywood. He borrowed five thousand dollars from Cecil B. DeMille, and he and Collins formed the Hollywood Baseball Association. Stock was sold to movie stars and town civic leaders, with the intent of creating a community-oriented franchise.

Bob was among a star-studded cast who held pre-game festivities. He and Barbara had bought into the Association, and as some of the biggest and most well-known performers of the day, and part of the Hollywood community, they were visible and active in their latest business acquisition. At one point, there was a development team in Billings, Montana, called The Mustangs, and Bob and Barbara were involved with that, as well.

In late April, Bob was in Hollywood, on the set of *Lady of the Tropics* (1939) after a quick trip to New York for the premiere of *Lucky Night* (1939). Barbara was on an across-the-west train press junket for the hyped premiere of *Union Pacific* (1939). The trip took her on a three-day celebration to Omaha, the headquarters for the Union Pacific Railroad. So many fans showed up the National Guard was called in to keep order. Franklin D. Roosevelt was included in the hysteria when he officially started festivities by pushing a button from Washington to open doors to the Omaha civic auditorium.

Barbara went on to her next production in early May, back home in Los Angeles. Bob was still working with Hedy Lamarr in *Lady of the Tropics*. On the evening of May 13, 1939, Bob and Barbara went to dinner with Zeppo and Marion. Their friends expected nothing but a night of relaxation with

**Bob and Myrna Loy in *Lucky Night*.
Courtesy Robert Taylor Family Private Collection.**

the tired couple. Early evening conversation centered on what they should do after the meal. Marion suggested they go to the Palladium on Sunset Boulevard. All agreed.

By eight thirty, they were still leisurely sitting around the table. Marion said, "We'd better hurry, or we'll miss the show."

Bob nodded. "Yes, let's get going."

They climbed into his car, and soon his passengers realized their evening wasn't going according to plan.

Zeppo finally spoke up. "Aren't we heading in the wrong direction?"

"Where are we going?" Even Barbara was confused.

Matter-of-factly Bob replied, "I just remembered. I have an appointment with a man in San Diego tonight."

Zeppo asked, "Are you kidding?"

Bob and Barbara out on the town with agent
and friend, Zeppo Marx and Marion, his wife.

Still watching the road, Bob's calm reply was, "No." He glanced at Barbara and for the moment spoke only to her. "Lady, you have a date with the man who is going to marry Barbara Stanwyck." They had already applied for marriage licenses, and she knew they were getting married, but this plan, this night and the arrangement, was Bob's doing . . . or maybe Bob's doing at the behest of Louis B. Mayer.

Mr. and Mrs. Marx were suitably impressed at how well the news had been kept from them. Marion remarked, "No one—except, possibly, Bob—can keep a secret as well as Barbara." Bob showed everyone that night how he was the one with the well-hidden secret. He managed to keep his bride-to-be unaware, also, though her beaming smile for the rest of the night showed him she was delighted to be on the receiving end.

He, Barbara, and the Marxes met up with Municipal Judge Phil Smith in San Diego at the home of friends, Mr. and Mrs. Thomas Whelan. All were waiting for them when they arrived. The evening had been organized nearly down to the minute, with the length of their relaxing dinner a key point in the timing.

The thirteenth was a Saturday, not a Friday, but still the ceremony was held off until after the clock chimed midnight to make sure they didn't marry on a superstitious date. Bob was susceptible to such things. For years, he wore a ring on his right pinky finger because the ring was given to him as a child, and "... I am convinced that it would be bad luck for me not to wear it." He always followed his hunches, never walked under ladders, and frowned upon people who whistled in dressing rooms.

Licenses had been taken out in the names of R. Stevens and Spangler Arlington Brugh, their earlier best efforts to foil any press attempts to root out their intentions. As soon as they both said, "I do," on paper they became Mr. and Mrs. Spangler Arlington Brugh.

Mayer, aware of the plan, made sure Ida Koverman was part of the wedding party; he wanted the event reported back in perfect detail to those who needed to know. Marion became the Matron of Honor and Barbara's Uncle Buck who, like Ida, "mysteriously" showed up at the right place at the right time, was Best Man.

Barbara wore a blue silk dress, and a hat she borrowed from her hairdresser that morning, at the last minute, because she didn't have one in the right color to match her dress. In somber stance, Bob was next to her in a brown business suit. They were subdued as they recited their vows, though Bob was a bit more so than his new wife, whose voice was at least clear and steady.

They had a press reception later at the swanky Victor Hugo's on South Grand Avenue in Beverly Hills. The restaurant was owned by Hugo Aleidas, and a meal considered moderate to expensive could be had for under five dollars. They served black coffee and scotch highballs to photographers who wanted picture-proof of the happy couple. Bob balked at the expected, forced show of affection. Never much for such public displays, he wouldn't

Officially Spangler Brugh and Ruby Stevens,
they legally become Robert Taylor and Barbara Stanwyck,
and as a couple, Mr. and Mrs. Robert Taylor.
Courtesy Judith Hanhisalo personal collection.

play to their tune just because that's what they wanted of him. In his usual sarcastic manner, he said, "We'll just smile and look silly. . . ." And they did smile, again and again and again. Some three hundred photos were taken.

Bob bemoaned the hectic manner of the wedding. He told a reporter, "Here I am married, and I've got to be back at work making love to another woman." His words referred to being expected on the set with Hedy Lamarr first thing in the morning. If this grand marriage scheme had been all a plan

Bob and Hedy Lamarr in *Lady of the Tropics*.

of his choice, he would have ensured the event was more sanctified, and the entire scenario would've played out naturally, with the time and respect such a union, in his mind, deserved.

To say his mother wasn't happy about this latest development was nothing less than an overwhelming understatement. After the festivities were over, Bob went to see her, and he didn't bring along his wife. Both he and Barbara knew he had to have this meeting alone. His mother was distraught over his marriage to Barbara and how the ceremony had taken place, and Bob felt he couldn't leave her by herself in such a state of agitation.

Ruth still regularly played the health card, especially when her histrionics suited her needs. Bob stayed in her home that night, while Barbara stayed at their house. This was not a good start to a marriage that had problems before the ink on the license was dry, but for a couple who had lived together almost as husband and wife for some time, their wedding night wasn't in actuality much different from any other night. The ceremony was little more than a technicality. Bob went straight to work the next morning. Directly after *Lady of the Tropics* had wrapped, he was on the road again on location in Payette Lake, Idaho.

Three months later in August, gossip tidbits whispered about Barbara having passport pictures taken prior to a "European trip." A Louella Parsons snippet declared that though the new Mr. and Mrs. Taylor had attempted to go to New York, they didn't get there because Barbara's "arm has troubled her much more than she thought it would." The reference to another injury was given no elaboration.

The piece indicated Bob was "feuding a little" with the studio over his next picture. Louella said MGM finally acquired a property for Bob that made both him and the studio happy, something called *Cause For Alarm*. Louella said the film was "as timely as today's news headlines, dealing with the espionage and sabotage activities" in a "mythical neutral European country." The original story, set in 1936 and based on a novel by Eric Ambler, showed a conspiracy to change the face of Europe, and dealt with Russians, Yugoslavians, Brits, and Italians.

Somewhere between acquisition and the beginning of filming, something went wrong. When the book was written, Ambler, the author, was a Communist sympathizer. By the time the making of this story as a movie was being considered, he had changed his viewpoints considerably. The original, written about Fascist Italy and predominantly sympathetic to that viewpoint, would have not been one Bob would have supported. The storyline would have required serious editing for him to sign on to the production. Whether the author didn't approve the changes, or the studio wanted something different from Ambler, or from Bob, or something else proved to be disagreeable, Bob never made the film. No one did.

All of this was a foreshadowing of real-world international issues on the horizon. A few months later Bob went to work on a light, easily-forgotten romantic comedy written especially for him. The title was *Remember?* (1939).

By November twenty-seventh, headlines proclaimed, "Back At Work" for the couple. Despite the unromantic start to their marriage, Bob and Barbara did take a brief honeymoon, ostensibly at the urging of Louis B. Mayer, for whom appearances were everything. They managed to sneak away on their first trip together as a married couple to Fair View Farm in Bucks County, Pennsylvania. Their respite was the home of writer Moss Hart and his wife, Kitty Carlisle. They obviously didn't get to Europe.

Bucks County was a literary colony of growing merit, as well as something of an entertainment enclave on the east coast. In addition to Moss and Kitty, George S. Kaufman, Pearl S. Buck, and Dorothy Parker lived there. This was a group that would ultimately, in less than ten years, include many of the same people who stood on the opposite side of the political fence from Bob and Barbara.

On well over seventy acres in Holicong on the scenic Delaware River, fifteen miles north of Trenton, New Jersey, the Hart place became a brief getaway from Hollywood for Mr. and Mrs. Taylor. This was the first time they spent any quality time together, alone, as husband and wife in a relaxing, easy-going atmosphere away from the glitz and glitter which brought them together. They liked the farmland and peacefulness so much they bought land and for a time, had a home there, too.

But their first official home as man and wife was Barbara's ranch, which adjoined the Marx property. Zeppo and Marion purchased the land to raise horses. Barbara had said early-on, "The only grass I've ever been close to was on a theater backdrop." Being able to have her own piece of earth gave her a sense of belonging. She had a ranch house built next door to Zeppo and Marion. "It would be great for Dion," she explained.

She and Marion became partners in a horse-raising business they named "Marwyck Ranch." At first, the distraction was exactly what she needed. Over time, that changed. She still loved the country, but seasonal rains added to the difficulty in getting from her home in the hills into Hollywood. She was forced to leave the house at four in the morning and drive winding roads in bad weather.

Bob and Barbara sharing a love of horses. Taken on their ranch days before he began filming *Remember?* Courtesy Robert Taylor Family Private Collection.

After she and Bob married, they reconsidered their living arrangements. With both making the trek into town at differing hours, and little time to spend together as much from the commute as from the work schedule, their discussions centered on how to have more time as a couple. Bob resisted the idea of moving. He didn't want to leave the first real home he had ever purchased. He'd selected his property next to hers, and he felt a sense of proprietorship in which he reveled. He didn't want to give that up.

Nonetheless, Barbara went looking for another home. She was tired of the commute and felt they needed something belonging to both of them. She found a furnished rental in Bel Air and signed a one-year lease. Bob wasn't happy and, at first, he refused to move. He didn't like the idea of living with someone else's furniture; she seemed unwilling to become a part of his male-dominated environment, which was full of guns and fishing rods and camping gear.

Barbara won the stand-off, and they moved to Bel Air. Eventually they purchased an Early American style home and in that, at least, Bob again had his own place. It was shared ownership, but his name was on the mortgage.

Horses were a genuine interest for both of them. At one point, Bob gifted Barbara with a buckskin roping-horse and later, a Tennessee walking-horse, which she kept at Marwyck. After the move, Marion and Barbara kept the stables between them until Marion and Zeppo also sold their ranch.

In the late 1930s and early 1940s, Bob and Barbara belonged to the settled, smart set of now-married Hollywood "happy couples," a fashionable and popular group including Bob and Barbara, Zeppo and Marion, Jack and Mary Benny, Basil and Ouida Rathbone. Relatively new to the scene were Ronald Reagan and his first wife, Jane Wyman.

Barbara was most often portrayed as a hard-nosed, tough woman. She was that, but there was a well-hidden side known firsthand by only a few people.

As her husband, Bob knew her to be more than a rough-and-tumble survivor. She allowed him to see her vulnerability, offering that part of herself to him in unvarnished intimacy. Only with those she trusted implicitly was she able to show a softer side. Barbara would often play such a woman on film, hard on the outside and vulnerable inside.

Marion knew the other Barbara. In an article in 1942, she told of instances where Barbara involved herself in community issues behind-the-scenes, not looking for publicity, but for a chance to give of herself, her experiences, and her understanding, to the type of young woman she would have been if she hadn't found her way into the movie world. "She started a sorority . . . called Athena," Marion said. "And she dodged publicity while doing it." Barbara founded the Athena National Sorority, and she took time away from her busy work schedule to speak with these young women. They weren't college students, not young ladies of high breeding, but the type of young women Marion Marx termed "working girls."

Barbara told no one for quite some time about the group, and Marion found out by accident. "Athena had been going two or three years before *I* found out about it. . . ." Barbara was getting dressed to go out one night, and Marion asked where she was headed. Barbara told her, "Oh, I'm making a speech tonight to some girls." And finally she explained.

She also contributed to rest homes, children's homes, and orphanages. She often found out about disadvantaged people through reading the newspaper, and would send off a check, or have delivered however many items would cover an organization's current need. She did these things without fanfare or outside discussion. Except for Athena, her actions weren't normally accompanied by personal contact.

Having lived a hard life contributed heavily to how Barbara interacted with Bob. By the time they were married, she had not only suffered emotional abuse at the hands of her first husband, Frank Fay; she reportedly had been physically abused, by Fay and others. The damage was done. She had a problem with intimacy, both psychological and physical.

Bob also had intimacy concerns. He held his emotions deep inside, second-guessing what his wife thought, what she wanted, trying to balance that with his own needs, and he was usually frustrated and off the mark all the way around. Often seeing her thick exterior as a casual feeling toward their union, he would follow her lead and stand back. The vicious cycle repeated itself, slowly at first but over the years, there was an attack-retreat tactic which became part of their make-up as a couple, and which wore away at the relationship. Work required them to often be apart; their personal issues naturally played on their separations.

Barbara was truly in love with Bob and he was good to her, if not always directly attentive. Whether or not he was wildly in love with her at any point in their relationship is in question. At first, he was in love with the fact that she was Barbara Stanwyck. As he became more of a celebrity in his own right, her fame mattered less to him.

Bob had a specific image of what a woman, and a wife, should be. Most of his interactions in Nebraska with the opposite sex had been with small, rounded, not heavy but shapely, dark-haired ladies. Definitely ladies. Their language was proper. Their public behavior was without stain. They came from solid, if not necessarily wealthy homes. They were educated.

And though most could easily hold their own with him intellectually, in society, and on the dance floor, their femininity stood out. They looked and acted like gentlewomen, and Bob Taylor innately appreciated a lady who acted like one. He also liked a woman who knew her way around a kitchen, who liked to be in the kitchen, and who liked to cook *for him*.

Once he was firmly ensconced in the Hollywood scene, and before he married, he had his choice of the most striking and often savvy women from varying backgrounds, many much more experienced than he. He seemed to split time between those that reminded him of girls back home, and others who saw him as an ingénue. He enjoyed the selection . . . and the selecting. Some ladies wanted him as a protector, some ladies wanted to mother him. Both experiences were welcomed, and he took advantage.

Promotional photo. Courtesy Robert Taylor Family Private Collection.

When Barbara came into his life, he found himself in a quandary. They grew closer and closer, and he saw less of other women. His hesitation to marry hadn't been because he didn't care for her. He was monogamous by nature. If he made a permanent choice, he'd be out of circulation. He accepted this, and if he made the decision, he would abide by that decision. Or that's how he thought at first.

Bob had sensed that maybe they weren't the most compatible pair, and he shouldn't have given in to the ceremony. He remembered his parents, whose love was strictly focused, so complete, that their relationship with him was routinely over-shadowed. In his heart, the institution of marriage had a lot to live up to based on what he had seen in his family unit. Would marrying Barbara bring him full-circle into the sort of happiness his parents experienced? The thought always nagged at him. He couldn't be sure.

That didn't much matter anymore, though. The act had been done; the choice in some ways was made for him. He *was* married and he *was* married to Barbara Stanwyck. In the beginning, everything seemed right. Eventually his mother was happy for him, or at least that's what she said. Despite many stories of how much Barbara and Ruth Brugh hated each other from the start, a note written by Ruth to a friend at Christmastime, 1940, gave another impression.

"Arlington is so grand to me," she related, "and now I have a daughter, she is so dear, too. They act like they could not give me enough...." The letter went on to talk about one of "Arly's" good friends who had, until recently, lived with them, but had married and taken on a home of his own. Speaking of Barbara and of the young lady Arly's friend had married, Ruth wrote, "... I love both girls so I just have too [sic] more to love. Most every Sunday I have one of them in for dinner in the evening."

Bob was still concerned about becoming a ready-made father, with a child attached to the act of saying, "I do." He wasn't comfortable around children. He didn't have a clue as to what to do with them. The closest child-centered relationships he'd had were in Nebraska during summers when, as a child, he got together with his cousins, but those times were still only in off-and-on doses, not extensive contact.

He was twenty-seven when he married Barbara, and certainly old enough to have been a father. Suddenly he now had a child living under his roof and that threw a wrench into his structured, adult-centered environment. He had been raised to follow rules, not get dirty or argue, and obey

Bob, Barbara, and Dion at the races in early days as a family.

elders without question. In other words, he knew he should make no waves whatsoever. Never act like a child. Period. He figured that's how Dion should act in *his* home.

Neither did the Taylor's lifestyle cater to a child. He and Barbara were constantly crossing paths, but rarely together in one place. If they weren't separately on set somewhere in the Los Angeles area, they were on location elsewhere. If they weren't on location, they were doing publicity. And on the rare occasions when they had a chance to be together, they socialized, as much a part of business, maybe even more, than a personal choice.

Barbara wanted her son to be tough like she had been tough. In short, she expected him to be a man, even though he was still only a little boy. In this respect, she and Bob were on much the same wavelength, and Dion was the one who suffered. Joan Benny, adopted daughter of Jack and Mary Benny, played with him when they were young. They enjoyed bike rides, and as Joan said with a smile in her voice, "He was my boyfriend." She added, "We were maybe five or six, and we did all the things little kids do together. I saw him often then, and I thought he was so cute! Freckles, blonde hair." Her voice changed. "But he was sad, lonely."

Joan believed Bob didn't have room in his life for a child as well as a wife. He was accustomed to and comfortable with the role of caregiver, so that wasn't the problem. The truth was . . . Bob was afraid of children, and Barbara was frustrated by them. With little time in their schedule to figure out how to solve the dilemma, Barbara decided to send Dion to boarding school. That may have been a logical solution for them, but not a good move for the boy's development. Dion grew up to be as lonely and forlorn as an adult as he had been as a child.

With Dion out of the way on a daily basis, this brought Bob and Barbara back to a couples-only household, and gave Bob a chance to try and reach for the idyllic type of relationship he had seen between his parents. His expectations on the marriage front may have been a bit too much for Barbara, not used to ever having such a solid, traditional relationship in her life. She had no basis of reference. This wishful scenario became a lot for Mr. and Mrs. Taylor to mirror day in and day out.

The specter of Bob's parent's perfect marriage still stood in front of him every day in the person of his diminutive, dark-haired, feminine and ladylike, but forceful mother; this, too, drove him. She was still opinionated and overly protective of her son. Still trying to dominate his life. This is where the rift between Barbara and Ruth really developed and took root.

Which one knew what was best for Bob? He usually felt as if neither one of them thought he could figure things out for himself, and this wore on him. He had two women telling him what to do, two women who were bold, opinionated and by nature, more vocal than he.

CHAPTER EIGHT:

It's War!

"I've heard about you . . . but I still want you to kiss me!"
– Lana Turner's character, from *Johnny Eager*

The Great Depression hit the United States in 1929. The world was in conflict in one place or another. By mid-1937, Japan had attacked China. Fascism took hold in parts of Europe, and England declared war against Germany in September of 1939.

The U.S. economy had taken a dive of nearly apocalyptic proportions, and by the time Europe officially went into battle, people were in desperate need. Everywhere. On the other side, there were those who had enough, and who led a fulfilled life. The conflict became a "those that have" against "those that have not." Robert Taylor began to be singled out as one of the most visible cinematic faces of the imbalance.

He certainly wasn't royalty. His father had been a simple but refined country doctor. He did well for his family, but theirs had been a working existence. They had moved from one home to another, a rented house to a rented house to, finally, a home purchased through the sweat equity of a hard-working father.

An article written about Bob in 1937 related, ". . . in the heart of the grain country, the families of Ruth Stanhope and Spangler [Andrew] Brugh were friends and neighbors. They shared their corn shocking and their ploughing

**Brugh family home in Beatrice, NE, still standing, 1995.
Courtesy author's personal collection.**

and harvesting and their husking bees. They sat on their front porches of an evening and talked of cows which were calving, of the prospect of drought or rain, of the goodly fields of golden grain."

Bob came from farmers, hard-working, salt-of-the-earth folks much like some of the people who would ultimately publicly represent the "other side." Someone who knew him well most of his life said, "To understand Bob, one must go back to Nebraska, to the kind of people there."

Despite his humble, American-heartland roots, he would come to be seen as one of "those that have." Much of this initially resulted from his looks, fastidious grooming habits, how he carried himself, and his nice clothes. The clothing, though, wasn't always altogether something of his doing.

His mother's insistence on dressing him in extravagant finery was one of the ghosts of his past, something which followed him into adulthood and from which he couldn't escape. Whether he was walking the streets of Beatrice, or was seen in Beverly Hills, people took note of him, and it wasn't only because he was Robert Taylor. He was at this point far beyond the stage where his mother still picked out his wardrobe, but that particular behavior had become ingrained in him. Now, his place as a representative of MGM ensured he continued to dress for the public, not for himself. Bob was singled out, for good or for bad, and he recognized this fact.

Bob's father had worked honestly for every dime he made. His mother raised him to be a sensitive, introspective and spotlessly-turned out young man. Between the two of them, they managed to send their boy to a decent college. Was there something wrong with the fact that he was smart enough to make his way, find his center, do well in school and get a good education, and then be discovered by a talent agent from a major motion picture studio?

All this came about in the mid 1930s when the world was looking for someone like Robert Taylor. Many places in the world, most of them, were bruising for a war, and the people of the United States wanted desperately to forget they might soon become part of that.

Louis B. Mayer, a brilliant judge of lucrative opportunity, was well aware of what someone like Bob could do for a hurting population. He knew a new star on the celluloid horizon could help them forget, and someone who looked like Robert Taylor, well, there was no telling how far he'd go. MGM dressed him up more and in different ways than his mother had, and paraded him around town and in front of cameras whenever possible. Before his marriage to Barbara, the studio sent him to lavish parties on arranged dates with the most exquisite, young, spectacularly-adorned starlets on his arm. After his marriage, he was still sent to the same parties; the difference, he now had his glamorous wife at his side.

After only a few years, Louis B. Mayer had smartly created a superstar named Robert Taylor out of an idealistic young man by the name of Spangler Arlington Brugh. The now-named Taylor went along willingly with the

Bob in a private moment, taking pictures before going out for the evening. Courtesy Robert Taylor Family Private Collection.

transformation, but he didn't always like the process. The image of whom he was in front of the cameras was not necessarily the reality of who he was when cameras weren't rolling, the basis of his struggle and the nucleus of the reluctant political animal he bit-by-bit publicly became.

Bob arrived in that limelight, voted there with each single purchase of a movie ticket by those with no real power, but definitely had the need. His star was created by those that had the power and a different kind of need, a need to make lots and lots of money off of someone with class and social ability, and someone who looked as good as Robert Taylor.

This was a natural marriage.

Bottom line . . . Bob was used to further Louis B. Mayer's professional and political aspirations. As the United States flirted with a full-fledged world war and the enemy lurked around every corner, the stage was being set, often intentionally and sometimes accidentally, for this man to become a center of international controversy. Though his literal physical appearance in this controversy in real time lasted only the length of a few light bulb flashes, the negative backlash of blacklisting affected the rest of his life.

War was definitely brewing. Everywhere. In the United States, the world, and in the mind, heart and soul of Robert Taylor.

Flight Command was filmed in 1940, from August to October. Newspaper headlines had threatened the breakout of war in Europe the year before. The movie, in which Bob starred, was released in December, credited as the first Hollywood production after the outbreak of World War II in which American military was used to entertain in a positively patriotic way.

At home in their rare down time, Bob and Barbara kept up to date through the newspapers and radio,

Bob in uniform for his role in *Flight Command*.

paying attention to what went on around the world in the same offhand way in which much of the rest of the country did. They were aware the growing unrest was critical, but at that point the agitation wasn't too directly or obviously threatening their way of life. Bob made nearly two hundred thousand dollars that year, and that was in addition to Barbara's considerable salary.

Flight Command was filmed on location in San Diego, introducing Bob to planes and flying in a hands-on sort of way. He found that airplanes and everything about them excited him. They liberated him from the burden of always being in the spotlight. In an airplane, there was nothing but him and the sky. This was his freedom.

He didn't realize then how planes would offer him a turning point, launching him into a passion unlike anything he had ever before experienced. His strength of character, always there but until recently without an avenue through which to really make itself known, found a way to fly somewhere up in those clouds.

He cemented a determination to serve in the Navy, and took on a driven, and surprising for him, public interest in the intellectual pursuit of American politics. He began to delve deeply into his privileges, and responsibilities, as a citizen. Barbara was right there with him, and while politics was something the couple shared for a time, and which brought them close, aviation pulled them apart.

Flying terrified Barbara. There was nothing about airplanes or aviation she liked. The fact that her husband was enamored became the core of a slow, painful parting of the ways. The more he wanted to fly and the more he wanted to be involved with airplanes, the more she felt he wanted to be away from her. He was so deeply into anything having to do with aviation that she became jealous of not only his air time, but also the time he spent at the airport talking to other pilots.

Bob had access to a single-engine aircraft based at Santa Monica Airport, and he took flying lessons there, as well as at Burbank Airport and the Indio/Palm Springs Odlum Ranch. Floyd Odlum was involved with both

RKO and Paramount Pictures at different points in his life. He shared the ranch with his wife, Jackie Cochran Odlum, a successful businesswoman and celebrated aviator. Harry Truman and Dwight Eisenhower were known to frequent the Odlum ranch; Eisenhower utilized the property as his home base when he wrote his memoirs.

In those early days of Bob's love affair with aviation, Jackie Cochran was setting records around the country and doing her civilian service to the growing war effort. She started the WASP program in 1941, and became the first woman pilot to fly a military bomber across the Atlantic Ocean. From the mid-1940s through to at least the late 1950s, the Odlum ranch was a meeting place for an amazing variety of learned people in an array of fields: film, politics, astronomy, military, aviation, and medicine. It is only speculation what Bob learned there, what conversations he had with any of the guests who crossed his path. With many around him in discussions of world events, he was certainly furthering his awareness of his world, and affairs of state.

Barbara continued to refuse to have anything to do with flying. Reports say Bob's interest became "obsessive," and MGM strongly urged him to "see the studio psychiatrist." MGM was a full-service employment operation. They had a police force, beauty salon and barber, commissary, zoo, elaborate gardens, cleaners and shoe-shines, and of course, a full cadre of medical personnel, including a doctor by the name of Eric Drimmer.

Though Dr. Drimmer called himself a psychiatrist, he was originally an osteopath, as was Bob's father. He was married to Eva Gabor for about three years, and was personal physician to Greta Garbo. MGM was known to periodically send their actors to the shrink; in fact, being on the couch became almost fashionable. Others seen by Drimmer included Bob's good friend, Clark Gable.

Though he followed through on orders from the brass and saw Drimmer for a short time, Bob adamantly would not consider giving up flying. He refused to back off. With Bob being seen as such a malleable sort within the industry, this "obsession," his resolve, came to be something of an anomaly.

The short-lived trips to the shrink were likely not much more than MGM's attempt to find out how their "golden boy" suddenly had a mind of his own; even more, they were trying to change his newfound sense of independent thinking. These sessions almost certainly came about at his wife's insistence.

When marriage issues with any of his stars started a murmur loud enough to be heard outside a couple's home, Louis B. Mayer considered that his business. Business always came before pleasure. If Bob and Barbara's growing rift became public knowledge that would put a chink in the idyllic appearance of the wonder couple. In turn, movie ticket sales would be affected. Questionable ticket sales would affect the studio's financial bottom line.

That as an outcome was not acceptable.

Many of the scripts Bob was given from then on reflected his determination to be in the air as much as possible, or at least be connected to airplanes whenever possible. Mayer realized if he catered to his need to fly, Bob eased off on his stubborn streak. Things were smoother that way, and Bob stayed content. Robert Taylor's name on the marquee meant a lot of profit for Louis B. Mayer, and keeping Bob happy was important. Mayer had a fine line to walk between making sure Bob was satisfied, and ensuring his deteriorating marriage didn't become an item in the gossip tabloids.

The world was moving closer into a dangerous, life-altering war, and MGM began to slide Bob into more heroic, war or flight-related films. Such products were a sign of the times. He had the persona, he looked fabulous in a uniform and no one, in the public and studio alike, found the idea of him as a military officer or national hero at all hard to imagine. Eight out of ten of his movies between 1940 and 1950 had storylines in which his character was either in the military, or worked with airplanes in service to the country.

Bob played Roy Cronin in *Waterloo Bridge* (1940), the first of his movies to see a 1940 opening, in the spring. This was one of the most critically-acclaimed performances of his career. He was visibly at ease in the characterization of a military officer.

The story had originally been made into a movie in 1931. This remake

Bob and Vivien Leigh in *Waterloo Bridge*.
Courtesy Robert Taylor Family Private Collection.

was weighed down under the restrictions of the Motion Picture Production Code. The newer version was grittier, with more realistic visuals but by 1940, political, moral, religious and ethical correctness had come into vogue, and the movie industry was responsible to the government's strict rules.

This idealized the Robert Taylor/Vivien Leigh romantic version. The blackout scenes in particular were heralded as bringing to the screen a darker, moodier environment. The film's Director of Photography, Joseph Ruttenburg, was particularly proud. ". . . We got effects never before possible, giving the camera greater scope and attaining a measure of realism that technically is the closest approach yet to perfection."

Roy Cronin was a complicated character. Bob had jumped at the opportunity to play the part when the script was presented to him, well aware he'd get second billing to Vivien Leigh, despite that she had played second fiddle to him a few years before in *A Yank at Oxford*. Roy Cronin was a meaty role requiring Bob to act, rather than parade around in front of the camera and show off his looks.

This was what appealed to him. The struggle between the physical and the emotional was an intrinsic battle always going on inside Bob. He needed a chance to show he was more than just his looks, though the studio still most often didn't want a whole lot more out of him. He made the effort to break out of that mold for his own personal satisfaction. As he said in later years, "It was the first time I really gave a performance that met the often unattainable standards I was always setting for myself."

That summer, he and Barbara were invited as dinner guests at Mayer's home. Mayer congratulated him on an excellent job in *Waterloo Bridge*. Matter-of-factly, Bob said he hadn't seen a final cut. He added that he believed he had done well enough, but as a general rule, he didn't watch his own performances. Momentarily speechless, the short and stocky Mayer stared at Bob, who stood in front of him with his hands casually in his pockets. After dinner, Mayer wasted no time in calling the studio. He ordered a copy of the film sent to his house, and had Bob and Barbara sit and watch the entire movie with him and his wife.

Bob had to admit that he *was* good. He was able that evening to fully appreciate his portrayal of the tortured British officer on the eve of World War II. Press reports were in agreement, saying Bob and Vivien Leigh had "vital, sympathetic roles which" damned the "evils of war." Critics said Bob was "surprisingly fresh and mature."

There was no romance between the stars. Leigh was initially upset that the role of Roy didn't go to her paramour, Laurence Olivier, with whom she was living though each was married to other people. She complained about the arrangement in a letter to her estranged husband, with whom she was on friendly terms. Ironically, he was a member of the British Navy. She told him the role had been written for "Larry," and nothing good could come of casting Robert Taylor.

It's War!

Bob as Roy Cronin in *Waterloo Bridge*.

Vivien Leigh ultimately took those words back. Filming came right on the heels of *Gone With the Wind*'s debut, and the film's success made her an immediate runaway star. She eventually admitted Bob had been a perfect choice for the role.

Escape (1940) was next to come out for him. This was his formal initiation into propaganda films, war vehicles which were beginning to take their place in the lineup of American movies thinly veiled as entertainment. Hollywood was already playing footsie with the government in the war effort. They hadn't yet gotten into bed, but they were slowly taking off their pajamas.

Bob played an American who went to Germany to rescue his mother, a well-known German actress. The storyline balanced a sense of American freedom against the totalitarian-run government of Nazi Germany. MGM made two endings, one for American viewers, and one for the international market. Bob was again second-billed when *Escape* debuted at Radio City Music Hall in New York City. On her way off the screen by this time, Norma Shearer, who played the countess, received top name recognition though Bob's role was more substantial than hers. He never balked.

In November of 1940, Bob and Barbara went to Canada for a month, and he hunted. Hunting and fishing were his solace, and along with flying, were the activities at which he found peace. He loved to go into the wild, and enjoyed the challenges of nature. What Barbara did during this getaway is unknown, but her activities likely included the lodge and a hot toddy. She did not share her husband's intense love of the outdoors, and hunting was out of the question for her.

Such a trip was a singular indicator among many of how the marriage was suffering. Bob had come into his sense of self, but he still retained recollections of his strict, mannerly upbringing, and his idyllic dream for a solid, grow-old-together marriage never left him. His inherent personality tried to make no waves, almost at any cost, while Barbara would stir things up and make noise. All of this created a whirlwind of growing discontent. Hunting and fishing and flying trips were Bob's way of asserting his place as the head of their family.

When he was angry, he let his emotion slip out in heavy sarcasm. He turned his frustration inward and lashed out with biting words, though rarely in a raised voice. The more time he spent at airports and outdoors in the wild, the more careful Barbara became with him. She loathed bringing about one of his rare outbursts, knowing she couldn't win. Bob was in love, really in love, and this was painfully clear to her. His airplane was his other woman, his mistress, and if she pushed him, the mistress would definitely win the battle. Even hunting and fishing seemed to come out in front of her on his list. She wasn't ready to force such a blow-out argument.

The asexuality of their relationship grew wings. According to a film reviewer, Barbara "was tomboyish, yet used sex like a loaded gun." Bob was a blatant sex symbol in his public life, and though he had a proclivity to be sexually active in his private life, his attentions weren't always toward his wife anymore.

His determination to stay monogamous faltered and, finally, disintegrated. Many of Bob's extramarital romances could be traced to his film credits. Moviemaking was an intense way to get to know somebody, a day-in, day-out world of make-believe. When a man and a woman were put in a situation where they were supposed to be in love, they were supposed to be in love. Selling tickets demanded believability. They had to make movie viewers feel the attraction. That often took an actor into a place where reality blended into storyline. They knew this was a job but in many ways, the job became real life, if only for a time. And if the chemistry was there, truth became make-believe and make-believe became truth.

"You're showing sides of yourselves," Chad Everett explained. "You're trusting each other. There's a lot of trust involved. A lot of cooperation involved. I can't imagine a better way to get to know somebody than to do . . . a movie with them."

This explained how an actor might fall for a co-star, if only for the duration of a film. And in the Hollywood of the 1940s and the 1950s, the world was still a man's world. Filmdom was an empire of play-acting. Many a man away from his wife for days, or often for a week or more, made sure he still found what he needed. Robert Taylor was no exception.

He was vocal in his appreciation of some of Hollywood's leading women. "Any girl . . . would have to go some length to be more beautiful than Lana Turner, Ava Gardner, or Liz Taylor. . . ." At least two of these women were Bob's paramours. Romantic entanglements required willing women, and of those there were many.

Johnny Eager started filming in September of 1941, over two years after Bob and Barbara married. From the beginning, there was a spark between Bob and Lana Turner, a blatant sexuality. Lana played Bob's love interest in a storyline which deviated from the sort in which Bob was usually seen.

Johnny was a reformed gangster, and Lana was the local high society girl who couldn't help but fall in love with him. One of Lana's lines, paraphrased, summed up her attraction to Bob in real life. "I've heard about you, Johnny Eager . . . but I still want you to kiss me!"

Lana had heard about him, all right. She knew Bob was a married man. At first she didn't seem to care. She aggressively went after him, and he re-

Bob in *Johnny Eager* title role, with onscreen and, for a short time, off screen, co-star, Lana Turner. Courtesy Robert Taylor Family Private Collection.

sponded. He really responded. Lana was only twenty, and already in the process of a divorce. Bob was ten years older. Their hook-up was the kind of stuff fan magazines panted over. In her autobiography, Lana said blatantly Bob was exactly the sort of guy that attracted her.

Some of the time they were together was surprisingly spent talking. Bob admitted to her he was unhappy with the direction his marriage had taken. He wasn't a man given to holding out for something he wasn't sure was ever going to be right, and he didn't have much patience for the waiting part. Lana was taken aback by the intensity of his discontent, and she didn't want to be responsible for the break-up of his marriage. He was clearly already headed in that direction, with or without her, and despite the attraction between them, she backed off.

"I wasn't in love with Bob," she stated, "not really." She claimed they had never physically been to bed together, though their "eyes" had already done the deed.

Bob and Lana Turner in a publicity still from *Johnny Eager*.

Bob was determined, though. Whether he thought he was really in love, or the lust factor overtook all logical thought, Bob was ready to leave Barbara for Lana Turner. Believing they hadn't slept together was difficult for gossipmongers in the face of their blatant and physical public flirting, and stories ran wild.

Bob's sole reason for getting married had been to create the sort of companionship his parents had shared within their sanctioned relationship. On the set of a movie filmed over only a few months, many doubted Bob's time with Lana could achieve such a long-term goal for them as a couple, lending credence to the widely-accepted idea of them as lovers. Common belief, from those who saw them together every day, indicated they did have a hot-and-heavy physical relationship, the sort of which to that point in his life Bob had never experienced. All else paled in comparison.

He said about Lana, "I have never seen lips like hers." Lana warned him not to tell Barbara how he felt about her. She said she cared about him, but she didn't want to be put in the middle of his domestic troubles. If he was going to break up with his wife, she didn't want to be the reason. Bob didn't listen to her. He went home and told Barbara right out he was leaving her. He wanted a divorce. He wasn't happy.

Barbara ran away from home and stayed for days with her maid, Harriet Corey. What Louis B. Mayer had wanted to keep quiet was finally irretrievably out of the bag. Gossip columnists went wild. There were reports of Barbara being taken to Cedars of Lebanon Hospital with a severed wrist. Official comment said "a window fell on her hand, necessitating many stitches." She was seen in public with her forearm and hand heavily bandaged, and her arm in a sling.

Barbara defended herself in a news conference, saying Bob, not she, had left home, not because of anything out of the ordinary, but because he was tired after a non-stop filming schedule. She said he'd gone to Odlum Ranch to do some flying, and took the explanation no further. She stressed she and her husband were not separated, and jealousy of some unnamed people was the source of the "false rumors." She added that she and Bob were building a home together in Beverly Hills and asked, "Does that sound as if we're getting a divorce?"

This brave front was the result of a quickly devised public relations effort. Helen Ferguson, Barbara's press agent and friend, took meticulous care of her, and made sure she was always protected, physically and emotionally. Bob was wisely nowhere to be seen, ostensibly off taking flying lessons. The divorce which had been wildly rumored and had, in fact, actually been considered on Bob's part, was played up as little more than gossipy attempts to drum up a juicy story on the Taylor/Stanwyck relationship.

A tidbit related to the cooling temperature of their married life came through a comment from Barbara. She wanted to make one point clear; except for supporting him and coaching him when he asked she did not interfere in her husband's career. "Outside of my pride in him I have no place in his work and we have always agreed that our professional careers should be

**Bob and Mary Howard in *Billy the Kid*.
Courtesy Robert Taylor Family Private Collection.**

separately maintained at all times." This was a somewhat lukewarm acknowledgement of Bob as his own person. She stepped in, she said, only if he asked.

From there, the marriage went on as usual. The public relations campaign to keep up appearances was a testament to the extensive, creative effort and the genius of the studio "fixers."

Barbara released *Meet John Doe* in mid 1941, in which she starred with Gary Cooper. Bob had just finished filming *Billy the Kid* (1941) and was getting ready to start *When Ladies Meet* (1941) with Barbara's good friend, Joan Crawford. On June eleventh, Bob and Barbara had their hands and feet forever imprinted together in cement in a ceremony in front of Grauman's Chinese Theater on Hollywood Boulevard. The media event was carefully orchestrated to be seen as a special moment between a celebrated and loving husband and wife, the fifty-seventh such official event held in a tradition started in 1927 with Mary Pickford and Douglas Fairbanks.

Barbara went into production next on *Ball of Fire* with Gary Cooper, one of the last "screwball" comedies made before the war. This sort of story was eventually perfected by the likes of Lucille Ball. Barbara's character's name was Sugarpuss O'Shea, a wisecracking, hard-living nightclub singer, and girlfriend of a mob boss. Cooper played a straight-laced professor.

Barbara was always on the set on time. She took her work seriously, allowing nothing to distract her. She knew her lines and was considered a true professional, not only with the job at hand, but also with her fellow actors. For her, the business of acting was a serious day on the job, and she was not given to unnecessary theatrics or any sort of histrionics during working hours.

The script called for thirty-three year old Barbara to throw a punch at fifty-six year old Kathleen Howard, one of the character actors. The Director, Howard Hawks, had urged the ladies to add more realism. Barbara was expected to go for Kathleen's jaw, and a specific camera angle used for such shots would make her action look like her fist connected. During previous rehearsals, Kathleen had asked Barbara to "hit harder."

And she did. Barbara miscalculated her swing and she floored Kathleen, a former opera star. She landed a "straight right" to the other woman's face, knocking her unconscious. Kathleen collapsed and was taken to the hospital with a dislocated jaw.

Barbara was known for always jumping right into her roles. In her days before Hollywood, she had seen the inside of a seedy nightclub, and she intimately knew Sugarpuss O'Shea's type of woman. Kathleen Howard turned out to be okay, but Barbara never forgot that afternoon. She became hysterical, and started bemoaning, publicly, her accident-prone nature.

Did this filter down into her marriage? Her relationship with Bob always seemed to be an accident waiting to happen.

CHAPTER NINE:

Hollywood vs. Washington

"Follow instructions and everything will be alright. Do this or else."
– Text from an extortion letter sent to Robert Taylor

Bob had recently turned thirty. Barbara was especially determined to hold on to him, and for his birthday, she had planned a blow-out party, without his knowledge.

He came home early that evening. Hearing his key in the front door, all the party guests hid at Barbara's bidding. They were ready to jump out and yell the traditional, "Surprise!" but the guests were the ones who were shocked.

Commotion and his footsteps were heard on the steps, in a hurry, and Bob called out, "Okay, I'm feeling horny, and I'm coming right upstairs!"

Everything unfolded simultaneously. Before he could get to the bedroom, the lights went on, and everyone came out of the shadows, yelling, "Surprise!" As the story is told, Bob Taylor stood there in all his naked glory, in front of his party guests, holding his clothes in his hands. It was a celebration to remember. Seems their relationship still had some amount of "romance" to it.

Bob and Barbara lived an outwardly charmed life, part of Hollywood's elite, secure and stable in their public lives, if not as much in their private world.

His mother, a big responsibility and always a concern, was in a good place—her own. They were physically close enough that he could visit and spend time with her, and far enough away that he didn't have to live with her anymore. He finally had an existence separate from hers.

This was as good for her as it was for him. She developed a social life, both as the mother of a top drawer celebrity, and as a woman. She joined clubs, had friendships with other celebrity mothers, and had a few male friends. She tried to keep a hand in Bob's affairs as often as possible, but he was by this time wise to her ways. He loved and respected his mother, but he had learned how to smartly manage her.

On December 7, 1941, only days after Barbara's film, *Ball of Fire* premiered, the United States was pulled into the war raging everywhere else around the world. Screwball comedies were put on the back burner for more serious fare. Everyone in the country had an opinion on the international state of affairs, and those in power in the States wanted desperately to keep the conflict away from home soil.

Bob was a wildly successful movie star living a life of luxury and ease. To hold to that course by doing his part for the cause of American liberty would've been easy for him. By lending his name to bond drives, publicity tours overseas, and starring in war-effort films made to mirror the war-crazy atmosphere, he would have been seen as doing his part. Old enough to have a solid hold on his place as one of filmdom's royalty, but young enough to manipulate the industry to work best for him, Bob could write his own career ticket.

And what he wanted was to enlist in the armed services, though he could have simply stayed home. The movie industry was utilized to support the allies; from 1941 to 1945, films praising Stalin and Soviet Russia as allies against Hitler were considered generally acceptable, even encouraged. Bob wanted to do more than support the effort as a movie star. His growing love affair with aviation fed his desire to fly for his country, and he started making inquiries at the studio about his chances of joining the Navy's aviation division.

His interest had grown wings during the filming of *Flight Command*. The production was filmed at Naval Air Station San Diego, with the government's buy-in for the growing marriage between Washington and Hollywood. Every effort was put into the movie to make war scenes realistic, packed with "air maneuvers at sea with aircraft carriers, battleships, and squadrons of fighting planes engaged in all hazards of the service." Bob's patriotic military image had been seen in all sorts of press, his spotless visage standing proudly in his at-that-time only make-believe uniform. The production went all out, winning an Oscar for Special Effects.

Bob wanted to be in the Navy, and he wanted to fly. He repeatedly made this clear to Mayer, and to anyone who would listen. He tried to get placed into combat as a fighter pilot, but the studio would have none of that. He was too valuable an asset to be put in direct conflict. Mayer argued Bob Taylor would be much more valuable to his country if his pilot skills were used stateside to teach and lead others. No going overseas for "The Man With The Perfect Profile."

There were few more fervent anti-Communists in Hollywood at the time than Bob Taylor. He didn't believe in any way Stalin intended good will for his own people, nonetheless for the people of the United States. Anyone who followed Stalin's line of thought was, in Bob's book, a Communist. An anti-American. He watched the progress overseas with growing interest and frustration. His newspaper-reading became voracious. He got together with others in the film community who were concerned over the direction in which the battle was moving. This became an odd, uncomfortable situation for actors; able-bodied men who otherwise would be welcomed and encouraged into the military were skated around because of their high visibility and international notoriety.

Louis B. Mayer continued to influence the strengthening relationship between Hollywood and Washington. His determination easily overrode that of his stars. If there was a decision to be made as to whether the star stayed in Hollywood or went to foreign soil to fight a dangerous battle for freedom, Mayer was always the final say. He would agree the effort was noble, but putting his stars, his assets, in harm's way was not an option. That would not be good for the studio's bottom line, financially or public relations-wise. He had a lot of dollars invested in these people.

As early as 1940, President Roosevelt's office was in talks with Nicholas

Schenk, President of Loew's, MGM's parent company. Roosevelt's administration wanted them to make films on defense and foreign policy. In February of 1941, Roosevelt publicly thanked the entire film industry for their "splendid cooperation."

The Office of War Information, (OWI), was put together out of Roosevelt's government by Executive Order on June 3, 1942. The OWI was abolished by an Executive Order, effective September 15, 1945. In those three-odd years of existence, the department had quite an effect on the movie industry. Their official purpose was to facilitate the collection of information, and put all the work into one place. Promotions told the world the OWI was created to help the public understand the war effort, and to be the liaison between press, radio, and motion pictures. Newsreels and radio shows were produced, monitoring design and content of government posters and putting out photographs to document the conflict. There was common belief their only reason for existence was to "sell" the war.

Records indicate many people working for the OWI were, at the least, ardent admirers of Soviet Union policies. Some were rumored to be members of the Communist Party. Whatever the reality, by the end of 1942, the OWI was in deep with movie studios at the direction of the highest reaches of the Federal Government.

OWI personnel organizing 1943 propaganda film.

Lowell Mellett was an assistant to President Roosevelt. Titled "Presidential Liaison to the Media," Mellett had an official office set up in Hollywood and opened a storefront physically run by Nelson Poynter, who worked for him. The office was the West Coast branch of the Bureau of Motion Pictures, under Mellett's direction, and a division of the Domestic Branch of the OWI. In December of 1942, Mellett issued what boiled down to an edict for the film industry:

"For the benefit of both your studio and the Office of War Information it would be advisable to establish a routine procedure whereby our Hollywood office would receive copies of studio treatments or synopses of all stories which you contemplate producing and of the finished scripts. This will enable us to make suggestions as to the war content of motion pictures at a stage when it is easy and inexpensive to make any changes which might be recommended."

In what was considered to be a free world society, the United States government started to sound as if they were issuing demands on what would, and would not, be produced. Mellett wasn't the heavy-hitter; he followed instructions from further up the food chain. The more the government leaned on studio heads to produce a product offering a favorable view of the war, and the allies of the United States, the more the studios realized they had little choice. Louis B. Mayer and his compatriots were told to "consider" the following questions when they began the production of a new film:

1. Will this picture help win the war?

2. What war information problem does it seek to clarify, dramatize, or interpret?

3. If it is an "escape" picture, will it harm the war effort by creating a false picture of America, her allies, or the world we live in?

4. Does it merely use the war as the basis for a profitable picture, contributing nothing of real significance to the war effort and possibly lessening the effect of other pictures of more importance?

5. Does it contribute something new to our understanding of the world conflict and the various forces involved, or has the subject already been adequately covered?

6. When the picture reaches its maximum circulation on the screen, will it reflect conditions as they are and fill a need current at that time, or will it be out-dated?

7. Does the picture tell the truth or will the young people of today have reason to say they were misled by propaganda?

Nelson Poynter physically attended studio story conferences. There were sometimes fifteen a week on his schedule, and studios were strongly encouraged to cooperate with his "suggestions." One can imagine what a problem this caused. Though executives had personal opinions, bottom line stated they were in business to make money. A good story would bring in profit; a good story that had Uncle Sam's hand overriding final distribution required a quagmire of what appeared to be forced collaboration. They were often required to buy into an end product not of their choosing. In some cases, the OWI became the final arbiter of what was offered to the American public as entertainment, a process sounding not much different from the government of one of our "allies."

Mayer had to put out work worthy of the public's money, while also showing the war and our allies in a positive light. This was, to be fair, a tall order.

The OWI answered directly to the Roosevelt administration. If there were ever any question as to which way the wind blew within the halls of the Roosevelt White House, one had to look only as far as many of the newspaper pieces of the day, most of which were repeatedly lauded by the Communist-directed press and were carefully, frowningly watched by Conservatives. The Red media spoke of those same Conservatives "trying to cripple the OWI's Film Bureau," and gave glowing accounts of numerous films called, in their words, "Government film productions" or "Government sponsored movies." In each case, the plots of these movies related directly to tenets of the Communist doctrine.

In spring, 1942, MGM acquired a story then called *Scorched Earth*. Earliest copies of script treatments were dated March. The tale was based on a universal love-story theme, telling of common interests between the United States and Russia, and their similar struggles and shared humanity. What has never been fully clarified is whether the studio decided alone to make the film and then the government got involved, or if the government instigated the production. Most records show MGM with the script ahead of the first OWI contact. This would indicate the product came to be as a result of studio effort, but quickly became a cooperative union with the government as they encouraged MGM to comply with OWI specifications.

About the second week of April, Bob received a letter postmarked "Peoria, Ill., April 18, 1942." There was no return address, and the only thing written on the envelope was, "Mr. Robert Taylor, Hollywood, Calif."

"Mr. Taylor," read the neatly handwritten-in-ink note on simple writing tablet paper, *"please put $5000 in a shoe box & put it in the 'General Delivery Department' of the Post Office in Los Angeles. You better do this or else. Put [marked out] on the package. To be called for in 10 days. You better do this,"* it reiterated, *"or else."*

Bob immediately got the studio involved, which in turn contacted the Federal Bureau of Investigation (FBI). According to the case file, a Springfield, Illinois Special Agent gave a report dated May 28, stating, "On May 1, 1942, the Los Angeles Field Division was advised by [name withheld], Metro-Goldwyn-Mayer Pictures, Culver City, California, that an extortion letter had been received addressed to Mr. ROBERT TAYLOR, the movie actor, and subsequently forwarded the letter in question to the Los Angeles Field Division, which was noted to have been mailed. . . ." and went on to give the date mailed, as well as, again, Bob's name.

There were a number of oddities. For starters, only one letter was officially indicated, citing letter and an envelope as evidence, but two letters were included in the file, clearly written by the same hand. Though they said much the same thing, there was a different slant to the words. The other note read, *"Mr. Taylor, I am demanding $5000 from you. Put it in a shoe box and address it [information withheld but quotation marks can be seen, as well as T-followed by 3 letters or numbers, X-ed out by typewriter] general delivery Los Angeles, Calif. Leave it there for 10 days. Follow instructions & everything will be alright. Do this or else."* There was more, apparently a signature, but that, too, was withheld.

Sheriff Guy E. Donahue of Pekin, Illinois called the Springfield FBI office on the second of May to report the letter-writer had "given himself up." A May fifth teletype from Los Angeles said the letter was forwarded to the FBI Technical Laboratory for examination. On May eleventh, the subject was interviewed at Sheriff Donahue's office, and an official complaint was filed in Peoria on May twelfth, before United States Commissioner, Robert W. Morgan. By May sixteenth, the Bureau advised, "it had not been possible to develop any latent fingerprints," but on May twentieth, the subject was indicted by Grand Jury. On May twenty-eighth, the Bureau advised, "it had not been possible to effect an identification of the handwriting on the letter. . . ." with any unidentified letters held in the government's "extortion letter file."

Paperwork of that same date indicated when the subject was interviewed, he was "informed that on April 19, 1942 he had written the above-mentioned letter." This was likely a typo, since the letter was physically postmarked on April eighteenth, and the date of the letter was an unusual detail to not check before filing an official report. To state the subject was "informed" that "he had written the above-mentioned letter" spoke either to sloppy report-writing or oddly-worded details.

The next dated fact was a report on June 23, 1942. In the sixteen days since the Bureau had been unable to identify the handwriting, "prosecutive action" was completed on a plea of guilty for a subject sentenced to "11 months to Quincy Work House by United States District Judge Leroy Adair on 5/25/42 . . . sentence to start 6/1/42."

The grand jury returned a decision on May twenty-second, and indictment was filed on May twenty-fifth, where the "defendant presented in court." He waived trial and examination before U.S. Commissioner W. H. Moore, and "judgment and commitment" was filed and entered. Bond was set, ironically, at five thousand dollars. The subject was unable to post the money and he was held in jail. Again, this was a curious chain of events. How could a judge in Quincy prosecute, and then sentence, a subject for a crime simultaneously handled by the FBI, when the FBI office in charge stated they couldn't identify the handwriting, three days after the individual was already sentenced?

The subject was reportedly twenty-six year old Richard Goodman of Creve Coeur, Illinois. He wasn't publicly identified anywhere in actual FBI documentation. Each time a name was indicated, and then blacked out. Instead, an obscure short newspaper clipping was kept in the file, giving Goodman's name, age, and hometown. The clipping also revealed a detail which hadn't been directly stated in any official documentation: "Sheriff Donohue said Goodman informed him he had sent Taylor a letter demanding $5,000 and threatened bodily injury unless payment was made." That Bob was in physical danger was not anywhere in the government's paperwork.

A description of the subject was marked out. A photo was "retained in the Springfield office," but wasn't included. Copies of Goodman's signed statement were also retained in Springfield. Throughout the paperwork, an alias was indicated, in some spots blacked out and in others a title was given as, "The Spider." Various papers show Goodman must have already had a criminal record under a different name, and his record going back to August 13, 1935 was outlined. Every bit, about half a page, was blacked out.

When all was said and done, a lab report dated July fifteenth concluded the right man had been nailed for the crime, verifying guilt thirty-four days after the accused had already started his sentence. That lab report used the words "threatening letters," but the "s" was removed and a comma substituted. The statement went on to say the "letter[s]" had been "previously submitted in connection with the instant case."

Who really was Richard Goodman? Why did he try to extort Robert Taylor for five thousand dollars? Why was the name of the MGM employee who reported the letter blacked out of the documents? Why was the name of the FBI Special Agent not included in a report publicly sent out over sixty years after the incident, when that Agent is likely no longer living, unless the document included a recognizable name?

Why were Richard Goodman's aliases and criminal record blacked out? And why did he sign his letter[s] "The Spider?"

"The Famous Crime Smasher Now Wars Upon The Nation's Secret Enemies!" was a tagline for the 1941 movie serial, *The Spider Returns*. The film debuted in the United States in May of 1941, about a year prior to when the extortion letter surfaced. "The Spider," a popular crime-fighting character of the day, was visiting homes and stamping out bad guys in comic books across the country from 1933 until 1944. The likelihood of any real connection is slight, but the possibility exists Richard Goodman, if that was his real name, felt he took on an important duty and in some way helped to wage war upon "the nation's secret enemies." Perhaps his politics didn't agree with Bob's politics.

While actual reasons for this incident haven't been discovered, the information was found as a result of a Freedom of Information Act request for anything related to Robert Taylor only during the House Un-American Activities Committee period. Hearings weren't a reality that early in the decade. They hadn't even received solid consideration. Why was such a file offered up?

On December sixteenth, Bob and Barbara petitioned the Superior Court to officially become Mr. and Mrs. Robert Taylor rather than, as they had been married, Mr. and Mrs. Arlington Brugh. Barbara had married as Ruby Stevens, and wanted to continue using Stanwyck as her public name, and the court also granted her that right. They were both known to the world under their screen names and had purchased, separately and together, various business ventures under those names. This was a matter of convenience, but Bob's concern may have been as much over being tagged as a possible Communist the year before because of his "phoney [sic] name."

A. Morgan Maree, Jr. was Bob and Barbara's joint business manager, and he facilitated these matters. Already well-known amongst the film community, Maree started with a small office in 1932 on Hollywood Boulevard. By the time the Taylors became his clients under both names, he was established as a savvy investment manager, one of the first to help movie stars wisely capitalize on their earnings.

Bob was summoned to see Louis B. Mayer in early 1943. When he entered his boss' office, he found they weren't alone. Lowell B. Mellett stood when he entered the room. Bob was introduced to him and the three had a brief talk which, according to Bob's later recollection, "didn't last more than five minutes." The subject of the meeting was the making of what had been called *Scorched Earth*, a film now titled *Russia*.

While some stories indicate this to have been Bob's first introduction to the assignment, official documents show Mellett personally made the trip to Hollywood for the "express purpose of overruling Taylor's objection" to being a part of the movie. A number of things clashed. Bob had already been inducted into the Navy. When Lowell Mellett, with his direct connection to the President, showed up in Hollywood for a meeting with Mayer, and with Bob, the drama which had gone on before to this "five minute" MGM get-together took on added importance.

Bob was offered the film prior to this meeting, and he had flatly refused to be a part of the project. This was an unusual move for him, notwithstanding any consideration of film content, or Bob's strong anti-Russian beliefs. There must have been some heavy leaning on Louis B. Mayer by the OWI, or

Mayer would have handled Bob's sudden rock-hard stubbornness internally. He was famous for great finesse in taking care of problems with his talent. He handled these matters in total privacy, within the ranks.

Available records indicate MGM acquired the *Scorched Earth/Russia* treatment in April of 1942 which, time-wise, curiously coincided with Bob receiving the extortion letter. Filming started in March of 1943. His previous assignment, *Bataan* (1943), another war film, had wrapped on February third.

Bob was sworn into the United States Naval Reserve that same month, dating this meeting between Bob, Mayer, and Mellett somewhere at a point concurrent with his official entry into the Navy in February, and six months or less after the extortion case had been finalized and the perpetrator punished. While there is no known indication that securing Robert Taylor as the lead in *Russia* and the attempt to extort him had any connection, the consideration is intriguing.

Bob with a military haircut, at home with Barbara.
Courtesy Robert Taylor Family Private Collection.

Also worth contemplating was why *Song of Russia* (1944), under any title, was made in the first place. War still raged in Europe. Pearl Harbor had been attacked barely a year before. While Russia was at this point considered an uneasy ally, they were not really trusted nor envisioned as a true friend in any true sense of the term.

The support of democracy, always the underlying theme of Americanism, saw a share of duplicity when the Nazi Party had initially come into power in Germany through democratic channels. One of the tenets upon which the Nazis won the election was a staunch stand against Communism. Not five years earlier, the Soviet Union had been expelled from the League of Nations for dishonest moves. They signed an agreement with Japan, facilitating Japan's efforts in the Pacific in April of 1941, eight months prior to Japan invading Pearl Harbor.

Who was to say Russia would play fair now that they had publicly changed their tune? Why was Hollywood, as well as the government, pandering to a force which had already proven their allegiance not to democracy, but to the power best able to further their cause?

This question has never been satisfactorily answered. Louis B. Mayer had a stock, uneasy reply when asked why his studio played nice-nice with an ideology mistrusted by many Americans. He said *Russia* was a film that married wonderful music and a touching love story, nothing more. The fact that the script was set in Russia didn't mean a thing. The setting could've as easily been any other country, with other music, and would have been as captivating. Official entry of the United States into the war in December of 1941, four months prior to MGM's acquisition of the script, makes his explanation suspect.

Documented accounts seem to show how MGM acquired the script prior to government intervention. Most likely his goal was little more than sheer pocketbook numbers. In 1942, Louis B. Mayer's income was reported at $949,765, a seriously tidy sum for the period, particularly considering this was war time. He was a smart man. He certainly also read newspapers and listened to the radio, as well as to his well-connected advisors, and he saw the writing on the wall. The acquisition of such a story, and the making of such a movie, was the right thing to do for the company coffers.

Notes indicate Walter Pidgeon may have been MGM's early-on choice to play the role of John Meredith, the American conductor who went to Moscow and fell in love with a local girl. Mayer, however, didn't want to go that route. Next, the studio attempted to secure a temporary release from the Air Force for Lieutenant Emmett Evan Heflin, Jr., known to the movie ticket-buying public as Van Heflin. No dice there, either. The Air Force refused the request. Interestingly, Mayer had once told Heflin, "You will never get the girl at the end." Would he have seriously considered him to play a dashing, romantic lead? Heflin himself claimed he didn't have the looks for such roles.

But that's how the story goes, and supposedly the series of events that came about prior to Bob finding himself in Mayer's office in the company of Lowell Mellett. By this time, the film was not only definitely on the schedule to be made, but already in production under the OWI's intense scrutiny and direction. Mellett had personally taken on the project and between him and Nelson Poynter, virtually every aspect was monitored.

There has never been any explanation as to why a temporary furlough for Van Heflin was impossible, but the task of procuring the initial deferment for Robert Taylor was simple. *Russia*, as the movie was called then, began filming in March, and the female lead, Susan Peters, was signed that month.

Whatever the reason behind the struggle, Bob did end up as the lead in this increasingly controversial film. There are records showing his name was probably bandied about quite early in the process, indicating that Mayer himself may have wanted Bob in the role from the start. Whether because MGM had already lost the option on the two other actors, or whether Bob was Mayer's initial choice, Bob learned in the meeting with Mellett and Mayer he would play John Meredith, Navy or no Navy, and he was not happy. In later years, he said, "They [the studio] wanted me to do it. I didn't want to do it because I thought it was definitely Communist propaganda.

In other words, it happened to paint Russia in a light in which I personally never had conceived it."

Bob's family members have vehemently stated he took the role only because he had no choice. He was "bullied" into playing a character in a script going against every fiber of his being, and all beliefs he held sacred. As an executive of the Screen Actors Guild (SAG), he was an outspoken anti-Communist and there was nothing about *Russia*, the country or the script, which he found to his liking.

Mayer somehow, for some reason, thought him "ideal," though, despite the fact he knew from the outset Bob "did not like the story." This in itself wouldn't have been unusual, since actors didn't always find an assignment to their liking for any variety of reasons. For someone like Bob, though, known to take whatever work was handed him and not argue with the brass, to be extraordinarily agreeable often to the point of submission; for him to speak against any role was a total shock to all involved.

That initial meeting must have been interesting, possibly volatile, in the short amount of time they were together, though Bob would've been nothing but icily polite in his determination to argue his side. He reminded his boss and the government representative of his commission in the Navy, already secured. He hoped, and probably at that moment believed, the signed fact of his upcoming military service would prove to be the end of his consideration for the lead in this film.

Mayer let him talk. He was well-versed in Bob's personality. He knew Bob's politics. He himself was considered conservative, though most thought his true allegiance was to the bottom dollar. Chances are, he finessed Bob and told him something that would've bought him time, something like, "Well see, Bob," or "I'll see what I can do about this," or "I'll do what I can for you, Bob." Mellett may have remained silent and let Mayer be the front man.

All the while, Mayer's think wheels were turning. After Bob left his office, and in correlation with a letter Mellett wrote to Secretary of the Navy, Frank Knox, Mayer called in his chips. He had a personal phone conversation with

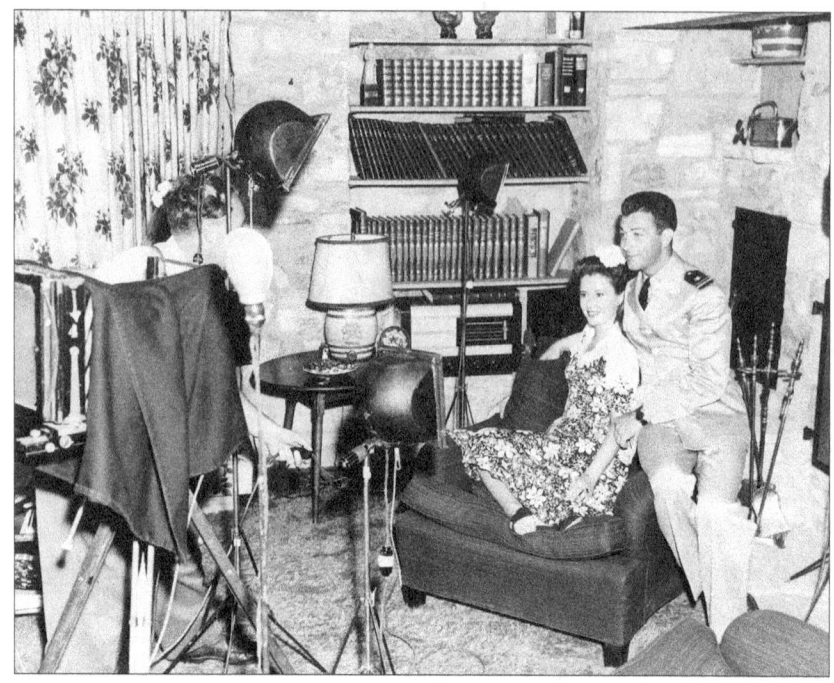

Bob in uniform with Barbara, in a formal photo before he leaves to serve his country. Courtesy Robert Taylor Family Private Collection.

Knox to explain the situation, "recalling the good that had been accomplished with *Mrs. Miniver* and other pictures released during the war period."

He asked for a deferment for Robert Taylor's Navy service. Knox listened, and then agreed to consider the problem. Ultimately Knox gave the nod so Bob could be granted "the time to make the film before being called to the service."

Done. Robert Taylor would star with Susan Peters in *Russia*.

No less than two deferments for Bob's military service were secured by the studio and/or the OWI. This must've been another slap in his face, more fodder for his already-angered state. His Navy experience started on paper in February, while he wasn't able to begin serving until August. An AP report on February 11, 1943 told the public Robert Taylor had officially taken the oath under the name of Spangler Arlington Brugh, and was scheduled to "report

Bob in uniform. Courtesy author's personal collection.

to Corpus Christie, Tex., within 30 days for training as a ferry pilot or instructor." Another piece published through the NEA on February nineteenth showed Bob smiling and wearing his field cap and uniform. The short text indicated he was soon on his way to Texas to start his stint as a naval aviator.

Years later, Ayn Rand, Russian-born writer and commentator and outspoken anti-Communist, related her recollection of Bob's involvement in the *Russia* production period, as well as his complicated naval connections. Rand stated that during a board meeting for an ultra-conservative Hollywood group, the Motion Picture Association for the Preservation of American Ideals, Bob had been vocal about his part in *Song of Russia*. He said that after he volunteered to join the Navy, but before he could leave on assignment, he was sent to Mayer's office and told "point blank" by the "man from Washington" that if he didn't take the part, he would not fulfill his commission.

This would back up Mayer's personality and business sense. He wouldn't have been the last call on such a decision. He would've toed the line if he had been given an ultimatum, especially if not following directions endangered his film kingdom. He would've done what he was told to do to ensure Bob Taylor took the role.

Bob continued to exhibit his displeasure throughout the filming of *Russia*. He noted later on he had "tried desperately to get out." His capitulation came only after he finally admitted that if he continued to fight, he might forfeit his chance with the Navy, and end up on the receiving side of other punishments meted out by Louis B. Mayer, Lowell Mellett, the OWI, and by default, the Roosevelt administration. He didn't give in quietly, though.

One has to wonder what other threats he may have faced. Since Bob was known across-the-board for keeping his feelings to himself and almost never publicly soiling his personal laundry, a look at surrounding facts helped tell the story, taking into consideration his personality and quirks.

Was only his Navy commission threatened? That had become of great importance to him. His awareness of the world's tenuous political atmosphere was heightening daily as he befriended and worked side-by-side with a growing group of ultra-conservative Hollywood-ites who believed as he did. Being part of the war effort became crucial, a way for Bob to give back to a country he felt had been good to him. He stepped up his public political profile. Along with Clark Gable, Gary Cooper, Robert Montgomery and others, all of them in unison repeatedly insisted that [group documentation] "the satisfaction of serving their country far outweighed any perks of stardom; moreover, they did not want their War service used in any way for publicity purposes...."

Their personal desires were trumped by the power of the studio over their lives. Bob's frustration boiled over. This was something being taken from him, something he felt strongly about, something which satisfied him in ways his career and his marriage never had. But were there other circumstances? Was his career also jeopardized? He was told he would, without question, at least be suspended if he didn't agree to make *Russia*.

What about his wife? He had Barbara to consider. Would her considerable body of work be in danger if he were to make waves? Barbara wasn't with MGM, and MGM wouldn't, in general, have any way of punishing her for something Bob wouldn't do, would they? MGM may not have had that power, but the OWI would have.

Bob was required by his own nature, not by any outside force, to take care of anyone who depended on him. As a couple, they both made more money than they could spend in any given year, and though Barbara could have arguably made more per film than her husband, she relied heavily on him. She had a considerable emotional investment in Bob, and many records indicate she was "blacklisted" early on when the union strikes started, making Hollywood a difficult place to work and live.

Bob, a man who had made his adult living in the world of make-believe was now faced with a real-life conundrum. He could've been seen as easily capitulating since the finished product clearly showed he made the movie. Whenever he and any of his industry friends got together they would, according to his stepdaughter, Manuela, "loudly argue politics well into the night." This indicates he never would have given in unless he felt genuinely threatened in a way that would have put him, his family, and/or his lifestyle in an untenable position.

The end result insinuated that Bob felt threatened, angry, betrayed. He saw only one way out of the growing build-up between his side and the other. He believed he had to follow the path put in front of him by a man he

Bob and Susan Peters in *Song of Russia*.

had come to trust, a man he considered to be like a father, a man who had always, or so Bob thought, had his best interests at heart.

But that was the problem. These weren't only personalities and family-style relationships anymore. Politics and profit were rough bedfellows and they trumped the old ways, the simpler, slap-on-the-hand, "do the film or get docked" rules. These times were tough all around and there was more at stake.

Bob contained his anger, if not his tongue. Pulling himself back into his structured, all-important, ever-present work ethic, he went to the studio each morning at the appointed hour, and knew his lines as well as the lines of all the other characters, a skill he utilized on every shoot. He did his job as the professional he was industry-wide known to be.

Complaining aloud to anyone but his closest family or friends, particularly about his work, was strange behavior for Bob. John Wexley, a writer who began on *Russia* in the summer of 1943 and a Communist, gave a telling interview in which he discussed his on-set interactions with Bob. He claimed he had been brought on as a "mollifier or a pacifier, a diplomat" toward Robert Taylor. Bob, according to Wexley, was a "very strong reactionary. He hated anything that had to do with the Soviet Union."

Opinions didn't necessarily fit with established definitions of different "sides." George Sokolsky, well-known anti-Communist journalist, offered up how to identify one's political inclinations in a discussion with founder of Random House, Bennett Cerf. Cerf, who leaned to the left, was seen as a fair and reasonable man interested in getting the best story from either side. Despite his more liberal beliefs, he didn't allow opinion to get in the way of a good story, or a good friend. His inner circle spanned the spectrum from both ends. He published Ayn Rand's controversial novels, while his second wife, Phyllis Fraser, was raised by Lela Rogers, ultra-conservative film producer and mother of Ginger Rogers, and one of Bob's cohorts in the Hollywood battle against Communism.

In a tongue-in-cheek rant at lunch one day, Sokolsky told Cerf, "... a liberal is supposed to be in the middle. At one end is the Communist. At the other end is the reactionary...." Wexley had called Bob a "reactionary" and that term wasn't arbitrary. During this time in American history, if an ultra-conservative was called a reactionary by a far-right liberal, the connotation was technical and intentional, a clear case of Communists vs. anti-Communists.

Bob was well aware he was being corralled. Throughout the production, MGM "kept trying to tell him it was his contribution to the war effort." He wouldn't speak to the other two writers, but for whatever reason he was comfortable with Wexley, who would "go into his dressing room or have lunch with him." Wexley said Bob would tell him how much he hated a certain part in the film or couldn't stand a certain line, and Wexley would placate him, asking how he wanted the offending piece changed.

As early as June, the set was "closed down indefinitely due to differences of opinion in the story." The reporting newspaper intimated Louis B. Mayer, Bob, or both had put their foot down. Filming was stopped "... after numerous reports of protests against repeated cutting and censoring of the original script on the part of the studio."

Bob and Susan Peters in *Song of Russia*.

Production resumed in late July. At the beginning, the film had been called *Russia*, but during hiatus the title was lengthened because "the previous titled was considered not a big enough name for the picture . . . too cold." Additional scenes and retakes were shot in September and October and, finally, *Song of Russia* was in the can.

Production had taken well over a full month to satisfactorily appease all warring opinions on how the movie should and shouldn't be made. There were constant revisions, reviews. They monitored and picked apart every little piece of storyline, dialogue, and even small things like clothing and set decorations. Input came from every direction, from the OWI, Mayer, Bob. Even The Hays Office put in their two cents which, after being born in the early 1940s, nitpicked away at every piece of work to come out of Hollywood to ensure morality and social propriety.

Wexley helped get Bob to the end of the filming, and from the sound of his words, that was done through the use of any means possible. Honesty didn't appear to be important. Wexley claimed, "That was part of my job—four weeks on the set keeping him happy." The set was clearly not a cheery place for any of the professionals involved.

OWI News Bureau.

Did Louis B. Mayer, or the OWI, hire a Communist writer to play nice-nice with Bob to get him to complete the project? At the time, did Bob know Wexley was a Communist? How much duplicity was involved in a well-planned project which required coddling and personal hand-holding between MGM and the United States government to keep the leading man on the set from beginning to end? How much trouble was Bob in danger of creating for either or both, for the OWI, or Mayer, to have gone so far as to bring in someone to babysit him, and keep him off the warpath?

The years of 1942 and 1943 are the least directly documented in Bob's life, though possibly the most crucial as turning points. He was the subject of a mysterious extortion attempt at the same time he was forced to be part of a film which ultimately stood at the crux of not only his career, but his adult life.

His naval effort had finally taken off, literally, and he seemed happier in the Navy and away from public view. His civilian pilot's license was an asset, bundled together with his natural ability to lead and influence. His first assignment was in Dallas, Texas. Bob was aware his celebrity status might cause ruckus within the ranks, and he carefully planned a "regular guy" campaign. He got a "real butch" haircut and shaved off his mustache. He bought an old car. His plan was to be as inconspicuous as possible, and he felt he succeeded because, as he related, he "had no trouble with the guys."

He was assigned to the Navy's Aviation Volunteer Transport Division. Bob's instructor was Ralph Couser, who ultimately became one of his best friends. After training, he was designated a naval aviator on January 11, 1944. *Song of Russia* debuted in New York City on February 10, 1944, a month after Bob officially started with the Navy. If not for his part in that film, he would've already been on active duty about a year.

His knowledge of acting and flying was an irresistible combination, and he became instrumental in the creation of training films for incoming aviators. As an instructor on film, and as a narrator, he made seventeen films considered to be some of the best ever produced during the war. In late 1944, Bob was assigned to work on a documentary titled *The Fighting Lady*, about a "battle-scarred aircraft carrier" of the same name. This won the 1944 Academy Award for best documentary, the only Academy Award to which Robert Taylor's name was ever attached.

Bob met Armand Deutsch when he was assigned to a Public Relations position to work on *The Navy Hour* in mid-to-late 1943. A radio program devoted to "dramatizing naval heroes," the show was based in Washington, and Deutsch was assigned the job of "shepherding" Bob through the process. Deutsch thought the naval officer was "quiet, pleasant, and reserved, all qualities that went unnoticed because he was so breathtakingly handsome."

Bob did his duty that day in Washington, and was shuffled off to New York for a short break prior to a second program due to be recorded a week later. Deutsch said Bob was "unreasonably despondent about spending the intervening time in a New York hotel."

Bob explained, "I can't leave my room without being mobbed. I'm a prisoner, plain and simple. I don't have any friends in New York and my only telephone calls will be to room service."

Deutsch was a bachelor with enough space for a guest in his Park Avenue apartment, and he invited Bob to be his houseguest. Bob was grateful but didn't want to impose, and he declined. Still, Deutsch gave him his phone number and told him to call if he changed his mind.

Three days later he called. Bob wanted to take Deutsch up on his offer if he were still welcome. Deutsch said, "He could not have been easier or more appreciative. He was disappointed that his wife, Barbara Stanwyck, could not join him for that week, but she was filming."

Deutsch found Bob to be "totally uncommunicative about his glamorous Hollywood life." When they tried to go out for dinner, he realized firsthand the star's predicament in getting around town with any semblance of ease. Deutsch said, "He had already made, among other outstanding films, *Magnificent Obsession* with Irene Dunne and been dubbed by *Time* as 'the most admired matinee idol since the late Rudolph Valentino.' Anywhere he went he was instantly surrounded and, although he knew it went with the territory, he disliked it."

Bob eventually completed his second *Navy Hour* program, which signaled the time for Deutsch to say goodbye to his houseguest, and return him to his base. Deutsch thought that would be the end of his association with the famous movie star.

In December of 1943, Bob was promoted to full lieutenant and stationed in Livermore, California for most of the next year. He was often asked to do War Bond appearances, and appreciated that his Commanding Officers always left that decision up to him. As a result, he was able to pick and choose his assignments.

Bob with a plane he flew for the United States Navy.
Courtesy Robert Taylor Family Private Collection.

He got his chance to fly in February of 1945 when he returned to the Naval Air Station in New Orleans as an active flight instructor. He felt the Navy had shuffled him around and used him for his acting background; finally he had received a reward for his patience. Joe Love, also assigned to NAS New Orleans and a fireman working in the overhaul shop, said, "He was... not an ancient by any means. I suspect that the Powers-That-Be simply used him in training rather than risk him in combat."

Joe explained how excited the WAVES, the army's volunteer women's unit, were to see *the* Robert Taylor in person. Joe was amazed Bob "had very dark hair, and he always had a five o'clock shadow... he always looked so clean-shaven in his films." Joe said Bob was "gracious to the WAVES who asked him for his autograph." Bob attended a dance held at one of the hangers, and he was "very friendly, and did not act as though he had an ego problem... seemed very affable."

By the time he was discharged in December of 1945, Bob was commended as one of the Navy's best flight instructors. Despite repeated requests for overseas duty, he had always been turned down. The reason given indicated he was "too old for combat," despite the fact that other actors, such as Clark Gable, were allowed to not only go overseas but participate in American raids on German soil.

Bob had recently turned thirty-two. Gable was four years older. Combat service was likely denied Bob based on studio pull and government intervention. Though Gable was still a leading man, he had crossed the invisible age line, and those four years meant a lot in the world of make-believe. He had a more rugged, manly image. Bob was usually cast as the urbane gentleman, easily not a battle-weary, front line sort. MGM wouldn't have wanted to put such a face as Bob's directly in the line of fire, and California draft boards were advised to go easy on actors. Bob was much too valuable in his current place in the movie world, and Mayer felt he best served the war effort as an openly patriotic, but well-heeled, movie star. The more dangerous assignments weren't going to be given to him.

Bob in front of his Beechcraft.
Courtesy Robert Taylor Family Private Collection.

After discharge, Bob managed to work some aspects of the situation to his advantage. Starting in 1946, as part of his contract package, MGM purchased one of the first Beechcraft D-18 airplane models made available for civilian use. The plane was given to him as his personal aircraft. Known as a Twin Beech, the registration number was N80356. MGM hired Ralph Couser to fly with him whenever and wherever, as well as to take care of the airplane. Ralph was by this time one of Bob's closest friends, and he was utilized by the studio as insurance and security, as much as he was officially on the payroll as Bob's co-pilot. In return, Bob agreed to make one picture a year for MGM. The plane was based at Santa Monica Airport and was always available for Bob at a moment's notice. Ralph was also on-call twenty-four hours a day.

Not a bad deal for Bob, all things considered.

Barbara thought otherwise.

CHAPTER TEN:
Washington Hunts Hollywood Communists

> "These investigations, the way they are being run in Washington at the moment, remind me more of a three-ring circus than of a sincere effort to rid the country of a real threat."
> – Robert Taylor

In retrospect, it may be difficult to attempt to understand the depth of emotion behind the actions of people who believed Communism threatened their way of life. Yet that there was a threat is hardly in question. How immediate was the threat is where the lines were drawn. In the early 1940s, an unnamed American citizen who had become a Communist Party leader returned from a trip to the Soviet Union. He gave a brief speech, parts of which were printed in the *Daily Worker*, the official organ of the Communist Party in the United States (CPUSA):

"I told the police the hell with the U.S.A. flag. I said that the flag I claimed was the one with the hammer and sickle, the Red Flag, which we will have some day. Not only the Red Flag but a Workers' and Farmers' Government here in the U.S.A."

While sympathizers weren't all card-carrying members of the United States' arm of the Communist Party, there were many who passionately took the party's philosophies to heart. The danger of sheer numbers became an alarming issue.

Martin Dies, around the time of the hearings.

A book written by Martin Dies, a member of the U.S. House of Representatives, *The Trojan Horse in America*, gave insight into the hysteria on both sides. Dies, a fanatical anti-Communist, was a Democrat and the first Chairman of the Un-American Activities Committee. Dies wrote, "If Stalin placed himself at the head of 150 divisions of uniformed Soviet troops and marched them through the streets of our cities, the American people would have no doubts about our being invaded by a foreign foe . . . If any American demanded in the name of 'civil liberties' that Stalin and his troops should have free access to our streets and highways, it would go pretty hard with him . . . If any high government official in Washington tried to ridicule those who were defending our homes against the Red Fuehrer and his troops, such an official would be dealt with as an obvious member of Stalin's fifth column. . . ."

He went on to say differences between "imaginary invasions" and a "real invasion led by an agent of Stalin" weren't all that dissimilar. Dies' was adamant the United States was being infiltrated slowly, methodically, surreptitiously, yet no less intentionally by individuals who wanted to sweep the nation with a change affecting the fabric of everything America held dear and crucial.

And Dies was not alone in this dramatic mindset. Ronald Reagan, vocally against Communism even then, and at the time a Democrat, showed that not only Hollywood conservatives such as Bob, and John Wayne, and Ward Bond stood up against the threat. A visible enemy was easier to fight and more believable to those who doubted. The nature of the Communist philosophy was to overtake with whatever means necessary. They would regularly do this by calculatedly shifting thought processes, for in changing the mind, the heart would naturally follow.

This concern was an undercurrent of the overall United States personality while a backdrop of real war waged around the world. Though the conflict wasn't physically fought on American mainland soil, the real threat affected every area of American existence, and the atmosphere of the country was testy. Villains were seen around every corner by both sides. Truth was regularly blurred and, as often, blasted away to create new truth.

Amidst this, the American royalty, the shared face of the silver screen, was expected to uplift the people as well as instruct and inform, all in the guise of entertainment. Movie stars were given a task, and their responsibility was to achieve that task at all costs. They had a job to do; their bread-and-butter depended on how well they could pretend, pretend, pretend, as they punched their imaginary time clock. They could hold their own opinions and feelings close to their hearts, but they were expected to never unleash those feelings on the ticket-buying public.

That as-yet unspoken demand from their bosses was nearly impossible to satisfy.

On February 4, 1944, approximately seventy-five people met at the Beverly Wilshire Hotel to officially announce the formation of the Motion Picture Alliance for the Preservation of American Ideals, called the MPA. As a voluntary, non-profit organization, membership was open to anyone in the industry, but applicants weren't approved for admission until they were satisfactorily investigated to keep out those with subversive tendencies. The only well-known actor visible at the initial event was Gary Cooper, who attended with his wife.

Director Sam Wood had more than a passing acquaintance with Bob Taylor. Wood was known as an elegant man who "liked to sip a half bottle of champagne after a day's work." The *Los Angeles Times* printed an article titled, "Leaders of Film Industry Form Anti-Red Group." Wood was the MPA's President, Walt Disney acted as First Vice-President, and Cedric Gibbons, arguably the most important Art Director in the history of film, was second Vice-President. The group's first meeting was held at the home of Jim McGuiness, MGM's Production Head and a Louis B. Mayer favorite. Several weeks of quiet organizational work followed.

Wood told the *Los Angeles Times*, ". . . these highly indoctrinated shock units of the subversive wrecking crew have shrewdly led the people of the United States to believe that Hollywood is a hot bed of sedition and subversion, and that our industry is a battleground over which Communism is locked in death grips with Fascism." A similar article appeared in the *Los Angeles Examiner* the next day, saying the MPA intended to wage war on industry Communists and sympathizers. The group saw them as attempting to spread their propaganda into screenplays through writers who were willingly utilized as weapons.

The MPA wanted everyone to know not all of Hollywood believed as the Communist Party believed, and Americanism was still alive and well in Tinseltown. They released a statement which read, in part, "As members of the motion picture industry, we must face and accept an especial responsibility. Motion pictures are inescapably one of the world's greatest forces for influencing public thought and opinion . . . In this fact lies solemn obligation. . . ."

Publicized founding officers were moderately and well-known industry names, though none were actors. Howard Emmett Rogers, an established writer, was a major player. He'd written *Billy The Kid* a few years earlier, in which Bob starred, and was part of the Conservative clique. In a speech Rogers made before the MPA, he said the group was the "first militant organization opposed to those subversive termites in the state of California" and he was "proud and happy to be a member of the executive committee."

Highly visible actors may have intentionally kept away from the foreground, either for professional reasons, or to see to it that the group's success or lack thereof wouldn't fall back on the celebrity of their names. But those names were in the game nonetheless. By mid-March, there were about two hundred and twenty-five MPA members, of which two hundred were believed to be employed by MGM. General records showed a few well-known actors as top-runners of the group, and they were called "moving figures behind the scenes."

The most prominent were: Clark Gable, who had only recently returned from overseas duty, and who was being addressed regularly as "Captain," Ward Bond, Gary Cooper, George Murphy, Adolphe Menjou and, of course, Robert Taylor, the only member actively in the military at the time of the group's inception. While Ronald Reagan is often listed as part of the beginning of the MPA, at this point he had not finalized his metamorphosis from Democrat to Republican. He wasn't an active MPA supporter, though he openly opposed Communism.

FOIA documents with names blocked out indicate one of these six was considered a "wheel horse." Another was called "logical and discreet," and he was singled out "because of his wife's influence." Another, who "for years" had furnished information to the FBI relative to Communist Party activities, was said to be "imaginative," but was "reported to have extremely bad credit and is usually in debt," though he made a considerable amount of money. The last was "not believed to be entirely reliable" and had "purchased several phony titles...."

Invasion of Privacy issues make verification of each man's description against the character sketches nearly impossible, but that Bob was the one who was "logical and discreet," and had a wife with influence, was the common assumption. Gable's wife, Carole Lombard, prominent in the industry, had recently died in a plane crash. Neither Menjou nor Bond had well-known spouses. The other three descriptions are up for discussion, though not hard to logically decipher.

The FBI actively followed John Howard Lawson, a Founder and the first President of the liberal-leaning Writer's Guild of America, as well as a known

Communist. Lawson avowed the MPA had no actual program and was composed of "just a bunch of agitators."

Through technical surveillance, as well as information turned over to the FBI by MPA members, the MPA learned the Communist Party had plans to attack them. The Party would label the MPA anti-Semitic, accusing them of being a political vehicle against Roosevelt and his administration. Most people believed the MPA organized as a direct effort to "combat a fourth term" for Roosevelt as President. There were clear-cut, documented indicators of both parties' intents against each other; the war was brewing.

The FBI accepted information offered by the Hollywood community against purported Communists, but was adamant not a single detail be made public knowledge. Agents were advised by no less than John Edgar Hoover that "under no circumstance should it be disclosed to officials of the MPA that the Bureau is presently conducting an investigation of the Communist infiltration of the motion picture industry." He told the Los Angeles office to ". . . continue to keep the Bureau advised of the general activities of the Motion Picture Alliance for the Preservation of American Ideals. Any information which may be received from this organization concerning Communist activity should be correlated with your current investigation regarding Communist infiltration of the motion picture industry."

The FBI monitored the MPA conjointly with the Communist Party, using information from one to feed the other. With each group standing for opposite sides, and each genuinely believing in their respective stance, the government had the perfect opportunity to bait one against the other. The FBI, and not any individual person on either side, created the hysteria to follow for many years. J. Edgar Hoover, a showman in his own right and a master at public relations, wanted a showdown, and members of the MPA, unknowingly at the time, fell right into place as part of his building screenplay.

In a politically-motivated move, the public declaration of the MPA's birth was timed to come out the day prior to a big dinner put on by the Hollywood Free World Association, the antithesis of the MPA. The Hollywood

Free World Association had been taunting the developing group, and the gauntlet was thrown down.

The anti-Semitic purpose for the MPA's existence, repeatedly denied with vehemence by Jim McGuinness, screenwriter and the organization's Executive Chairman at the time—". . . the most active opponents of Communism in the United States are members of the Jewish race. . . ."—was an official argument utilized by the Communist Party. The MPA received growing attention within Hollywood, and a lot of it wasn't positive. Rumors abounded as to whether or not the organization was truly an enemy of the Jewish people. The Communist Party made sure to milk every last drop of possibility out of that confusion.

Another piece of the Party's attack against MPA members was a dirt-digging effort. They hired someone at fifty dollars a week to find salacious details about the lives of members of the MPA. Those most actively targeted were visible people in the Hollywood community, with most being actors and well-known directors.

Despite his Navy service, despite being stationed away from Hollywood for most of 1944, Bob managed to stay apprised of MPA activities. Most often, his wife kept him in the loop. Barbara was photographed on April 28, 1944 with Sam Wood and Clark Gable for an article that appeared in the *Los Angeles Times*. They had attended a big meeting over which Wood presided. The get-together was held at the Hollywood Chamber of Commerce, with an audience of "two hundred leaders of the industry, including producers, writers, stars, and labor representatives." The faces eventually seen in front of the 1947 HUAC cameras were already coming forward to be counted. Along with Wood, others who spoke that night were Lela Rogers, Ginger Rogers' well-placed mother; and Captain Clark Gable, who said he was "happy . . . to hear that an active campaign had been started against Communist groups in the motion picture industry."

Barbara, Robert Young, Hardie Albright and Cliff Edwards in *Red Salute*.

As far back as 1935, before Bob and Barbara romantically crossed paths, and before Bob became a star in his own right, Barbara had made films addressing a potential Communist threat. She had been part of the focus of a Red-directed smear campaign a few years before, and her movie, *Red Salute* (1935), was touted as an "anti-Communist comedy" with a message. She was master of her career, and took on projects which aligned with her strong beliefs. Bob was now standing near the forefront of the growing concern, but Barbara had been an active participant for quite some time.

Bob had had enough of the growing threat to his country. The whole scene brought out the stubborn fighter in him. He saw their chosen way of life being put in jeopardy and both he and his wife had been targeted in the ongoing dirty fight. *Song of Russia* debuted in the United States days after the first notices went out about the MPA's creation. This was certainly no coincidence; Bob still smarted from that trying experience. He had been raised as a conservative. His Midwestern values were strict and unbending, everything

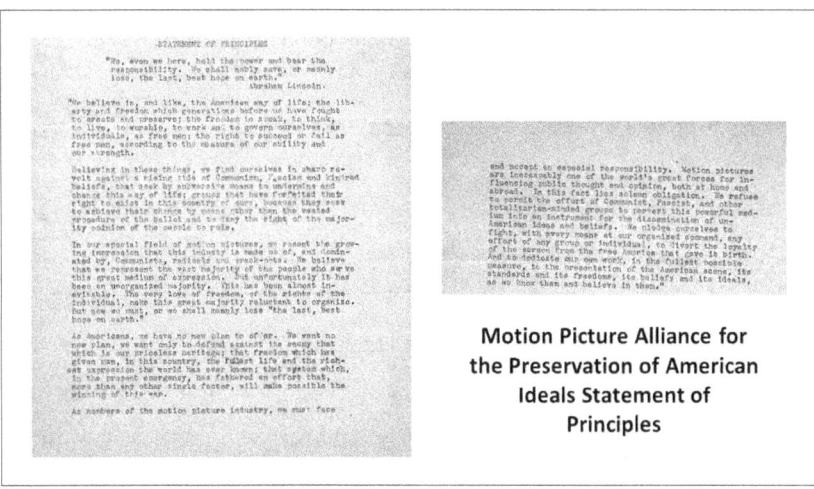

Motion Picture Alliance for the Preservation of American Ideals official Statement of Principles.

the liberal-leaning Communists were not. He was an easy-going fellow, but even the most sedate personality had limits, and Bob had been pushed to his.

Becoming a part of the MPA was the right ticket at the right time, and the organization's rise-up against the Communist Party was a showdown waiting to happen. J. Edgar Hoover would get his way. MPA members went along willingly, going so far as to encourage eventual anti-Communist hearings. They eagerly offered tidbits of information to the government, in every way they could openly worked against the Communist Party, which in Hollywood was usually seen as synonymous with the Screen Writers Guild. The Guild, in turn, saw most anything ultra-Conservative as virtually indistinguishable from the public face of the MPA.

The group's Statement of Principles began: *"We believe in, and like, the American way of life: the liberty and freedom which generations before us have fought to create and preserve; the freedom to speak, to think, to live, to worship, to work, and to govern ourselves as individuals, as free men; the right to succeed or fail as free men, according to the measure of our ability and our strength. Believing in these things, we find ourselves in sharp revolt against a rising tide of communism, fascism, and kindred beliefs, that seek by subversive means to undermine* and change this way of life; groups that have forfeited their right to exist in this country of ours, because they seek to achieve their change by means other than the vested procedure of the ballot and to deny the right of the majority opinion of the people to rule."

A line had been crossed in the minds of MPA members; as an organization they were willing to be "in sharp revolt" against Communism. Terminology was intentionally hard-core. The MPA's brand of Americanism was a rally cry against liberalism. The MPA believed if one wasn't with them, they were against them, against the United States as a whole, and everything their countrymen had ever stood for since the signing of the Constitution. In the group's collective opinion, there was no room to fight for another way of life in the U.S. by using the precepts of that Constitution against itself.

Bob shaking hands with Walt Disney.

The battle had long brewed under the surface of public view. Woods was bold and not shy about making his views known. Along with the activities of Walt Disney at the group's outset, and a host of right-wing celebrities, including Bob, Barbara, John Wayne, Adolphe Menjou, Ward Bond, Gary Cooper, Ginger Rogers, and Clark Gable, Wood's actions were the most obvious, the most blatant to that point. John Wayne said after he was sensitized to the change in the air, he began to "... be aware of cracks at our president, the flag, patriotism ... a kind of sneering." His words echoed the feelings of his compatriots. They weren't going to put up with this attitude anymore.

Active MPA members determined to do whatever necessary to work against Communist infiltration within the borders of the United States. These influential actors and actresses were box office draw and an important part of the economy. Film's universal ability to carry pointed messages to the people was crucial, and gave the stars a voice to be heard. A camera was around every corner at any event headlined by a movie star.

This was another natural marriage between Hollywood and Washington, and this union started to worry Louis B. Mayer, as well as some of the other studio heads. CPUSA attempts against the MPA were finding some success in the public arena, and this didn't show studios and their product in the best light.

Washington took notice when the MPA came on the scene; each contingent courted the other. The MPA would become crucial in bringing Washington to Hollywood for the 1947 House Un-American Activities Committee hearings. But in 1944, battle lines were only yet being sketched. The stage was slowly set. Influential connections were in the making. Important liaisons were forming.

Studios had their own complicated political personalities. Built on the belief structures of not only the studio heads, but also the influential producers, directors, and writers, they had well-formed, separate and easily-identifiable personas. MGM was considered the most ultra-conservative. At heart, Louis B. Mayer shied away from liberalism and gathered like minds around him. Somehow, the studio's image had grown a life and surpassed any right-wing ideas Mayer originally held, as if the son had taken on the father's beliefs, and grown into someone more formidable. MGM began with Mayer's ideals and had blossomed, growing more vocal with each conservative voice added to the mix.

Since the MPA was largely a MGM-created animal, MGM had a lot at stake in this battle. In theory, Mayer agreed with all the MPA supported. Hollywood was his town, and he felt if Communism went ahead full steam, the structure of filmdom's money-making abilities would tumble down.

On the other side of the coin, artistic pursuit, by nature, was a liberal venture. Politics and movies were already intricately entwined. Louis B. Mayer was in Roosevelt's pocket, Roosevelt was in his, and Mayer wanted that way of things to continue. The MPA's activities had the potential to threaten that lucrative relationship because the group did not support the core of the Roosevelt belief system.

Mayer viewed the personalities in the motion picture business as American equivalents to the British Royal Family. He felt that basic human nature was to need someone to look up to and revere. Since the United States had no official royalty, stars of the silver screen came closest to fitting that need. People hung on their every word, delighted in what they wore and ate, who they dated and married and divorced, and how they handled their public and private lives.

He knew there was a definite worship factor involved, but when the public turned sour on a star, the ostracization was immediate and complete. What they did, how they were treated, and their overall images were, in his mind, points of crucial national and political interest. Especially during a time of war, the stars' peculiarities could and most definitely did affect official interests of the United States, the bank accounts of Mayer's studio, and the government.

He was careful how he handled his assets, but no less determined to run the show, not the other way around. This filtered down to how the public viewed his studio because the studio was the structure under which Hollywood royalty lived, in essence, the "royal household." Mayer's purpose was to ensure American royal persons were always seen in the best light, and to ensure his household was never publicly sullied. While Hollywood was up to their earlobes in political activity, Mayer attempted to lessen the awareness of that fact; the monarchy's official tradition was to be above politics and to never indicate personal opinion. He was determined his stars would be no less circumspect.

Mayer did well, sidestepping any show of direct opinion, but his stars weren't all as careful and this arose to be a significant bone of contention. He had to be the mediator and blur lines only enough to never be seen as supporting any popular wind. He was doing a fast dance behind the scenes.

This was a presidential election year, and the war brewing in Hollywood, a sideline to the war aflame around the world, was coming to a head. The MPA made a conscious move to suspend any organized activity for two months prior to the election. They put out an official press release, stating

Louis B. Mayer in his office.

they didn't want to be seen in any way as a partisan political organization trying to steer the outcome of the vote.

That didn't slow down Martin Dies. As an American politician and unapologetic anti-Communist, he had wanted to investigate Communist infiltration in the moving picture business as far back as the late 1930s. Now that he had a footing within the industry, he gravitated toward the MPA. This organization had been most active in rooting out what he saw as the forces of evil. He had amassed a great deal of information specific to the Communist faction of Hollywood's elite. Dies and his supporters, with the help of the MPA and other factions, now had a growing dossier against what he already knew as a matter of record to be card-carrying Communists.

Many MPA members were in Mayer's stable of talent, in front of and behind the camera, and he had some explaining to do. He made a public display of minimizing the connection, and by the time the election was over, the MPA's existence was clearly in trouble. Negotiations were ongoing at the behest of studio producers trying to force the group to dissolve. As of late 1944, those negotiations looked as if they might succeed; the group showed signs of disintegration. Studio heads announced they didn't want the interference, and they did not want to be a part of this Communist hunt. Earlier informal questioning had involved Samuel Goldwyn, while an interview with Jack Warner said he "refused to interfere with his writers...."

Enter Edgar Dunlap into Louis B. Mayer's life, a Georgia attorney and Roosevelt supporter who put a lot of money into the presidential campaign. He was rewarded with growing visibility in the Democratic Party, as well as enhanced connections in his business and political life. Democratic Congressman John S. Woods of Georgia was Chairman of what was in 1945 to 1946 called the House Committee on Un-American Activities, and to him fell the job to begin the official investigation into Communism in Hollywood.

The Committee was supplied with information on Communist film writers, but Woods didn't follow through. The Committee had worked this angle since at least 1942, but only recently had their efforts been visible. Woods left his post without ever actually instigating the inquiry. Why? When the Committee began to seriously snoop around in Hollywood studio affairs, Louis B. Mayer, along with other leaders, looked to hire an attorney to protect interests. Edgar Dunlap got the job and did so well that Congressman Woods appeared to have little left to use to publicly move in any closer.

How did Edgar Dunlap, an obscure Democratic deep-South lawman, become Republican Mayer's attorney? He was an insider with the Roosevelt bunch, as was Mayer. Did Dunlap assert pressure on Congressman Woods to give up the fight?

What would've happened if Woods went through with his investigation at that point? The studios hadn't had a chance to line up their ducks. Their bottom dollar couldn't have survived at the going rate, and producers, writers, and actors would have gone down in the scandal. The public would have hung onto every salacious detail coming out of Hollywood, forming opinions as to who was, and was not, a Communist, not an overall popular label to wear in America at that time. Many would have stopped buying movie tickets which, again, would have affected the studio's pocketbook.

Louis B. Mayer and his associates knew the timing wasn't right to take this show on the road. There would have to be some sort of non-partisan effort to achieve that purpose.

***

In early 1945, Bob and Barbara made a trip to New York City. Before they left Hollywood, he called a man who, a few years back, had been a friend when he'd needed one most. Armand Deutsch still lived in Manhattan and worked on Wall Street. He was happily surprised when his phone rang and he discovered Bob Taylor on the other end. An invitation to dinner and the theater with Bob and Barbara was quickly accepted.

"He sent me my ticket and we met at the theater. Luckily I went early. The arrival of my hosts produced massive aisle-jamming that was contained only by the rise of the curtain." Deutsch was again reminded of the difference of his world in stark contrast to that of Robert Taylor and Barbara Stanwyck.

Once the show was over, "Getting away from that theater was far more hazardous than any experience I had in the Navy. With the help of a policeman and the doorman, we were stuffed into their limousine. Before police reinforcements arrived in sufficient number to let the driver inch his way out of this unholy mess, the densely packed crowd rocked the car and hammered the windows to the point where I truly feared for our safety...."

Deutsch enjoyed himself. "We had supper in the Cub room at the city's posh Stork Club. The patrons . . . for the most part, did not approach the table. But the ogling at these two people was truly Major League. The Stork Club was a favorite hangout of mine...." Of Barbara, he said, "... she of the sexy voice and sultry looks, was far more outgoing than Bob. Her only interest in the evening, after all, was helping her husband reciprocate for hospitality. I loved her salty style and gave her an A-plus for effort. We parted with the time-honored 'Let's do this again' dialogue."

They went their separate ways at the end of their pleasant evening. Deutsch felt Bob had taken him out on the town in gratitude for his hospitality when they were in the Navy together. As he watched the couple leave, Armand Deutsch was sure he was seeing Bob Taylor in person for the last time.

<hr>

Mr. and Mrs. Taylor went to London in March for the premiere of her film, *The Other Love*. Both were wildly popular and always in the news, international as well as stateside. They could go nowhere without creating a mob scene. Though most were well-meaning fans, there were some who seemed intent on crossing their paths in a destructive way, and Bob and Barbara became more careful when they had to make public appearances. The expected throng was outside the theater when they arrived, and there was no way to get inside without assistance. Police guards, atop their horses, were forced up against lobby doors by the masses. The horses neighed nervously, and the scene threatened to become a riot. Crowds blocked traffic and, in a sudden display of their fervor, smashed a glass display advertising Barbara's film.

A plan was formed. First Bob was freed from the vehicle and police hoisted him on their shoulders, carrying him safely inside the theater. Women followed, pulling on his coattails and trying to grab at his evening clothes. Another group of police did the same with Barbara. Finally safely together again inside, they sank onto a divan to catch their breath. Bob rubbed Barbara's feet to calm her. "It was overwhelming," she said. "I was terrified for a few minutes." Looking at her husband, she reassured him, "I'm not hurt."

<hr>

Political tides once again turned in Mayer's favor. Any hard-hitting, difficult questions which might've been posed to him prior to Dunlap coming into the picture were swept under the rug. John Parnell Thomas had taken over the House Un-American Activity Committee, and questioning started in earnest behind closed doors at a Los Angeles hotel. As an "invited" guest, Louis B. Mayer was asked how many pictures he'd made for MGM, and if he had received any public, media, or government criticism about any of the movies he made. This was a lead-in to the *Song of Russia* issue, to which Mayer eagerly responded. He said there had always been great response to the MGM product, until *Song of Russia*.

He went into an eloquent, long-winded discourse on his filmmaking philosophy. The Committee wanted to hear directly from him as to why *Song of Russia* had been made. He was asked only questions which could easily be answered based on issues he had indicated to his attorney ahead of time he would answer. He was queried, he responded. The conversation was civil, easy, all well-coached and carefully orchestrated. His words would not have been as well-received if this exchange had taken place a few years earlier.

All in the timing. Mayer's best interests were served by putting off the inevitable until he could intelligently play both sides to the middle. He was still balancing the growing vocal discontent of some of his talent. Also not in his favor was a power struggle behind the scenes with an up-and-coming executive named Dore Schary. Schary was a Democrat on his way up the MGM leadership ladder and a member of many liberal organizations; he did not see eye-to-eye with Mayer on most issues.

The country wasn't long out of a war where Russia was viewed as an uneasy partner. The Soviet Union had never really been trusted. For many Americans, their philosophy had shown them to be the enemy, not the friend. The government also walked that middle line, much like the studios, and they were making every effort to hold on as long as possible to a tense peace with a country wielding power and influence around the world. The Roosevelt government put pressure on Mayer and the other studio leaders to cooperate; they didn't want the hearings to get out of hand. They were planned as a good show, a vehicle to indicate to the American people their leaders were there to help and protect them from any perceived bad guys.

In reality, the government couldn't sincerely take on those bad guys.

The international situation was still too precarious. What the White House faction of the government really wanted out of the House hearings was a Hollywood production, not a serious, honest investigation.

The effort was put out to help the public feel they were sheltered from what in many corners was believed to be a threat, though in reality, Roosevelt's administration may have been playing ball behind the scenes with the Russian government. There was still a need to keep lines open for trade, as well as political stability, whether one believes in that or not. Politics wasn't a clear-cut business any more than was movie-making.

Louis B. Mayer was still concerned over losing untold amounts of money if movie-goers got wind of the orchestrated connection between Hollywood and Washington. He was thick into a growing, seemingly inevitable battle between labor unions and the film industry's blue-collar workers, and some of his film stars. This business war, definitely on his home turf, threatened to take down the studio system, and this he could not allow. He was never known as a Communist sympathizer, not even when some of his fellow top producers were pegged as such. He did have a business to run, though, and he had to figure out how to find a balance and make all factions work together.

He tried hard to force his brass and his stars to dance to his tune. Some of his best box office draws, and Bob Taylor was one of them, didn't want to follow him on this one, and their dissension became obvious. Whether intentional or simply the way the game ultimately played out, Bob somehow became Louis B. Mayer's focused point of contention.

On May 14, 1947, Bob appeared as an "invited guest" in front of the closed-session meetings held in Los Angeles. The same assembly had heard Louis B. Mayer's testimony earlier in the month, and listened to J. Edgar Hoover in March. When Bob was called in on that early spring day, he answered ques-

Bob interviewed by U. S. Representatives McDowell and Thomas in the first meeting prior to his public testimony at the House Un-American Activities Committee. Courtesy author's personal collection.

tions for an hour.

Whereas Mayer's testimony was carefully crafted toward answers to questions he had pre-arranged, Bob wasn't afforded the luxury of a custom-designed line of inquiry. He was asked primarily about *Song of Russia* and how he came to be cast in the lead; about the MPA and his involvement in that group; and was forced to field questions on any other issue the committee thought would further their cause. He knew he was putting his entire career on the line. He had agonized over this moment, dreading the time when it would become necessary.

He had a responsibility to his personal belief system, though, and as Manuela, his stepdaughter, once said of him, "He never lied and wasn't phoney." He responded as he would to any official body of the United States government, with respect and honesty, believing the session was private and understanding that his remarks would never be made public. He told them he resisted starring in *Song of Russia* because he thought the movie to be nothing more than Communist propaganda. He flatly stated he'd been forced to make that movie, as much by the United States government as by his own studio.

He shared how his active service in the United States Navy was dangled like a tasty treat in front of his face, threatened to be snatched from him if he didn't "willingly" take the assignment. Bob was under the assumption he was offering information behind closed doors for background purposes only. He left the hearings and told the press, "I want to make it clear that I was not invited as a suspected Communist. I'm strictly 'agin' it and that's why, I guess, I was called."

No more than twenty-four hours after he walked out of that meeting, Bob's words were ceremoniously revealed to the world via newspapers and radio by J. Parnell Thomas under the guise of applauding Bob's "courage." He told all that Bob felt *Song of Russia* favored "Russian ideologies, institutions and ways of life over the same things in our country." He proclaimed the actor's testimony proved his side's beliefs that what was going on in Hollywood was ". . . another instance where persons in our government have been aiding and abetting Communism, even to the extent of getting one of our most prominent actors to play a leading role in a picture to which he had already objected."

The "leak" of Bob's testimony was a calculated public relations move on the part of Thomas and his camp. They knew his impassioned words would be considered sensational, and the media would take to the sound bites in his testimony as fast as they could transcribe and print them. They were also aware any actions they would take could cause a rift between Bob and his boss, and this could be a workable ploy for them. Thomas quoted Bob as saying he "relished" appearing in front of the committee, clearly a blatant lie.

Bob was incensed over how the situation had been handled. Revealing his words was a dramatic breach of his trust on Thomas' part. The production couldn't have been more of a camera-worthy Hollywood event had there been a script carefully put together by Hollywood writers.

The ensuing buzz made Bob the centerpiece of a nightmare for MGM. He had expressed his views outside of his studio community, an act seen as a breach of "home" etiquette. Mayer, in many ways, had no choice but to trump him because of how the situation would look to the world if MGM really had "forced" a top star to go against his convictions to keep his job. Mayer couldn't let such a thing appear as fact, whether or not the United States government had "suggested" that exact same thing.

He was required to carefully respond all over again to critics about his personal part in *Song of Russia*. He issued a statement saying, in part, "I am assuming that the excitement growing out of Robert Taylor's testimony before the house un-American activities subcommittee here last week was due to the mistaken belief that the film, *Song of Russia*, was communistic in plot and action . . . *Song of Russia* is simply a love story about an American symphony conductor who was invited to Russia to direct a series of concerts. While there he met a young Russian girl, a music student, and they fell in love. The picture contains no Russian ideology, to my knowledge. . . . "

After all, he was the boss. Damage control was absolutely proper and necessary in this case. If he had to make Bob look like a fool in the process, that's what he would do. MGM was his world, and his world was in serious danger of disintegration if all this got out of hand. Bob and his boss had come to the first public spot in their shared history where they didn't see eye-to-eye. Bob would most definitely not rise to the top on this one.

Lowell Mellett, a name previously unknown to the general public, received wide recognition, once again with a questionable thanks to J. Parnell Thomas. Thomas revealed the meeting between Mellett, Bob, and Louis B. Mayer, and fingered Mellett as the "government man" and a "federal government administration agent." He continued, saying Mellett "came to Hollywood in 1943" on orders of his superior to "see that Mr. Taylor played that leading role" in *Song of Russia.* While Mellett didn't refute the meeting was held, he vehemently denied he forced Bob into anything. He said the accusation was "too damn silly to deny," adding, "I certainly didn't compel Robert Taylor or anyone else to do anything." He ended with a challenge, ". . . if Thomas wants to know what I know about the matter, I'll be glad to tell him. . . ."

Bob thought that throughout their years together, he had built an important relationship with Louis B. Mayer. He felt a sense of loyalty to the older man, a quality intrinsic to his nature and of ultimate importance to him. He had a great deal of his life wrapped up in MGM. His duty to those he supported would have been a serious consideration as he decided how to proceed. His dependents and what he had to do for them would have weighed heavily on the direction he took.

Lowell Mellett, about the time of the House Un-American Activities Committee hearing.

That one day in May of 1947 put Bob not only on the line with MGM, but also placed him smack amidst an international drama in a way he did not appreciate. Official records made clear the May hearings were to have been "conducted in secret." Bob's words had been shared in private and he had trusted in the honor of his hosts. Having his testimony resounding in every newspaper and over every radio wave throughout the country, and the world, angered him as little had ever angered him before.

Bob wrote the House Un-American Activities Committee a letter blasting their tactics, and accusing the members of playing their hand for the sake of the most salacious publicity. This was a common opinion, both from those for whom this was personal, like Bob, and the private citizens who watched the drama unfold from the outside. Drew Pearson, in his "Washington Merry Go Round" column, stated Robert Taylor was "one of the most highlighted witnesses ever to appear before the Un-American Activities Committee." He noted how Bob's testimony "made front-page news across the country."

J. Parnell Thomas said a few years later the public release of Bob's private testimony was not cleared with him; he was never given any chance to approve or disapprove the move. Whether he was trying to take his name out of the scandal, or this was true, was never revealed. When Bob found out what he had spoken of under the guise of a private discussion with government personnel was revealed for all to hear, he showed a rare fit of electrified anger living deep inside him but, in true Robert Taylor fashion, he did not vent his feelings in public. He made his anger known only in his letter to the Committee.

"I've never cared a whole helluva lot for politicians, whether they be Republican or Democrat," he started. "And I've certainly never believed it inherent in my job as a motion-picture actor to aid in feathering any of their nests for them via publicity from my name—a name, by the way, which I have worked hard to build and maintain without any blemish." This is what incensed him most. He was a public figure, and for that reason, he was being used as a pawn in the career advancement of a group of political figures.

He continued, "My last appearance to testify was valuable only insofar as publicity was concerned; my appearance in Washington can be valuable purely for the same reason. I firmly believe this to be utterly ridiculous and a waste of time, both for me and for the Committee!"

Bob didn't want to appear at the upcoming public hearings to be held that fall. If he was to be there, which he knew was already expected of him, his appearance would be nothing less than a command performance. He wasn't going to go willingly. In this letter, he stressed how forcing him to go before the cameras would do nothing to get to the root of the issue which was, he stressed, Communism in Hollywood and in America. Having him appear at the hearings would only serve to bring crowds and wholly-inappropriate attention to the ludicrous party atmosphere. If the issue wasn't brought under control soon, all of the hoopla could harm the cause, and never actually solve any problems inherent in the system.

"These investigations, the way they are being run in Washington at the moment, remind me more of a three-ring circus than of a sincere effort to rid the country of a real threat. There's nothing any of us are going to tell them in Washington that the FBI didn't know five years ago. Maybe it's easier, to call twenty friendly names from Hollywood than to have a look at the FBI files! Maybe it's better publicity for the home-state electorate too!"

He laid his impassioned feelings on the line, which probably only served to ensure more that his place would be front and center at the Committee's table, rather than help him dodge the appearance. The whole thing had gotten horribly out of control. Headlines screamed, "Everybody Wants To Get Into The Commie Probe Act!" All of Hollywood had to pick a side and then figure out how best to become visibly for, or against their choice. If they didn't make a stand for themselves, they well could have one made for them. Bob had learned this the hard way.

One article said, "The most sought after role in town is a chance to speak a piece at the committee's coming hearings at Washington. Scripts now being prepared for the affair indicate it should be colossal. Approximately 50 top Hollywood names will make the exclusive subpoena list... The word is that it's still a wide-open race. They're saying that you can't rule out even such names as Margaret O'Brien, Betty Grable, Bebe Daniels, or the Marx Brothers."

Hollywood went mad for politics. The entire event had turned into a production worthy of an Academy Award, with the cast going on location to Washington for the final reveal. "Within the motion picture industry," copy indicated, "Communism is now being hailed as the slickest publicity gimmick since the discovery of the swoon ... Since Robert Taylor made headlines all over the country recently by claiming he was forced by the White House to appear in a pro-Russian propaganda film, there has been a rush to climb aboard the red bandwagon...."

Bob didn't have to show up for the casting call. He already had the lead. As his letter to the Committee indicated, he was sick about the direction events had taken. Robert Taylor didn't choose to appear in front of the House Un-American Activities Committee in 1947. His testimony was a done deal because he was a camera's dream; because the public loved him; because he had a friendly persona and people paid attention any time he spoke or was seen; because his politics were clearly and vocally anti-Communist. For whatever reason, his studio had chosen him to star in *Song of Russia*, one of the movie world's most flagrant Communist-loving films. His role and his displeasure, led to his starring role in the government's upcoming production.

Since his letter to the Committee was never-widely promoted, the world saw only what appeared to be a willing Bob, speaking as if he wanted to tell the world MGM and the government had done him wrong. The whole thing looked almost like a pout in the choreographed presentation. Everyone not intimately involved in Bob's life surely though he was thrilled to be a star of the upcoming show of shows.

Media outlets ran with the false impression. *Izvestia*, a Russian daily newspaper, printed a piece by Aleksandr Gerasimov, an award-winning artist, and the article received international distribution. Bob was attacked for lacking "political morality." Gerasimov said, "Conscience, honor and even the very elementary representation of decency are tied up conveniently with the dollar, for which Taylor, according to his own statements, sold his 'American convictions.'" This was a reference to Bob having said he was "coerced" to make *Song of Russia*. Gerasimov said Bob should have held out for his convictions.

Bob could have changed public opinion. He could have told the world what he told the Committee; if he had, he would have at least in part exonerated himself. He would have made clear he was a man with defined convictions, and not a man seeking to destroy the career of fellow artists, or ruin the profitability of his studio. He would've shown he was not happy with the spectacle the Committee had made of the proceedings, or of him and of his career.

Instead, he stayed quiet in the face of public scrutiny and negative feedback. Why?

As late as August, he was one of a group of actors who refused to publicly debate the topic, "Is Communism really a threat to Hollywood?" The ABC network put on the show, and most who refused the invitation were members of the MPA and ultimately called before the Committee in October. Those who wouldn't appear were: Hedda Hopper, Howard Emmett Rogers, Edward Arnold, Adolphe Menjou, Pat O'Brien, Ronald Reagan, Sam Wood, Barbara and Bob.

These people were the industry insiders who found the issue most serious, and they would not make any effort in public which could look as if they were capitalizing on their views.

Bob made his mark on the 1947 House Un-American Activities Committee meetings in October, called "the biggest show of the fall investigating season." Chairman J. Parnell Thomas and his bunch didn't hide the fact that "right from the start" they planned to "begin naming names." That was their focus. They also intended to finger the Roosevelt administration for forcing the production of "flagrant Communist propaganda" in moving pictures. The day before the proceedings, "the stage was being set in the big, marble-lined caucus room in the old house office building. Movies, radio, television and the press busily moved in equipment for recording the investigation."

Lawyers and agents showed up to make sure their clients were featured in the best light. The appearance schedule was carefully reviewed, edited, and rearranged. Last minute notations were included. Press reports continued to call Bob's May testimony "secret," though by now everyone knew not a single word had been kept under wraps.

Lowell Mellett was no longer with the government; he had become a columnist for the *Washington Star*. Still doggedly denying his part in Bob's participation in *Song of Russia*, he requested a hearing to tell his side of the story. The Committee refused his request, though they said he had been subpoenaed two weeks earlier. Mellett issued a public statement after he was denied the chance to speak.

J. Parnell Thomas knew Bob was a "reluctant witness." That approved label, connected to his name, wasn't widely disseminated in press reports. Officials would not go into detail as to why he was considered "reluctant," when most other scheduled witnesses were called "friendly."

Bob's letter had been received after his first appearance and before his public testimony, and Thomas was clearly aware Bob wasn't happy but not a single citizen readying to watch the proceedings was aware Robert Taylor was anything but a willing participant; the Committee wanted that image to stick. The best interest of the Committee was to let the belief grow, and lump Bob in with those being called "friendly."

And the publicity machine spin continued. His appearance took on a favorable light before he had shown up in front of a hearing camera. If anyone caught the well-oiled publicity machine's change of heart, no waves were made. In early October, headlines said "ex-navy officer" Robert Taylor was called as a "friendly witness" by Chairman J. Parnell Thomas, a Republican from New Jersey, to appear at the third session of the committee's investigation hearings. This was the follow-up to his private testimony five months earlier.

When Louis B. Mayer, Jack Warner, and Sam Wood opened the hearings, Mayer revealed the new joint studio tack. Newspapers screamed, "Ban Reds, Film Executives Ask." The scene looked as if a movie production were rolling out. Klieg lights glared, camera bulbs popped, microphones strained to hear them speak. Media hung on their every word.

This time around, Mayer, along with Warner and Wood, gave an account of efforts to keep Communists out of Hollywood. When the Committee first quietly nosed around in 1942, Mayer said he had tried to deter them. He had fought their actions in a pseudo-public manner ever since June of 1945, when the Committee announced intentions to staunchly stand up against any attempt by film stars and producers to "overthrow the government."

Times had changed, though, and the trio now told the Committee they favored a bill to make the Communist party illegal in the United States. Mayer went a step further. He wanted a law allowing industrialists the legal right to keep Communists off their payrolls.

Sam Wood declared Communists had tried to win control over Hollywood for the last ten years. He named four directors whom, he said, "attempted to scare us into the Red view." He claimed writers were now predominantly at the helm of the movement.

Jack Warner testified that leftwing writers tried on many occasions to slip un-American doctrine into films. He said he fired or "dropped" half a dozen writers, some nationally known, when he learned they were Communists.

Mayer declared, "The motion picture industry employs many thousands of people. As in the case with newspaper, radio, publishing and theater business, we cannot be responsible for the political views of each individual employee. It is, however, our complete responsibility to determine what appears on the motion picture screen." He requested the committee "perform a public service by recommending to the congress legislation establishing a national policy regulating employment of Communists in private industry. It is my belief they should be denied the sanctuary of the freedom they seek to destroy."

This was a change from his original stance. The winds of opinion had altered, and those who ran the studio system were desperate to hold on to their large piece of the American dream. They willingly sold out any personal beliefs for the deep-breath relief of being able to continue their business as usual.

Mayer was put on the hot seat once again over *Song of Russia*. He called the finished product a "pat on the back for our then ally, Russia." He said the project had been discussed with government coordinators who lauded the ideas as "good." *Song of Russia*, in their eyes, was an excellent vehicle in which to "use the music of Tchaikovsky." Standard answers. Nothing new.

When Bob's participation was brought up, all Mayer would say was that he had thought Bob Taylor "ideal" for the lead male part. His only possibly out-of-the-ordinary input, he stressed, had been to discuss with Frank Knox a request for Bob to be "given time" to make the picture before "being called into service." This was an interesting choice of words since there was no *before* involved. Bob had already been "called into service" at the time the request was made.

Mayer vehemently denied the movie was prompted by any government official or entity, or produced as war propaganda. "I am convinced that there were no political implications . . . I will be convinced of that until I meet my God." He included, "Mention has been made of the picture *Song of Russia*, as being friendly to Russia at the time it was made. Of course it was. It was made to be friendly. In 1938 we made *Ninotchka*, and shortly thereafter *Comrade X* (1940) with Clark Gable and Hedy Lamarr—both of these films kidded Russia."

Mayer's speech was impassioned. "According to research I have made, our newspapers were headlining the desperate situation of the Russians at Stalingrad . . . Admiral Standley, American Ambassador to the Soviet Union, made a vigorous plea for all-out aid. He pleaded for assistance second only to the supplies being provided the United States Fleet, and emphasized the best way to win the war was to keep the Russians killing the Germans, and the most effective way was to give them all the help they needed . . . The final script of *Song of Russia* was little more than a pleasant musical romance. . . ."

The MGM executive was asked to explain government involvement in general film production. He said representatives made periodic studio visits during war years to discuss what pictures might aid the war effort. He called them "coordinators," and said they did not "attempt to tell us what we should or should not do. We made our own decisions." When point-blank asked why he hadn't fired anyone he thought to be a Communist, he explained his attorneys advised him that unless he had solid proof, the studio could face damage suits.

The day was grueling, long and full of emotion and frustration. As activities wound down, someone from the other side of the argument labeled the hearing "the best example of undemocratic procedure I've ever seen."

Bob's role in *Song of Russia* was at the heart of the HUAC journey. There had been for some time a sizeable group of rabid anti-Communists in the film industry. Many were more vocal than Bob, and many more openly political, but none of the others had the lead in a film going against the grain of their strongest beliefs. This was the reason he became the "forever" whipping boy for the Hollywood anti-Communism hysteria, second only in many circles to Eugene McCarthy. And whereas McCarthy may have arguably deserved the arrows thrown at him, Bob's place in history was created against his will.

On October 22, 1947, *The New York Times* stated "as all Washington knew, Robert Taylor would appear." He did what he was expected to do. Cameras clicked away madly when he was shown "conferring" at a table with J. Parnell Thomas. Photographers didn't know they weren't talking about anything important. Headline-conscious Thomas had beckoned Bob to the side of the room, aware his picture was being taken. The difference between the two men was striking, and the media had a heyday capturing shots of the short, rounded, shiny-headed and bald Thomas next to the tall, slender, photogenic Bob Taylor.

With his words not loud enough to be picked up by the microphones, Thomas coached Bob, "Go ahead and say just what you told us in Hollywood." As the cameramen became more curious, asking for placed shots, he said, "These photographers get crazier and crazier." The conversation was

J. Parnell Thomas chatting up Bob before official start
of the House Un-American Activities Committee hearing.
Courtesy Judith Hanhisalo personal collection.

haphazard, with little meaning. They were asked to pose; Thomas beamed into the lenses, pretending to talk about the hearings. With flashbulbs going off, the picture which ultimately went around the country the next day had Bob sitting at the table, looking up at Thomas, who stood next to him. Thomas' expression said they were speaking on matters of national importance. Yet the moment the camera snapped the ultimately distributed photo, Thomas was discussing a friend who had broken a leg.

The face-time for the cameras turned serious, though, when Bob was called to the stand. The room was filled to capacity with 391 spectators ready to hang hungrily on his every word. He took his place. He was somber, as prepared as he could be for his nearly-scripted part of the show. He was aware he'd be led in a certain direction, and he was painfully certain the public and the press were not. His was hardly the most sensational testimony of the day; that mattered little, though, because his testimony would undoubtedly end up as the most remembered.

Bob under oath, testifying before the House Un-American Activities Committee.

What he did say is important to note because the press of that period manipulated his words to fit a certain typecast.

Before he sat, Bob raised his right hand and swore his words would be "the truth, the whole truth, and nothing but the truth, so help [him] God." He was asked to state his full name and address, "Robert Taylor, 807 Rodeo Drive, Beverly Hills."

Suddenly, Robert Stripling asked still photographers to remain "for a few more minutes, take a few shots, then come down here and take your positions." The flash bulbs were blinding, with so many pictures being taken a stir was created before Bob said anything of note. This was natural, since he was who he was, but the maneuvering looked to be on cue, a way to ensure Bob's visibility on that witness stand. The press would have no problem showing him to the world after cameras had been strategically situated.

Stripling then asked Bob to speak a little louder. He was asked when and where he was born. Stripling posed the question, "You are here before the Committee on Un-American Activities in response to a subpoena which was served upon you on October 3, 1947, are you not?" Bob replied, yes, he was there because of the subpoena.

In other words, because of a summons of the law.

The subpoena was made to be part of the record before Strickling asked Bob his current occupation, and with whom he was employed. Audience giggles, then gales of laughter, were heard throughout the packed hearing room when he was asked how long he'd been an actor, and how long he'd been in Hollywood. Had he been "in the last World War?" In what branch of the service, and what was his rank?

Then they got into the real reason he was there. Bob's cigarette was lit, one, after the other, after the other. An ashtray, a glass of water, and a pitcher sat before him on the dark wood table whose glassy shine was marred with water spots and dotted with paperwork.

Stripling: "During the time you have been in Hollywood has there been any period during which you considered that the Communist Party or the fellow travelers of the Communist Party were exerting any influence in the motion-picture industry?"

Bob: "Well, of course, I have been looking for Communism for a long time. I have been so strongly opposed to it for so many years; I think in the past 4 or 5 years, specifically, I have seen more indications which seemed to me to be signs of communistic activity in Hollywood and the motion-picture industry."

Stripling: "In any particular field?"

Bob: "No, sir. I suppose the most readily determined field in which it could be cited would be in the preparation of scripts—specifically, in the writing of those scripts. I have seen things from time to time which appeared to me to be slightly on the pink side, shall we say; at least, that was my personal opinion."

Bob's comment about "the past 4 or 5 years" encompassed both the start of *Song of Russia* and his work with the MPA, corralling the period when the Communist issue had started coming to a head. That was when the more visible people against the perceived Red menace, including him, began to stand up and make noise.

Here the audience got rowdy. Stripling's next words were, "Could we have a little better order?" The Chairman, pounding his gavel, demanded, "Please come to order." Newspaper reports indicated that repeated "surf-like murmurs were heard among female fans old and young."

Hearings were open to the public. Only Bob's appearance was publicized ahead of time. All the other actors were scheduled, and everyone knew they'd be there, but there had been no public indication of the order in which they would be on the stand. With masses of people aware, thanks to the press, of the date and time Robert Taylor would be in Washington, and exactly where in Washington he would be, people showed up in droves to see him in the flesh.

Many in the hearing room, the halls, even in the streets may have had an opinion one way or the other if asked about Communism. More likely, most were there not because of a commitment to or against Russian interference in America, but because they might catch a glimpse of Robert Taylor, the movie star. The crowds were predominantly made up of women, but a good number of men were there, too. The mass of people had to be contained and wooden barricades were hastily thrown up in the corridors to try to keep them in order.

Stripling went back to his questioning: "Mr. Taylor, in referring to the writers, do you mean writers who are members of the Screen Writers Guild?"

Bob: "I assume that they are writers of the Screen Writers Guild. There seem to be many different factions in skills in Hollywood. I don't know just who belongs to what sometimes, but I assume they are members of the guild."

Stripling: "Are you a member of any guild?"

Bob: "I am a member of the Screen Actors Guild; yes, sir."

Stripling: "Have you ever noticed any elements within the Screen Actors Guild that you would consider to be following the Communist Party line?"

Bob: "Well, yes, sir; I must confess that I have. I am a member of the Board of Directors of the Screen Actors Guild. Quite recently I have been very active as a director of that board. It seems to me that at meetings, especially meetings of the general membership of the guild, there is always a certain group of actors and actresses whose every action would indicate to me that if they are not Communists they are working awfully hard to be Communists. I don't know. Their tactics and their philosophies seem to me to be pretty much party-line stuff."

The Chairman intercepted here. "May I interrupt for just a minute? We are going to recess for about 2 minutes and we hope everybody will keep their seats."

A somewhat odd place to jump in with an un-scripted break. Records show a "short recess." Upon return, the Chairman announced they were back in session and Stripling could continue.

Stripling: "Mr. Taylor, these people in the Screen Actors Guild who, in your opinion follow the Communist Party line, are they a disrupting influence within the organization?"

Bob: "It seems so to me. In the meetings which I have attended, at least on issues in which apparently there is considerable unanimity of opinion, it always occurs that someone is not quite able to understand what the issue is and the meeting, instead of being over at 10 o'clock or 10:30 when it logically should be over, probably winds up running until 1 or 2 o'clock in the morning on such issues as points of order, and so on."

While this may seem an inane line of questioning, "disruptions" were a common tactic officially used by Communist Party members. Disruptions were repeatedly inserted during all sorts of meetings—in this case, SAG meetings—when CPUSA members were intent on insinuating their agenda. The question was intentionally calculated on Stripling's part.

Bob testifying before the House Un-American Activities Committee. Courtesy author's personal collection.

Stripling: "Do you recall the names of any of the actors in the guild who participated in such activity?"

Bob: "Well, yes, sir; I can name a few who seem to sort of disrupt things once in awhile. Whether or not they are Communists I don't know." He was clear; he was not naming anyone to be a Communist.

Stripling: "Would you name them for the committee please?"

Bob: "One chap we have currently, I think, is Mr. Howard Da Silva. He always seems to have something to say at the wrong time. Miss Karen Morley also usually appears at the guild meetings."

Bob was responding directly to a question. He had been asked to name actors who intentionally participated in disrupting Guild meetings. He had already plainly stated he was not calling anyone a Communist.

Stripling: "That is K-a-r-e-n M-o-r-l-e-y?"

Bob: "I believe so; yes, sir. Those are two I can think of right at the moment."

Stripling: "Mr. Taylor, have you ever participated in any picture as an actor which you considered contained Communist propaganda?"

Howard Da Silva.

Karen Morley.

Bob: "I assume we are now referring to *Song of Russia*...." He was being led into a scripted issue. "... I must confess that I objected strenuously to doing *Song of Russia* at the time it was made. I felt that it, to my way of thinking at least, did contain Communist propaganda. However, that was my personal opinion. A lot of my friends and people whose opinions I respect did not agree with me."

Louis B. Mayer, perhaps?

Bob continued: "When the script was first given to me I felt it definitely contained Communist propaganda and objected to it upon that basis. I was assured by the studio that if there was Communist propaganda in that script it would be eliminated. I must admit that a great deal of the things to which I objected were eliminated.

"Another thing which determined my attitude toward *Song of Russia* was the fact that I had recently been commissioned in the Navy and was awaiting orders. I wanted to go ahead and get in the Navy. However, it seems at the time there were many pictures being made to more or less strengthen the feeling of the American people toward Russia.

"I did *Song of Russia*. I don't think it should have been made. I don't think it would be made today." Right there Bob told the world he hadn't wanted to make the movie, and had already been commissioned into the Navy when the film went into production. This wasn't an almost-issue, not a maybe; his commission had been a done-deal.

Stripling: "Mr. Taylor, in connection with the production of *Song of Russia*, do you know whether or not it was made at the suggestion of a representative of the government?"

Bob and Susan Peters in *Song of Russia*.

Bob: "I do not believe that it was made at the suggestion of a government representative; no, sir. I think the script was written and prepared long before any representative of the government became involved in any way."

Stripling: "Were you ever present at any meeting at which a representative of the government was present and this picture was discussed?"

Bob: "Yes, sir; in Mr. L. B. Mayer's office. One day, I was called to meet Mr. Mellett whom I met in the company of Mr. Mayer and, as I recall, the *Song of Russia* was discussed briefly. I don't think we were together more than 5 minutes.

"It was disclosed at that time that the government was interested in the picture being made and also pictures of that nature being made by other studios as well. As I said, it was to strengthen the feeling of the American people toward the Russian people at that time."

Stripling: "The Mellett you referred to is Mr. Lowell Mellett?"

Bob: "Yes, sir."

Stripling: "He was Chief of the Bureau of Motion Pictures of the Office of War Information?"

Bob: "That is right. However, may I clarify something?"

Stripling: "Yes; go right ahead."

Bob: "If I ever gave the impression in anything that appeared previously that I was forced into making *Song of Russia*, I would like to say in my own defense, lest I look a little silly by saying I was ever forced to do the picture, I was not forced because nobody can force you to make any picture.

"I objected to it but in deference to the situation as it then existed I did the picture."

Stripling: "Did you have any special qualification, Mr. Taylor, for the particular part they wanted to fill? I understand you were selected, among other reasons, because of the fact that you were a musician...."

Bob: "Well, I assume that that might have been a qualification for doing a part in *Song of Russia*. Yes, I had studied music quite extensively in college and previous to going to college."

Bob testifying before the House Un-American Activities Committee.

This was a case of fishing. In no documented records about the movie's creation or selection of cast members was there mention that Bob got the part because he was "a musician." Merrill, the lead male character, was a pianist. Though Bob knew how to play the piano, he wasn't an expert.

Stripling continued with a lengthy inquiry as to scripts in Hollywood submitted to Bob which might have been seen as "un-American or Communistic." Bob replied that "from time to time" such reviews were bound to happen, and "lines and situations and scenes" would be objectionable.

Stripling then got to the writers. "Mr. Taylor, there has been quite some testimony here regarding the presence within the motion-picture industry of a number of writers who are considered to be Communists. Are you personally acquainted with any of the writers whom you consider to be Communists or who follow the Communist Party line?"

Lester Cole.

Bob: "I know several writers—I know of several writers in the motion-picture business who are reputedly fellow travelers or possibly Communists. I don't know about that."

Stripling was still leading him to reveal a name. "You have no personal knowledge of it yourself?"

Bob: "I know one gentleman employed at the studio at which I am employed. Mr. Lester Cole, who is reputedly a Communist. I would not know personally." While Bob did go out on a limb with this comment, Cole had previously been pegged as a Communist. By speaking his name in the same sentence with the term, Bob wasn't telling anyone anything new, and he clarified his words were hearsay. He clearly knew others who were less visible, people he could have named openly; for example, the writers of *Song of Russia*.

Stripling then asked Bob if he felt Communist activities in Hollywood had increased after Pearl Harbor. Bob said they "quite obviously" had. When he was asked if he had ever joined any Communist-front organization, Bob replied, "No, sir; believe me."

The next probe indicated the Committee's determination to show Bob as an ultra-conservative reactionary, and overtly anti-Communist.

Stripling: "Have you ever played in any picture with people whom you had any doubts about as to their loyalty to the government?"

Bob: "Not that I know of. I have never worked with anyone knowingly who is a Communist. Moreover, I shall never work with anyone who is a Communist." Again, this was dangerous for Bob to admit under oath. By doing *Song of Russia*, he had worked with people he believed to be Communists, but he did so under strict orders.

He was in an untenable position.

Stripling clarified: "You would refuse to act in a picture in which a person whom you considered to be a Communist was also cast; is that correct?"

Bob: "I most assuredly would and I would not even have to know that he was a Communist. This may sound biased; however, if I were even suspicious of a person being a Communist with whom I was scheduled to work, I am afraid it would have to be him or me, because life is a little too short to be around people who annoy me as much as these fellow travelers and Communists do."

Stripling: "You definitely consider them to be a bad influence upon the industry?"

Bob: "I certainly do; yes, sir."

Stripling: "They are a rotten apple in the barrel?"

Bob: "To me they are and I further believe that 99.9 percent of the people in the motion-picture industry feel exactly as I do." This was spoken from a place deep inside the man. He was rabidly anti-Communist. This was no secret around town. He had his opinions, as did those who followed the principles of the opposite viewpoints. He was as vocal as they were.

Stripling: "What do you think would be the best way to approach the problem of ridding the industry of the Communists who are now entrenched therein?"

Bob: "Well, sir, if I were given the responsibility of getting rid of them I would love nothing better than to fire every last one of them and never let them work in a studio or in Hollywood again. However, that is not my position."

Louis B. Mayer's recently-changed official studio position was important in the context of Bob's next words. "If I were producing a picture on my—and I hope I never do—but if I were, I would not have one of them within 100 miles of me or the studio or the script. I am sure the producers in Hollywood are faced with a slightly different problem. They are heads of an industry and as heads of an industry they might be slightly more judicial than I, as an individual, would be.

"I believe firmly that the producers, the heads of the studios in Hollywood, would be and are more than willing to do everything they can to rid Hollywood of Communists and fellow travelers.

"I think if given the tools with which to work—specifically, some sort of national legislation or an attitude on the part of the government as such which would provide them with the weapons for getting rid of these people—I have no doubt personally but that they would be gone in very short order."

Did Bob believe everything he said? Yes. Did he really want to make such a speech in front of the world, vehemently proposing exactly how studios should take care of Communists? He was only an actor and had never claimed to be anything more. Why would he put forth a plan to solve the problem, virtually the same plan offered by his boss a few days before? Had his boss clarified for him how he should publicly toe the studio line? Answers unknown, but Bob was practically making a commercial endorsement to the suggestion Mayer had made during his Committee appearance.

This was not Bob's style. He'd been clear a few lines before when he said he never wanted to be a producer; why would he give such an expansive opinion on production matters? Was he coerced? He was still in the dog house with Mayer for telling the world he'd been "forced" to make *Song of Russia*.

Bob was too big a star, a gold mine, for Mayer to chastise him for his previous testimony in any overt way. Mayer knew any overt public wrath leveled at Bob wouldn't bode well for the studio. However, slapping Bob's hand privately, getting him to reinforce the studio stance in the guise of helping to strengthen MGM's position, would have been something he would have done.

This seemed all too scripted.

Stripling went on to ask Bob about the use of entertainment as a vehicle for propaganda. Did he think the industry would "be in a better position if it stuck strictly to entertainment?" Of course Bob wholeheartedly agreed and expounded a bit, still playing the cheerleader to the hilt.

The next questions once again surrounded *Song of Russia*, and they were more directed toward ideology and not necessarily Bob's direct involvement. Again, Stripling solicited his opinion, in this case about freedom of religion and how that freedom was handled. He finished his questioning and turned Bob over to other committee members.

Richard Nixon was a little known political figure about to make his first noticeable mark on history. As a committee member, he initially passed on questioning. Richard Vail also passed.

Next was John McDowell, Republican representative from Pennsylvania, and he made a curious comment. "Mr. Taylor, you have been interested in this matter for quite a long time, and probably know as much about the situation in Hollywood as any person who lives there. . . ." Why would Bob, of all the prominent actors questioned, know that much about Communist infiltration of Hollywood, "as much . . . as any other person who lives there?" In the face of the growing and extensive awareness and participation of Ronald Reagan or John Wayne, Bob was behind-the-scenes. Even Robert Montgomery had more "face time" with the issue.

McDowell finished with, ". . . many statements made since Mr. Thomas and I were to Hollywood last May . . . to the effect that the Committee on Un-American Activities was attempting to control thought or frighten the producer out there into producing some sort of picture. Has that been your impression?"

Bob dutifully replied that he never had such an impression. McDowell was "very glad to hear" this. He felt such ideas were "silly," that the Committee on Un-American Activities was "attempting to find the enemies of the Nation . . . we are hunting enemies of the Nation."

He thanked Bob for coming, as if they were at a cocktail party. Before the actor was allowed off the stand, the Chairman gave Richard Nixon one last chance to speak.

Nixon went for it this time. "Mr. Taylor, as a result of your appearance before the Subcommittee on Un-American Activities in Hollywood, a few months ago, you were subject to considerable criticism and ridicule from certain left-wing quarters were you not?"

Bob: "I am afraid so; yes, sir. It didn't bother me, however."

Nixon: "And as the result of your testimony and your appearance before this committee today and the stand you have taken on this issue you will be the subject of additional ridicule and criticism from those quarters; will you not?"

Bob: "I suppose so. However, any time any of the left-wing press or individuals belonging to the left wing or their fellow traveler groups ridicule me, I take it as a compliment because I really enjoy their displeasure."

Nixon: "You realize, however, that your success as an actor, your livelihood as an actor, depends to a great extent upon the type of publicity you receive?"

Bob: "Yes, sir."

Nixon: "And that ridicule and abuse heaped upon you has a much more serious effect than it would have upon a person who does not depend upon public acceptance of what he does? Yet you feel that under the circumstances it is your duty as an American citizen to state your views on this matter?"

Bob: "I most assuredly do, sir."

Nixon: "As far as you are concerned, even though it might mean that you would suffer possibly at the box office, possibly in reputation or in other ways

Richard Nixon doing his part to find Communists in Hollywood.

for you to appear before this committee, you feel you are justified in making the appearance and you would do so again if you were requested to do so?"

Bob: "I certainly would, sir. I happen to believe strongly enough in the American people and in what the American people believe in to think that they will go along with anybody who prefers America and the American form of government over any other subversive ideologies which might be presented and by whom I might be criticized."

The audience went wild with applause and Bob smiled at them, as well as for the cameras. He was giving an impassioned speech, a speech in which he undoubtedly believed, and one he may have been encouraged toward in such a pseudo-patriotic environment. No other actor had been asked such questions. No other actor had been publicly warned about the real chance of being ostracized.

Bob's letter to the Committee written after his private meeting in May gave credence to the likelihood that on this day in October, he was playing a role as much as he had played a role in *Song of Russia*. This one, however, had all the right ideals. Bob had no problem with the message; the method in which the message was delivered was what bothered him.

He was caught in a web. If he wanted to keep his career, his elevated place in Hollywood, and the lifestyle to which he had become accustomed, Bob had to magnify his position as a patriotic countryman. He had to make clear his place as a "company man" for Louis B. Mayer.

His testimony was nearly over. He was asked by the Chairman if he were in favor of the motion-picture industry making anti-Communist pictures, to which Bob said he would be, if and when the time came for that to be necessary. Howard Stripling asked if he thought the Communist Party should be outlawed.

Bob: "Well, in order to answer that, I personally, with all due regard to Mr. Hoover, whose opinion I respect most highly, certainly do believe that the Communist Party should be outlawed. However, I am not an expert on politics or on what the reaction would be. If I had my way about it they would all be sent back to Russia or some other unpleasant place . . ." Loud applause, ". . . and never allowed back in this country."

The Chairman made a great show of asking the audience not to applaud. "We are trying to get the facts here," he said. "This is not a show, or anything like that."

A show was exactly what the event had become, and everyone knew this. Soon, Bob was again thanked "for coming here today," congratulated for his "very frank statement," and escorted from chambers. As he left the building to go out onto the street, more than half of the spectators followed, stampeding the door and trying to surround him. They were obviously there only for his appearance; now that he was finished, the show was over.

He was accompanied by police officers for his protection, and they tailed him for more than a block to where a car awaited him. As he readied to hop into the waiting vehicle, he caught sight of a smiling young blonde-haired girl dressed in blue. She held out a book and asked for an autograph, which he gave her. He asked her for a kiss. She refused, to the shock of the surrounding crowd. He laughed, winked and waved at everyone as he jumped into the car's back seat, and was driven away.

The next day, an extra detail from the Capitol police was added to the hearing room, as a result of Bob's appearance. While he was in front of the cameras, officers were "bruised and shoved about by a stampede of sighing women." The Committee didn't want to take any chances this time. However, the preparations were unnecessary. Crowds never reached the same fervor for the rest of the hearings.

Bob amid a well-behaved mob of fans, protected by police officers, as he leaves the hearing. Courtesy author's personal collection.

For whatever actual behind-the-scenes reasons, Bob was tossed into the murky world of Hollywood-mixed-in-with questionable politics. After his HUAC appearance, he became the MPA's third President, from 1947 to 1948. He served with a veritable "Who's Who" of Hollywood royalty who, like him, made their feelings known during the hearings. Adolphe Menjou was third Vice President, and Ward Bond, Gary Cooper, Clark Gable, Lela Rogers, John Wayne, and Sam Wood sat on the Executive Committee. They had letterhead and were a well-organized group with a honed message. The MPA was considered the official organ of Hollywood conservatism.

As MPA President in June of 1948, Bob sent a letter to J. Edgar Hoover, asking him to be part of an "Americanism rally" to be held that fall. His letter stated in part, "In the war against Communism, the fight in Hollywood has a

Bob, Barbara, and Clark Gable.
Courtesy Robert Taylor Family Private Collection.

definite importance. The battle in this sector has been fought for five years now by the Motion Picture Alliance for the Preservation of American Ideals...."

The MPA would sponsor the rally, Bob's letter said, and the American Legion, VFW, AMVETS, Kiwanians and "various others of the service clubs of this community" were invited. He asked if Hoover would be in Los Angeles "any time between Labor Day and the end of September." If so, could they count on him to be the rally's "principal speaker?" Would he check his calendar and "... please advise us ... what date within the month of September would be most convenient for you?"

Hoover responded immediately, his return letter dated only four days after Bob's invitation. He called the request "gracious" and "appreciated" and said, "I do wish it were possible for me to accept." He had to decline, however, because of his "official schedule." He wished the MPA "every success in this endeavor." The tone of his response was favorable to the cause.

CHAPTER ELEVEN:
And What Are Friends For?

"Don't make such a big deal out of it. We're friends...."
– Bob Taylor to Armand Deutsch

After the hearings, as the 1940s turned into the next decade, Bob's political world calmed down and he got back to the act of living his life. He was still astoundingly-attractive and recognized everywhere. There was nothing material he could want and not have. If a schedule didn't appeal to him, he usually wheedled his way around the shooting. Sundays were the one day he had to be with Barbara, if she was available, and he stayed away from the set at least that one day, if at all possible. This was his last-ditch attempt to keep his marriage alive.

But a good part of that year, and those Sundays, was spent attending to his mother. She was in her mid-60s and while she would have an occasional date, a beau now and then, she was not much of a mixer. Bob held steady as the substance of her life, and that wasn't easy on him with all of his other responsibilities. She got involved in local activities, some including mothers of other Hollywood stars. Still, her health was always an issue. Not only her body but, also, her state of mind concerned Bob. As he said, she suffered from "lonesomeness." In a letter to a Nebraska friend, he confided, "... wish I could find some good woman to live with her but they're few and far between, especially one who can drive in this California traffic. I've tried to

Ruth Brugh. Courtesy Robert Taylor Family Private Collection.

get Mother to sell her house and take a nice apartment but she seems to fight the idea...."

He helped her in every way he could, despite Barbara's growing frustration. The tension between him and his wife had thickened during the political upheaval. She supported him throughout and was of a like mind, but his vocal stance had grown overwhelming and wearying for her. Now there were mounting issues with his mother to add to that rift, and they required larger chunks of his time and energy.

Their marriage was on life support.

Bob had one film come out in the United States in 1949, *The Bribe*, with Ava Garner. *Conspirator* (1949), while released internationally that same year, didn't hit the screen in American theaters until early 1950. There wasn't a single Robert Taylor film which debuted in 1948, and this was unusual. Except for his military service, he had not had a year without a film since he hit the screen in 1934.

Conspirator, a dark story, had begun filming in '48. His co-star was a breathtaking young starlet only beginning to be recognized. Elizabeth Taylor was seventeen. Bob was thirty-seven. While she was a mere baby in relation to him, a man is a man, and she didn't look like a baby. They played husband and wife; during their "love" scenes, Bob was said to have told the cameraman, "You're going to have to shoot me from the waist up" because of the visible results of his unavoidable physical attraction to her. He really got into his role, and unintentionally slammed her up against a landing wall during an intense kissing scene. Later in life, Liz credited Bob, as a result of this act, to be the cause of what ultimately became her life-long back condition.

Bob with Elizabeth Taylor during
filming of *Conspirator*.

Bob's part was that of a British military officer who was also a spy for the Soviets. To get the script to pass required censor issues, MGM had to pussyfoot around the dialogue, character names, and how they handled diplomatic relations between the United States and Russia, and some European countries. The State Department was worried the "depiction of Russia in an unfavorable light" could be banned by censors in England when the film was submitted for international distribution. The studio still scurried to finesse political angles.

Promotional spin continued in all directions, and not only political but romantic innuendoes were played out. MGM's promotional department worked overtime to use the innocence of their new young actress against the maturity of the film's leading man, touting the on-screen romance as something akin to a wild love affair.

Overseas in London, Bob got sick of hearing the ridiculous unfounded rumors. The press was going wild, and he finally called the studio. He told the publicity head, in no uncertain terms, MGM needed to immediately lay off of Liz. "Stop exploiting the poor child!"

Liz didn't help matters much. She was starry-eyed over what she called her "first adult role," and told a reporter, "To be kissed on the screen by Robert Taylor means I will never again be considered a little girl."

Wind of the over-done publicity finally filtered down to Dore Schary, who was leading this production, and he declared the set off limits to any more press. He was savvy enough to know this kind of notoriety wasn't good for MGM, or for Liz's too-old-for-her leading man.

The 1950s came about with, again, two movies for Bob. *Ambush* (1950) was his only production with Sam Wood, the director with whom he had shared much during early MPA days, and the second he made since his return from the Navy.

His MPA work may have had something to do with his lower-than-usual production numbers. While there is little to document exactly what he did for the group during his tenure as the President, the organization's biggest rally was planned that year, and he had a considerable amount of involvement.

When he returned from Navy service, the atmosphere in Hollywood had changed. His political period, and his stint in the Navy, had altered the direction of his career, and his life. Bob was no longer the young heartthrob, matinee-idol type, but he continued to be, without question, a bona fide established movie star. He still brought in box office dollars, and he well knew his status. He had come to accept his place as a celebrity, and he willingly used that status when he saw a benefit to others, as well as to himself. If the end result was a good one, Bob was not above throwing his weight around a bit.

Armand Deutsch with wife, Harriet, in 1951.

The next year, Armand Deutsch again figured into Bob's life. Deutsch became a MGM producer through the good intentions of his friend, Dore Schary, but hadn't gotten his hands on a meaty project. Louis B. Mayer was on a professional decline, and Schary was more often the one in command. He called Deutsch into his inner sanctum and told him he had a script for him. Almost magically, Deutsch was given a private office with decent furniture and his own secretary; the lot of a producer was directly connected to the real estate, and the perks which were attached. This was Deutsch's dream come true.

The same day, Bob entered Deutsch's new office, and sat down in the chair opposite his grand desk. Bob was done up in costume and make-up, but still, he lit a cigarette before he did anything else.

"It just doesn't seem right," Deutsch told him, "that I work so hard and you look so great."

Bob's answer was classic Bob. "You can look like you look forever and I can only look like this for a few years." The comment was straightforward. As he puffed down the second half of his smoke, he acknowledged the body in which he lived, and how he looked on the outside. At the same time, he made clear he was aware of, and accepted, the fact that the physical part of him was slowly fading away.

Bob had come in to welcome his friend to his new world. The visit was short, and he soon went back to work. A few weeks passed as Deutsch started preparations for *Ambush*, the gem handed to him by Schary. He was thrilled, and treated the script with utmost care, following the well-set, long-standing rules of the studio. Deutsch knew that at MGM, the process of moviemaking was revered and all-important.

The story had been with the Production Department for awhile as they went over cost breakdowns, when his secretary buzzed to say Robert Taylor was in his waiting room. As soon as they were sitting across from each other and Bob had lit a cigarette, he confided he had a "problem."

The studio was transitioning away from Louis B. Mayer and toward Dore Schary. Mayer wasn't completely out of the loop, but he was slowly losing favor. Bob was still making money for the studio and held on to his spot as a box office draw, but he wasn't yet wise to Schary's ways and he had difficulty relating to him.

Schary had slated him to star in one of his pet projects, a war film titled *Battleground*. The ensemble cast would highlight more than one character. Bob felt at this point in his career, he needed something to be his alone. He had given great thought to this, and was concerned about how the casting would play out. Deutsch wasn't sure why Bob came to him for help and direction, except he was believed to have Schary's ear, and Bob possibly considered him the perfect vehicle for a message he wanted delivered to the new boss.

Still, Deutsch didn't want to be that vehicle. He told Bob he didn't think he would benefit by being Robert Taylor's messenger boy. He suggested Bob allow his agent to do the job, since that's what he was paid for. During the conversation, Bob noticed newly-covered scripts in a neat pile on his friend's desk. He asked about them, and Deutsch, caught off-guard, delightedly gave him the low-down.

Bob listened to the story's description. He sat quietly for a moment, put his cigarette into the ashtray, and told his friend he wanted to read the script. Deutsch was adamant; that was out of the question. MGM had a strictly defined process for script distribution, and Deutsch, a "neophyte producer" as he called himself, would be party to a great breach of etiquette if he were to personally hand over a not-yet-in-production script to one of the studio's most established stars. This wouldn't be acceptable procedure on Deutsch's part, and he knew that. He probably couldn't make a dumber move. He told Bob exactly that in no uncertain terms.

A few beats of silence went by before Bob calmly replied, "Bullshit." He picked up his cigarette in one hand, and a copy of the script in the other. "Don't make such a big deal out of it. We're friends. I'll just read it and get it back to you in the morning."

Bob had pulled rank faster than Deutsch could blink. The script was in Bob's possession. End of discussion. Despite how this may have at first seemed to Deutsch, Bob wasn't being callous. He did care what happened to his friend's junior-level career. Bob was well aware of his place in the pecking order. He knew he could maneuver the process, shortcut the steps, get what he wanted out of the deal, while also sweetening the pot for Deutsch.

He was, however, playing with him a little by not letting on to any of this. He waved the script in the air as he left Deutsch's office, and called him the next morning, as promised. He loved the story. Perfect, he said. And he planned to get out of his part in *Battleground* and star in *Ambush*. That simple.

Oh yeah, sure. What sounded uncomplicated coming out of Bob's mouth reached Deutsch's ears as more of a panic alarm. Why was his friend doing this to him? His thoughts went everywhere but toward the same easy understanding Bob seemed to have. Deutsch told him without gentleness he had "no intention of setting out on a course which would terminate" his job "instantly." He was coming to Bob's house immediately to pick up the script. He punctuated his agitation "in very forceful terms," telling him "not to tinker with [his] newfound, pleasant life." He thought Bob agreed, though Bob was clearly amused when he told him "it had been a long time since a producer had been so vociferous about not wanting [me] in a film."

Which may have been part of the joke. Bob was enjoying the game. He admired Deutsch for having the guts to talk back to him. After all, Bob had worked the system for years. He knew what rules could be ignored and who could, and could not, successfully ignore them. He recognized his place in the chain-of-command and knew he wouldn't get any flack from what he was doing. He also knew his plan would benefit Deutsch. Bob had all intentions of good-naturedly utilizing his friend in this plan prior to walking into his office the day before.

There was a more pressing question to consider. Why didn't Bob want to star in *Battleground*? He was the lead. His name would carry the film. And though he would share a portion of the marquee with other known box office draws, they would take second billing to him. Were his motives based only on the fact he didn't want to share? That he wanted to be the only true star?

Although that's the exact argument he gave Deutsch, the real answer was more complicated. *Battleground* was considered an "A" list film. *Ambush* was at that point on the "B" list. *Battleground*, the new bosses' baby, did have more than one actor in the lead roster. Bob would do well for himself if he played nice-nice with the guy taking over Louis B. Mayer's office, a win-win for him. At first glance, wanting to get out of the more visible film made no sense.

Closer inspection showed a few other things. *Battleground* was a war film. Bob had had more than his fill of those. *Song of Russia* had irreparably burned him. *Conspirator* was less of a struggle, but, still, didn't impress him much. He didn't trust war films anymore, especially ones directed by the studio's new regime, and he was, plain-and-simple, tired of doing them.

More telling was the uneasy alliance between Bob and Dore Schary. Schary's politics were in question in Conservative circles, and in Bob's mind, he was no Louis B. Mayer, in any capacity. His beloved Mayer may have been the one who sold him down the pike for *Song of Russia*, but Bob and his mentor had a long, mostly positive history. On the other hand, he was unsure of how well he and his new boss would communicate.

Bob knew that in toying with Deutsch, he could get what he wanted without directly going up against Schary. He was planting a seed in Deutsch's mind, offering him a great opportunity through the use of his name. This would aid Deutsch in furthering his career beyond a simple "B" movie, which *Ambush* would be without Robert Taylor in the starring role.

For days after retrieving the script from Bob, Deutsch had visions of how he could snag his friend to star in *Ambush*. He worked the possible scenarios over and over in his head, and rehearsed potential discussions. All the while, he thought he was wishing and dreaming. Bob Taylor, though he called him

Dore Schary with Louis B. Mayer.

his friend, was too far beyond him in the studio's human food chain, and there could be no chance to get Bob as the star of his first production.

Several uneventful weeks later, Deutsch was called to Schary's office. Knowing the time had come to go over *Ambush*'s preliminary budget, and discuss casting, he was sure that was the subject of the meeting. He entered Schary's office prepared with his talking points, only to find someone else already there.

Bob's agent.

With a suddenly queasy stomach, Deutsch sank into the first available chair, while Schary explained how Bob had somehow managed to read the script for *Ambush*, and all of sudden he was eager to take the lead. Deutsch uncomfortably looked at the floor, the ceiling, even Bob's agent, anywhere but directly into Schary's eyes. His boss' voice was quiet and controlled. Deutsch knew the words coming out of Schary's mouth were calculated to create a squirm factor for his benefit alone. After a few moments of measured silence, Schary continued talking. He informed Deutsch "the studio" had given Bob's request great consideration, and finally decided to go ahead and give him the lead. This would, he added, require him to let Bob out of his obligation to do *Battleground*.

The decision had been made. Bob's agent got up to leave, and as he passed Deutsch, he said, "You're a lucky guy." Thinking he was also expected to go, he began to follow the other man out the door, but Schary stopped him. One can imagine the tension in the room and the look on Schary's face. He didn't speak immediately, and he let Deutsch stew. The question of how Bob had gotten hold of the script was never brought up, but the air between them was stifling, heavy, bearing down on the already-thick silence.

Finally, Schary said, "You're a lucky guy," and let him out of his office.

Deutsch's blood pressure would get the chance to rise again over this production. The next step was to assign a Director. He was once more called to Schary's office and informed Sam Wood would do the film. As he was told, "Wood likes the story, likes the script, and likes Robert Taylor." This was a man with a legendary reputation and a great body of work. What had started out as a small, beginner's project for Deutsch had, with Bob Taylor added to the mix, become a major production. Literally. And Deutsch knew his days of perspiring had only just begun.

Schary played with him in that meeting, too, probably unable to resist a chance to pay him back for the under-the-table way Bob secured the script. Deutsch was told that since Wood had signed on to direct, he must realize he could be removed. This was business. Wood had worked with many "front-rank" producers and "none . . . would be wasted on a Robert Taylor film," Schary said matter-of-factly. Deutsch bravely asked Schary if he would allow this to happen. The boss quietly said, yes, he might accede to Sam Wood's wishes. Again, Deutsch was reminded he had to realize he was in the big-time. This was serious business, and a lot of money was at stake.

What had Bob done to him and his project, his first chance to prove his abilities as a producer? He called him his friend. Deutsch didn't understand.

He knew he had little to lose, and he made an appointment for the next morning with Wood, "who had a reputation of being crusty, direct, and cantankerous." He then called Bob, and in no uncertain terms he "told him bitterly that he had managed to transform the nice little pictured that [he] was going to produce into a nice big picture which [he] was not going to produce." He then hung up.

The next day he arrived promptly at Sam Wood's office. He walked in and found Bob casually sitting on Wood's sofa, the ever-present cigarette dangling from his fingers. With little preamble or time spent looking in Bob's direction, Deutsch went into a practiced speech. He told Wood how he had gotten to where he was, why he was originally given *Ambush* to produce, and his fervent hope that Wood wouldn't take him off the project. He left nothing out. He finished with promises to "shine his shoes, get his lunch, back him to the hilt in everything, and even try to get Bob to play the girl if that's what he wanted."

His previous night without sleep, and his floor-pacing preparations, proved to have been a waste of time. Only a few beats after Deutsch finished speaking, Wood responded, "You'll do. Most producers are stupid as hell anyway. You couldn't be any worse than they are."

Deutsch knew he had escaped another bullet, and he quickly slipped out of Wood's office, offering Bob a backwards scowl as he left. Bob still sat on the sofa, and hadn't spoken a single word throughout the entire exchange. He seemed to have no interest in anything but his cigarette.

From beginning to end, the scenario was carefully, artfully, and intentionally orchestrated by Bob. He didn't want to do *Battleground*. He had become fond of Westerns, that being his natural proclivity. After getting wind through the studio grapevine *Ambush* was going into production, he decided that suited him best. He owed Armand Deutsch a favor for Deutsch's thoughtful hand-holding a few years back, and this was Bob's opportunity to repay him.

Shooting *Ambush* took about three months, two of them on location in Gallup, New Mexico. Deutsch ultimately came to understand Bob's brilliant maneuvering.

Bob and Ava Gardner behind scenes of *The Bribe*. Courtesy Robert Taylor Family Private Collection.

Bob and Ava Gardner had a fling on the set of *The Bribe*, which was filmed in late 1948, and released in February of 1949. She was a knockout, and he wasn't happy at home. That was a recipe for an affair. Ava cared little that he was a married man. "We hurt no one because no one knew. . . ." Their sexual interlude lasted maybe four months, and Ava was impressed with her paramour. "Bob, despite all his efforts, couldn't break the mold of the beautiful lover. The film world remembers him that way, and I have to say that I do too." She sighed. "Bob wasn't some effeminate type trying to hide reality under a macho exterior. . . ."

Despite all sorts of female companionship within his reach, Bob was still an excruciatingly lonely man. That changed in 1948, in the most unlikely way, when an important woman entered his life through his acquaintance with David Niven.

Niven married Primula "Primmie" Rollo in 1940. She and a man named Leonard Pearson grew up in the same English village. When Primmie and Niven prepared to come to America after the war, they signed affidavits of support allowing Leonard Pearson and his wife, Ivy, to emigrate with them. Len was David's secretary. Once in America, Ivy took on the job of managing the Niven household.

On May 21, 1946, a few days after their arrival in the States, the Nivens attended a party at Tyrone Power's home. While playing a game of hide-

and-seek, Primmie walked through a doorway, thinking the door led to a closet. She was moving quickly, and everything was pitch black as soon as she closed the door behind her. A fall down a flight of stone steps caused a fractured skull and brain lacerations. She died the following day, leaving David Niven bereft and the single father of two young sons. Leonard and Ivy lived in the Niven guest house at the time.

Niven slowly put the pieces of his life back together with the help of the Pearsons, but in 1948, he had to go back to England to make the film, *Bonnie Prince Charlie*, and suggested Ivy and Leonard find other employment. He had no idea when he would return to the States.

Len and Ivy had made connections in the Hollywood community, and Len began a valet service for such stars as John Garfield, Gene Kelly, Dick Powell, and Mr. and Mrs. Robert Taylor. Bob and Barbara were among his first clients.

Len and Ivy rented a room in a nearby small house. Their funds were limited, and though Ivy was pregnant, she had to add to their income. She found a position as a live-in nurse for the child of an up-and-coming actress. When a call came in to do an off-site shoot, the mother, the baby, and Ivy found themselves as houseguests to Gene Kelly. The job was expected to last three months, but dragged on and on. Ivy stayed until she went into the hospital to have her own child.

Ivy took in sewing to make enough money to take their new son, Mike, back to England for his christening. When she later on returned to California, she learned her husband had rented a home in Topanga Canyon. He had decided to start an import business, yet another venture, and without her knowledge he depleted their funds to buy the company stock.

At first, Ivy was angry. Len's behavior was completely out of character. There were arguments and many tears, and eventually appointments with many doctors. Soon she learned he had a malignant brain tumor and was in need of surgery. This had slowly altered his behavior, and his illness left him permanently disabled with an organic psychosis.

Ivy Pearson in later years. Courtesy author's personal collection.

By late 1948, Ivy was forced to take over as head of her household. She also had to manage Len's round-the-clock medical care. She was taking courses at UCLA for credentials to become a kindergarten teacher when she had learned of Len's illness. Despite her other responsibilities, she refused to give up her studies. She was driven; she had to acquire the financial means to raise her son and tend to her husband's needs. Because Len's business was floundering and they still owed money, there were no other options . . . and added on top of everything else, Ivy assumed management of the valet operation.

Throughout the ordeal, she and Bob Taylor were becoming friends.

CHAPTER TWELVE:

Lia DiLeo—*The* Affair

"There were hundreds of girls. I don't know why he picked me."
– Lia DiLeo

MGM began work in 1949 on a large-scale production. The stars were cast, with Elizabeth Taylor and Gregory Peck in the leads. *Quo Vadis* (1951) was a story of epic moviemaking proportions. Given a budget of $6,500,000, the biggest ever for a film to that date, the final effort employed thirty-seven thousand extras, thirty-two thousand costumes, twenty-three lions, and for dramatic effect, included a chariot race, as well as an elaborate scheme to recreate the burning of Rome. There were one hundred and ten speaking parts. Action figures were put on the drawing board to be released along with the movie, one of the earliest examples of mass product marketing connected to film distribution.

The movie was so long in preparation that by 1950, there had been a director change, and the show languished in seemingly never-ending preproduction. Mervyn LeRoy was now at the helm and casting changed. Elizabeth Taylor was replaced by Deborah Kerr as Lygia, the young servant girl. Stewart Granger wanted the role of Marcus Vinicius, the Roman soldier who fell in love with her. He refused to sign a long-term contract, though, and with the uncertainty of who would take the lead, Bob tested for the part. This was Mayer's last big budget production, and he still favored his Golden Boy of earlier days for the title. Bob got the role.

Bob's friend, Stewart Granger, wanted to play Marcus Vinicius in *Quo Vadis*.

Years later, Bob told Granger, "Do you know what they did when they put me in *Quo Vadis*? They showed me your test and told me to play the part just like you!"

Granger laughed and replied, "But that's typical, Bob. If I was so great, why didn't they use me? They chose you because you're a bloody fine actor. Just look at those arseholes . . . stunted, pot-bellied and bald, most of them. They were just jealous."

Granger thought a lot of Bob, but was concerned about his friend's self-image. "He was such a nice guy, but he had even more hang-ups than I had . . . Bob Taylor was the easiest person to work with but he had been entirely emasculated by the MGM brass who insisted that he was only a pretty face. He was convinced he wasn't really a good actor and his calm acceptance of this stigma infuriated me." His friend's acquiescence to the status quo never failed to frustrate Granger. He often told Bob, "Your problem is that you're too bloody good-looking and it's fashionable to say that good-looking guys can't act."

Bob in wardrobe review, without makeup.
Courtesy author's personal collection.

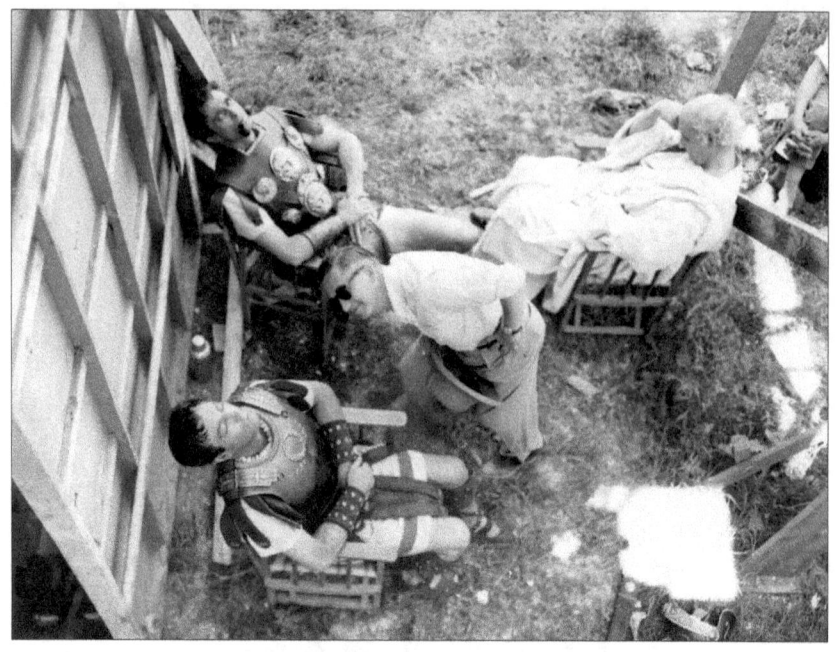

**Bob resting between takes of *Quo Vadis*.
Courtesy Robert Taylor Family Private Collection.**

Bob was forty years old and a chain-smoker, hardly what would normally be considered the best profile for a virile character such as Marcus Vinicius. He still had the looks, though, along with the physique and an austere persona. He had aged gracefully, and carried himself as the larger-than-life movie star Louis B. Mayer had made of him. Bob's smoking, possibly at work within him as a future health issue, hadn't outwardly affected him at this point.

This role was meant to revive Bob's career. The part of an arrogant centurion brought him back into the public eye in a big way, and put him in period costumes for years to come, typecasting him into epic-style films for the second half of his career.

At the time, however, all he knew was that the shoot would last more than six months. He would have to be far away from home, and Barbara, for however long the production would require. The heat was horrible. Working conditions weren't any better. The cast was often out in the hot sun for hours

**Bob taking photographs between scenes of *Quo Vadis*.
Courtesy Robert Taylor Family Private Collection.**

at a time. The atmosphere was thick, and air-conditioning was a problem. What was that problem? There wasn't any that worked.

They managed to find a few things to take their mind off their problems. An audience with the Pope was arranged for Bob, Deborah Kerr, Sam Zimbalist, and more than ten others. When His Holiness was introduced to Zimbalist, he said, "I suppose you are the star."

Zimbalist said he wasn't, he was the producer; Bob Taylor was the star. Smiling, the Pope replied, "Well, you do look Roman."

Other distractions were not as innocent.

Bob's aggravation at being away from his wife for such an extended period, particularly amidst their rising marital concerns, was at the root of his unease. They were growing apart more every day, and he had an added sense of apprehension about this trip. Location filming, and the sheer magnitude of distance, had separated them, mind, body, and heart. The stress which, for Bob, was as much physical as emotional was starting to be too much. The time was never available to rekindle any sort of intimacy. She got testier; he pulled away more. He wasn't much of a verbal communicator. She had a propensity for allowing her emotions to take her far over the edge. The recipe was written for a less-than-happy marriage.

This is where they were as a couple when Bob left for Italy. Enter Lia DiLeo.

Lia was young, busty, long-legged, and she hardly spoke a word of English. She'd recently left her husband and had no means of financial support. Someone suggested she go to Cinecitta in Rome, the big movie studio where many international moviemakers and stars came to make films. They were hiring extras for what promised to be an American extravaganza.

Lia DiLeo, model and *Quo Vadis* bit actress, had an affair with Bob during filming. Courtesy Robert Taylor Family Private Collection.

She secured a part in *Quo Vadis*, nothing more than a blip across the screen, but an appearance nonetheless. Lia said Sophia Loren was in the crowd as an extra. "People say she did it for the fun," Lia remarked. "She didn't. She was fifteen at the time. She did it for the money, like the rest of us."

In a group scene, Lia played the manicurist to Peter Ustinov's Nero; many women were staged to fawn over the emperor. She and Bob never appeared together onscreen but, once Bob caught sight of her, they were seen as a couple nearly everywhere else in town. "There were hundreds of girls. I don't know why he picked me." She sounded amazed. "I don't know why." With a laugh, she went on to say there were "a bunch of beautiful girls there, but somehow he kind of gave me the eye."

An understatement. "And then he invited me to dinner that night, and from then on, we were together practically every evening. We went everywhere where the public could see us so we went dancing, in all the famous places . . . he was still shooting, and I used to go every night and have dinner with him at the commissary."

When this famous man started courting her, she didn't know what to make of the attention. He wasn't pushy, he was intently focused on her. "He was very nice, a gentleman."

She became his constant companion. They had a "long romance going, around two or three months." He would walk her to her car at the end of the day's work. He'd take her to dinner at the finer restaurants, and they usually went dancing afterward. Bob seemed careless in how public he was, how flagrantly he displayed his interest in this young Italian beauty. He would often take her to his place late in the evening. "He had a butler serving a wonderful dinner."

Many years later, she spoke wistfully. "He was so very handsome." Her words were heavily accented, despite many years of living in the United States. Again she stressed, "He was nothing but a gentleman." What did they talk about? "Well, you must understand, I knew very little English. I carried a dictionary with me. What little English I did know . . . I learned from being with him." She insisted they talked mostly about the film and the day's shooting.

"He wasn't really a talker." She added quietly, ". . . just a few words . . . 'hello,' 'goodbye.' 'I love you.'" She laughed.

Bob took her on day trips to local tourist spots when he had a lull in filming. From the time he set eyes on her until the day he left Italy, they were together nearly every evening, and often during the day. He was being seen everywhere in public with a captivating young woman. It didn't take long before this became an issue for him, especially with a well-known, frustrated wife back home in the United States. Such news traveled fast; gossip columnists on both sides of the ocean were blaring reports about Bob Taylor's love affair with the sexy Italian ingénue.

He still didn't seem to care. He was flaunting his relationship with Lia. His actions spoke loudly, indicating that he was gunning for a showdown with Barbara, and she played right into his game when she flew to Rome to see for herself what her husband had going on.

"Yeah," Lia said, "she came over."

Barbara arrived while filming was in progress. Lia said Bob ". . . was on the set and he was looking at me. . . ." Bob was caught in the act of watching his paramour as his wife watched him. Lia and Barbara never spoke. "Of course," she said, "I didn't see him . . ." for awhile. "I never asked him, he never told me what happened."

Barbara stayed with her husband for six weeks and he played the dutiful husband the entire time. They played tourists in virtually every corner of Rome. Shopping, seeing the historical spots, dining at the best restaurants—they did it all together. Lia was clearly missing from the picture during this period.

Yet once Barbara left Italy, Bob was again back to his old ways, even seen frequenting a Roman whorehouse. One night, back in the swing with his special local lady, Lia, he walked her to her car after shooting, and, as she related, ". . . we saw this flash . . . lots of photographers everywhere and the day after it was in all the papers and magazines. There was nothing I could do about it."

The story grew legs and could not be contained. Soon after, Bob left the

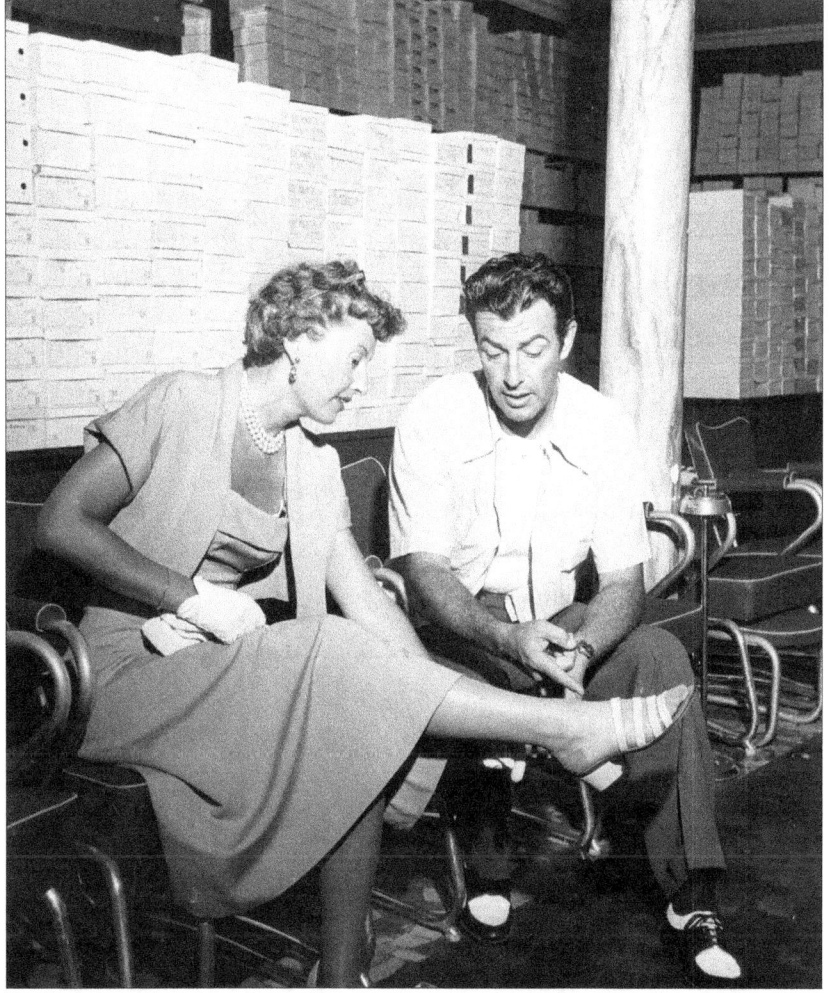

Bob and Barbara shoe-shopping in Rome.
Courtesy Robert Taylor Family Private Collection.

country. Before he departed, he saw Lia one last time in Rome, and he was livid with her. She explained, "... when he left, he accused me to ... to ... um, to provoke this publicity but, you know ... we were out in public all the time, together ... I didn't have to call anybody. They already knew. Everybody knew." She stressed again everyone was aware of them as a couple while Bob was in Rome, and the photographers made sure their continuing affair was

Bob reviewing wardrobe in costume on set of *Quo Vadis*.
Courtesy Robert Taylor Family Private Collection.

well-documented. "We were there, every night, eating at the commissary, laughing, and talking, going to his house every night...."

Lia was philosophical when asked if Bob discussed his marriage with her. She reiterated she didn't really know the language. "I'm a person who never asks questions." When they talked, she would nod and act as if she knew what he was saying. He didn't say much about his personal life. "He wanted a divorce, I understand." She emphasized she was with him enough to sense a lot of what he was feeling. Not understanding the actual words wasn't a deterrent to their brand of communication.

"I heard . . . it seems like he was tired of his wife and probably she could not understand that he was just tired of her. And she . . . took him to a doctor. . . ." Lia's tone was derisive. "Yeah. She was so, you know, ignorant about these things. She didn't realize that after so many years of marriage, the guy didn't want her anymore, and she thought something was wrong. You know, people get tired of the same thing."

"The same thing," meaning sex, was the unsaid end of her sentence. "He was a man!" she finished vehemently. She sounded amazed at her memories. "He was so handsome, that was the problem! He certainly was very macho, a rather macho man in his mannerisms, his way of thinking . . . like fly a plane, horse riding . . . a cowboy."

When two people who didn't speak the same language spent much time together, they had to find some other way to communicate. The scenario was a prescription for intimacy. Lia talked about their sexual relationship without offering specifics. She said they had ". . . a few months of, you know, love affair." She went on to stress he was ". . . a very great, good lover. Maybe I inspired him," she laughed. With her, he was ". . . friendly, nice, a very gentle person, very, very gentle. . . ." She finished, "I have a good remembrance of him."

After he left Italy, contact between him and Lia stopped abruptly and completely, or that's how the story went. ". . . he left mad at me because he thought I had used him for the publicity. The man should've known better. I couldn't care less. I wasn't married at that time. Didn't have a boyfriend. I didn't care if someone saw me with him. But he should've known better than to take me around to all the fancy places, where all the movie people go."

Bob knew what would happen if he carted such a strikingly-attractive young woman around town for months. He was aware his every move was noticed and word of his brazen affair would get back to his wife, all the way across the ocean. Whether intentionally, or out of subconscious frustration, Bob had created his own nightmare.

Over their years together, starting early on, he tried to leave Barbara on numerous occasions, but one thing or another changed his mind. Often, her histrionics nearly drove him to the edge of his usually-calm persona. His Italian escapade was the first face-off he had actually orchestrated, and he wanted the confrontation to play out in the public arena. He was searching for a way to completely sever the ties of his marriage, and he made Lia DiLeo part of his plan. He had been advised, by numerous people on more than one occasion, to tone down public appearances with her, but any such urgings fell on deaf ears.

Barbara dealt her last card in this scenario. She did not want a divorce; she wanted to keep hold of Bob forever, and she got on an airplane and flew all the way to Rome to be with him, and to be seen with him. Flying petrified her, and nothing less than absolute necessity would have been important enough for her to make the flight. Once he had finished filming and was back in Los Angeles, their inevitable face-to-face happened. She gave Bob an ultimatum to behave in public, or she would meet him in court. She was sure if she called his bluff, he would back down. He always had before.

This time, she underestimated him.

He took her up on the divorce, which turned out to be a challenge Barbara lived to regret, later calling her hasty move "the biggest mistake of [her] life." Barbara Stanwyck carried a torch for Robert Taylor until the day she died, reputedly swearing that his ghost visited her in her bedroom right after his death, standing at the foot of her bed. He was the one true love of her life, and she went to her grave avowing that love.

CHAPTER THIRTEEN:

In Transition

"That'll be enough. Divorce granted."
– Superior Judge Thurmond Clarke

Bob made sure he returned to Hollywood from Italy in time to vote in the 1950 Presidential elections. Sheilah Graham said, "Bob is as interested in politics and good government as are George Murphy, Dick Powell and Humphrey Bogart—to name a few of our top politically minded stars." He had "dashed back... in double-quick time because he wanted to be sure to be here...."

Politics and his disintegrated marriage vied for the top reason for his "double-quick" return to California. To take his mind off his problems, he went back to work. His next film was an interesting choice for him and for the industry, adding another facet to his already-long resume. He found his way to *Devil's Doorway* (1950) when Director Anthony Mann, specifically asked for him in the lead role of a dark-skinned Shoshone.

Many thought Bob was miscast, but he liked the stretch of playing a full-blooded Indian. He welcomed the chance to portray a Native American in a positive way. He explained, "... I admired the characterization because of the fact that the Indian, previously considered the 'heavy' in early Westerns, is a regular guy. For once he gets a chance to tell his side of the story." He ran with the part.

On the front-side of the aging process, he was losing his soft prettiness in favor of a rougher, craggy-faced masculinity which seemed to attract just as

Bob as Lance Poole in *Devil's Doorway*.

many female fans. His changing looks, as much as his willingness to step out of his comfort zone, helped lead him into roles offering him more personal satisfaction. These were roles he would've never been offered in earlier years.

The script for *Devil's Doorway* was far ahead of its time. Studios had begun to explore how they presented the Western way of life, and in particular, Indians. That year saw the beginning of an evolution away from the always "bad guy," unintelligibly grunting, one-sided bow-and-arrow image, toward a multi-faceted real-life human depiction.

Two films came out delving into this. Both were sensitive depictions, and each showed Indians as persons who were not blood-thirsty savages. The first to hit the screen was Twentieth Century Fox's *Broken Arrow* (1950). Though *Devil's Doorway* was completed and ready for theaters first, MGM hesitated because of the delicacy of the subject matter. The vacillation cost both the studio and Bob a great deal of public acclaim.

Broken Arrow stole the thunder. When MGM saw that the public could receive such material in a positive light, *Devil's Doorway* was released in September. The film's impact was greatly diminished by the other's fanfare, and what might have been a picture of important historical implication came out as nothing more than a follow-up. Historians have since seen *Broken Arrow* as having less realism, using words such as "preachy" and "patronizing" as descriptions. *Devil's Doorway* was grittier, more realistic and hard-hitting, and production values were considered brilliant. The movie "refused to fall back on the clichés of the genre." *The New York Times* said *Devil's Doorway* was "a Western with a point of view that rattles some skeletons in our family closet."

Timing was everything, though, and MGM missed the boat. *Devil's Doorway* did give Bob added confidence and in that way, the role was an important one for him. From then on, he chose his parts with a changed eye, intentionally reaching out to play edgy, predominantly Western characterizations.

By Christmas time, Bob's unconcealed affair with Lia DiLeo had become the last straw for Barbara who had tried for years, in her own way, to hold together a marriage going down the tubes almost from the get-go. He was not the same man she had married, and that didn't sit well with her. On December 15, 1950, they officially separated.

The Robert Taylor who had wed Barbara Stanwyck had been young and green, not only chronologically, but emotionally and experience-wise. At the outset, she was the teacher and he the student. In every way. He was learning his craft, learning about the business and the studio system, learning about how to be a celebrity. He was learning how to be a man. She, on the other hand, was years ahead of him in experiences, and willingly shared what she knew. At one point in those first years, a member of the press had remarked on their age difference, to which Barbara saucily replied, "The boy's got a lot to learn and I've got a lot to teach."

He'd had previous relationships, but Barbara was a glamorous, sexy, older woman, and there was much she could school him on in the romance department as well as other facets of life. Bob told her, "It was really something to be socially acceptable to an actress of your caliber!"

As their relationship continued, his career rose in meteoric proportions. His star made a straight shot into the heavens. The training his new wife had given him served him well; he was a fast learner. Their relationship followed something of a timeworn formula: experienced older woman takes a nice-looking younger man under her wing and into her bed, and the younger man soaks in everything offered him, eventually moving on.

There was nothing intentional or mean-spirited about how Bob treated his wife. Those who knew him well said he really tried to make the marriage work, over and over. His naturally peaceful personality and his quiet nature could find no way to meld with Barbara's often unrestrained and domineering behavior. Ivy Mooring said Barbara would yell and screech at him, often getting so drunk, particularly on champagne, that she would verbally abuse him. Rather than physically strike back, Bob used his best defense; he separated himself from her, at first emotionally, but as time wore on and the situation became severe, he would literally walk out on her. This angered her more, and she became strident, bossy, overbearing; sometimes her verbal abuse cut him to the core.

The process of her leading and he following had initially been a good thing, but ultimately her "motherly" ways became an unbearable weight around Bob's neck. The more comfortable he was in his Hollywood lifestyle, the more Barbara's behavior bothered him. Friends and acquaintances saw her as trying to handle him, making him look to the public as the sort of man he really was not—submissive, meek, and effeminate. A malleable man who could easily be led around and dominated by a fiercely strong woman.

Finally Bob had enough. That image was beginning to stick, and he was tired of being demeaned. He had built his career, served in the Navy, made noise and stood up to the government, and become at ease with his quiet and stoic, old-fashioned male sexuality. A hard-core, brassy, sometimes mean woman didn't appeal to him.

He felt cornered.

Barbara had turned into the mirror image of the one person a man never wanted in his bed. Ivy stated bluntly, "A man doesn't want to sleep with his mother, does he? That's how she acted."

Everything came to a head at Christmas. Bob was back from Italy, and his affair with Lia was fresh in both of their minds. Barbara felt Bob's public and unashamed cavorting with another woman was the ultimate insult to her. Everyone who could read, or listen to a radio, was aware her husband had cheated on her. She desperately wanted to hold on to him, but he clearly wanted something else, and he had crossed an invisible line. She couldn't let that pass.

Barbara said she waited "a reasonable time," but finally the story of their break-up was leaked. Louella Parsons was one of the first to release the headline: "Stanwyck, Taylor Split Up." Barbara told her, "It all started when he got that airplane...."

The official statement came out on Christmas Eve and blamed everything on their careers. "In the past few years, because of professional requirements, we have been separated just too often and too long. Our sincere and continued efforts to maintain our marriage have failed. We are deeply disappointed that we could not solve our problems. We really tried...."

Each in their broken way had really tried to make the marriage succeed. Despite all their baggage, there was a long-standing affection between them, though the shine of sincere love had long ago slipped away. Over the stretch of their eleven years together, numerous quiet splits had been patched, and each time they once again showed their public a happily-married face. Parsons' comment gave the perfect summation. "I don't know when the breakup of any marriage has come as a greater surprise...."

This time there was no way to fix the problem. The statement continued, "There will be a California divorce. Neither of us has any other romantic interest whatsoever."

The truth, and a lie. There was no actual romantic involvement on either part at that point, but Bob's sexual tryst with Lia DiLeo and previous liaisons were the obvious catalyst to start the ball rolling irretrievably down the hill. Barbara officially filed for divorce. She was said to be "ailing and staying in seclusion," and "neither she nor Bob [were] happy over the prospect of freedom."

Forever the pacifist, Bob may have never left Barbara if she had played the part of the wronged wife with less pressure. He might have continued to be married to her, at least in name, if she hadn't forced him into his final move. If their confrontation had been orchestrated differently on her part, he likely would've come home to her again and pretended to be the happy husband, at least to the outside world.

But this production was headed straight for court. Bob was recovering from hernia surgery in Palm Springs at the time of the announcement. A week prior to telling the world of their split, Barbara had spoken to Louella Parsons about Bob's operation. She told the gossip columnist the "three hours he was on the operating table were the worst" of her life. She bought him a Cadillac for Christmas, a present she said she would drive until he had recovered enough to get behind the wheel.

Obviously, the 1950 holiday season wasn't to be as joyous as Barbara presented to the press. Her interview with Parsons was a smokescreen to give Bob enough time to get beyond the operation, leave town, and put room between them to make their separation look affectionate, and sadly amicable.

When an AP photographer showed up poolside while Lia DiLeo sunned herself in Italy in January of 1951, the caption showing along with the photo quoted her as saying her relationship with Bob was "a friendly one, nothing more." Lia proved she had the power to haunt his marriage to its last breath.

The Taylor/Stanwyck split was finalized on Thursday, February 15, 1951. Barbara arrived at the courthouse wearing a toast-colored suit and matching hat. Bob was still in Palm Springs. She told the judge, "He said he had enjoyed his freedom during the months he was in Italy. He wanted to be able to continue his life without restrictions." She pulled out all the stops, bringing out the actress in her. "I was very shocked and very grieved over it. It made me quite ill. For several weeks I was under the care of my physician."

Barbara after divorce from Bob was finalized.

Helen Ferguson, Barbara's press agent, was there for support. "I went to Barbara's house and found her in a tragic emotional state." She sighed dramatically and added, "Barbara said: 'I'm giving Bob the freedom he wants.'"

The judge barely allowed each woman time to finish their commentary before swiftly ending the eleven-year marriage with five simple words: "That'll be enough. Divorce granted." Tall and well-groomed Superior Judge Thurmond Clarke sided with Barbara. Maybe he thought Bob had done her wrong. Maybe he didn't like Bob's womanizing. Maybe he was a big fan of Barbara's movies. He had presided over other high-visibility divorce cases, and his track record showed he most often favored the wife. He granted Barbara possession of not only the $100,000 Brentwood mansion she and Bob owned together, but he officially gave her back her maiden name and fifteen percent of Bob's gross earnings . . . until she died, or until she remarried.

No one considered the idea *Bob* might die before either of those things happened.

※

Recovering in Palm Springs, Bob called Ivy. She and Bob weren't really close friends yet, but her family issues were known within the Hollywood community serviced by the valet business, and Bob felt sorry for her. He assured her the paycheck would continue in the same amount, with no change since Len had run the business. He offered to help her and the family in any way he could.

They started to talk more often. Bob still utilized her business, mostly because she needed the money rather than because he needed the work done. Ivy was a good listener. Bob saw her as the sister he never had, and he was drawn to her as a confidante. In the course of their conversations, he urged her to take her husband to England where he could be hospitalized under that country's National Health Scheme. Since Len wasn't a United States citizen or a veteran, stateside private hospitalization would be too expensive. Without insurance, Ivy's mounting bills could easily get out of control. She was on the verge of a real financial crisis.

Since his divorce from Barbara, Bob needed a new home. He rented an apartment in Beverly Hills and was, as Ivy said, "sad and lonely," but more than willing to be of assistance to this British couple he had come to know and appreciate. The cost of his divorce settlement had the intended effect, and that filtered down to those who relied on him. He was still supporting his mother. Few people ever realized how much Barbara depleted his bank account; this wasn't common knowledge. She essentially demanded he "pay" for leaving her, and pay for the rest of his life.

By the time the divorce was over, he well knew the score. His new status affected every aspect of his life, particularly his finances. After consultation with Morgan Maree, still his business manager even though Maree also handled Barbara's affairs, Bob acceded to her demands without public argument or challenge. He let himself settle into his old habit of not wanting confrontation. He didn't need a private matter to become a public boxing match, which is exactly what would have happened if he had contested her terms. He never aired his personal laundry, if he had any control over the situation. This, along with his thorough distaste for face-to-face conflict, had him opening his pockets and telling Barbara to take what she wanted. And she did. She was tragically hurt and wanted to make him hurt, too, in whatever way she could.

All this happened in a short period of time and forced him to give up his newly-rented Beverly Hills apartment. Against his better judgment but with few other options, he moved in with his mother in Westwood. He was paying the mortgage, anyway, though he had bought the house specifically for her. The address was 1063 North Selby Avenue.

The house was large enough. Simple economics illustrated how Bob could no longer afford his own place as well as one for his mother, and he was determined to not burden her finances or comfort. He wouldn't make her give up any part of her lifestyle because of his marital woes. Part of this equation was his desire to not provide her any cause to tell him, "I told you so." She hadn't wanted him to marry Barbara, and prophesied at one point the union would ultimately cost him lots of money. Unfortunately, Mother had been right. He didn't want to hear this fact hammered back at him.

Lia DiLeo may have still been in this picture somewhere, though there is no direct indication as to whether a relationship was all in her mind, or if Bob was a willing partner. A February report talked of her reading newspaper pieces about their affair. The short article re-told the story of their "romance," and then asked Lia about their current status. "If it depended on him alone," she avowed confidently, "I am sure we would marry," but she added she was reluctant to marry again. Hardly likely Bob would've again said, "I do," especially this soon after signing off on his divorce.

But Lia milked the publicity for all she could. The article said she hesitated after her last comment, but then continued, "I might yield eventually to his persistence."

Bob and Ivy empathized over each other's situations. Ivy commuted from Topanga to UCLA for studies. Her husband was under constant hospital care. No longer able to afford their house, she moved into a room over a garage. She was working furiously to pay off the huge hospital bill with the small income from the few valet clients she still serviced. In addition to work and school, she cared for her son.

Seeing Ivy struggle pained Bob, and he was compelled to do whatever he could to alleviate her stress. With no clear motive other than making her life easier, he invited her to move into his mother's house. He offered her the guest room with a private bath, next to the master bedroom. He explained he would continue to live there, too. If she moved in, his burden over again having to live with his mother would be eased. This would be a big help to him. Her presence in the house would make the set-up more bearable.

He planned to take over the small maid's room in the back, and he adamantly said that was what he preferred. Not having his room on the top floor would give him privacy and let him come and go without his mother listening for his footsteps on the stairs at night. All this despite the fact she herself had a steady beau, and he was old enough to do as he pleased.

What he didn't say, though Ivy already knew, was that he would not have taken the smaller room if she hadn't moved in. The arrangement was worded to sound as if this was to his best advantage. She was aware he explained his offer to ensure she wouldn't feel guilty about taking up residence in what was essentially his home, putting him in a tiny room in the process.

At first Ivy wasn't keen on accepting the generous offer. He wouldn't take any money from her for living expenses. She felt she would be imposing, but as much of a concern was the issue of her son. He was still a small child, and she knew she couldn't bring him into such a unique, blended arrangement. That wouldn't be right for any of them, especially her son.

Bob had proven to be a thoughtful person, but Ivy already suspected he didn't take well to young children. Despite her protestations, he continued to offer, saying they could work this out. Her financial obligations were growing out of control and that, and his persistence, slowly wore away at her. She could no longer refuse the only solution available to help her get out from under her debt. Finally she gave in, arranging to have her son sent to England to stay with her parents, and she moved in with Bob and his mother. The deal was to last only as long as Ivy needed to financially recuperate enough to put her family back together.

Ivy saw Bob as the heart of generosity, but she didn't want his charity and she made that clear. She started out cooking for him; that proved to be a minor disaster. Her idea of a meal was mutton well-done to toughness, with boiled potatoes and watery cabbage. The first time she served him, the disaster was immediately evident. Next, she tried making a steak. She seared the meat outside on the barbecue, turning the steak over and over to ensure thorough cooking. Since he wasn't home by the time the meat was ready to be served, she put his plate in the oven for warming.

Once he walked in the front door and sat at the dinner table, the food was tentatively placed in front of him, and he took a bite. After minutes spent attempting to chew the meat, he looked at Ivy, grimaced, and said, "Maybe it's the knife that doesn't cut well." The next day he brought home four steak knives and a cookbook, fairly well summing up her experience as his house cook.

His mother wasn't any better. Her lavish meals of his childhood had deteriorated to where her specialty was now lemon pie and, as Ivy said, "not much else." Bob had learned to enjoy eating-out; even Barbara hadn't been much of a cook.

He never complained.

Bob was scheduled to go to England to make *Ivanhoe* (1952). Still concerned about Ivy, he suggested she come with him during summer months while school was out. She could be with her son, and spend time with her family. He hired her as his secretary, even though, as she related, "I could type about three words an hour." Despite her office inadequacies, she felt she

Bob "cooking" for himself in a photo opportunity.
Courtesy Robert Taylor Family Private Collection.

earned her keep because she pressed his pants and his suits, shined his shoes, and she listened to his every woe.

A note he wrote to her, early enough in their relationship that he still called her "Mrs. Pearson," said, "The June 1st departure for England seems a very dubious date at the moment." He was in the middle of filming *Westward the Women* (1951), and going back and forth between California and Utah. "We're about two weeks behind schedule on this picture (weather, illness, etc) and I have no way of knowing just when we'll finish."

He had asked MGM to pay Ivy's way, first class, to and from England. "The studio still has not given me a definite answer regarding their paying your transportation," the letter continued, "but I feel certain that, in the final analysis, they'll 'come thru.'" He signed with, "My kindest regards, R.T."

The plan did go through. During the week, she would work for Bob. On Fridays through Sundays, she would go to the country to stay with her family and son. The arrangement was ideal. Ivy's husband remained hospitalized in England, every day lapsing deeper into a serious state of physical illness and dementia, and she needed a strong shoulder. Bob and Ivy emotionally supported each other.

In the same timeframe, Lia DiLeo made clear to anyone who would listen she was on her way to the United States. Newspapers said she was "stalking the handsome movie star, for a showdown." She said she knew he loved her. Lia arrived in November; Bob left for England in September. The timeline shows they didn't see each other in the States; in fact, their ships probably crossed in the open seas.

Bob knew this was a hard time for Ivy. Her husband was gravely ill, her son and she were together only a short time, and she would soon have to once more leave him behind with her parents, to return to California. This was the only way she could afford to support her child, her critically sick husband, and pay down the debt which never seemed to lessen. On one of her weekend trips from the city to her parent's home in the country, Bob sent her on her way with a huge ham, since food was still scarce in Europe, admonishing her not to "boil the damn thing!"

He tried to lighten her emotional load by taking her out on late afternoons and weekday evenings. They went to the ballet; he didn't enjoy the dancing art, but knew she did. He also took her to the theater, and on shopping trips to quaint markets. On one outing, her pocketbook was stolen with her passport inside. Bob went to considerable effort to make sure she got a new one. This was all a large dose of kindness on Bob's part. Ivy was alone and had too much to handle. Still, the companionship was as much a salve to his hurting heart as a comfort to hers. They were good for each other at a point when they both desperately needed the support.

Ivy said, "Bob was the most lonely man I have ever seen, and spent most of his spare time in his suite at the Dorchester [Hotel]. We leaned on each other in our mutual misery and I began to see through his shyness and get glimpses of the kind, vulnerable human being who became my friend."

Bob relaxing between scenes of *Ivanhoe* with his two favorite pastimes—coffee and a cigarette.

In Transition

By the time he and Ivy left England, they were comfortable with each other; truly friends, not lovers. They departed the country at different times, he before her, but he ensured she had tickets and everything she needed, and knew how to get hold of the studio employee making the arrangements.

Bob unintentionally left a watch behind. In the note which included final preparation details, he asked Ivy to contact the studio employee, and "... perhaps you could simply leave the watch at the hotel where he intends me to stay the one nite. I'll be in New York." He then became playful. "Have a good trip—and hang on to that Emergency Passport!" With the letter addressed to "Ivy," he signed off, "As ever, Me."

Bob may have gotten wind of Barbara being ill around this time. She was under-the-weather enough to cancel an appearance, and threaten a trip east she had long had planned with Nancy Sinatra. There were no details as to the type of illness, but hints said she still pined for Bob, and this affected her well-being.

Once he got home after *Ivanhoe*, Bob was blindsided with an accusation he "ran up exorbitant expenses on his trip to London." Sidestepping feelings of anger was much easier for him than expending the energy and having things get out of hand. Still, there were moments when he couldn't help himself. When he got to his snapping point, he became sarcastic, biting . . . darkly humorous if viewed in the right light.

He responded to the news of his alleged indiscretion in typical Bob Taylor style. He went to his typewriter, got comfortable, and proceeded to draft a response to Eddie Mannix, MGM Vice President, and the one who had sent down the edict outlining his extravagance. Bob explained how he flew in a small plane from Los Angeles to New York to save money. He stopped in Jackson, Wyoming, to catch trout for dinner. After all, he was hungry, but he knew he had to save money. He tried to sleep under the plane that night.

Why? Well, of course, to save money. But the mosquitoes decided he was their dinner, and his plan didn't work.

On his way to New York, and the ship which would take him to London, his next overnight stop was Mattoon, Illinois. He gave in and rented a hotel room, acknowledging, "I realize that $5 is an exorbitant price to pay for a hotel room, but I hasten to assure you that I did not take a suite. I confess to having a private bath . . . but this was only as a last resort after I learned that several people on my floor had dysentery. I assure you," the letter continued, tongue firmly planted in cheek, "that I shall check with the health department of each city I visit before stopping at a hotel. I quite agree that it's expenditures such as this which can bankrupt our studio."

Bob had barely warmed up. "The New York expenditures are self-explanatory. Only one item would I like to explain. Mr. Gil Cote, our very efficient special services man in New York, accompanied me to the boat and, [despite] my continued protestations that Coca-Cola is very bad for the teeth, the digestion and disposition, [he] insisted on drinking two of them before the boat sailed. They appear on the statement as an item of 20 cents and I am truly embarrassed by it.

"During the crossing, aboard ship, I endeavored in every way," he stressed, "to minimize expenses as much as possible. The following examples will, I trust, serve to authenticate this statement:

"Through the use of extreme charm, the displaying of faultless manners, and the casual reference to the fact that I was a friend of Bunny Dull [Orville Dull, aka Bunny, Producer/Director], I succeeded in persuading innumerable passengers aboard ship to buy me drinks during the evenings. Some of these included Vincent Astor, Mr. and Mrs. Wellington of Dumont Television, and Mr. and Mrs. Reid, editor of the *Herald-Times*."

In case this wasn't enough to make his point, Bob continued, "I avoided the rental of a deck chair, blanket and pillow by making my appearances on deck before anyone else was out of bed or after everyone else had gone to bed. Sitting on other passenger's chairs didn't really bother me much, especially when I knew I was saving the studio a lot of money. Moreover, by changing chairs continuously, I had a change of scenery which I couldn't have ever gotten with my own chair.

"I completely avoided buying any wine during the entire crossing. This I accomplished by dining as late as possible and by drinking the dregs out of all the old unfinished bottles which passengers had left before me. The mixing of white wines, red wines, still wines and sparkling wines became a little nauseating at times. But again I realized that was the least I could do for a generous studio which could only look forward to an even break on such complete flops as *King Solomon's Mines, The Great Caruso, An American In Paris, Show Boat, Quo Vadis*, etc., etc."

Was he angry? His words were pure mockery. This was but another instance of Bob Taylor secure in who he was, especially who he was in the MGM Studios pecking order. He was aware such a letter would not get him in trouble, but would make his point.

"I endeavored to press my own clothes," he stressed, "but the small electric iron I carry for this purpose blew out a fuse in this section of the main deck, and the ship's electrician recommend [sic] that I discontinue its use. I tried to clean my own room and make my own bed at the outset of the trip. However, the room steward caught me the second day out and threatened to report me to the Steward's Union. After weighing the possible consequences I decided that it might be cheaper for the studio to permit a tip to the steward for such services rather than to fight a case against a powerful international union. In this I hope my conclusions were correct." This passage threw a well-directed jab at the Hollywood union troubles of a few years back.

"These are but a few examples of my never-ending efforts to save the studio money. If I have failed I shall never forgive myself. If I have succeeded I shall, at least, rest happy in the knowledge that a lowly actor has contributed if only in a small measure to the financial well-being of his studio. Perhaps the executives of our organization can, in the future, travel in even greater splendor at studio expense, and we shall emerge upon a new and brighter era for our product and will once again start making a few bucks. It would be so nice to have a deck chair again!"

Bob finished his sad tale with a most polite, though skewered, sign-off. "My very kindest regards, Mr. Mannix, to your good self and all the other members of the executive branch of our MGM family." He signed the letter, "Very Respectfully, Robert Taylor."

Bob never again heard anything more from the studio about his spending habits.

CHAPTER FOURTEEN:

Ursula, and Bob's Exotic European Women

> "I have set 'traps' at all the more likely Pubs, Bars, Clubs, Rooming Houses, and intersections but, thus far, nothing's fallen into them. I've obviously lost my touch. . . ."
> – Robert Taylor

Ursula Schmidt-Hut was born in Hamburg, Germany, the only child of a prosperous importer. When she was fifteen, she was taken from school to spend a year "pulling Pflichtjahr," compulsory farm labor under Hitler's government. When her father lost his business and fortune, her home was bombed a few steps ahead of advancing Russian troops, and the family had to flee for their lives. The easy life was no more for Ursula.

She joined a theater stock company, and in 1942 she married George Thiess, a film director. The union was not a happy one. In 1943, she was pregnant with her first child while the Allies bombed Hamburg into rubble. Her daughter, Manuela, was born in the Finkenau Clinic, the same place Ursula had been born. Her son, Michael, arrived in 1945.

By 1947, Ursula was divorced and alone with her children, taking any job she could to keep them fed. She modeled, wrote and sold short stories,

Ursula Schmidt-Hut on German stage in Clare Booth Luce's *The Women*.
Courtesy Robert Taylor Family Private Collection.

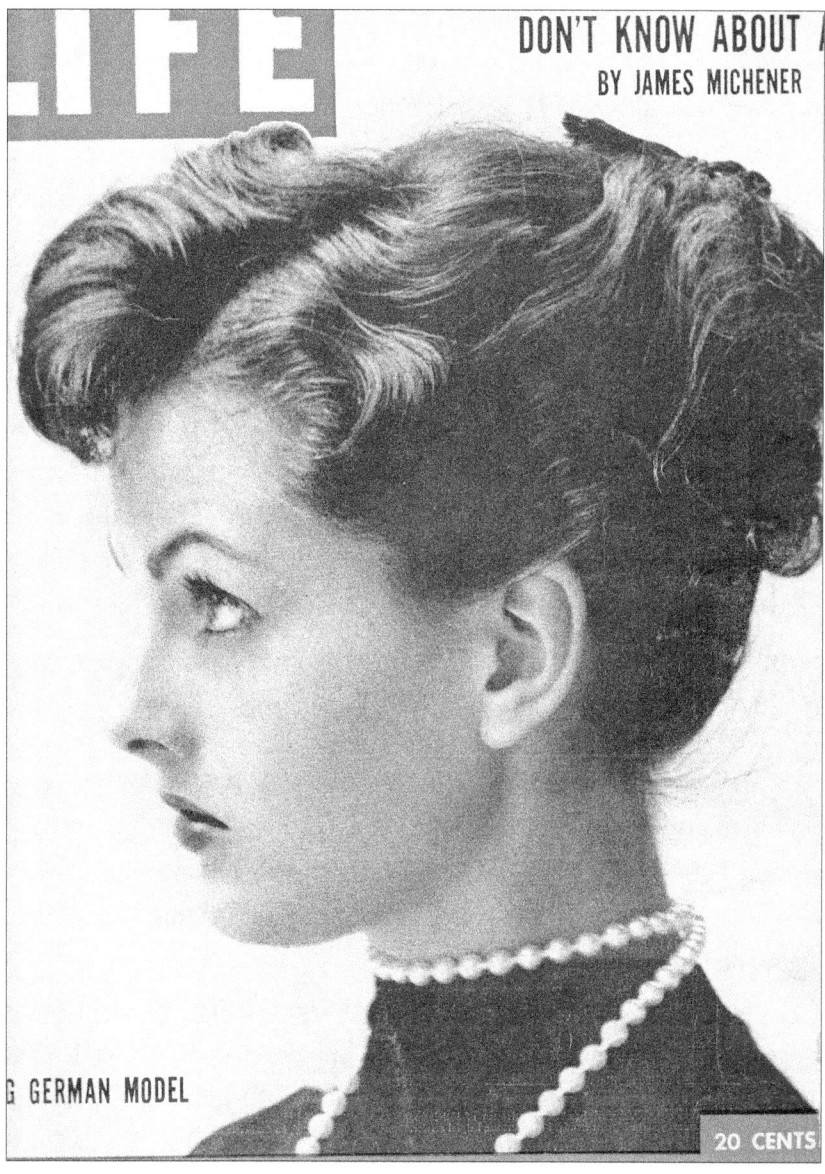

Ursula found her way to America, and the cover of *Life*, in part thanks to Howard Hughes. Courtesy Robert Taylor Family Private Collection.

and acted in minor theater. She was credited in one German movie production, *Nachtwache*. Her monthly income averaged about thirty-five dollars, and there were days when she would ensure the children had something to eat, only to find nothing left for herself.

This changed when a talent scout saw her picture in a German magazine. Howard Hughes learned of her; he was enamored with her striking beauty and sent her a cablegram, offering her a contract with RKO Studios. She thought the cable was a joke and threw it in the trash.

The cable had not been a joke, and Ursula finally came to the United States in 1951 when another effort to contact her was successful. She left the children with her mother to travel to America to work for RKO under the tutelage of Howard Hughes. She couldn't speak the language but that didn't matter much. She was in the United States and about to become the protégé of a well-known American. Life would never again be the same for Ursula.

Amidst repeated media reports he and Barbara might reunite, Bob was gun-shy about getting back into the Hollywood dating scene. One line in *Westward The Women* seemed to sum up his feelings about embarking on any serious relationship after his divorce. "Only two things in this life scare me, and a good woman's both of them."

Still, he was, as Ivy said, lonely, and he and his ex had parted company in a pseudo-amicable manner, at least without public emotional bloodletting. They seemed to genuinely enjoy each other's company now that they were no longer married. They were occasionally photographed as they laughed over a shared late-evening dinner. When a reporter asked Barbara about rumors, she quipped, "There's nothing to them. Every day I read something new about us. You know something—it's even exciting reading for me."

But Bob was seeing someone other than Barbara, actually more than one someone. On a trip to New York City in January of 1952, he was caught

Yvonne DeCarlo, an "intimate friend" after Bob's divorce from Barbara.

shopping on Fifth Avenue, giving some young salesgirls a thrill. He bought nylons and other intimate feminine items, but refused to offer the slightest hint of the identity of the lucky recipient. Rumors were rife his paramour was still Lia DiLeo.

There was another possibility. He had been keeping company with thirty-year old Yvonne DeCarlo. One night on a dinner date, they had a heart-to-heart conversation. Eleven years her senior, Bob gave her advice. She had been in movies since 1941 but hadn't made a memorable picture. "Always set your sights high," he told her.

Yvonne didn't have her career on her mind at that moment. She listened to him, looking into his eyes, watching his lips, and all the while wondering how much higher she could possibly set her sights than on him. "We got very little sleep that night," she later reported with a grin, "but it didn't seem to matter." She also said in her older years that Bob Taylor had been "an intimate friend."

In June, something he had long tried to deny seemed verified when he was "caught cabling posies and baby-talking" to Lia over Trans-Atlantic phone. His travels did take him to England and Scotland. They may have met overseas. Reports said he tried to forget her but he still carried a torch.

Truth was, he was playing the field. He had enjoyed his time with Lia, and his marriage with Barbara was behind him. He was finally responsible to no woman. The thing with Lia was a casual dalliance. By August, their tryst was clearly over. Lia was quoted as saying she planned to sue Bob for "breach of promise," something which intimated he had money invested in Italy. Nothing ever came of her threat.

All the game-playing surrounding any new relationship, with any woman, took a different turn one lovely night in 1952. Bob was coerced by his agent into going to Mocamba, a glitzy club on Sunset Boulevard opened eleven years earlier. His agent told Bob he would "bring along a starlet who was a nice and beautiful girl."

The set up was intentional, a blind date and maybe a publicity ploy, but the night changed his life. That "nice and beautiful girl" was Ursula Thiess. Bob discovered his agent had been right, and more. A reporter spotting them together said they "certainly acted as if they meant it." Another said Bob was finally dating someone prettier than he was. RKO's press people dubbed Ursula "the most beautiful woman in the world," and the title stuck. If the statement wasn't true, there was no way to tell by looking at her. She was built to make a man dream, with long legs and a busty, hourglass shape. Her thick wavy hair and huge eyes completed a picture of a woman born to be seen on the silver screen.

That night upon his return home, he went to Ivy's room, as was his habit.

They traditionally visited late in the evenings to chat about their days. Her light was on, meaning she was still awake. He walked in and perched on the end of her bed. His first glance scanned the books strewn around her; he shook his head and made a face. He was always telling her she read and studied too much. Her nose was forever in a book. He teased her, saying she should "get a life."

Ignoring his antics, Ivy asked what he thought of Ursula. "She's a knockout!" was all he could say. From the look on Bob's face and the sound of his voice, Ivy could tell he was floored by the exotic German woman. "But," he continued, "I don't understand her . . . and she doesn't understand me."

Young, beautiful Ursula Thiess. Courtesy Robert Taylor Family Private Collection.

This was only partly because Ursula's English was spotty, and more a result of Bob's almost in-awe response to her appearance. They got along, he said, though they didn't talk much. Their first meeting was strongly based on physical attraction.

Subsequent dates weren't always easy sailing. The problem wasn't that they didn't care for each other. What made waves between them may have actually been the result of much the opposite. They appeared to regularly one-up each other, trying not to seem too interested in any general connection they had. Not long after they started being seen together, Ursula was asked about the relationship. "He's a nice guy," she replied without commitment. She insisted their dating wasn't serious.

They by no means saw each other exclusively at this point. Ursula was noticed on the arm of many dashing men, and Bob still had his pick of women. On his forty-first birthday, though, she was the one he wanted with him. He had Ralph fly Ursula to Kanab, Utah, where he was filming *Ride, Vaquero* (1953). Ralph's wife was along as "chaperone," and the four spent a happy twenty-four hours together. Bob had been noted in Ursula's company often enough by this time to have the gossip tongues wagging. When the trip was discovered by the press, one columnist said, "... a man's birthday is a sentimental occasion. Could mean something."

Bob gravitated toward the more exotic European type. His growing association with Ursula received regular note in the gossip rags, but he wasn't ready to be tied down again. He saw other women, and one was a Russian/French ballerina-turned-actress.

Ludmila Tcherina was born in Paris in 1924 to an exiled Georgian prince and a French mother. She started in ballet almost at the same time she learned to walk, and she and her mother moved to Marseilles when the war broke out. At sixteen, she starred with the Ballet de Monte Carlo. Billed as Tcherina, she danced in Paris, New York, Milan, and with the Bolshoi. Ludmila returned to Paris with screen actor, dancer, and choreographer Edmond Audran. They married in 1946; he was killed in a car accident in July of 1951.

She was willowy, buxom, with dark hair, long legs and big expressive eyes. Bob crossed her path in early 1952. He was in England making *Above and Beyond* (1952), a film whose working title was *An Eagle On His Cap*. He was still a head-turner and he had a newfound sense of sexual confidence. Not cockiness. Bob Taylor was never seen as cocky. He still didn't envision himself as the sex symbol most of the rest of the world saw in him, but he was secure in his place in Hollywood, and he was finally really enjoying his celebrity.

For Ludmila, their meeting helped assuage the hurt over the death of her husband. Bob was exercising his independence and freeing himself of the demons of his failed marriage. In an interview a few years later, Ludmila said they "consoled each other."

Bob enjoyed women whose natural language was not English, women with whom he could not easily and automatically communicate verbally. This was likely not intentional. He wasn't a talker by nature, and preferred

Ludmila Tcherina, another love interest for Bob.

ladies not given to chattiness. Columnist Harrison Carroll wrote in April of 1952, "I called the ballerina at her hotel and she speaks very little English. Bob's French is equally limited." A language barrier had proven more than once to not be a deterrent. Lia, Ursula, and now, Ludmila. Each was exotic, fine-looking, European, and physically similar. Not one of them spoke much recognizable English when they met Bob.

Bob readily admitted to "location romances." His trysts resulted from basic sexual need, but as important for him was female companionship. He was rarely without intimate female relationships, though they weren't always sexual. Whether the woman was his mother, or Ivy, or Barbara, or Lia, or Ludmila or Ursula, or any of his "location romances," he made sure he had a woman around him.

His romance with Ludmila was reported in the press as early as January of 1952. They may have never been as serious as gossip columnists wanted the public to believe, despite the March headlines which blared, "It's Orson Welles vs. Robert Taylor in the fight for French ballet dazzler, Ludmilla Tcherina's heart." Walter Winchell, famed newspaper columnist, reported "the Robert Taylor and Orson Welles 'feud' is over Ludmila Tcherina. Taylor's crush is the one she prefers. . . ." Later that month, Winchell added, "Ballerina Ludmila Tcherina is It with Robert Taylor, and now has a blazing boulder on that tattle-tale finger to verify the speculation here. . . ."

Did Bob give Ludmila an engagement ring, or were gossips fueling fires to sell publicity? For Bob to hastily jump into a relationship with Ludmila would have been odd, especially with his growing attachment to Ursula.

Ludmila and Ursula were almost two different versions of the same woman. European children of the war, each had difficult younger lives. Their physical appearances were hauntingly similar. Both learned to speak English, at least in part, with Bob's help, though that hadn't been his intention, and they'd had previous relationships which ended badly.

No accounts have been found with an exact telling of what Bob felt toward Ludmila, except that she was a lady with whom he enjoyed spending time. He genuinely liked her. Soon after the "blazing boulder" story hit the papers in March, another report said the couple had "a lets-talk-it-over date in London [while] he completes *Eagle on his Cap* at MGM." The same tidbit continued, "They were introduced to each other on Bob's last night in London months ago. When Bob flew back to see her, Ludmilla took a rain check on romance talk, explaining that she was still in mourning for her late husband. . . ."

This alludes to the idea Ludmila broke off their relationship. Meanwhile, stories closer to his personal camp had him pining over Ursula more and more each day. The Ludmila–Bob courtship was a see-saw. She was quoted as saying,

"There is a great friendship between Bob and me and he is so very kind to me. I am still in mourning for my husband. It is only nine months that I lost him."

Columnist Dorothy Kilgallen wrote the next month Bob's "sudden decision to concentrate on Linda Darnell has the Cinemaland gossips confused. Everyone thought he was daffy about ballerina Ludmilla Tcherina." Darnell's name added to the mix may have resulted from a single date, a passing and friendly time in front of cameras, the studio throwing off the scent of his Ludmila/Ursula indecision . . . or to add to the intrigue. His name in gossip columns still sold many movie tickets and fan magazines.

Maybe he and Linda Darnell did have a fling; if they did, it didn't amount to much. By May, Ludmila was in Paris, though as papers said, "not to see Robert Taylor" but to make a film. She was married again by the turn of the New Year, and not to Bob Taylor.

He was again on his way to England in the summer of 1953, this time to film *Knights of the Round Table*. He saw that Ivy had reservations to join him, ostensibly as his secretary but, like the last time, her real purpose was to serve as his sounding board. Bob couldn't decide what he wanted to do about his growing attachment to Ursula. He seemed afraid of his feelings for her, and Ivy was always able to help him make sense of his confusion.

She would take the trip to England when school was out, with the same arrangements as the last time. She would stay in London during the week and on weekends, go to the country and visit her son, her family and her husband.

Bob camped out at his favorite place in England, the Dorchester Hotel. He stayed in his "old stand—Suite 617-8," as he affectionately recalled the room number. Ivy said he "spent most evenings writing letters and fretting about whether Ursula really loved him." Before Ivy could make the journey, Bob, who was already there, bent her ear via the written word.

He joked about the weather. "Come on over; the weather's fine—*TO-*

DAY! It's rained all the past week and will undoubtedly be raining again tomorrow—but *TODAY* it's fine!"

He mentioned his health. "My 'old creaking back,' as you so aptly put it, seems to be on the mend. It was a little troublesome on the boat for a few days but, toward the end of the crossing, seemed to perk up and now is infinitely better."

He talked about the state of the city. "London seems to be going quite mad with preparations for the Coronation." His dislike for crowds was evident. "Spectator's stands are everywhere, even on roofs of buildings and certainly in every nook and cranny along the processional route. I'm almost hopeing [sic] that I will be out of town at that time; it'll be utterly impossible to move!"

And he teased her about how his "sex-life has suffered badly since leaving home." He referenced people he had met during previous visits to the Dorchester. "'Winnie-Poo', my maid—'Ray the Pooh', the valet—and all the floor waiters I previously knew are still here and all asked about you."

But back to his sex life. "Winnie has lost several pounds and, I'm sure, thought I'd insist upon her crawling smack into bed with me. However, she's still not *quite* my type!" He was really feeling lost. "Actually, I may end up with Winnie . . . I have set 'traps' at all the more likely Pubs, Bars, Clubs, Rooming Houses, and intersections but, thus far, nothing's fallen into them. I've obviously lost my touch; either that or the *beard* is scaring everything away!"

He'd started a unique-looking goatee and beard required for his role as *Ivanhoe*. This would be part of his appearance for his entire time in England until filming was over. He was self-conscious and never really comfortable. Ivy often had the opportunity to watch him during a day's work. "The shooting is . . . done in huge fields, and there's a castle made out of papier-mâché!"

When he wasn't in front of the camera, and after Ivy had arrived, they took trips away from the crowds. Ivy and Bob visited a favored spot in Cornwall, enjoying the slower pace and the countryside. They stayed in a cottage, with the host couple doing their best to accommodate the American movie star and his guest.

Ivy called Bob "the easiest person to work with . . . the best boss in the world—and one of the finest people you could wish to meet." This was no surprise considering her job description, and Bob's intense determination to see to her happiness and comfort as much as she was hired to see to his. They told each other everything and trusted each other implicitly. And everyone in each of their respective lives, including her husband, his wife and/or girlfriends, her family, and his mother, they all accepted the relationship between Bob and Ivy as a natural and healthy one.

Bob was physically and materially a self-sufficient man. For the most part, he took care of his own personal correspondence, could type faster and better than Ivy, cook a meal much more palatable than she, and if he were in the mood, iron and wash his own clothes. When he was away, he didn't have a lot of time to do these things, except to write his own correspondence, and his letters were mostly lovesick notes to Ursula. Ivy's presence was a big help in those ways alone, but she earned her salary predominantly as moral support.

When he was on location and she was keeping the home fires burning, she did facilitate facets of life for a man who, while flying from one end of the world to the other, still had the everyday details of living to handle. Without large blocks of time to devote to those details, an assistant was a necessity. Ivy saw to his bills when they came in, knowing what to handle on her own and what to bring to his attention.

One letter from Bob in December of 1953, while he was in Egypt wrapping up *Valley of the Kings* (1954), gave insight into his business mind. "Thanx," he said, "for your letter of December 9th and the many enclosures. The bill from the English tailors will be filed for future reference—glad you didn't send it to the office because I fully intend to 'trim' it slightly before remitting." He paid attention to his affairs but leaned on Ivy to eyeball things, certain she would know what he should handle directly. She processed other issues without his intervention. Morgan Maree handled bigger business matters.

Over and over in his many letters, Bob sang the same sad song Ivy had become used to hearing, one of uncertainty over his relationship with Ur-

**Bob in action on set of *Valley of the Kings*.
Courtesy Robert Taylor Family Private Collection.**

sula. He didn't understand how he could long for her so much. That seemed to really amaze him.

Ivy wrote back, sending pointed, intentional tidbits about Ursula's comings and goings, her dates with other men, and her determination to move on if he wouldn't wholeheartedly commit to her. Ivy's actions were carefully designed to raise his blood pressure, and they worked. "As for any 'off the cuff' news," he told her in one note, "I suppose that's unnecessary and inadvisable. You'd probably tell me about her many new boy-friends and that, strangely enuf, would upset me. And I'm upset enuf by being over *here*, without seeking additional sources of annoyance."

Whether Bob was more intrigued with Ursula, or she with him, is in question but, ultimately, Ursula cried wolf first. Awhile after he had returned to the States, she let Bob know she was ready to be married. If he wasn't, then she'd go elsewhere. He would often say, "If we were to get married...."

Finally, she blew her top. "Bob, I don't want to hear 'if' anymore! Don't talk to me about 'if' anymore. If you say that to me again, I want to hear you say, '*When* we get married.'" This became a growing source of agitation.

Ursula in the early days of her courtship with Bob.

Despite Ursula's impassioned speech, Bob continued to see other women, even as he found himself pining for her late at night, dreaming of her when he went to sleep, and having thoughts of her during the day's work. In another note to Ivy, again on location for a film, he said, "Actually I've missed Ursula more on this trip than I ever have before. And that's not because I've not been 'taken care of' in the romantic way while I've been gone. A little 'location romance' has developed which will end the minute I get home and the only result therefrom has been that I realize more and more what a nice companion Ursula really was."

While in Egypt, Bob was being "'taken care of' in the romantic way" by his leading lady, Eleanor Parker. Ivy said Eleanor would have married Bob "in a minute" if he'd have asked. Unfortunately for her, he had another woman on his mind while he was squiring her around.

There was an exchange in the film between Bob's character, Mark Brandon, and Ann Barclay Mercedes, played by Eleanor. Mark said to her, "You know what they say: Egypt is like a man without a woman."

Ann responded, "Why do they say that?"

His nearly-prophetic reply was, "Hot by day, cold by night."

Bob was not one to be "cold by night" if he had a choice. He made three movies with Eleanor Parker, released

Bob and Eleanor Parker in a scene from *Valley of the Kings.*

between 1952 and 1955. Their "location romance" didn't start with this film, the second of the three, but after he committed to Ursula, his dalliance with Eleanor ended. The last, *Many Rivers to Cross* (1955), debuted after he married Ursula and she would sometimes visit the set.

From looks alone, Eleanor had a similar-to-Barbara Stanwyck appearance. She was blonde, self-assured, and had a take-no-prisoners way about her. One comment on Eleanor's work in *Valley of the Kings* gave an overview. "She emits . . . a source of radiant energy of a young woman who knows exactly where, and with whom, she wants to be. . . ."

The movie was the first ever made on location in Egypt, which was a coup for international business relations between the United States and the Middle East. Filming was done all over the country. Some scenes were staged at the actual spot of discovery of Pharaoh Cheop's funeral boats, where worldwide media excitement had been centered only a few weeks before. Others were done at the site of the Pyramids, with one of Bob's intense fight scenes during the movie's climax filmed atop the statues of Ramses II.

Despite the history around him and the history-in-the-making of which he was a part, Bob had more practical, down-to-earth concerns . . . he had physical issues. His knees were giving him trouble. "It all started, very subtly, while I was hunting up in Canada—then went away and didn't start up again

Ursula visits Bob between takes on the set of *Many Rivers to Cross*. Courtesy Robert Taylor Family Private Collection.

until the first day I worked here and had to jump off a camel several times," he said in a letter to Ivy.

None of this showed in the final film product, but the ailment was threatening his daily movement. ". . . and last Sunday morning, I got up scarcely able to walk. I got to work but, when we finished for the day, I got a Doc from the Anglo-American hospital here who examined me, insisted upon X-Rays, and pronounced my condition as something which sounds more like an Italian Liqueur than a bone ailment . . . 'Pelligrini-Steida's [sic] Disease.'" This was a calcium deposit on the outside edge of a bone in Bob's knee joint. Tendons and nerves rubbing on that joint caused the pain.

True to form, he made a joke of the problem. "Anyhow, for the past four days I've been hobbling about like a tired old character actor. . . ." He went on to say after each day's shooting, he had "deep X-Ray treatments" to dissolve the calcium. After all was done, he'd have to be careful for several weeks but "... it apparently is not serious and is in no way related to arthritis which I originally feared." The problem did turn out to be a form of arthritis and an activity-related injury, something unknown at the time, and in that geographic location. Bob had done the damage on his Canadian hunting trip, but the pain didn't start seriously dogging him until he got to Egypt.

Bob with his ever-present cigarette.

He finished his letter by telling Ivy he had related "all the grizzly facts" to Ursula but "warned her not to mention it to mother" unless, somehow, the newspapers got hold of the news. If that happened, she'd have to know because she would "fret." He asked Ivy to get with Ursula, if needed, and to talk with his mother, "... then you both can give her the details and calm her jangled nerves. You can also assure her that it has nothing to do with '*smoke* and *drink*'!!!!"

Bob's mother was always, always concerned about his smoking. Early on, she foretold of his habit becoming the bane of his existence, certain nothing but harm would come his way because of cigarettes. The ravages of smoking many packs a day, most often unfiltered Camels, had started to show on him. He was physically aging fast. His skin had creased in deepening lines, his posture wasn't as straight, and his voice grew grainier each day.

He also exhibited signs of chronic respiratory problems. Another note to Ivy explained, "The picture, thus far, has been a rough one for me." He was sick with a bronchial infection before he left for the States and attributed the malady to, "... badly heated rooms, poor food, and terribly dry and dirty air...." He related the solution, "... the Doc gave me a gallon or two of penicillin...."

Bob never vocally recognized how these ills could be connected to his smoking. "My cold is gone," he told her, "and all that remains of it is a little cough, the result of a certain amount of drainage from my sinuses... Apparently, despite the dryness of the climate, there's a great amount of dust in the air which irritates and causes the sinusitis. I'll get that fixed up, however, as soon as I get home."

Later on, Bob wrote, "Our hotel accommodations... expire on January 1st so I have a feeling we'll rush through the work...." The shoot was hectic and he was already familiar with the landscape. "The weather in Luxor is invariably fine this time of year," he continued, "so I don't expect we'll be held up there once we get started." Bob said work was "going Okay, although, strangely enuf, we're having more trouble getting sunshine here than we did in Cairo." Still, they managed to keep to schedule. "I think," he added, "we can finish by the 1st if nothing more serious than a few clouds crops up to bother us."

He was anxious to get back. Such a trip was not a fast journey in those days. "I'll be out of here as quickly as possible and will only be stopping en route home long enough to rest up overnite in Rome, Paris, N.Y. and then good ole L.A. It's just too rough a trip if you try to do it all at once." He interjected a bit about the European political scene. "Paris is now on 'strike'—nothing going in or out of there—so we may have to bypass it and go either via Lisbon or London—won't know until almost time to leave."

Health concerns continued to dog him. "The leg is still bothering me considerably and I'm not at all certain that an accurate diagnosis has really been made ... I seem to have very little strength in the joint. My personal theory is that there's a slight dislocation of some kind which can only be remedied by manipulation." This harkened back to his experience as the son of an osteopath. "That, too, I'll investigate when I get home."

The separation from Ursula had been a good thing for him. By Christmas, she was all he could think of, and he asked Ivy to help him get her a special present. "I'm enclosing a card and a personal check," he wrote. "Would you please take it to a very, very good florist and have a beautiful basket or something made up for her at Xmas time. I'd even prefer that you take it out to her *yourself,* if you have time!" He started cajoling. "Wouldja? Couldja? And make it as nice as possible."

He warned her, "That's about the only plans I have for Xmas so don't you and mother be disappointed at not getting presents—willya? I'll see if I can't remedy it all when I get home." Bob still took care of his women. While he felt the responsibility, he also found deep satisfaction in knowing he was their provider and their protector. He was again able to afford this role without any financial stress, and that felt good to him.

The shoot was finally finished on elaborate MGM soundstages. In assessments many years afterward, *Valley of the Kings* was credited as the precursor to the likes of *Indiana Jones and Raiders of the Lost Ark*. Bob played a macho, outdoorsy character similar to Indiana Jones.

Bob and Ursula continued to play hide-and-seek or, more accurately, he hid and she sought. As time went on, she barely put up with him. He was on and off the road, and she worked on her own burgeoning career. In 1952 she was in *Monsoon*. The Golden Globe Awards voted Bob, along with Alan Ladd, male "World Film Favorite."

One day, Ivy received a phone call from Ursula, who had tears in her voice. "Can you come over here?" she begged Ivy, who dropped everything and went to her friend. She found her amidst an organized pile of items given to her by Bob. "Please take these away," Ursula requested. "Give them back to him." Ivy solemnly collected the gifts and brought them to Bob's house.

When he returned in January of 1953, Ivy let him know Ursula was through with him. Their on again-off again relationship was off, for good, unless he could figure out a way to finally make a commitment.

The biggest impediment to marriage for Bob this time around was similar to the problem he'd had with Barbara: Ursula would come into their union with two children. Her son and daughter had already had a tough life in their short years. They were raised in war-torn Europe. Ursula, like Bob, also had a mother to financially care for, and her mother was, at best, a difficult woman.

Ursula in *Monsoon* (1952).

The kids had been left with their grandmother for long periods of time, away from their mother, and the separation hadn't been easy on them.

Once Ursula was discovered by Howard Hughes and sent to America, her time away from her children lengthened. She had plans to bring them over, but that required money and time, as well as a lot of governmental red tape. She lived in the States, returning to Germany as often as she could. All the while, her professional and personal life became a whirl of activity. She was suddenly famous and sought-after, and had regular movie work. Not only cameras and film beckoned, but so did men.

She had more attention than she could handle. She was still being called, "The Most Beautiful Woman in the World," and the weight of such a lofty title, coupled with her family responsibilities, became a burden she no longer wanted to handle on her own. Her on-again-off-again courtship with Bob needed an adjustment. Ursula wanted stability, and her children deserved nothing less.

Bob became moody for a few weeks, knowing he had to propose marriage to Ursula, or say goodbye. She would accept nothing less. If he was going to continue to play the field, his days with Ursula were over. Did he want that? Did he really want his freedom? Or did he want her and a family?

Bob proposed to Ursula in April. She showed up at the studio wearing an engagement ring, and they made a public announcement when they celebrated at lunch in the MGM cafeteria. Bob said he "wanted to tell the world she belongs to me." He added, "Ursula and I have been considering marriage for some time . . . We have set no definite date for the wedding because she has film commitments and I have to do another picture after I finish my current assignment."

He was engrossed in her beauty, but he finally had to admit to himself her down-to-earth personality was what really attracted him, and her standoffishness during the last part of their courtship kept him coming back. During his time of introspection, he continually returned to the fact he couldn't see himself living the rest of his life without her. His decision came down to that one final thought.

This all meant he had to now figure out how to be a father. Manuela had come to the United States the year before to meet Bob, to make sure they could get along. She didn't know the language, and was accustomed to a female-driven household. Staying with her grandmother while her mother

Bob and Ursula. Courtesy Robert Taylor Family Private Collection.

was away, Manuela had done her best to take care of herself and her brother, and when necessary, her grandmother. She was an uncertain young girl eager to learn how to relate to her new father figure.

Except for Ivy's son, who hadn't really lived in Bob's home, and for whom he had never had real responsibility, Manuela was the first child in

**Ursula and young Manuela, before Ursula left Germany.
Courtesy Robert Taylor Family Private Collection.**

Bob's life since Barbara's adopted son. Children in his house were a disruption to his well-planned lifestyle.

Bob was strict. He had rules in place and expected them to be followed. He had been brought up that way, and in his mind children were supposed to be compliant. He had been obedient and had never given his parents any arguments or disagreements. That was what he knew of the experience between adults and young people. That was how he figured he should operate with Ursula's kids.

His plan, however, didn't work with Manuela from the start, and Bob was at a loss as to how to settle this. He was overly generous, showering her with gifts at the beginning of their relationship, and continuing for birthdays and holidays. This was how he showed affection; he wasn't comfortable with fatherly sorts of physical or emotional exhibitions. Taking her fishing and flying was his way of trying to share his life with her.

"He was very kind," Manuela said. "Even when we went fishing. He wanted me to take the hook out of the fish carefully, and then whack it over the head quickly, so it didn't suffer. He was always concerned about suffering."

In return for his efforts, Bob wanted obedience out of Manuela, but he soon found out that one behavior didn't necessarily follow the other. Manuela was later to comment on his generosity, his honesty, his strong beliefs, and his good heart, but she also admitted that for quite some time, they had a rocky connection. He was stern and unbending. She said of herself she had been "hard to like," an unfortunate commentary for a young girl thrown into a world she didn't necessarily understand.

As the adult, Bob was at the helm of their burgeoning father/daughter connection, and he certainly realized he had to take the reins. He was willing to make the effort, but didn't know how. Ursula was a good mother, and he wanted to show her how, together, they could work through this.

He was impressed with her skills in the kitchen and the house; she was a master at the art of homemaking. Nothing made Ursula happier than to be able to cook her family a good meal and have them around the table together. In an interview years later, Bob told columnist Hy Gardner, "I found she could cook. When I courted her at first I'd bring the vittles up to her tiny place and we'd let down our hair," the next words were pointedly to the reporter, "without you column fellows reporting every move."

They married on May 24, 1954, in a semi-secret ceremony at picturesque Jackson Lake, Wyoming, at the base of the 13-thousand foot high Teton Mountains. The wedding took place aboard Jess and John Wort's cabin cruiser in the middle of the lake. The Wort brothers were local hotel operators, and Bob regularly stayed at their place. One brother told the press they were "old friends and old fishing partners."

Bob was totally at home in the area. Justice of the Peace Russell Robinson performed the ceremony. By design, the only witnesses were Ivy and Ralph. The party had flown into Wyoming from Los Angeles the day before.

The newly-married couple had a one-night honeymoon before Bob re-

Bob and Ursula, Mr. and Mrs. Robert Taylor, after their wedding.
Courtesy Robert Taylor Family Private Collection.

Bob and Ursula, with friends Ivy Pearson and Ralph Couser, after their wedding.

ported to Cloverdale, California, the next day, to start a new project, a Western titled *Many Rivers To Cross*. Ursula had no assignment at that point and she accompanied him. He did an article for the UP, the occasion being his flight to Cloverdale, in which he discussed his love of flying. The rest of the film crew, "some 100 strong," was on chartered flights. He and Ursula flew in his plane. He remarked, ". . . a recent check of my flying log showed that since World War II I have covered more than 300,000 trouble free miles in my own plane. . . ."

His love affair with being in the air had not ended. ". . . Flying a private plane gives a man a pleasant respite from timetables. You take off when you are ready. Many private pilots I know look upon a plane as just another car—with wings. The romance and adventure which once went with the open cockpit and goggles have been replaced by speed, safety and comfort." That his new wife enjoyed this with him was the icing on the cake. He had never been able to share this part of his life with Barbara.

In October of 1954, Ursula was in *The Iron Glove* with Robert Stack. December saw her in *Bengal Bride* with Arlene Dahl and Rock Hudson. Press reports called her "the highly publicized European star," and said she lived up to her "advance heralding." Various European film organizations avowed she was "the woman with the most beauti-

Ursula plays female lead opposite Robert Stack in *The Iron Glove* (1954).

ful eyes in the world." Her gray-green eyes caught the attention of *Bengal Bride*'s cinematographer. He said of her, "This girl can do more with the flicker of an eyelash than a lot of actresses can do with a full shot in Technicolor and dressed in a Bikini bathing suit."

The Americano hit the screen in early 1955 with Glenn Ford and "exotic Ursula Thiess." The movie was filmed the latter half of the previous year in South America against the "savage and scenic splendor of Brazil's Matto Grosso jungle." The experience was a rugged one, and Bob wasn't happy with his wife being gone, or with her living and working in such difficult conditions.

Much of his concern was because Ursula found herself pregnant with his first natural-born child during the last months of that year. He couldn't have been prouder when on June 16, 1955, she delivered a seven pound, eleven ounce son. They named him Terence, and called him Terry. Bob decided, and Ursula agreed, she would stop work and stay home with the children. Some reports stated, ". . . we might as well call her Mrs. Taylor because that's apparently who she's going to be." Ursula laughed, "Now Bob says I'll be doing pictures only if it's something I really want to do, if he thinks it's worthwhile and if it doesn't involve a location."

Terry Taylor about four years old.
Courtesy author's
personal collection.

Terry was born into a secure household, and that his arrival coincided with the next chapter in the life of his half-brother, Michael Thiess, was not intentional. Terry was entering a family structure free of baggage and into the eagerly-awaiting arms of a father who had never known such a thrill. Michael would come into the same family, but as an outsider desperately wanting to be accepted. He was leaving a life that may not have been the best, but was the only life he'd ever known. The mother they shared was soon to become an American citizen, and she was the glue between them . . . the cohesive hold that would hopefully bring them all together. As soon as Michael came to the United States, this new chapter could begin.

While recuperating from an emergency appendectomy before leaving Germany, Michael received regular letters from his mother and sister, sometimes photographs of Manuela enjoying the wonders of her new life. One such set of pictures showed "Daddy, (Bob) and Dickilein," a nickname for Manuela, beaming over a fish she had caught with his help. The caption written on the back in German by Ursula said, "How nice it will be when you can join us fishing."

Late 1955 finally brought Michael to the States to live. Since he was fourteen days old, he had been raised primarily by his grandmother. They had a "dreary two-room flat." As soon as he knew his new home would be with his mother, his sister, a new brother, and his new "daddy," in a big house in a new country, he started worrying. With all the innocent fear of an uncertain young boy, he asked, "Do you think Robert Taylor will like me?"

He and Bob had never met, and the whole concept was frightening for a nine-year old child who not only didn't speak the language, but had never stepped foot on American soil. Neither had he any remote way of knowing what life would be like as the child of a world-famous movie star. His mother had tried to bring him to California the year before, but according to his grandmother, "Michael became so upset at the thought of leaving me that he almost suffered a nervous breakdown."

Most people believed Ursula's mother had deep-seated emotional issues. In fairness to her and Michael, she had raised him, and though he well knew his mother, his grandmother had been the only steady presence in his life. He called her "Omi," and often said he would never leave her. How much was encouraged by Omi is not known, who stated in a magazine article how Michael had "spent his whole life" with her, and "when my daughter arrives I will tell her the truth. I do not think that the child will go off to America without me." She continued, "I merely want to help Michael get adjusted. You have no idea what a sensitive artistic boy he is."

That one comment proved to be prophetic and painfully-true. Once Michael was in the country and settled into life as Robert Taylor's stepson, a title the press seemed determined to hang on him every time his name was mentioned, he tried hard to assimilate, but he was clearly troubled. The emotional hurt was engrained in him long before he became a part of Bob's family.

Now a bona fide father, Bob started to see himself as a husband and a family man. He had not only a mother to support, but a wife and young children who depended on him for everything. This weighed heavily on his mind; paradoxically, it also energized him. He began what was probably his most creative period in the mid-1950s, particularly in the professional choices he made, and the roles he accepted. His pictures were stronger, and they had a depth his work had previously been missing. He felt complete, both personally and professionally.

Quite possibly, the most striking role of his entire career came in 1956 when he took on the part of Charley in *The Last Hunt* (1956). Up to then, he had moved between the happy-go-lucky upper class gentleman and the gritty frontiersman. This role was a characterization of the sort Bob had never portrayed. Charley was a psychopath, a sadistic, kill-crazed, demented, immoral man. The movie was a shock to Bob's dedicated viewing public. Reviews said the story was "not for the squeamish," and "it might be Taylor's best performance ever." The role allowed him the freedom to show how good an actor he could be, and he submersed himself in the idiosyncrasies of Charley's character.

Prior to the start of filming, he had returned from England and France, where he wrapped *Quentin Durward* (1955), a movie he considered a flop. *The Last Hunt* was on location in the Black Hills and Badlands of South Dakota. To work in the vast countryside was another draw for Bob. Wide open spaces signified freedom for him.

The storyline told of the last chapter in the history of the American West, when bison roamed free and were hunted and ultimately wiped out. Bob couldn't resist the chance to play such an against-type role. This was a man's movie and the production company, made up of 167 men, proved that. There was only one woman in the cast. Debra Paget played the love interest between

**Bob behind scenes of *The Last Hunt*.
Courtesy Robert Taylor Family Private Collection.**

Bob's character and his nemesis, Stewart Granger, the good guy in the story. Charley was a kill-hardened shell of a man who had no real human contact in his life, except for a ragtag bunch he had put together to go on one last buffalo hunt. He relished killing the animals . . . and the Indians. He was cruel to the animals, to the natives, to his companions, and even to the woman who tried to get close to him. The man, Bob Taylor, was none of these things, and to act the part realistically, he had to pull from somewhere deep within.

Scenes of buffaloes being hunted and slaughtered were real. The production was filmed during the annual thinning of the protected herd at Custer State Park in South Dakota. MGM took a chance on this, and on Bob in the starring role, and the result was startling. The realism gave the picture a graphic quality uncommon in Hollywood productions.

Bob's interpretation of Charley surprised everyone, opening another chapter in his acting career. By this time, Louis B. Mayer was no longer at the helm, and Dore Schary held MGM's reins. He and Bob had a much different relationship, and Schary didn't have the "soft gentleman's image" of him Mayer had never relinquished. Bob's work, particularly in Westerns, took on a hard edge, and he was happy with the results.

In 1957, Bob and Ralph Couser decided to terminate their contractual relationship with MGM. For personal reasons, Ralph gave up his job as Bob's personal pilot, though the two men remained close friends and Ralph recommended a man named Hal Bowen to take his place. Hal had been flying out of Santa Monica, working for Wade Air Service as a charter pilot, ferry pilot, and flight instructor. He and Ralph were acquainted through Santa Monica Aviation, and though he had never met Bob, Hal knew of Ralph's association with him and MGM.

Hal's first flight with Ralph was on September 3, 1957. They flew Bob to Sheridan, Wyoming, left him there, and returned to Santa Monica. The trip was uneventful except that Hal now worked for Robert Taylor, the movie star. They started an alliance which endured to the end of Bob's life.

Hal flew Bob somewhere nearly every week in "Old Betsy," his Twin Beech airplane. Most of the trips were to Sheridan. On their second visit together, Bob invited him to stay at the ranch, but ever the professional, Hal preferred to be in town, close to the plane. He wasn't comfortable with the distance involved between the two locations. That plane was his responsibility, something Bob understood and respected. Bob knew Hal took his job seriously, and he never again offered him the chance to bunk at the ranch.

According to Hal, Bob rarely flew the plane solo, maybe no more than every three months. He did, however, always sit in the co-pilot's seat, called the "right" seat. They would take turns with the dual controls. Though he was piloting the plane with less frequency, Bob's flying skills remained excellent. When he chose to take the left seat, the pilot's chair, he was at the top of his game in much the same way he had been in the days when he taught flying.

Both men were smokers, and the cockpit, according to Hal, "was always full of cigarette smoke." Hal thought Ursula was "very sweet and charming," and if she was onboard, Bob sat in the cabin part-time with her and the other time he spent in the cockpit. Rarely did anyone else fly with them. Only occasionally was there a studio representative along.

There were many reasons why Bob may not have been the pilot-in-command during these flights. He was still a star and, as such, a financial commodity for MGM. Since the studio had a hand in the fact that Bob had the plane, they most certainly laid the ground rules. Insurance concerns were the major culprit, and at all times, he was required to have a current license, regular physician exams, multi-engine ratings, and ninety-day currency ratings. This added a lot to his already-filled schedule. By maintaining a regular pilot on staff, Bob had the best of both worlds. He was still a part of flying the plane, which freed him from having to take commercial flights, especially on professional trips where the schedule would be tight and hectic. At the same time, there was independence in having his own plane, and the chance to fly without maintaining government-regulated requirements appealed to him.

Bob and Ursula bought their first and only permanent home together in 1958 in Mandeville Canyon. Over one hundred acres of land became the ranch Bob had always wanted, his own property where he could roam, keep animals, and be king of his kingdom. He lived as a gentleman rancher, finding peace with his horses, hens, dogs, and other assorted creatures. He raised Australorps, a hearty black chicken originally imported from Australia, for their eggs and firm meatiness. He'd fly Old Betsy to Murray McMurray Hatchery in Webster City, Iowa, to buy chickens. He was a stickler for fresh eggs, and though the trip was expensive, the eggs and the chance to fly were worth the cost.

The sprawling but unpretentious traditional-style ranch house was eleven thousand square feet, designed by architect Robert Byrd, and sitting

The Taylor home on Mandeville Canyon Road in Los Angeles.

at the foot of the Santa Monica Mountains. Tall eucalyptus trees framed the front and were allowed to grow without being trimmed. The circular driveway made up much of the front yard, which didn't sit too far off the street behind a gate and a fence. A small swimming pool and a boat-playhouse were in the backyard, mostly for the children. Other outbuildings were on the grounds. Well-manicured yards and extensive paved riding trails covered the back of the property where the wild, overgrown southern California brush hills created an idyllic backdrop to Bob and Ursula's paradise.

This was his pure heaven. He and his family rode the hills, on any given day seeing deer, coyote, rabbits, mountain lions or bobcats. They swam in the pool, and ate many dinners on the back deck. His life was filled with good food, children, holidays and traditions, and he was finally creating memories he would pass down to the next generation.

Their home was near that of Ronnie and Nancy Reagan, Bob and Ursula's closest friends. Bob now lived a pseudo-private life, going out in the public only occasionally. He and his wife would invite friends over for an evening of barbecuing, drinks on the patio, sharing current lives and details on the world around them, and the comfort of similar pasts. These were

**Ursula, Bob, Ronnie and Nancy Reagan
celebrating Ronnie's birthday.**

some of Bob and Ursula's happiest recreational moments.

Hal Bowen would still come to the house and help with chores when an extra hand was needed. He installed light fixtures, upholstered new bar stools, and once supervised the building and the work for a "very elaborate trailer" carrying Bob's hunting dogs on trips. Occasionally, he would share a meal with Bob and Ursula, or have a drink at Bob's beloved bar. "Bob was a gracious host," he said, "but early in the evening he would retire, saying, 'You folks enjoy yourselves, I'm going to bed . . . see ya later,' and he'd leave."

By the early 1960s, Bob and Hal were seeing less of each other. They continued to share the occasional phone call, and Hal received interesting "colorful" letters, "all neatly typed." Their friendship was solid, but Bob had become more and more of a homebody. He had everything he needed right there, and unless he had an assignment and had to go out on location, he was where he wanted to be.

CHAPTER FIFTEEN:

Family Life . . . Finally

"I see no reason why an actor *shouldn't* go into politics."
– Robert Taylor

The 1960s found life truly changing, not only for Bob, but for the world all around him, as well. The movie industry had become drastically different. In a letter to a Nebraska newspaperman, Bob said, "The Motion Picture business in this country is in one Helluva bad condition . . . Costs of making films have risen to a prohibitive 'high,' due to a lot of causes, and entirely too many pictures are now being make [sic] in Europe at much lower prices. I don't see the end of the dilemma."

Bob had his last contact with MGM in 1958, and then the studio system became part of his past. The organized, official "studio system" itself was no more, disintegrating into days gone by for everyone who had ever worked in films.

"There was a 'style' in living and making motion pictures . . . [it] has been coldly modernized into something very factual, very efficient—and, I'm afraid, not much fun." Bob went on to say that making movies had become all about a group of people ". . . working for themselves on a one-picture-every-two-years basis."

In 1961, with outstanding contractual obligations to MGM fully satisfied, their airplane agreement with Bob was terminated. He and Hal got together and bought the plane at a reasonable price, making Old Bessie his and Hal's without outside interference. The arrangement was half-and-half, and when they weren't flying, they offered their investment for charter through Wade Air Service at Santa Monica. For liability reasons and partnership clarification, Bob's business office set up a corporation called Bowlor, a combination of Bowen and Taylor.

They continued this way for another year, at which point they decided to sell Old Bessie. Bob had diminished use for the plane for many reasons. Hal's other business matters didn't allow him to take proper care of her, and keeping the plane outside wasn't good for the value. There was no longer a profitable, or logical, reason to keep her. This signified the end of another era for Bob, speaking directly to his age and changing lifestyle.

He went through a good amount of soul-searching. Studio days were over, he'd gotten rid of his beloved plane, and he was experiencing a new way of life. On being a MGM star, Bob said, "I was part of the MGM 'stable.' We called Metro the campus—and even the seasons became semesters. Camaraderie was shared at work and at play, up and down the line . . . We associated with each other in those days for fun—not just publicity. The Trocadero was the Clubhouse. . . ." As for his long-term boss, "There was nothing predictable, except perhaps sunrises and L. B. Mayer—and not necessarily in that order. . . ."

He ran down a list of the Who's Who of Acting. "Wallace Beery was special; he'd upstage his own mother, but was always a warm, loyal friend . . . Lionel Barrymore had forgotten more about acting than most of us would ever know . . . Jean Harlow, despite some . . . unkind publicity, was a wonderful gal. The studio sent her and me to the first President's Birthday Ball for the March of Dimes . . . off we went, riding with J. Edgar Hoover in a bulletproof limousine, and escorted by screaming motorcycles expertly ridden by State Troopers. It was exciting. . . .

"And good old Gary Cooper—'Coop' to just about everyone, whether they knew him or not. To my way of thinking Coop was the handsomest man—and certainly one of the two or three best actors—ever to honor the ranks of the motion picture business. And one of the most beautiful and talented ladies ever to grace a motion picture screen—Vivien Leigh."

After all that had been between them, he had only good things to say about the last person on his list, his ex-wife. "... Wonderful Barbara Stanwyck, one of the finest actresses in show business. A lot of young actors and actresses could have profited then and now from a few 'seminars' with 'Missy' on their professional attitudes—their regard for the business of being an actor—on their on-stage and off-stage deportment as it were—because I doubt that there ever has been, or ever will be, a greater 'pro' than Barbara."

Bob knew full well the old way of making movies was gone. Another of his letters told that, "... the motion picture business is not, at the moment, one of the most thriving industries in our country. Costs of production, via Union demands, and taxes, have made it almost impossible to create a good picture at a price from which any net profits can be expected ... As a result money for production purposes is scarce. The big studios, which were at one time our main source of production money, are known largely as rental organizations—and distribution agencies—and the Banks do most of the financing ... With them it's strictly a matter of dollars and cents—which motion picture making has never been and will never *be*!"

He understood the ins-and-outs of not only the acting side of his business, but also the production side. His words showed his intimate awareness of the technical side of moviemaking, as well as how unions figured into the evolution. He revealed that he'd been paying attention all those years, even if he hadn't seemed to be, and always had said he wasn't.

Robert Taylor Productions formed in 1958 to organize incoming opportunities so he would have a place to put his money, offering a viable avenue through which that money would make more for him. The company would also give him a steady hand in the direction of his career, something he had little of during studio days.

Bob made some memorable pictures during the transition and directly after the end of his MGM contract. He needed the kickstand punched out from under him to solidly stand on his own and believe in his worth as a talented actor, and to realize he was a truly viable, bankable talent. He started to

**Bob as Tommy Farrell in *Party Girl* with Cyd Charisse.
Courtesy author's personal collection.**

believe he had the ability to carry a character, and he also realized his aptitude as a businessman made him capable of steering the direction of his future.

One outstanding role for which he received a considerable amount of public acclaim, if not critical attention, was *Party Girl* (1958), his last MGM film. Bob shared the screen with Cyd Charisse and Lee J. Cobb, playing an attorney who made his living defending crooks and underworld figures. The character, Thomas "Tommy" Farrell, was crippled as a child and walked with difficulty, using a cane. He believed he could do no better in life because of his handicap. He quietly accepted his place in the human food chain, until a lovely dancer came into his life. She made him see he had more to offer, and could rise above the seamier side.

Bob and Cyd Charisse in *Party Girl*.

The script might have been trite if not for Lee J. Cobb's performance as the cruel gangster, the antithesis of everything Farrell would like to be; as well as the striking way Bob played the tortured, blemished lawyer. After having a career which had relied almost solely on his physical image through the motivation of MGM's star machine, the part of Tommy Farrell gave Bob the opportunity to crawl out from underneath his striking features. He gave a performance which in many ways went against everything his "pretty boy" persona had ever done for him.

Farrell wasn't by any means unattractive, but his handicap, not only physical but solidly psychological, made him a man used to being behind the scenes. This concept was one Bob really bit into, and which he played to the hilt. He was most often personally comfortable behind the scenes, and he took this part of Farrell's psyche to heart. His portrayal made the character intrinsically, appealingly human.

He had a formula to decide how to pick his projects. "The play's the thing," he stated. "The one thing I don't look for is Robert Taylor stories. I fit myself to the part, not the part to me." This became fully evident after twenty-four years when he stepped out from behind MGM's shadow. As Bob drove away from MGM for the last time, the longest-held contract actor of the official studio system, one of the few remaining senior executives said, "In all the years he worked on this lot, he never once behaved like an actor."

During his down time after leaving MGM, Bob made more and more trips to Wyoming. He loved the peace and beauty, and he and Ursula bought property. They brought the family out when his schedule permitted. Bob said, "The elk and deer come down almost into your front porch and the people in the area are wonderful."

The Taylors became a common sight in and around town, and they were treated like locals. Bob especially liked that he was not fawned over. "The hunters and fishermen couldn't care less about my being a movie star. Sport is their primary interest . . . no one comes up to talk about a movie he saw me in." He frequented the local Elks Club for lunch and companionship, and an elderly lady in town escorted Ursula to Penney's to buy sheets and towels. Her daughter was "mortified" that her mother took Robert Taylor's wife to such a common store, but Ursula was charmed.

Another person recalled meeting Bob at the Elks Club where his mother worked. He was a young man dressed like a cowboy, upset he didn't have a bolo tie. He admired Bob's, intently telling him how much he liked the style. Several days later, his mother came home and handed her son a bolo tie made from a deer antler.

She smiled before speaking to her son. "Mr. Taylor told me to give the tie to the 'tie-less cowboy.'"

Once the townsfolk realized how much a "regular guy" this movie star was, a man who dressed and comported himself as if he were nothing more than another local rancher, he was enveloped into their scene. Bob and some of his neighbors would have coffee together in the morning at the Post Office Coffee Shop.

His hobby was to write letters, and he wrote to people for almost any reason and sometimes for no reason; everyone and anyone he met and with whom he became friends got letters from him. Sometimes even strangers, before they became bona fide friends, were his favorite correspondents. His new coffee buddies received letters when he went overseas to do a film. One note complained about local coffee, and in response the guys sent him a pound of American beans, a gesture which delighted him.

He was in awe of the rough Wyoming land. Bob needed to be comfortable and in wide-open surroundings. He was "just another cowboy" as he visited the coffee shop, the Elks Club, the bakery or the grocery store. The environment offered him a sense of peace and anonymity he hadn't known since fame had started following his every move.

Bob made investments in Wyoming in May of 1954, prior to his marriage to Ursula. He knew then, as he was about to enter another union, he would need a diversified portfolio under his belt. He was going to have to support not only a new wife, but with Manuela and Michael, a family.

He had partial interest in an oil well showing "signs of producing more than 50 barrels an hour." Near Newcastle, a town on the old Cheyenne-Deadwood stagecoach trail, the field was 7,130 feet high in the mountains in what was called The Black Thunder area, and Bob and his partner, Maurice Yates of Salt Lake City, started a "10-well drilling program." This was one more indication of how much Bob had going on behind the scenes. He didn't let his celebrity slide him along through life.

In between and here and there, Bob did a few pictures in Europe. He had to pay the mortgage, take care of his mother and send his kids to school, and schooling now included Terry. One other big chunk of his income still went to Barbara. Their divorce settlement had not changed, still requiring him to fork over fifteen percent of his annual income until the day she remarried, or the day she died. He wasn't about to let this or anything else get in the way of him ensuring a comfortable lifestyle for his family.

Throughout, the greatest constant for Bob was his hometown of Beatrice. He made more trips back there after his MGM days, when he was able to be a better master of his time. He often stayed at The Paddock Hotel, a Beatrice landmark right in the center of town. If he went without the family and had made the trip by private plane, he usually arrived with Ralph. They stayed on the fifth floor, getting adjoining rooms with a balcony. Paddock management ensured the entire floor was blocked from other patrons. Bob and Ralph would often request meal trays sent to their rooms. Occasionally they would venture into the hotel's coffee shop, always later in the day to ensure the least amount of traffic. When they left the hotel on their way out of town, they exited out the back door because there was usually a standing crowd waiting for Bob and his party at the front.

Bob Marvin, who wrote a column for the *Beatrice Daily Sun*, became one of Bob's regular correspondents. In 1963, after a copy of the newspaper was sent to him at home in California by a friend, Bob sent in his money for a subscription. He included a note to Marvin, reminiscing over his love for his home state. Reading the *Daily Sun*, he said, gave him a "lump right where it's hardest to swallow." He told the columnist "what the people back home think has always been a very important thing to me—and many a time a decision on my part has been influenced largely by what I figgered my old friends and associates back in Nebraska would think of it." He added he'd always felt "the best people in the country either lived in or came from that part of the USA."

His words summed up what spurred him on in virtually everything he had ever done as a public figure. The subscription gave him a direct lifeline back home, and offered him a way to have the "early evening porch chats" he had known he would miss many years before when he left Nebraska for California. He read those papers from first to last page, every word, often going to his typewriter to jot off a note to nearly anyone whose story caught his eye, or who gave him the slightest glimpse into his past.

Armand Deutsch once said, "There certainly was no such thing as a Robert Taylor until he was invented. Spangler Arlington Brugh, not Robert

Family Life ... Finally

The Paddock Hotel, now an assisted living facility in Beatrice, Nebraska.

Taylor, was born in 1911 in Nebraska. His roots were deep and his values were set long before his good looks came to the attention of talent scouts and he made the transition to Robert Taylor, California resident and film star. The transplantation never really took with Bob...."

Whether he was called Arlington Brugh, or Robert Taylor, Bob was a Midwesterner at heart. According to Ivy, mirroring Deutsch's words, one had to only look into the collective conservative and "of the earth" Nebraska mindset to understand Bob and why he was the man he became. He held onto a no-nonsense lack of flamboyance, strict values governing how he handled his marriage and raised his family, and hard-core right-wing political views. All of this was easily traceable back to the state in which he was born and bred, a state of mind he never really left, and a place in his heart as much as a physical place in his beloved United States.

The adulation which had been shown Bob over the many years by fawning females was turned around on him on the evening of August 16, 1959, when he became the father of a seven-pound, four-ounce girl. He and Ursula named her Tessa. Bob called her his "Puss Face," and he became the most pliable father the world had seen, a Robert Taylor no one had ever known or expected. He was awestruck. She was a precious and adorable blonde-haired child, and all she had to do was upturn her picture-perfect face and clear blue eyes, so much like his, to her "Ol' Dad," a name he had started calling himself, and she won. No arguments. Manuela said he treated her like a "delicate little flower," and he "couldn't get enough of her."

Bob with young Tessa. Courtesy author's personal collection.

Christmas was always a big thing in the Taylor household. Bob's dad had played the role of Santa Claus from Bob's youngest years until he was old enough to know the truth, and Bob carried on the tradition with his kids. The house would look like a holiday wonderland. As he said, "Ursula has been decorating, and bakeing [sic] cookies and cakes . . . our home is beginning to take on a very festive appearance." When the Christmas season rolled around every year, the stage was set at Bob's place.

Ursula was "Mutti," an affectionate German name for the family mother. She would cook a big meal, and they would sit down at the elaborate, elegantly-set table. Bob was at one end, she was at the other, with the children surrounding them. Their holiday feast always included Bob's mother and Ivy, and as the years went on, her family members, as well as other close friends. The affair showed off Bob's role as a "family man" to the hilt.

At some point during the happy after-dinner conversation, once their stomachs were full, Bob would excuse himself to go out to the barn. A

Ursula—her favorite role was as Mrs. Robert Taylor.

little while later, the front door intercom would ring. As Ursula responded to the buzz, jingling bells sounded from the other end, along with a boisterous "Ho, ho, ho!" Then the door opened, and in came Santa with bags and bags ... and bags of presents.

The children fell for the good-natured ploy every time. Manuela was already aware who was behind the Santa suit, and when Terry became old enough, he also kept the secret and played along. In the mix were Tessa, Michael, and Ivy's son, Mike, who had finally come to the States to live with his mother after his father died. The one who likely enjoyed the tradition most, though, was Bob. His Santa suit got at least as much use as any other costume in the history of his acting career, and this role was his favorite.

Bob made his first television appearance as a guest on a show called *The Thin Man*. Afterward he vehemently stated, "This is my first and last TV appearance. I don't like the medium. Can't say that I enjoy watching it, either."

He soon ate those words. Bob allowed a TV show to be created especially for him when the direction of film obviously started moving away from old-school moviemaking. He saw that he would need to start making more varied professional decisions, and he offhandedly commented in an article, "What can I lose by getting my feet wet?" He had come to realize how good TV could be for his finances. When asked by a reporter why he changed his tune, he replied honestly, "The motivation is a five-letter word pronounced m-o-n-e-y. If you get the right vehicle, TV is a harmless and lucrative racket."

Another reason he had stayed away from the small screen was an edict from Louis B. Mayer years before whom, Bob said, "had the foresight to think that television would ever be a threat to movies." Mayer had a clause inserted in Bob's last contract forbidding him from doing TV work. When the contract ended, his responsibility to Mayer's concerns also stopped.

An interesting project came Bob's way for the 1958 to 1959 television season. The plan was for an anthology series focusing on the development of the United States defense system. The title was to be *The Price of Peace* but, for whatever reason, the project never panned out.

The Detectives (1959), however, was written for him, and proved to be the "right vehicle." Conceived soon after Bob's break with MGM, the show ran ninety-seven episodes, into 1962. A half-hour sponsored by The Procter & Gamble Company, and increased to sixty minutes for the last thirty episodes, the show went through a change in names along the way, from *The Detectives*, *The Detectives Starring Robert Taylor*, and finally ending as *Robert Taylor's The Detectives*.

Bob during *The Detectives* period.
Courtesy Robert Taylor Family
Private Collection.

Bob found TV work relatively easy compared to films. He enjoyed being able to pick up a script, memorize his lines and action, and go in and do his job, then go home. Once the show caught on, he planned to "sit back and deposit residuals without ever having to look" at himself on the screen. He was again clear in his mind about why he was doing the show. The money wasn't really the only deciding factor; the lifestyle the work afforded him and his family drew him in to the new medium. "I work so many weeks, spend the day shooting, learn my funny jokes at night for the next day's filming and go to bed. Then I take a week or two off and go hunting."

His production schedule was, these days, arranged around his recreation. Bob was always most at ease with a gun or a fishing rod in his hand, and his calendar made certain when duck shooting season opened, he was not in the studio. "I can never get enough hunting, fishing, or loafing."

Bob had paid his dues. Loafing was something to which most now considered him entitled. He had spent nearly twenty-five years in the business, and made almost seventy films. There were few years at any point in his career not attributed to a movie release with his name in the starring role. He was hardly loafing.

The ranch was a handful, and with his busy professional schedule requiring him to sometimes be away from home, Bob had to hire help. Jim Burk worked for him while he also carried on an acting and stunt career. John Wayne was preparing to film *The Horse Soldiers* (1959) and Jim was hired as his stuntman. This took him away from Bob, who began interviewing to refill the position. Jim suggested Art Reeves, a horseman he knew and trusted. Art was working on "Wild Bill" Elliott's ranch, and living in the bunkhouse with a number of other ranch hands when Jim asked him to interview for the job. Art went to talk with Bob. He got there in time to see Bob chatting with another applicant, and Art was certain the other guy would get the position. He went ahead with the interview, but told Jim later he was sure someone else had been chosen.

Bob did hire the other guy, but not more than a week later, a phone call came in at Wild Bill's bunkhouse. "Bob Taylor for you," someone called out to Art.

After the usual pleasantries, Bob got down to the reason for his call. "Are you still interested in the job, Art?"

**Art Reeves, Taylor ranch foreman, good friend and
"like a member of the family." Courtesy Robert Taylor Family Collection.**

"Sure am, was interested the day I came in."

That was the start of a relationship which made Art a member of Bob's family, forever much more than an employee. He moved on to the property, living there and taking care of the place like his own, until and after Bob's death.

Bob and Ursula on the set of *The Detectives*. Courtesy Judith Hanhisalo Personal Collection.

The Detectives was produced in part by a company developed by Bob, and aptly titled to reflect his personal stamp. Ursulor Productions was a name formed from the combination of his wife's first name and their family name. Four Star Films was also part of the team. Bob's good friend, film actor Dick Powell, ran the company bought into by Bob and others of the same era, men who all came out of the studio system. Powell was the one who suggested Bob give TV a try.

Ursula got into the act on the set of *The Detectives* after fans started clamoring for Bob's character, Matt Holbrook, to have a personal life. Matt was all-work-and-no-play, and the guy needed a girlfriend. A suggestion was made that Matt "ought to interrupt his pursuit of the bad guys occasionally to at least wink at a pretty girl." The first ninety-three episodes portrayed Matt with tunnel-vision. He fought crime, and had no time for play.

Bob wasn't keen on the idea of adding a love interest, and he would have nothing of bringing in any actress to play such a part. When the viewing public grew adamant Holbrook should loosen up a little, Bob relented, but only by asking Ursula to come out of retirement and take on the character of Lisa Bonay, newspaper reporter, and she became a recurring cast member. This satisfied viewers and added spice by letting them see Bob playact alongside his real-life love, while Bob was able to stay true to his personal world.

He had become something of a hermit in relation to the Hollywood social whirl, interested in little else other than his family, his ranch, and outdoor recreation. When he threw a party to signal the end of shooting for the first season of *The Detectives* at Chasen's, considered the most famous celebrity restaurant in town, everyone in the star community was surprised, and those invited were thrilled to be on his guest list. According to the media, the "beautiful bash" was co-hosted by "Bob's beautiful better-half."

Terry, Bob, Tessa, and Ursula relaxing together.

His love life was totally inhabited by Ursula. Her appearances on *The Detectives* weren't for fame or attention, and not even really for the money. They calculated that, in their tax bracket, she ended up netting about ten dollars a day after taxes and paying for daycare.

Ursula took on the role for Bob, and only for Bob. She did most everything for him. When she agreed to the part, she said, "It could be fun doing an occasional show with Bob. But I would never allow a career to keep us apart." And she was serious. Acting and modeling, the glamour, were no longer the highlights of her life. In fact, they had most often been only a means to an end. Her world had changed; now she spent her days taking care of Bob's house, their family, and him. She let him pick out her clothing because, as she said, "After all, I dress to please him." She was called a "woman who does everything to please her husband."

Bob and Ursula. Courtesy author's private collection.

In many ways, this was the perfect time in Bob's life. In a 1960 interview, after extolling the virtues of his new TV schedule he said, ". . . I've got more time for my family. . . . I'm a very happy man."

Bob was mature, he knew his strengths and weaknesses. He had grown into his family life, and he enjoyed this latest stage. He turned down a lucrative offer in Europe for what would have been a television series. "It's just not for old dads," he said. "I like it too much here. I'd have had to spend six months out of the year there, and that's not for me."

He did hope for a good, old-fashioned western series; Westerns held fast as his favorite genre. He had enjoyed the "cowboys and Indians" game as a kid, and that hadn't changed, though he was certainly no longer a kid. Despite fancy clothes, glamorous leading ladies, and colorful filming locations, Robert Taylor was a cowboy at heart.

Bob in a cowboy hat.

He was really in control of his career for the first time since he started in the entertainment world. He selected the films he made and, more and more, TV work suited him and his tastes, rather than arbitrarily accepting assignments required of him by studio bigwigs. He finally had a family, and he could take care of them without worry as to their future financial welfare.

There were difficulties. Serious issues surrounded the lives of his stepchildren created a dynamic which threatened Bob's sense of well-being and family structure. Yet he felt more adept at handling these problems. He had a better handle on how to work the press, and keep them at arm's length when things going on at home were not for public dissemination. He also knew which writers and reporters he could count on to be fair, no matter the subject.

Hy Gardner, well-respected Hollywood columnist.

Hy Gardner was one press connection Bob held on to over the years. Born only a few years before Bob, Hy and Bob got along well, and they understood each other. Hy was always respectful, even though he managed to ask all the pointed questions to which his reading public wanted answers. Bob appreciated his approach, and their professional relationship lasted out his career.

The two men had lunch one day in October of 1959. Bob was comfortable in his middle age, adding an appealing edge to his appearance which continued to draw women to him. He was older, but no less striking.

Hy was recently married and brought his bride with him on their lunch date. He carried a photo of him and Bob taken in 1938.

"Why is it," Hy's new wife asked, "that columnists age faster than movie actors?"

After their laugh was over, Hy asked Bob, "Do you feel any older than when we did this interview 21 years ago?"

"Nooooo." Bob smiled. "Not unless I watch myself in those old TV movies. Which is why I avoid them like a plague . . . I think there's something sadistic recalling the way you looked and felt and acted in earlier days. The big kick is enjoying today to the hilt, not wading in yesterday's sticky triumphs or memories."

He didn't watch much TV, nor did he often let his children watch. On most occasions, he did "avoid it like the plague." Despite his lack of enthusiasm for the new medium, he was aware TV was the future of entertainment. He may not want to be a regular consumer, but he knew he had to embrace it in his professional life.

In mid-1960, Bob wrote a guest article for *TV-Radio News* outlining his thoughts on his first year in the newer medium. ". . . There's very little of the camaraderie that springs up on a movie set . . . In TV, you arrive on the stage around 8 a.m.; you're shooting your first scene a few minutes later. There's not a dawdler in sight, and you're lucky if anyone takes time out to introduce you or anyone else to anybody."

For someone who always seemed to want to be on the outside looking in, Bob was actually forever trying to be part of a group. Art Reeves said he "wanted to be liked," and went out of his way not to offend people. He took great pains to appear as if he didn't care if he was included, but being included was one of his greatest desires, and well may have been the core reason behind what led him to a career in films. Publicly noting the lack of personal contact in the TV world was a clear-cut statement for him.

He didn't want to alienate his new bread-and-butter, though. "That's the way it goes in TV. You have three days of shooting for a half-hour show... Such social amenities as introductions get kicked way down to the end of the day's long list of what must get done."

Bob compared the two, giving the better points of both. "Television is an exciting business; I love it. I like the staccato tempo... and the efficiency... I also love making motion pictures and hope to do a few more before they decide to put me out to pasture... Movies and TV are the greatest businesses in the world, and I'm grateful to the guy—or guys—who invented both of them. Else, where would I be?"

That same year, Bob had his first conscious brush with insidious, ugly illness. He went in for a check-up, which showed a spot on his lung. This wasn't big news. He'd had the spot since he was a child, and each time before, check-ups had shown the source of the unnamed speck to be benign. During this medical visit, further tests indicated a need for additional attention, and he underwent a minor procedure at St. John's Hospital in Santa Monica. He came out of the hospital in tip-top shape, or at least that's what he was told. Everything seemed handled, and Bob went on with his sedate, scheduled, and highly satisfactory life.

In 1961, a reporter made note Bob had a pipe with him on the day of their interview. He regularly smoked three packs of cigarettes a day. The pipe wasn't unusual, since he'd been known to occasionally puff on one over the years, but this time he may have been attempting to cut down on his cigarette habit. Though pipe-smoking wasn't necessarily a healthy alternative, in the early sixties, a pipe was still considered a gentler option.

Not gentle enough, though. Before 1961 had ended, he entered St. John's again for "minor surgery" related to his lung condition. Each trip to the doctor's office, and then to the hospital, took a toll, making Bob more and more leery of the medical profession, and bringing out his natural "worrywart" personality.

Doctor's told him he had "Valley Fever," an air-borne lung infection caused by organisms found in soils of the Southwest and West. Dust and dry air were close friends, and people with weak immune systems were most likely affected. Bob had never considered himself to have a weak immune system, but his multiple stays in Egypt in dry, dusty and not-always-sanitary conditions may have heightened his odds, which were already worsened by his never-ending smoking.

He dared to speak of his concerns with Art. "I just had x-rays, and I don't know if I have cancer." Art suggested he dig up his old records of the spot on his lung, and check the size and shape. Had there been a change? While everyone around him celebrated the fact that, again, everything was okay, Bob silently considered the possibilities, all the negative possibilities.

As he dealt with these health issues, the lives of the people around him weren't any calmer. In 1962, Manuela's problems started to come to a head, though the process would be a painfully slow one. She had pled guilty to being under the influence of drugs and was put on probation, which she was later arrested for violating.

In early 1963, Bob spoke to a reporter about his marriage, and how he and Ursula spent time together as a couple, and individually. "Married people need to get away from each other occasionally for one reason or another," he said, "but they should also have vacations and recreation together." This recipe worked for the Taylors.

Amidst the family upheaval in his household arising from efforts to raise Ursula's two children from her first marriage, Bob did walk away from the conflict at times. This was a testimony to how tight he and Ursula were as a couple—to have him hold on through those years of late-night calls from the police station, visits with the kids in and out of drug rehab, alcohol-related arrests, and the emotional turmoil caused by attempts to blend a high-profile father figure and two kids with many-layered and long-standing emotional concerns. There was no easy fix.

But Bob knew what he had with Ursula was good, and Ursula understood his need to occasionally distance himself. As each year passed into another, they grew closer. Ursula took note of what made her husband happy and molded her life to his, while continuing to deal with the escalating special needs of her children. In this way, she engaged the spirit of a man who, in turn, enriched her life and ultimately became fully dependent on her.

Bob loved having his wife by his side when he went hunting, fishing, and skeet shooting. "Ursula didn't cherish the idea, but I put my foot down to start off," he laughingly stated about the skeet shooting, "and pretty soon she was nearly a pro. She likes dogs and horses so the rest came easy." She became an excellent shot, though Clark Gable actually taught her. She had never done these activities prior to her relationship with Bob, but before long, she was an extraordinary outdoorswoman. Bob said she "earned her camping wings" when they went on "one camp deal that was absolutely murderous. She didn't squawk as much as I did."

Ursula didn't lose herself in the process. She held on to her feminine side, enjoying writing and baking and sewing and taking care of their home, and she did all of that regularly. She was also a movie buff. Bob said, "She likes to do the things I do . . . though I suspect sometimes that she'd rather spend a weekend seeing three movies. She's crazy about movies."

Bob was a man's man, which had become openly evident long ago once he allowed himself to be comfortable with his place in and out of Hollywood. After having had lady fans "in a swivet for 30 years as the beau of the boudoir, the darling of the drawing room, the suave city slicker," he found that not to be his true self. He had made friends with like-minded men such as Clark Gable, John Wayne, George Montgomery, Robert Stack, and his best friend, Ronald Reagan, and he kept company with them throughout his life. His social circle was tight . . . they understood each other.

But his closest confidante in those days was Art Reeves. He and Art had coffee together in the mornings, rode the property during the day, and cared for the family week after week with almost equal love and concern.

There were often times when he would offer Art personal opportunities under the guise of work. One such instance came in 1963. He went on location for *Cattle King* (1963) in Kernville, some three hours drive from the ranch. Ursula was visiting for a few days, and Bob suggested Art drive her car up and she would then be able to get herself back home. Art made the trip, and Bob asked him to stay. Figuring there would be work for him, Art took the room at the local hotel which Bob had already held for him. In the evening, he told Bob to give him a holler in the morning. He planned to accompany him to the set and take care of whatever his boss needed done.

Bob didn't get Art up the next morning. Instead, he hopped on the bus with the other actors and went off to work. He didn't take his car, even though he was the star and well could have pulled rank. He considered himself "just one of the guys," and expected to be treated no different than anyone else. Nor did he expect Art to work while he was there; his offer had been made to give Art a break from his job at the ranch. Bob figured Art wouldn't take the opportunity if presented to him as recreation. He had been right.

Another time, he and Art were on the road to Audie Murphy's ranch to buy horses. Bob didn't like to stop in public places when he was driving. He preferred carrying a few sandwiches and his ever-present thermos of hot, black coffee. This afternoon the men decided to take a rare break out of the truck, and rolled into a small restaurant for a piece of pie and coffee. They slipped into seats at the counter, and soon the cook came out of the kitchen.

"Don't I know you?" he asked Bob.

"I don't think so."

The guy shrugged and went back to his post, but in a few minutes he was back at the counter in front of Bob. "I'm sure I've seen you," he persisted. "Have you worked in the movie business?"

"Well," Bob drew the word out as he finished the last gulp of his coffee, "yeah, once in awhile."

The guy couldn't get Bob to say the words. He liked people fawning over him less these days than in his earlier years as a movie star. The men paid their bill and left the restaurant, and Art, who said he wasn't "very impressed

Bob with hunting dog. Courtesy Judith Hanhisalo personal collection.

with himself," had a good laugh over the incident as they again made their way down the road.

As he aged, Bob was clearly aware of what made him happiest, and he accepted how his station in life allowed him the opportunity to do almost anything he wanted to do. He didn't abuse the gift, but he became at ease with the perks. If for a few weeks he wanted to go hunting or fishing and Ursula didn't want to go, he went anyway. This wasn't a slight to her or to their relationship; he had a need which he satisfied as he chose. He liked to "jump in the car with another guy and a couple of dogs and take off on a little hunting trip." No insult intended, no insult taken.

They often played together outdoors as a family, too. Their camp at Big Horn Mountain, Wyoming, was a favorite spot where Bob and Ursula, and

Terry and Tessa would ride, fish, hunt, and go "frog-giggin.'" At seven-and-a-half, Terry caught "all the fish in the stream," Bob said proudly. He bought his son a twenty-two gauge shotgun and they went skeet shooting. He supervised Terry's use of guns, carefully teaching him the proper way to use them.

He was still a strict father, and did what he could to ensure the kids got their recreation in natural surroundings rather than in front of the TV set. "Terry earns his TV hour each day by doing chores, homework, eating his dinner, and then reading for a half-hour." He added, "It's reading that suffers when kids get the television bug."

He used the television himself primarily as a way to get his news fix. He also voraciously read the newspaper. "He was a news junkie," Manuela said.

When the Taylors were together away from home, Ursula continued to do family maintenance duties. According to Ivy, Bob had no idea how hard Ursula worked, but he was actually paying more attention than others thought. "Ursula does the laundry, cooking, cleaning, child care and her own horse care in Wyoming," he said, then laughed. "She also does the decorating." He had changed his line of concentration from being outdoors with his wife and family, to being at home with them. "That's the ideal time for a man to go on a fishing trip, which is exactly what I do."

One telling indicator of how secure Ursula was in her position as Bob's wife, and his only love, came in 1964 when he took on a new film titled *The Night Walker* (1964). This was a campy, creepy thriller, another genre to stretch his range. He played an attorney with a dark, less-than-appealing personality, working for a wealthy man certain his wife was having an affair. Hayden Rorke, who would a few years later become a household face thanks to his part in *I Dream of Jeannie*, played the tortured husband. And who was to play Hayden Rorke's wife?

Barbara Stanwyck.

The whole thing was arranged by Bob's agent without talking with him before signing the contract. The offer was lucrative, and his agent made a quick decision to accept the role for him. At first, Bob wasn't happy he had no say in the final choice, but before he made any rash attempts to get out of the obligation, he gave the opportunity serious thought. The money was good, the script was superb, and the part gave him the chance to play a bad guy... something he really enjoyed.

And the press was already on top of the story. They'd gotten wind of plans to put him back together with Barbara, if only for one movie.

Ursula could've easily said, "No," and there would've been few who blamed her. While the film didn't call for overt romance between Bob and Barbara, they did share a questionable romantic entanglement. There were physical moments, though quite tame by most standards. This was the third film they had made together and the first since they split up. Their impending reunion was creating quite a fuss in Hollywood and in the media, but little fuss in the Taylor household. Ursula was a regular visitor to the set, and she was genuinely friendly toward Barbara. At one point, Bob said his marriage to Barbara seemed like a dream.

Barbara's reaction? "A job is a job."

They treated each other cordially. Almost fifteen years had passed since their official split, and they were both still topnotch professionals. William Castle, the director, was thrilled with his actors and how the production progressed. At one point during a few moments of down time, they chatted about "the old days." Castle guessed Bob had been about thirty when he made *Camille*. Bob corrected him, saying he had been twenty-five.

"I was the one who was 30!" Barbara shot back, and they all laughed, an easy-going rest between takes.

Minutes later they were back at work, shooting a scene in a spooky chapel with only the two of them. After a run-through, Barbara wasn't satisfied with how she delivered her lines. "It was too pat," she announced. "As a matter of fact, it stunk." The make-up folks ran in, coaxing her hair into place while Bob pulled a comb through his.

They tried once more and this time, everything was perfect. Cameras rolled, the scene was captured, and Castle announced, "Cut—print it!" He

Family Life ... Finally

Bob and Barbara make *Night Walker*, their
first get-together since the divorce. Courtesy Judith
Hanhisalo personal collection.

wistfully looked at Barbara and Bob, now going their separate ways until the next scene. "This is how movies should be made." A nostalgic comment about a time long gone ... in many ways.

Bob started work on a new hour-long TV drama, titled *The Robert Taylor Show* (1963), a series about a bureaucrat in the Department of Health, Education, and Welfare. About four segments were filmed with each costing Four-Star Productions more than one hundred thousand dollars per segment.

Something happened between pre-production and the government's overall involvement in the storyline. When the problems started, Tom McDermott, President of Four-Star, issued a media statement. "We are not in breach of our agreement . . . and we are now, as we have been in the past, prepared to meet our obligations in all respects. We have always had the cooperation of the department. Recently we went to Washington to improve our liaison and . . . discuss the procedures of a closer working relationship with the department. . . ."

McDermott made known that whatever was wrong wasn't on their end. He continued by saying HEW representatives were "desirous of cooperating with the series in the public interest." After more talks and meetings going nowhere, the government wasn't willing to engage in a continuing product. The series was finally cancelled with all plans for further negotiations scrapped. As soon as this was made known to Bob, he shrugged, wrapped up his end of the deal, and took off for Wyoming.

Amidst growing problems in his step-children's lives, Bob also had to play the role of a parent to his mother. She was in a Santa Monica nursing home and, as he said, she had "practically lost all her memory and is more of a 'vegetable' than a person." With his heart heavy, he wrote in a letter to Nebraska friends, "I sometimes feel it would be better if she could just die peacefully." He spoke of people who lived in the state of mind in which she lived. "They're not happy—they're not unhappy—and really don't know what's going on." Bob and Ursula visited her, but she rarely knew who they were. "It's terribly sad to see," he finished, "and I'm only grateful that she's at least comfortable."

Michael had returned to Germany to live with his natural father in early 1961 after a stint in a United States military school. Ursula and Bob finally admitted they couldn't handle him, but even going back to his native Germany didn't help Michael confront his demons. In February of 1963, he and his father had a horrible argument. Not long after, acting as if all was well, Michael served his dad a cup of tea. George Thiess sniffed before drinking because, "It smelled funny." He suspected his son of lacing the drink, and reported him to the police. While the state prosecutor investigated the case, Michael was arrested and held for attempted murder. He was officially charged in December.

Meanwhile, in October, in the United States, Michael's sister was picked up on suspicion of forgery. Manuela was arrested in Santa Monica, and police reported she and two men had tried to cash a forged check for twelve dollars. Five months earlier, she had completed a year's probation for being under the influence of drugs in a public place.

A West German juvenile court sentenced Michael in the spring of 1964 to one year in a reformatory for the aborted poisoning of his father. He was accused of using a de-lousing chemical in the attempted murder. Michael told the court, "I'm sorry."

Manuela was found drunk in September, lying mid-morning in the streets of Venice, California. The arresting police quoted her as saying, "I was drinking wine, beer and whisky with two dudes who left me in the alley." She sang a different tune in front of the judge. "I want a meaningful life," she beseeched him when she was sentenced to thirty days in jail for public drunkenness. "I'm making every effort to rehabilitate myself. I'm working steady. I'm going to a psychiatrist. I have not been drinking."

The judge wasn't sympathetic. "People have done too much for you," he told her, fixing her bail at two hundred and fifty dollars because of her previous indiscretions. "You've been mollycoddled too long."

Manuela cried as she pled guilty. "I really, really thought at last I had a chance to overcome my problems."

Walter Scott's *Personality Parade* ran a reader's question during this difficult period for the Taylor family: "Actor Robert Taylor's stepchildren by Ursula Thiess—are they both in jail?" The reply was indicative of the sort of press the family was receiving. "As of this writing, they are...."

**Bob with Terry and Tessa, playing at home.
Courtesy Robert Taylor Private Collection.**

Bob tried to balance these disturbing reports with chatty messages to friends. "Terry is back from his summer camp—seems to have grown at least 6 inches vertically and lost about 8 pounds in circumference. He had a great time and is naturally reluctant even to think of the start of the new school year . . . Tessa seems to be real happy about the idea—but of course about all she has to do, being in what they call 'Primary' Grade, is play all day. . . ."

He alluded to the fact there were only four of them in the house in the closing of another letter. "Our housekeeper takes her vacation during August so Ursula and I and Tessa will stick pretty close to home, I guess." Terry was off at summer camp.

Bob had become part of Hollywood's old regime, and was now considered something of a relic. He told a friend he'd "slowed down to a . . . pea-pickin' walk." He was the last member of a studio system, a kingdom seen from the tail end by many new and upcoming actors. In his late fifties, he was suddenly a historian and sage of the Golden Era of movies. In the unofficial capacity, he was often asked for interviews. Everyone wanted him to talk about the "good ol' days." Bob good-naturedly chatted with reporters, most of whom were quite young. He gave telling insight into a world of glamour and make-believe that would never again reach the same dizzying heights.

"A director once told me that there were two kinds of stars in Hollywood. First, there were the actors and then there were the personalities." Bob was still not convinced he was anything special, despite his long and illustrious career. He cocked an eyebrow and added, "I'm a personality." Then he qualified. "I'm not . . . one of those dedicated actors who has always wanted to play Shakespeare. I was tested once for *Romeo and Juliet* with Norma Shearer and old Bill must have turned over in his grave."

He had his own theory of acting, utilized every time he was stymied over a part. "When I was making *Johnny Eager* or *A Yank at Oxford* I would think to myself, how would I—Robert Taylor—feel about this. . . ." He hesitated. "Sometimes something special happens. It's hard to say just why, but somehow all factors—the writing, direction, acting, even wardrobe and set design—seem to jell and, as a result, you have a great picture." Bob felt his downward career spiral began when "*Quentin Durward* was a bust, and then we started getting into mediocrity." In reality, he hadn't had a downward spiral. The studio system had gone away and the old way of creating entertainment was evolving.

No matter how much he tried to downplay his place in movie history, these people who came to hear about old Hollywood from him had a well-grounded sense of the real essence of Robert Taylor. "Taylor comes across," one article said, "as a professional—a craftsman sure enough about his strong points to admit his weak ones and joke about them."

Did he regret he no longer had women hanging on his every word, willing to follow him wherever he led? "All things equalize themselves," he said with a shrug. "When I was first starting out I needed the girls. They were an indication of a certain kind of success and that was more important to me

Bob and Ursula in a relaxing moment alone.

than money." Reporters could easily see, these days, his contentment with his wife and family far surpassed any thrill of his romantically dazzling past.

During another interview, Bob was asked to talk about the state of the industry, the way things had been, as opposed to the new way of making movies. He placed the start of the "Golden Era's" demise in the late 1940s, "... with the unexplained but seemingly premeditated murder of glamour. Television, taxes, actors pricing themselves to the skies are all part-causes, but not the definitive one... Perhaps if someone could correctly explain the phenomenon of rock 'n' roll, Beatle haircuts and beatnik wardrobes we will start to understand. In any case, it was 200 years ago."

As of the mid-to-late 1960s, Bob Taylor's earlier life, his days as a movie star

Family Life... Finally

rather than an actor, did seem to be two hundred years in the past. He was now a gentleman rancher with many business ventures. He was still well-known in the industry and to the entertainment-enjoying public, and he was well-respected. When he wasn't roaming his more than one hundred acres in Mandeville Canyon, he and his family went off to Wyoming or to a comfortable mobile home at Lake Mohave on the Colorado River. All avenues open to him had resulted from his long and illustrious career. He had worked to get where he was.

Bob had few complaints about his life.

He released two films in 1964 and none in 1965, but this was a big time for his business ventures. In the latter part of 1963, he bought into Nebraska's fledgling cable industry. The investment, called Multi-Vue TV, was headquartered in Grand Island. Along with Bill Moore, former broadcaster and head of a local public relations firm; Bill Martin, ex-President of KMMJ, Bob's radio station from the old days in Nebraska; Telesis Corporation of Indiana; and locals Darrell McOstrich and Howard Eakes, he brought Multi-

Bob and Multi-Vue TV business partners, Darrell McOstrich, Bill Martin, and Howard Eakes. Courtesy Robert Taylor Family Private Collection.

Vue to Grand Island and Kearney, and Colby, Kansas, becoming one of the earlier executives of Midwestern cable TV.

Their plans didn't stop there, and they built franchises across the area. In September, he flew into Omaha and rented a car to drive to Beatrice for dinner, and an overnight with friends. Early the next morning he was on to Grand Island for the Broadcasters Banquet, which he called "a nice affair."

"I might be able to run out for a little chat . . . Sunday morning, the 20th," he told friends. "If ya happened to have a cuppa coffee I'd love to drink it with you—then shove." As usual when he was in that part of the country, he had a Wyoming trip figured into the mix. This time he was looking around for another piece of land for a new cabin, before moving on to Denver for more business. Finally, he took a commercial flight back to Los Angeles, eager to get home to Ursula.

For someone who started out suspicious of and vocal against the television industry, Bob caught on quick to future potential, and he made it work for him. He was finally making good on his college degree. In January, Multi-Vue had three-and-a-quarter million dollars worth of equipment in Grand Island, offering eight different channel selections. Original negotiations included the city of Lincoln, but after Lincoln added restrictions to expected programming, Multi-Vue withdrew the offer.

A number of instances came together to bring this venture to Bob. He had been in college with Darrell McOstrich, who lived in Grand Island, and he knew Bill Martin from their time in radio. Bob had kept in touch with his old friends throughout the long years, and when he got the opportunity to get together with them to start Multi-Vue, he had eagerly accepted.

That summer, after taking care of his mother who had suffered a "small" stroke, Bob, Ursula, and the kids relaxed on the Colorado River, south of Hoover Dam. The fishing was great, and they kept a boat on the river. He told friends there wasn't much to do except "ride around in the boat—pull up on a sandy beach for some swimming, resting, and picnicking—or go fishin'!" They stayed in a little motel with kitchens and did their own cooking. A "loafing-off" period followed the trip. As he said, he was "sittin' around lookin' at the fog and drizzle...."

For all the rest he got that year from not often being in front of a camera, Bob made up for his relaxation the next year. He was ready, "... looking around for another picture to do...." as he told a friend. "One project is being discussed ... and it looks very good. The contracts aren't signed yet but I'm hopeful." Once technicalities were out of the way, he went deep into the Florida Everglades near Wekiwa State Park and on October nineteenth, work began on *Johnny Tiger* (1966). The shoot lasted until nearly Thanksgiving.

The film's title was the name of an Indian. Chad Everett, who played the role, said, "We worked sixteen to eighteen hours a day. It was a very low budget film." He spoke of how pictures were billed. "The studios ... were in control of all of the theaters. So you made pictures to make someone a star and you double-billed with someone who was already a star. That's how it was done." Bob was already the star. Chad was the up-and-coming wannabe.

"To get the money to put it on the screen, we had to do it with long work days. It was a very hard picture for all to do." *Johnny Tiger* was panned upon debut, with little fanfare except a few brief newspaper notations without photographs. The project was an important one for Bob, though; through those long months of work in the Florida swamp, he found a good and lasting friend. Despite their age difference, the bonding between him and Chad was immediate, and it was real.

Some of Bob's die-hard, old-fashioned fans were unhappy with his portrayal of a crotchety, arrogant, and usually-bespectacled university professor who, as one newspaper reported, was "blacklisted" by colleges for his unpleasant way of relating to others. Though Bob had managed to break free of the more urbane roles, there were fans who held stubbornly to his early, beautiful and well-groomed image, and they wanted nothing else.

Bob as a crotchety professor in *Johnny Tiger*.

Bob, on the other hand, was delighted with not only the part and his growing friendship with Chad, but he reveled in the shoot's location. "I've always loved the woods," he told a reporter. "And here we are in one of the most picturesque settings in America. It's just like it was when the Seminole Indians lived here. In fact, they're living here with us right now in their native chickees." He was thrilled with the environment, and he was in his

Family Life ... Finally

element working outdoors. "In the morning," he continued, "the pungent smell of smoke from their fires fills the air ... and I have to pinch myself to remember that I am living in the space age and not primitive times."

The movie revolved around a Seminole reservation school. Bob's character, an outsider hired to teach native children, had a lot to learn about the people he was suddenly living amongst. The plot required him to figure out how to deal with a rebellious daughter who accompanied him to the reservation and who, not surprisingly, fell for the unschooled, self-proclaimed half-breed grandson of the local tribal chief, the defiant lead for which the movie was named.

Paul Wenkos was the director who chose Chad, who was thirty, to play the lead. Bob was fifty-five, old enough to be his father. Tables had finally turned. Rather than him looking up to an older man for guidance, Bob became the role model. "When I was growing up, going to movies like everybody else ... Taylor was one of my favorites," Chad said. "I knew when I had the opportunity to work with him, early on, that it was something I wanted to do very badly. I was not going to miss a chance to do that."

Chad said Bob was "... just exactly almost the hero that he played ... well-founded, steady, honorable. ..." He expounded on Bob's work ethic. "He would get up very early when he was fresh, and he would do the majority of his studying for his day's work at that time ... He was always prepared." The younger man couldn't say enough. "He was a giant ... there was not a contemporary of mine ... that wouldn't have walked across the United States to do that part ... That's how much we felt we had to learn ... from working with that kind of man."

Brenda Scott with Chad Everett in *Johnny Tiger*.

Watching and listening, Chad took away a technique he made a part of his own work ethic. "... He knew... the whole scene. I mean, he knew everybody's stuff. And he... never flaunted it or showed it off. I just became aware of it one time when he threw somebody a cue that wasn't a line that came from him or came after his or one that was going to go before his. He was in the mix, and I found that's a great way of learning the story...."

Bob was known for having two "creature comforts" throughout his adult life, his cigarettes and his coffee. "He was a man who taught me, both verbally and by example," Chad said, "to decide what made you comfortable and be responsible for those things... don't relegate that responsibility." Chad was sad to talk about what cigarettes did to his good friend. But as for the coffee, "He liked simple things... he always had his own thermos ... that *he* made, in the room, that morning, that he brought along with him for himself. That wasn't being selfish, that was just, as he said, deciding what gave him comfort... and being responsible for it."

Bob said the role of the professor in *Johnny Tiger* was "part of" him. He got into the essence of the character, feeling as if he had come full circle. In early years, he needed learned advisers to guide him, especially after the death of his father. He had been hungry for mature male support to help make decisions to put him on the right life path. One had even been a professor.

The personal dynamics between Bob and Chad, and the storyline in which they acted, brought Bob to a place where he felt comfortable tak-

Bob as Professor George Dean in *Johnny Tiger*.

ing on the role of the teacher. Something in Chad encouraged and spoke directly to him. Friends and family remembered him as one of Bob's favorites, a man of a younger generation with whom he connected. "He treated him like a son," Manuela said.

Chad summed up his image of Bob. "When he said he would do something, it was done ... He was terribly loyal to his friends ... he was calm, he was a together guy ... what you saw was real ... He had a lot of compassion ... he *cared* about his family and he *cared* about his work and he *cared* about his friends. ..."

The movie wasn't promoted well, and didn't do for Bob what he had hoped. He was deflated, and the whole experience seemed to take the final shine off of Hollywood for him. His words were hard when he proclaimed, "From now on, I'm a strictly for *money* actor."

Bob had to care about the weight of his pocketbook because he still had mouths to feed. He spent the rest of the fall, and until November, on a shoot in Spain. Ursula came over for a three-week visit; otherwise he was alone for an extended period for the first time in quite awhile. He "enjoyed the people," but missed his wife and kids. As a result of that job, he signed a contract to do two more pictures there in 1966, and for those he would bring Ursula and the kids over. Plans fell through, though, and the family never got the chance to enjoy Spain together.

The year of 1966 turned out to be a political one. Hollywood was again playing a visible role in the public's vision of international goings-on. Conservative members of the California Republican Party were searching for a few good celebrity-types to take their message to the people in a run for governor. There were some natural choices.

Ronald Reagan had been extremely active in behind-the-scenes political activity in Tinseltown in the 1940s and 1950s. He knew his way around the process, and was a shrewd, intelligent voice. He and Bob had a slight falling-out during the years when Ronnie embraced the Democrats and vacillated between the parties, but ultimately he returned to the Republican philosophy, and to their friendship. Asking him to run as the Republican candidate for governor was a logical move for the party bigwigs. There was really little surprise when he agreed to take on the race.

The tightly-held secret, however, was that Bob had also been asked to run. His part in the direction in which Hollywood went in those earlier years was most significant behind the scenes, more than Reagan's, who more often stood in front of the podium.

Bob was a solid potential candidate; he was photogenic and classy, quietly and seriously political, ultra-conservative, above scandal, well-liked and respected. His inner circle knew he was plugged-in and aware. In the early 1960s, he would repeatedly tell people, "The Middle East is going to get us into the third World War." One person said Bob Taylor was the one individual who most consistently influenced Ronnie Reagan's eventual history-making views on the world.

Bob was ripe for the picking, but he didn't want the job.

He and Ronnie had many long discussions, and did some serious soul-searching. Though the fact that Bob was asked to run never became wide-scale knowledge, family members knew, and each had their opinion. The effort to get a celebrity in office was led by an Eisenhower Republican, a wealthy Los Angeles Ford dealer named Holmes P. Tuttle. He, along with others determined to maneuver the direction of their state, created what became known as the "Kitchen Cabinet."

At the 1965 Golden Globe Awards, held at the Ambassador Hotel, Ronnie and Nancy were chatting with Bob and Ursula when columnist Sheilah Graham approached.

"Are you planning to run?" she asked Ronnie.

"No, I'm not."

Bob smiled during their exchange, looking as if he was bursting to get in on the conversation. After Ronnie finished speaking, he piped in, asking Graham, "Aren't you going to ask *me* whether I plan to run?"

He was giving her a hard time. Bob was fiercely protective of his family's privacy. He refused to allow publicity photos of them, and unless questions were informal, he usually sidestepped interviews about his home life. At one point he said, "The public should not be entitled to anything I do not feel they should have. I'm aware of the necessity of publicity, but I don't go out and look for it." His step-children's problems had to be a big concern; keeping Michael and Manuela away from the trash-digging which would accompany a political run was a big consideration. They were part of his family. According to Art, he never considered them "step" children. They were nothing less than his kids.

And Bob wasn't any more comfortable as a public speaker in his mature years than he had been as a teenager. He was a pro with people one-on-one, could work a script with little more than a glance, and did well when required to chat off-the-cuff with a group. The medium made the difference. He had never been really at ease delivering specific points in a speech to a large audience. Basing a public platform on nothing but his persona, and his words and personal opinion, no matter how deep his conviction, was the dividing line for him. His memory of the days during 1947, his House Un-American Activities period, still haunted him.

Despite the overtly public career he had built, Bob wasn't happiest under an intense direct public gaze. To intentionally go out and seek the limelight, not as an actor but as a leader, wasn't his style. That required representing himself, not a make-believe character. He was known to campaign for others, behind the scenes and out of the way of prying eyes. He was interested in changing the course of the issues without being the one at the head of the charge.

Something he worked on that summer was a perfect example. He took a trip for Multi-Vue requiring a "very fast—and hot schedule." He said the "little caper . . . looks real good. We have franchises in Grand Island, Kearney, Broken Bow, Colby, Kansas and we look very good in Hastings, Mc-

Cook, and North Platte. Billings also looks fairly good and would be a real 'Klondike' if we get it."

Bob took some time while in the Midwest to do some stumping for Nebraska Republican Senator Carl Curtis' reelection. He told friends he received "considerable sniping by Democrats who figgered I shouldn't have taken sides for Sen. Curtis but I honestly didn't feel it was harmful. The concensus [sic] seemed to be that Curtis would win—and I actually did the job for two reasons—a) I think Curtis is and has been a good man, and b) my old buddy, Sen. George Murphy from California had called and asked me to help out."

He went on to discuss Ronnie's run. He said he "looks good for Governor." He, Ursula, and the kids had recently visited the Reagan's "little beach house for some swimmin' and a steak bar-b-q . . . and Ronnie looks better than he has for quite a spell. He's gettin' rested up for the resumption of the campaign next month. Naturally the AFL-CIO is against him—and the entire colored vote in the State will go to Brown—but I think Ronnie has a fightin' chance." He got in his usual shtick. "Actually he's too nice a guy for Politics [sic]—and I wouldn't envy him the job—but maybe it's time some *good* people got into that racket!"

Bob felt he could work the system from both sides without putting his family right in the middle, under added scrutiny. He wanted to be Robert Taylor, actor/public activist, and Robert Taylor, American citizen, but he wanted to do his part on his terms.

"Mind you," he told the editor of the Beatrice paper two months later, "I see no reason why an actor *shouldn't* go into politics. It seems to me that honesty, intelligence, a firm belief that America is one of the finest countries in the world and that our political philosophy is the best in the world should be all the requirements that *anyone* should need." He had become unhappy with how actors were, in his eyes, being used. "I believe that we need fewer *professional* 'Politicians' and more just plain *good people* in politics." He finished with, "Before I sound like I'm makeing [sic] a campaign 'pitch' perhaps I'd better sign off."

There was one last, heavy consideration against any sort of personal political campaign, a concern at least as influential as all others. Bob knew deep inside something wasn't right. He was certain he was not well. He tried to deny what he was feeling, managing to halfway convince even Ursula everything was okay. She knew more than anyone else, but his family and friends had little awareness of the intensity of his medical problems. A serious illness was working bad magic on Bob.

For all these reasons, Bob felt he should keep his finger on the pulse of politics through Ronnie, and he was more than willing to throw his weight and name behind his friend's campaign. He thought Ronnie had not only the celebrity, but also the awareness and intelligence, and he was the candidate to get the job done right. Ronnie had been in the trenches. If he won, the victory wouldn't come because people were voting in "the glamour."

Bob campaigning for Ronald Reagan as California's governor.
Courtesy Judith Hanhisalo personal collection.

Ronnie didn't like to fly, though, and once he accepted the challenge of running for governor, he had a hectic campaign schedule to follow. Meeting obligations via road transportation wouldn't be practical. Hal Bowen asked Bob to vouch for the reputation of Santa Monica Aviation, and him as a pilot, allowing him to offer his professional services. He and Ronnie had met awhile back at the Taylor house. As a result of Bob's recommendation, Hal became the pilot-in-command on about fourteen trips across the state for Ronald Reagan and his party. They flew in a two-pilot twin-engine corporate jet Commander, with Santa Monica Aviation as the provider.

Instead of going on the road for the country, Bob went back on the road to promote his films. He did another movie with Chad Everett, *Return of The Gunfighter* (1967), and accepted an assignment in Egypt, though "several years ago I must confess I didn't look forward very much to coming back."

He was still writing letters, lots of letters, which was his best tool against loneliness. The stationery read that he was at the Nile Hilton, complete with hieroglyphics at the bottom of the page.

In late 1966 he explained to Ivy in a letter why he had returned to Egypt. "... It was a 'job'—and I needed the money ... Living conditions haven't changed for the better ... but the prices are higher than ever. I paid my first week's hotel bill yesterday and it was $590—and I've *not* been living extravagantly." A reference to the Eddie Mannix's slap-on-the-hand for his wasteful habits years earlier? "The food is unbelievably bad ... and everything is so darned dirty one almost leans toward giving up eating ... I'm useing [sic] bottled water entirely." This couldn't have been good for his health. "... I had a bad touch of stomach cramps yesterday, which I guess happens to just about every tourist who comes here." He called Egypt "the jumpin'-off place of the world" and told her he expected to miss Christmas at home, but would be back by mid-January.

Bob's deeply tanned face accentuated clear, deep blue eyes, and gave evidence to his love for the rugged outdoor life. The lines creasing his brow were created from hours-on-end spent in the sun. He had been more often on his ranch than in front of a camera that year, when an offer came in which he couldn't refuse. He agreed to become the host and occasional star of *Death Valley Days* (1966), taking the reins from Ronnie, who had to leave the show because of his run for governor.

Bob during *Death Valley Days* period. Courtesy Robert Taylor Family Private Collection.

Seen in one hundred and thirty cities in the United States and Canada, *Death Valley Days* was solely owned and sponsored by the U. S. Borax and

Chemical Corporation, best known as 20 Mule Team Borax. After fifteen years, the stories were still based on true incidents and characters from western pioneer days. The show never hyped action in favor of the story, and refused to include unneeded violence. Bob found the work "fun," especially since he only had to appear about four weeks a year. "It's much easier than doing a weekly series as a character," he said.

When he was asked if he was interested in going into politics like his friend, Ronald Reagan, he still gave his standard answer. "Not on your life! I'd rather go huntin' and fishin'." At this point, he was likely speaking from the heart. In light of his medical problems, he knew what he considered the most intelligent use of the time available to him, and that wasn't politics.

In March, he had another round-the-Midwest tour. He went to, ". . . Grand Island for board meetings of various CATV corporations. . . ." as well as making stops in Denver to pick up an American Legion award for *Death Valley Days*, and two days in North Platte for "Centennial goin's on." He was happy with the direction his work with Multi-Vue had taken, and the benefits it offered the family. ". . . Things look real healthey [sic] for our Cable efforts and, a few years from now, that caper may be worth some money for Ol' Dad and all the little Taylors."

Bob had a great time being Ol' Dad to all the little Taylors. That same month, during Easter vacation, he and Ursula went back to the Colorado River for "boatin', fishin' and fun." He'd found a new pastime he wanted to share with "Tar," his name for Terry. "I also bought one of these here-now Yamaha Trail Bikes with which I'll cover a lot of those remote desert areas where the Dodge Four-Wheel-Drive won't take me. Figger on teachin' Terry how to ride it too—'n that'll probably be the last we'll see of him for days on end. Can't very well get lost up there; just point 'her downhill and yer a cinch to end up at the River sooner or later."

Bob, Ursula, and Terry and Tessa together as a family. Courtesy author's personal collection.

Before the trip they had the "annual Taylor Clan Easter Egg Hunt." As patriarch, Bob got into this with his family. The day's events started only after he had the chance to "shake the sheets and get 'em outa the sack." Once the kids were up and ready, festivities began and the day was full of kiddie fun. The only reference to the Thiess children, in the early-morning Easter letter to friends back in Nebraska, came in one line, "So—we've been havin' 'Weddins' (and that's the first and last of that little gesture). . . ." This indicated an ill-fated marriage for Manuela.

He and Tessa had developed a tight bond, an intense father/daughter connection. She went into his study almost every afternoon, to visit with him as he typed letters to his friends. She crawled into his lap, and he did his best to type, using one finger as he always typed, and never getting angry or telling her she was interrupting him. She enjoyed the mixed smell of her father's warm typewriter and his aftershave, and it was part of her daily routine to play with those funny-looking round erasers with the pointy-edged brush on the end.

He would type around her wiggling body as she leaned into his big desk, digging for treasures he had long ago put away. Those items were the source of joy from which her playtimes with Daddy were made.

One treasure was a little pouch with a drawstring. Each afternoon, sitting on his lap, she opened the bag and poured out the contents onto the corner of his desk. She would ask him what everything meant. Day after day, he called her his "Puss-face," his pet name for her, and told her the same old stories.

He said the pouch had been given to him by his buddies right before he went off to war. One of them had the pouch made, and different friends each added something special and important. There was a capsule with a tiny Jesus figure, a Mother Mary medal, a 1942 penny, Jesus' cross, and many more goodies. She never tired of hearing what each piece was, and how it had come to be in that small bag. He never tired of telling her. Every day, she asked him. Every day, he answered.

A considerable number of publicity trips were expected of him in connection to his various business interests. In May, he and Ursula attended the HemisFair in San Antonio, visited Dallas and, "... came home pooped. They really do get their money outa ya on deals of that kind." *Death Valley Days* assignments kept him going, but he was tired, and he really started to look the part. He was off to Idaho in October for show introductions and, he hoped, a "coupla days of steelhead fishing."

He and Ursula were traveling all over for business, but a few trips were made for relaxation. They went to the Colorado River, to Florida to visit friends in Sarasota, and back to Beatrice. In the fall of 1967, Winchester Rifles took Bob on as their spokesperson for their Clay Target Championships. They issued a statement lauding his love of the outdoors and particularly shooting, his acting, and his gentlemanly ways. They said, "We feel his association with this Claybird Tournament will greatly add to the luster of the shooting sports."

Bob and Ursula flew to Grand Bahama Island to act as Honorary Hosts for the tournament and then did a "world trip" in February of the following year. They went to Honolulu, Sidney, Bangkok, Rome, Frankfurt, London, New York, and back to California. "This is all on Winchester," he said, "and I've got so damned many guns and cases of ammo around here I don't know where to put it. But—it's fun!"

Bob and Ursula in the Grand Bahamas. Courtesy Judith Hanhisalo personal collection.

Bob was still running around in the spring of 1968, though he felt more and more out of sorts. He tried to ignore hints that his body was giving up. He was always fatigued and winded, not a surprise considering his schedule,

Bob in *Death Valley Days* garb.

but he felt in his bones this went beyond simply running around too much. His chest hurt, he wheezed a lot, and he coughed up blood. When pain threatened to slow him down, he drank a scotch, and if his aches worsened, he drank another. If that didn't work, he smoked another cigarette, which helped to calm his nerves.

He and Ursula flew to Chicago on the thirtieth of March for a formal dinner given by ABC. The next evening, they were at a cocktail party hosted by The Borax Company. Their time was theirs only for the next three days, and on the following Wednesday, Bob went to another party to accept an award for *Death Valley Days*.

As this journey finally ended, Bob had a heavy, deep-in-his-heart sense he needed to go home. Not to California, but to Nebraska. *Home.* He knew he must see Beatrice. Ursula went on to Los Angeles, and he flew to Omaha alone, where he rented a car. No one but his wife knew where he was, and that was what he wanted. He drove through Beatrice and out of town on the old Holmesville Road, then toward Filley. He had a leisurely drive through the country before he turned around and returned to Beatrice.

Bob roamed his old haunts and relived the familiar, hauntingly bittersweet sights of his childhood and adolescence, all from the privacy of his rented car. He drove down Main Street, and hesitated a moment in front of the Rivoli, remembering his days as an usher. He smiled as he passed the Paddock Hotel, and the building across the street where his dad's medical office had been. He took a pass down Sixth Street, stopping at the corner in front of his family home . . . that brown bungalow held many memories for him.

There was no one he had to answer to, and that was exactly what he needed. Passing by the home of his old friends, Spiv and Abbie Eyth, he noted that no lights were on and no cars were in the driveway, and he didn't stop. His next destination was the local Holiday Inn, where he checked in for the evening, took a long, warm shower, stretched out on the bed, and fell into the first truly peaceful sleep he'd had in a long time. The next morning, he watched the *Today Show* and listened to the local weather. Bad stuff was coming, forcing him to regretfully end his trip down Memory Lane. Before going on his way to the airport, he made one last stop, driving to Bob and Flossie Tyser's farm south of town to have coffee with them.

A letter he wrote to Spiv and Abbie Eyth after he was back in California was spunky, philosophical, and even prophetic. Talking of his trip to Beatrice he said, "It would have been wonderful to see you guys . . . but if you won't 'bother' us when you come out here I'm damned if I wanta bother *you* when I come back there. Maybe all of us should decide to be a little more bothersome—OK?"

<hr>

Hal Bowen wasn't aware Bob was as sick as he was until the men happened to be at the same place at the same time in the fall of 1968. Hal's private physician, Dr. Brandsma, was a good friend of Hal's, and he was also Bob's doctor. Hal was visiting his office when Bob came in. The three men got comfortable and Dr. Brandsma asked, "When are you going to quit smoking, Bob?"

He'd recently had a brief hospital visit, and wasn't in the mood for pleasantries. He looked the doctor in the eye, and with a gritty tone to his voice, he replied, "When are you going to give me a reason to quit?"

With a sinking, queasy feeling in his stomach, Hal realized his friend was in deep, deep trouble.

A few days later, during a night at home with friends, Bob was feeling especially bad, and he went to bed early. Ivy was there, as was Loyal Davis, Nancy Reagan's step-father. Dr. Davis called Ursula into another room. They had a closed-door conversation, and when they emerged, Ursula was, as Ivy said, "white as a sheet."

She put her arm around Ursula's shoulder and sat her down. "What happened?"

Tearfully, Ursula replied, "You know, Bob has cancer and he's going to die."

"Dear," Ivy replied, her heart breaking for her friend, "how could you not know? Yes, I knew. Didn't you?"

"Not until this moment." Bob had been in denial for years, hiding his worst moments so well that he'd taken Ursula down the rosy path of denial with him.

Not more than a month later, Bob was in the hospital. Again. He was still trying to support the "Valley Fever" theory, at least in public, but an abscess had formed, and he had to have his right lung removed. He finally

Bob in an early print ad for Lucky Strikes cigarettes, long before he learned what smoking could do to him. Courtesy author's personal collection.

agreed the time had come to give up cigarettes, but only because the situation was that dire and he had no other choice.

Family assured the public he was "feeling just fine" and doing well. He wrote a letter to Spiv and Abbie with the same sugar-coating. "My second session with surgery seems to have done the job," he said. "I presently have a hose comin' outa my chest, and they tell me I may hafta carry it for a few more months. . . ."

Bob knew the truth, but he wasn't quite ready to make his condition widely known. He had contracted a staph infection during the operation, and that coupled with the surgery made reality impossible to ignore much longer. "The cobalt treatment knocks Hell outa ya but they say it's workin'," he told his friends positively. "We plan on staying home until after New Years—then Ursula and I hope to go to the River for a coupla weeks by ourselves. . . ." He wasn't really all that upbeat, though. ". . . I just ain't got enough 'spizerinctum' to write a long letter—but I'm sure you'll understand and forgive."

He knew he was dying. There was no way to sugarcoat the facts. One article said he was "slowly ebbing." He was aware he'd been the subject of much speculation in the press. A handful of visits in and out of St. John's Hospital were fertile fodder for gossip pages. The TV carried stories about him. Newspapers followed each admission and release. Bob found humor in all the sadness, somehow, that now, at the end of his life, he was again receiving a celebrity's share of fame, fame for something which no one wanted to be known . . . fame because death was knocking at his door.

Attention came from people of all ages, young as well as old, which was somehow comforting. Newspapers and magazines received letters, many, many letters, asking about him, wanting to know if he could possibly get better. The youthful ones seemed especially curious. Maybe they had rented some of his older movies when they first heard of his illness. Maybe they started watching his films on late night TV when they saw his name in the papers.

Bob went into, and out of, the hospital a total of seven times before his last admission. He was surely seen on TV in *Death Valley Days*, a show whose title was eerily prophetic, and in reruns of *The Detectives*, and replays of his movies. People were becoming acquainted, and reacquainted, with him. However he was being found, a younger generation was learning about Robert Taylor, and the older generation was re-celebrating him.

The four youngsters who meant the most to the man himself, though, were *his* children, Michael; Manuela; Terry, fourteen; and Tessa, his eleven-year old cutie. These kids knew him intimately and were most affected by his life and now, his illness. They saw his pain, day in and day out.

Before he left the hospital for his latest stay, he thought back about his experience as a father. On his first try, he didn't do such a good job. Barbara's son had been a sad child. Dion hadn't known where he belonged, to whom he belonged, and if anyone really cared. Bob liked him and tried to be good to him, if not actually a father figure. Dion had wanted to bond, but didn't know how. He hadn't been shown much love in his short life, and had no awareness of how to love others. Years later, Barbara disowned him. The boy had never had the emotional tools to equip him to relate to a masculine figure, and his mother wasn't really motherly.

Bob knew Dion, a troubled boy, had since become Dion, a troubled adult. He knew the time had passed for him to be able to change anything, and he was willing to accept his part in the tragedy.

In each case, with Barbara and Ursula, Bob had children the minute he said, "I do." Each wife had come to him with a pre-arranged family. He had done much soul-searching prior to marrying Ursula. Having learned a few lessons through his relationship with Barbara, he felt more attuned to the responsibility put into his hands the second time around. Not even his awareness, though, could equip him to handle Michael, who was already emotionally disturbed when Bob met him. He also found no amount of looking into himself put him up to the task of knowing what to do with a pre-teen girl who desperately needed a father, and who wasn't shy in saying so.

The job of being a parent had never been easy for him. The role had forever been an uphill battle. He felt as if he had lived his entire life as an adult, even as a child himself, and understanding how to intimately communicate with anyone had forever been his biggest challenge. Still, he had come to love having Manuela and Michael in his life. He saw Ursula in both of them in happier moments.

Difficult times happened all around him, but he tried to turn them into positives. It meant that for now, at least, he continued to live and be part of a unit that cared deeply for each other. The trouble surrounding him indicated he still could do what he did best. He was a part of the lives of those people who depended on him, still responsible for them . . . his dear wife, and his blended family.

Manuela had slowly put her life on track. Bob helped her get a role in a movie, *Buckskin* (1968), through A. C. Lyles, a producer and an old friend. She had small parts in a half dozen *Death Valley Days* episodes, and a bit part in another film. She was in her early twenties, and this was a good start for her. She felt how much Bob wanted to be involved in her life. They were coming together.

Michael wasn't doing as well. He made the effort, also looking into acting opportunities, but nothing panned out. He was a long-standing tortured soul, and had recently tried to commit suicide by slashing his wrists.

Children had ironically become the single most motivating factor in completing Bob's life. Unspeakable heartache on one end, and great joy on the other, with little in between, summed up his interactions. From Dion, to Michael and Manuela, and then Terry and Tessa, they each made their own acutely personal imprint on him.

The nurse with him in his hospital room had been at his bedside during previous stays. She'd known his face over the years, watched him in the movies and on TV, and now she cared for him as he approached death. They'd had conversations, and now she saw him smile through the physical pain which was his constant companion, right alongside his memories. She swiped at tears threatening to stain her cheeks, not wanting him to see her cry.

He looked at her, and she was certain he recognized her sorrow. He knew. When he spoke, she couldn't resist his whispery smile as he told her of a moment in time between him and Terry, about a year earlier. He was in one room of his house, and Terry was in another, giggling as he watched the television.

"My son suddenly tells me I'm on TV. I . . . go in to see what it is that strikes him as terribly funny—and he . . . says, 'You look so different, Dad.'"

The nurse knew beloved memories such as this helped him take the next breath, and the next one, each more difficult to draw than the one before. The edges of her lips turned upward slightly as she helped him get more comfortable on his pillow.

After surgery this time, Bob was released on November twenty-six from St. John's Hospital. Newspapers reported he was able to eat Thanksgiving dinner at home, though, in truth, he wasn't much interested in dinner. The entire family was subdued that holiday, and Thanksgiving dinner was the last thing on their minds.

Ursula told reporters he "felt just fine." Bob explained in a letter to a well-wisher how he'd been "running in and out of the hospital and to and from doctors. The way things look now, however, I think I've got it made and recouperation [sic] shouldn't take much longer."

Bob didn't really believe his words, and putting on the act was getting to be too much. Ultimately, he and Ursula had to confirm the truth to the world. Robert Taylor, movie and TV star, would soon be dead. Cancer was about to claim his life.

The dawn of 1969 showed how far down illness and treatments had taken Bob. His efforts to win the battle were overwhelming him, and he had little strength left to fight the fight. He told Spiv and Abbie in February, "Some days I think I'm winning—others I'm not so sure and couldn't care very much. It's been a really rough ordeal due largely to unexpected complications and the end surely isn't in sight."

Tessa knew her dad was hurting, and she was crushed to realize there was nothing she could do for him. Two years earlier, during a party at their house, she had watched him prepare to show home movies to guests. He stood at the front of the room, next to the projector. Suddenly, he coughed. A lot and he kept on coughing.

The sound was loud to her ears, and it lasted too long. When he finished, he made no move to indicate if all that coughing had been anything serious, but she knew. He shouldn't cough like *that*. He turned his head to the side, away from his company, and wiped his mouth with a tissue. When he faced everybody again, she saw blood on his collar. Something was definitely wrong with her father.

Yet no one else seemed to take notice that night. No one, including Daddy, made a comment, or acted as if anything was out of the ordinary. That incident had confused and frightened Tessa. She adored her father. She couldn't let anything happen to him.

She had no power over the situation, though, and she was aware of that sad fact. Daddy was now hardly able to move without assistance, or sit in his living room chair long enough to watch the TV evening news. Tessa knew the truth, even if Daddy and Mother refused to say much about what was happening.

<hr />

The first drainage hole in Bob's chest was cut in the wrong place, and that had to be fixed. This added stress to his already-weary body, and caused additional physical damage. He had to lie down for the hole to seep, and those closest to him said the hole probably would've never healed had he lived.

One hospital trip came as a result of weather, rather than in direct response to his health. Torrential rains hit southern California, "... the worst I've ever seen..." by Bob's estimation. "... My doctor insisted that I go to the hospital rather than run the risk of being stranded...."

Going home after the storm was short-lived. He needed a third operation that spring, and had to return to St. John's. He absolutely refused to be seen in a wheelchair, and forced himself to walk into the hospital, though in truth, he could hardly breathe. Art was right beside him, holding on to his arm when he was sure no one could see him being helped along. Gasping, making every effort to do this for himself and by himself, Bob was determined to show a strong front. He knew the brutal truth, but he still didn't want anyone else to know the depth of that truth.

This experience, he said, "... was far and away the worst of the bunch and it looks like it will take me a long time to recuperate. I feel that they finally accomplished, medically, what they wanted to do but I'm sure getting tired of being a Guinea Pig . . . Fortunately Ursula seems to be holding up amazingly well in her role of chief cook, dishwasher, housekeeper, bus service, nurse, and wife. I get scared everytime [sic] she sneezes because I'm damned if I know what I'd do without her. . . ."

While he was in the hospital, Art Reeves took Terry to the bicycle shop, explaining his dad finally agreed to buy him a new bike. The presentation of this gift frightened the boy. His father had been denying him the same bicycle for over a year. Dad repeatedly insisted he had to work for his bike; it would never be handed over to him. This afternoon with Art, there was no big explanation, no excuses as to why Dad suddenly changed his mind, but Terry knew. This time, a new bike might not be a good thing.

After it was bought and loaded into the back of the truck, Uncle Art drove toward the hospital instead of going straight home.

"Wouldn't you like to go in and see your dad, Terry?" Art asked.

Terry couldn't find the words to answer. He didn't know how he felt. He wasn't sure he wanted to see his father like an almost-dead man. His mind flashed briefly back to the sight of Dad not too long ago, at home in his recliner, after the first surgery to try and stop what had finally been classified, without question, as cancer. In his mind, Terry still saw his dad in his chair, a blanket wrapped tightly around his body, a tube coming out of his chest.

And that hole!

He clearly remembered the hole the doctors had made in his father, a hole almost the size of a golf ball, a hole showing Dad's insides, a hole which had not closed. He would *never* forget that hole.

When he didn't immediately answer Uncle Art's question, the older man continued, telling Terry his mother would be pleased if he held himself up like a man and visited his dad in the hospital. Terry felt as if the decision was taken from him. He had no choice, and he reluctantly went with Uncle Art to his dad's room.

It was difficult to see him in there. Where there had been only one tube in Dad at home, now there were many, and they were in different parts of his body. At home, Dad had been able to sit in his own chair and watch his own TV. Now, he had to lay on a hard, stuffy white bed that didn't belong to him.

Dad was much the same, attitude-wise. He laughed a little, said silly things, and tried to make him and Uncle Art and Mother laugh. But there was heavy sadness around and in his eyes, a look telling everyone in that unfriendly room how he knew what would soon happen to him, and he, too, was afraid.

Terry couldn't grasp the thought of his father being afraid. Dad was a gruff cowboy. He had always been a no-nonsense, "men-don't-get-scared" kind of guy. Terry already realized Dad didn't allow himself much time to consider things that bothered him, or anything at all which might seem almost un-manly to spend too much time thinking about. Death was surely one of those subjects.

His father was happy to see him. Terry knew, even though Dad didn't come out and speak the words. Terry didn't know what to say, either. In his fear and uncertainty and hurt, he used Uncle Art as physical support, and mumbled his thanks for the new bicycle. Then they left for home.

Those last months were hell on earth for Ursula. After the latest operation, Bob quickly deteriorated to a point where no one could be sure of his next breath. He was moved home, and then shortly returned to the hospital. "I'm going to take the situation by the horns," he vowed in another letter which, these days, he had to transcribe, often with Ivy taking the dictation. He refused to stop communicating, though. Letters were his lifeline to the many important people in his world. "You're damned right I am. I'm going to whip it, knock it down and stomp on it."

Ursula was at her wit's end. She was determined to be with him, finally accepting that he would not overcome his illness. The cancer had already whipped him, and now this day-to-day waiting was only a matter of time. Life, for her beloved Bob, was only a matter of time.

She also had Michael to care for. He lived in a hotel room while he worked as a construction company clerk. He had been diagnosed with a "mental problem," and released the month before from Camarillo State Hospital, reportedly later-on the inspiration behind the song, "Hotel California."

The institution already had a checkered reputation, and this turned out not to be the best place for someone like Michael. Because of his ongoing drug problem, he couldn't be trusted on his own to properly administer his weekly doses of legitimate medication. Ursula was forced to deliver them to him every day. He had been back in the United States since 1965, and in and out of the legal system ever since. His convictions ranged from possession of marijuana, to battery on a police officer.

One Wednesday in late May, Ursula drove to see Michael in his motel room, as she usually did. She closed her car door, and nothing seemed out of the ordinary. There was a note stuck to his door, written in German and asking her to wake him when she arrived. After unlocking the room with her key, she went inside and found Michael lying across his bed in his pajamas, unnaturally still. As Ursula moved closer to her son, she knew something was wrong.

She reached out to touch him; his skin was sickeningly cold.

Emergency personnel were immediately called to the scene. Medics assessed Michael's body, and appearances gave the impression he intentionally overdosed. Though everyone involved tried to keep things quiet, the newspapers found out and jumped on the story. As gentle as they had been with Bob since the announcement of his illness, this situation was much more salacious. With little caution, reports came out proclaiming Michael Thiess, stepson of dying actor, Robert Taylor, had committed suicide.

Ursula believed otherwise, but she was more than aware how the situation looked. The coroner ordered toxicological studies to determine the actual cause of death since the autopsy, done the day after he was found, failed to come up with an official answer. Final reports showed her son had unsuccessfully tried to take a managed dose of medication.

The days directly after Michael's death went by for Ursula in a fog, as she bounced back and forth between the shocking loss of her son, and the imminent death of her husband. Bob had lapsed into a coma. Ursula was grateful he no longer felt the constant, excruciating pain he had rarely ever expressed, but of which she was aware, having been at his side through the entire ordeal. He was emaciated, barely a sliver of the image of his former self, old far beyond his fifty-eight years, no more the picture of vibrancy and virile masculinity he had seemed to be even a few short years earlier.

Manuela tried to support her mother, and she spent time at her stepfather's side. Gently holding his hand, she whispered to him, finding comfort in knowing they had finally made their peace.

Only the day before, she hadn't been sure. As they loaded him into the ambulance, he looked straight at Manuela standing there in her pajamas. His eyes were clear and she knew he saw her. "Mani, you did this!" he croaked. Ursula assured her daughter his words didn't mean anything, that he thought he was going on location and he didn't want to go, and he needed to blame the move on someone. His direct words pained her and stung her eyes with tears, despite her mother's attempts to soothe her.

Manuela had been sure Bob's outburst was a result of something she had said in these last days to comfort her mother. She had wanted to counsel her, and Ursula asked for her advice. Ursula was afraid the younger children would walk into the room and find their father dead. This thought petrified her, and Manuela gently suggested Bob would be better off, and the children sheltered, if he returned to the hospital. After his outburst, Manuela was afraid he somehow had heard the whispered conferences between her and her mother. Somewhere in the fog of his pain-filled mind, Manuela was sure her stepfather knew what she had said to her mother.

But now, as she sat quietly with him, her fingers entwined with his still-warm ones, she looked at his closed eyes and listened to his ragged breathing. He was holding on to her. Somewhere in his touch, she knew they were finally right with each other. She felt at peace with him.

On Sunday morning, June 8, 1969, the press was told Robert Taylor was again in a sterile hospital bed at St. John's, "resting as comfortably as can be expected and . . . not in too much pain." The hospital spokesperson announced death was "inevitable in the immediate future." He added that Bob's condition was "rapidly deteriorating," and he was aware he was about to die. Ursula, Bob's physician, his attending nurse, and Art were there. Ursula and Art had been in the room with him nearly around the clock for the last few days.

As did everyone, Ursula knew the end would come fast now. Tired beyond human endurance, she had spent the night with her beloved, watching the clock tick. The man she had looked upon with favor and love ever since her teenage years, would soon pass away. This he'd have to do without her. She could not do this for him, or with him, though if there had been any possible way, she would have. She loved him that much. And she knew he loved her as deeply.

Art told his wife that morning when he awoke he had to see Bob immediately. There was no time to waste. Through his many visits to St. John's, Bob had been attended by a kind nurse who admitted she had "worshipped" him since she was a kid. She had tearfully told Art she didn't want to be there when the time came; sadly, she was on duty when Art arrived, and stayed late into the night.

Nancy Reagan flew to Los Angeles from Sacramento as soon as she heard the news. Her daughter, Patti, was at Bob's bedside. Nancy stayed for the day and when she left, she told Ursula she'd see her in a few days. "I got out in the hall, and something made me turn back," she remembered. "I returned to his room and kissed him on the cheek."

By the time she landed in Sacramento, she was given the bad news. It was over. Bob was gone. She returned on the next plane to be with Ursula.

The news that "Robert Taylor is dead" was broadcast before Ursula could get home from the hospital. In those early morning hours directly after Bob's death, Ursula was taken care of by Manuela, and Art Reeves. Art had always been there for Bob, for her, for the kids. He became their rock, somehow more than ever before. They also received support from Ronnie and Nancy, and Art's wife, Barbara.

Nancy was Ursula's emotional rock, coming in and taking over when Ursula finally collapsed. The funeral had to be taken care of, and thankfully, Bob had planned the entire process down to the last detail. True to his living persona, in death he didn't want any fanfare. When his obituary printed on the front page of *The New York Times*, an unheard of honor at that time, the *Times* ran his picture with the tagline, "Death Ends an Era."

Governor of California, best friend to Golden Era film legend Robert Taylor... Ronald Reagan gave the eulogy, although he confessed to his wife on the morning of the service he wasn't sure he could get through his tribute without breaking up. The funeral was held on June 11, 1969, two months before Bob's fifty-ninth birthday. Glendale's Church of the Recessional at Forest Lawn Memorial Park was the site of the ceremony conducted by the Rev. Gary Demarest. A whole host of celebrities were in attendance, including Barbara Stanwyck.

Tributes poured in from all corners of the entertainment community. Richard Thorpe, who directed Bob in six films, said he was a "no-nonsense, untempermental actor who efficiently and quickly learned his lines." Thorpe added Bob was "really a nice guy and it comes through on screen."

Shelley Winters had starred with Bob in *A House Is Not A Home* (1964). She said of him, "... he was the sweetest man to work with. By that I mean he was co-operative and understanding in contrast to most leading men today, who try to either elbow you out of camera range or are off in a corner somewhere practicing 'Method' acting."

Bob's own commentary on his career would have served him well as a tribute. "Films were never an art form to me. Acting is a job, a respectable way to make a living—like truck driving. I think back on the parts I played—different costumes, long hair or short hair, but I played the same character." Bob had never been too concerned about his image. He figured the "fixers" would take care of everything. He always played variations of himself, and his public, his friends and his family had been not only satisfied, but impressed.

The ceremony took only twenty minutes. As he had predicted, Ronnie's eyes were filled with tears as he broke down, trying to speak about his best friend; some said Bob had been his only true friend. In front of two hundred attendees, choked with emotion, he called Bob "one of the great and enduring motion picture stars of all time." He added, "He was also the most handsome. But he was more than a pretty boy, an image which embarrassed him because he was a man who respected his profession and was a master of it."

Toward the end of his speech, Ronnie looked directly at Ursula, Manuela, Terry, and Tessa. He again hesitated, forced to do so by the tears now freely threatening his composure. "I spoke to Bob only a few days ago," he told Ursula, as if she were the only person in the chapel, "I think there was something he wanted me to tell you . . ." he indicated the entire family, ". . . he wanted me to say, 'Ursula, be happy.'"

When they left the church, Manuela physically supported her mother as Ronnie and Nancy walked behind them with the other children. Bob had wanted the service simple, and his wishes were respected. Among attendees were Senator George Murphy, Bob's good friend elected to the Senate in 1964; as well as George Montgomery, Van Heflin, Walter Pidgeon, Keenan Wynn,

Ursula supported by Manuela leaving the church after Bob's funeral. Ronald and Nancy Reagan follow. Courtesy Judith Hanhisalo personal collection.

Gilbert Roland, Robert Stack, Chad Everett, and even Barbara Stanwyck, who wore a yellow suit. She didn't want anyone to accuse her of acting like the widow.

Ruth Brugh watched the major media event on TV in her nursing home room. She felt no emotion. Her face was blank. She didn't cry. She was detached; she seemed to have no idea who had died, whose funeral played out in front of her on the screen. She didn't know. Although she had physically outlived her son, Ruth wasn't aware of this. She didn't even know she had a son. As Bob had said about her in a letter barely a year before, "Life means nothing at all to her anymore."

One of Bob's last requests was to have his best friends return to his home after the funeral and "have a drink with him." Barbara was ready to leave the church directly after the ceremony when Morgan Maree, their shared business manager, went to her car and told her Ursula wanted her to

Barbara Stanwyck leaves Bob's funeral in her yellow suit.

come to the house with the rest of Bob's family and closest friends. She hesitated, but Maree said Ursula really wanted her there. She didn't want Barbara to be alone.

Chad Everett was at the house, invited at Bob's request. "I went up to his house and stepped up to the bar and ordered a double and . . . said, 'Here's to you, Bob,' knocked it back, and left." Tears held back his words. He cleared his throat, and continued, "Whoa . . . ! That was about all I could handle of that. I'm sure everybody handled it differently but . . . you know if you worked with a guy and you cared about him, hell, you loved him. It was just that way."

No one stayed long. Before Barbara left, she and Ursula went for a walk in the Taylor gardens. Bob had saved a few things from his marriage to Barbara, including his wedding ring and some photographs, and Ursula gave these items back to her. Their time together was cordial, private and respectful. They had each lost the man they loved.

At the beginning of Bob's career, in September of 1936, he was considered a "spectacular new star," and a movie magazine gave him a list of questions to answer for a glossy article layout. One question asked what he wanted most out of life, and Bob replied, "I suppose you could sum it up by saying I want happiness—and happiness to me implies success, financial security and, eventually, a family and a home."

Nothing could have been more prophetic on that long ago day in 1936. Thirty-three years later, Robert Taylor had fulfilled his dream life.

Postscript

An article written by columnist Hy Gardner was published right after Bob's death. The heartfelt piece was a collection of Bob's answers to questions Hy had asked him over the many years of their association. At the end, Hy added:

Robert Taylor never won an Oscar. May I suggest that, at the next Academy Awards ceremonies, his peers vote him a Special Oscar, posthumously. I think he earned that dignified distinction. For close to 35 years' devotion to an industry that needed his dedication to decency, principle, and self-effacing behavior. For uplifting the too-often tainted image of a motion picture star. I think, wherever he is, he'd like that.

This author agrees wholeheartedly. The time has come for Robert Taylor to be un-forgotten.

Bibliography

Albert, Jr., Edward. Interview with the author. 1994.

Benny, Joan. Interview with the author. 2006.

Bourbon, Ray. *Don't Call Me Madam: The Life and Work of Ray Bourbon.* "Vaudeville." Unpublished, courtesy of Ernest Cunningham, owner of manuscript, and Randy Riddle, agent.

Bowen, Harold [Hal]. Interviews and letters with/to the author. 2006.

Brewer, Roy. Interview with the author. 1994.

Brugh, Ruth. Personal letters. 1936, 1937, 1940.

DiLeo, Lia. Interview with the author. 2000.

Everett, Chad. Interview with the author. 2000.

Gates, Larry. Interview with the author. 1994.

Keller, Beth Naden. Interviews, letters from/to the author, and personal effects (scrapbook) 1994 - 1997.

Kral, E. A. Interviews and letters from/to the author. 1994 - 2006.

Leigh, Janet. Letter to the author. 1995.

Love, Joseph. Letter to the author. 1995.

Mooring, Ivy Pearson. Interviews with the author. 2000 – 2006.

Parmerter, Robert. E-mails to the author. 2005 – 2006.

Reeves, Arthur. Interview with the author. 2006.

Rippe, Rosemary. Letter to the author. 1994.

Stack, Robert. Interview and letters from/to the author. 1993, 1996.

Stanhope, Eva. Personal letters. 1937.

Taylor, Robert. Personal letters. 1936 – 1969.

Taylor, Terry. Interviews, letters and e-mail from/to the author. 1993 - 2006.

Taylor, Tessa. Interviews and letters from/to the author. 2000.

Thiess, Manuela. Interview with the author. 2006.

Thiess, Ursula. Interview with the author. 1993.

Newspapers:

Associated Press (AP)

Associated Press International (API)

Bristol United Press (BUP)

International News Service (INS)

National Education Association (NEA)

United Press (UP)

United Press International (UPI)

Ames [IA] Daily Tribune, Dec 18, 1954.

The Charleston Gazette: April 9, 1933.

The Chillicothe [MO] Constitution – Tribune: Jun 12, 1937.

The Chillicothe [MO] Constitution – Tribune: Jun 29, 1940.

Great Bend [KS] Daily Tribune: Jun 21, 1958.

Los Angeles Times: Jan 18, 1998.

Lima [OH] News, June 21, 1937.

Lincoln Evening Journal; Feb 27, 1937.

Lincoln State Journal; Mar 2, 1937.

Lincoln Sunday Journal and Star: Nov 1, 1936; Feb 21, 1937; Mar 14, 1937; May 2, 1937, Nov 24, 1967.

The Modesto Bee, Jan 29, 1961.

Newark [OH] Advocate and American Tribune; Mar 28, 1952.

New York Times: Mar 1, 1956; Aug 25, 1984; Jul 15, 1991.

Oakland [CA] Tribune: May 19, 1966.

Sunday Post Crescent [WI]; Aug 6, 1967.

Sunday Times Signal [Zanesville, OH], Oct 29, 1950.

Syracuse [NY] Herald, Sept 10, 1935.

Wardsville [IL] Intelligencer, May 23, 1942.

The Washington Post: Jan. 17, 1988; Jun 26, 1987.

Winnepeg Free Press, Aug 29, 1947.

Books:

Berg, A. Scott. *Goldwyn*. Alfred A. Knopf. 1989.

Bessie, Alvah. *Inquisition In Eden*. The Macmillan Company, 1965.

Billingsley, Kenneth Lloyd. *Hollywood Party: How Communism Seduce The American Film Industry in the 1930s and 1940s*. Forum, An Imprint of Prima Publishing, 1998.

Broman, Sven. *Conversations with Greta Garbo*. Viking, 1992.

Clarke, Donald. *All or Nothing At All, Life of Frank Sinatra*. Fromm International, 2000.

Davis, Patti. *The Way I See It*. Jove; 1993.

De Carlo, Yvonne with Doug Warren. *Yvonne: An Autobiography*. St. Martins Press, 1987.

Deutsch, Armand. *Me and Bogie, and Other Friends and Acquaintances from a Life in Hollywood and Beyond*. G. P. Putnam's Sons, 1991.

Dewey, Donald. *James Stewart, A Biography*. Turner Publishing; 1996.

Bibliography

Dies, Martin. *The Trojan Horse in America*. Dodd, Mead, & Company. 1940.

D'Souza, Dinesh. *Ronald Reagan*. Free Press; 1997.

Finch, Christopher and Linda Rosenkrantz. *Gone Hollywood*. Doubleday, 1979.

Fried, Albert. *McCarthyism: The Great American Red Scare, A Documentary History*. Oxford University Press, 1997.

Friedrich, Otto. *City of Nets: A Portrait of Hollywood in the 1940s*. Harper and Row Publishers, 1986.

Gardner, Ava. *Ava: My Story*. Bantam, 1992.

Golden, Eve. *Platinum Girl: The Life and Legends of Jean Harlow*. Abbeville Press; 1991.

Graham, Sheilah. *Hollywood Revisited: A Fiftieth Anniversary Celebration*. St. Martin's Press; 1985.

Granger, Stewart. *Sparks Fly Upward*. William Collins and Sons and Co., 1981.

Grononucz, Antoni. *Garbo, Her Story*. Simon and Schuster, 1990.

Guiles, Fred Lawrence. *Hanging on in Paradise*. McGraw-Hill, 1975.

Higham, Charles. *Merchant of Dreams: Louis B. Mayer, M.G.M., and the Secret Hollywood*. Dutton, 1993.

Leyda, Jay. *The Voices of Film Experience: 1894 to the Present*. Macmillan Company, 1981.

Madsen, Axel. *Stanwyck*. Harper Collins Publishers, 1994.

Mayhew, Robert. *Ayn Rand and Song of Russia: Communism and Anti-Communism in 1940s Hollywood*. The Scarecrow Press, 2005.

Radosh, Ronald and Allis. *Red Star Over Hollywood: The Film Colony's Long Romance with the Left*. Encounter Books, 2006.

Reagan, Nancy. *Nancy*. Morrow; 1980.

Tornabene, Lynn. *Long Live the King: A Biography of Clark Gable*. G. P. Putnam, 1976.

Turner, Lana. *Lana: The Lady, The Legend, The Truth*. G. K. Hall, 1983.

Walker, Alexander. *Elizabeth: The Life of Elizabeth Taylor*. Grove Press, 2001.

Walker, Alexander. *Vivien: The Life of Vivien Leigh*; Grove Press, 1989.

Wayne, Jane Ellen. *Robert Taylor*. Robson Books, 1973.

Wise, Jr., James E. and Anne Collier Rehill. Stars *In Blue: Movie Actors in America's Sea Services*. Naval Institute Press, 1997.

Articles:

Associated Weekly Screen-Radio. "Allan Jones—He Married the Girl Robert Taylor Dated." Oakland Tribune supplement: Sept 19, 1937.

Associated Weekly Screen-Radio. "Reel Romances, How Can You Tell When They're Real?" Oakland Tribune supplement: Feb 18, 1940.

Babcock, Muriel. "His Old Home Town Gives Hero's Welcome to Robert Taylor." 1930s

Brugh, Izetta. "My Cousin Arlington." Nebraska Alumnus, December 1936.

Brugh, Ruth. "Fate, Fame, and Robert Taylor." Movie Classic: September 1936.

Cheatham, Maude. "Movie Man at Home," 1930s

Hartley, Katharine. "How Bob Conquered A Hostile College Crowd and, Incidentally, Paved the Way to his Later Screen Success." 1930s

Hill, Gladys. "Robert Taylor's True Life Story." Dell Publishing. 1937.

The Inquiring Reporter. "Robert Taylor Answers." Movie Classic: September 1936.

Madden, George. "When Bob Taylor Decided to Quit the Screen." 1930s.

Maddox, Ben. "A Real Day with Robert Taylor." 1930s.

McNamara, Francis J. "The Early Years of the Committee on Un-American Activities." Human Events: Mar 3, 1990.

Ramsey, Walter. "Robert Taylor's Always Been in Love." 1930s.

Rooks, Lyle. "Born to Be an Idol." Screen & Radio Weekly, 1930s.

Stuart, Cedric. "Fooling the Public with Fake Love Affairs of Film Stars," Unidentified publication, 1930s.

Surmelian, Leon. "24 and Very Fickle! Bob Taylor Postpones The Day for the Ball and Chain." March 1936.

Taylor, Robert. "Anything Can Happen In Hollywood." Ladies Home Journal. Oct 1936.

Taylor, Robert. "Pilot Taylor is Free of Travel Worry." United Press. Oct 21, 1954.

Taylor, Robert. "Robert Taylor Tells of First Video Year." Associated Press. July 16, 1960.

Taylor, Robert. "The Golden Age." Film Fan Monthly: June 1969.

Tildesley, Alice L. "Let Me Live My Own Private Life," Oakland Tribune supplement, 1930s.

TV Week's Cover Close-Up. "Robert Taylor—At Home in the Old Corral." 1966.

Publications:

Nicholson LL.D, S. E., Secretary Anti-Saloon League of America. "Proceedings of the Twenty-Fourth Convention of the Anti-Saloon League of America." Detroit, Michigan, January 15 – 19, 1930.

Time Magazine. "Hollywood on the Hill." November 3, 1947.

Hollywood Foreign Press Association. "11th Annual Golden Globe Awards for 1953 Achievements," Jan 21, 1996.

Beech Log & Beechcrafter (magazines). Various short articles. Jan 3, 1947; Mar – Apr 1948; Jan – Feb 1949; Mar 29, 1956.

Miami Herald Publishing Co. "People etc." Aug 24, 1969.

Nebraska State Journal. "Robert Taylor's Own Life Story." March 1 – 3, 6, 8 – 9, 1937.

Columnists & Nationally Syndicated Writers:

Allen, Irwin. "Meet The Stars"

Brown, Vivian

Carroll, Harrison. "Behind the Scenes"

Connelly, Mike. "Mr. Hollywood"

Considine, Bob

Gardner, Hy

Graham, Sheilah

Handsaker, Gene.

Harrison, Paul. "In Hollywood"

Bibliography

Johnson, Erskine.

Kilgallen, Dorothy.

Lake, Talbot. "Profiles for Today"

MacPherson, Virginia.

Morriss, Frank. "Here, There, and Hollywood"

O'Brian, Jack. "On Broadway"

Parsons, Louella. "Hollywood"

Pearson, Drew. "Washington Merry-Go-Round"

Scott, Vernon. "The Hollywood Scene"

Scott, Walter. "Personality Parade"

Shearer, Lloyd.

Smith, Dave.

Taylor, Robert. "Stage and Screen"

Thomas, Bob.

Winchell, Walter.

Witbeck, Charles. "TV Keynotes"

Government Documents & Websites:

Federal Aviation Administration. Online Registry. Airmen Inquiry/Name Inquiry. 2006.

Federal Bureau of Investigation. Freedom of Information Act Request: Communist Infiltration-Motion Picture Industry. 2006.

Federal Bureau of Investigation. Freedom of Information Act Request: Motion Picture Alliance for the Preservation of American Ideals. 2006.

Federal Bureau of Investigation. Freedom of Information Act Request: Robert Taylor. 2006.

U. S. Congress. House. Un-American Activities Committee. 1947. Testimony of Robert Taylor.

Internet:

Columbia University Libraries Oral History Research Office. "Notable New Yorkers." re: Bennett Cerf. Transcript Session 9. pages 418 and 423.

http://www.columbia.edu/cu/lweb/digital/collections/nny/cerfb/index.html

Internet Movie Database. http://www.imdb.com

Newspaper Archive Database. http://www.newspaperarchive.com

Ancestry Database. http://www.ancestry.com

Index

20 Mule Team Borax 381

A House Is Not A Home 398
A Yank at Oxford 98 - 100, 172, 367
Abney, Officer Glenn 141- 142
Above and Beyond 308
Adair, Judge Leroy 189
Albright, Hardie 216
Aleidas, Hugo 150
Alexander, Helen 36
Alexander, Ross 125
Alpha Psi Omega 48
Ambler, Eric 153
Ambush 260 – 261, 263 – 265, 267
An American in Paris 299
American Legion 256, 381
American School of Osteopathy, The x, 4
Americano, The 328
AMVETS 256
Anti-Saloon Archives of America, Archives of The 10
Anti-Saloon League 10, 44 – 45, 408
Arnold, Edward 144, 234
Arterburn, Lesa x
Astor, Vincent 298
Athena 157
Audran, Edmond 308

Bachman, Senator Nathan L. 113
Baer, Max 104
Bahamas: Grand Bahama Island 383
Ball, Lucille 180
Barkley, Senator Alben W. 113
Barry, Philip 108

Barrymore, Lionel 144, 338
Bataan 192
Battleground 262 – 265, 267
Beatrice Daily Sun 344
Beery, Wallace 136 – 137, 338
Bender, Kathryn 39, 49 – 53, 57
Bengal Bride 327
Bennett, Constance 89
Bennett, Joan 89
Benny, Jack 156, 161
Benny, Joan 10, 161, 405
Benny, Mary 156, 161
Bern, Paul 104
Bessie, Alvah 10, 38
Bessie, Dan 10
Beverly Wilshire Hotel 211
Billingsley, Lloyd 10, 406
Billy Gray's Band Box 132
Billy the Kid 179, 212
Blondell, Joan 132
Bogart, Humphrey 283
Bond, Ward 210, 213, 218, 255
Bonnie Prince Charlie 269
Bourbon, Ray 65, 67 – 68, 108, 405
Bourbon and Sherry 65
Bowen, Hal 10, 332, 335, 338, 379, 386, 405
Bowlor 338
Dr. Brandsma 386
Brazil: Mato Grosso 328
Brent, George 139
Brewer, Roy 10, 405
Bribe, The 258, 268
Broadway Melody of 1936 85, 98
Broadway Melody of 1938 98

Broken Arrow 285
Brown, Gilmor 136
Browning, Steve 10
Bruce, Virginia 84, 124 – 125
Brugh, Izetta 20, 83 – 86, 407
Brugh, Ruth XIX, 5 – 10, 12 – 20, 22 – 23, 25 – 26, 28 – 32, 34 – 35, 37, 39 – 40, 42 – 44, 54 – 62, 70, 72 – 74, 77, 96, 101 – 103, 106, 108 – 109, 120, 122, 127, 130, 135, 137, 146, 152, 160, 162, 165, 181 – 182, 257 – 258, 29 – 293, 310, 313, 318, 320, 330, 343, 346, 364, 370, 400; aka Ruth Stanhope 163
Brugh, Spangler Andrew 1 – 13, 17, 20, 22 – 23, 25 – 26, 28 – 29, 35, 39 – 41, 45, 53, 55 – 58, 61 – 62, 66, 70 – 74, 77 – 78, 85 – 86, 107, 123, 163, 165, 169, 374
Brugh, Spangler Arlington xxii, 5 – 23, 25 – 37, 39, 41 – 47, 49 – 62, 65 – 78, 80 – 81, 84, 86, 91, 97, 104, 109, 122, 135 – 136, 150, 160, 165, 190, 196; aka Arly Brugh 10 – 19, 21, 27, 29, 36, 40, 44, 55, 60, 160
Buck, Pearl S. 154
Buckskin 390
Bucquet, Harry 74
Burbank Airport 168
Burk, Jim 349
Burke, Senator Edward R. 114
Butler George 102 – 103
Byoir, Carl 112
Byrd, Robert 333

Cagney, James
California: Beverly Hills 77, 110, 150, 165, 178, 240, 290 – 291; Burbank 168; Claremont 56; Cloverdale 327; Culver City 62, 187; Hollywood vii – ix, xv, xvii, 39, 63, 65 – 66, 70 – 71, 73, 77, 79, 81, 84, 87, 89, 92, 97, 112, 114 – 115, 117, 122, 124, 128, 130 131, 133 – 134, 139 – 140, 142 – 144, 146 – 147, 154, 156, 158, 167, 175, 179 – 183, 185 – 187, 191, 193, 198 – 199, 201, 205, 209 – 210, 212, 214 – 215, 219 – 223, 226, 229, 232, 234, 236, 238, 241 – 242, 248 – 253 255, 257, 260, 269, 283, 286, 290, 299, 304, 308, 331, 352, 354, 363, 366 – 367, 375 – 376, 406 - 409; Indio 168; Kernville 359; Livermore 205; Los Angeles 27, 66, 74, 83, 102 – 103, 132, 144, 147, 161, 187 – 188, 212, 214 – 215, 225 – 226, 282, 297, 325, 334, 370, 376, 385, 397, 406; Mandeville Canyon 334; Palm Springs 168, 288 - 290; Pomona 56 – 62, 66 – 67, 69, 71, 107; San Diego 148, 150, 168, 182; Santa Monica 168, 208, 332, 334, 338, 356, 364 – 365, 379; Tinseltown 134, 375
California Republican Party 375
Camarillo State Hospital 395
Camille 92, 94 – 95, 98, 362
Cancer 19, 357, 386, 391, 393 – 394
Cantwell, Archbishop J. J. 144
Capra, Frank 144
Carlisle, Kitty 154
Carroll, Harrison 309, 408
Carroll, Madeleine 89
Castle, William 362
Cattle King 359
Cedars of Lebanon Hospital 178
Cerf, Bennett 201, 409
Chaplin, Charlie 20, 114
Charisse, Cyd 340 – 341
Chasen's Restaurant 352
Cigarettes 118, 241, 261 – 263, 267, 296, 318, 333, 356, 374, 384, 387
Cinecitta Studio 276
Clarke, Superior Judge Thurmond 283, 289
Cobb, Bob 147
Cobb, Lee J. 340 – 341
Cohn, Harry 123
Colbert, Claudette 140
Cole, Lester 248
Collins, Victor Ford 147

Index

Communist Party 136, 184, 209, 212 – 215, 217, 236, 241, 243, 248, 254
Communist Party of the United States (CPUSA) 209, 219, 243
Conspirator 258 – 259, 264
Cooper, Gary 142, 179 – 180, 184, 198, 211, 213, 218, 225, 255, 338
Cote, Gil 298
Couser, Ralph 204, 208, 307, 325 – 326, 332, 344
Cox, Stephen 10
Coyne, Representative Francis X. 143
Crawford, Joan 88 – 89, 117 – 118, 179
Crewe, Regina 107
Crosby, Bing 144
Cukor, George 94
Cunningham, Ernest 10, 405
Curtis, Senator Carl 378

Daily Worker 209
Darnell, Linda 311
Da Silva, Howard 244 – 245
Davis, Dr. Loyal 386
Death Valley Days 380 – 381, 383 – 385, 388, 390
DeCarlo, Yvonne 305
Delta Omicron 48
Demarest, Reverend Gary 398
DeMille, Cecil B. 104, 147
Democratic Party 222
Dempster, C. B. 19
Dempster Mill Manufacturing Company 19
Denham Studios 100
Detectives, The 348, 351 – 353, 388
Detectives Starring Robert Taylor, The 348
Deutsch, Armand 204 – 105, 223 – 224, 257, 261 – 267, 344 – 345, 406
Deutsch, Harriet 261
Devil's Doorway 283 – 285
Dies, Martin 210, 221
DiLeo, Lia 10, 271, 276, 282, 285, 288, 291, 295, 305, 405
Disney, Walt 212, 218

Doane College 29, 41 – 42, 47, 50 – 51, 55, 60: Doane Players 44, 46 – 48, 50, 52, 55; Doane String Quartet 54; Doane Symphony 44
Donahue, Sheriff Guy E. 188
Dorchester Hotel 311
Drimmer, Dr. Eric 169
Drive-In Theater 83
Dull, Orville "Bunny" 298
Dumont Television 298
Dunlap, Edgar 221 – 222, 224
Dunne, Irene 86, 205
Durbin, Deanna 144

Eagle On His Cap, An 308
Eakes, Howard 10, 369
Edwards, Cliff 216
Egypt 313, 315 – 316, 318, 357, 379 – 380
Egypt: Cairo 319
Eisenhower, Dwight 169, 376
Elks Club 35, 342 - 243
Elliott, "Wild Bill" 349
England 89, 100, 163, 259, 269, 290, 293 – 295, 297, 306, 308, 311 – 312, 330
England: London 100, 224, 260, 297 – 298, 310 – 312, 319, 383
Escape 173
Everett, Chad 9, 19, 175, 371, 373, 379, 400, 405
Eyth, Abbie 385
Eyth, Spiv 385

Fair View Farm 154
Fairbanks, Douglas 179
Farah, Joseph 10
Fay, Dion 128, 144 – 146, 154, 161 – 162, 389 – 390
Fay, Frank 128, 139, 145 – 146, 157
Federal Bureau of Investigation (FBI), United States Government 187, 213 – 214, 232, 409: Los Angeles, CA 188; Springfield, IL 188 – 190
Ferguson, Helen 178, 289

Fighting Lady, The 204
Fitzgerald, F. Scott 99
Flaws, Robert 2
Flight Command 167 – 168, 182
Florida 371, 383
Florida: Everglades 371; Wekiwa State Park 371
Flynn, Errol 136 – 137
Ford, Glenn 98
Ford, Peter 10, 98
Forest Lawn Memorial Park, Church of the Recessional 398
Fortitude 1
Four Star Films 351
France 104, 330
France: Paris 308, 311, 319

Gable, Clark 67 – 69, 79, 87, 137, 144, 169, 198, 207, 213, 215, 218, 237, 255 – 256, 358, 407
Gabor, Eva 169
Gage County Historical Society and Museum, The x, 3
Garbo, Greta 74, 87, 92 – 96, 98, 104, 169, 406 – 407
Gardner, Ava 137, 175, 268, 407
Gardner, Hy 325, 354, 403, 408
Garfield, John 269
Gass, Dr. P. Y. 11, 57, 61
Gates, Larry 10, 405
Gaynor, Janet 90
Gem, Gina xi
Gerasimov, Aleksandr 233
Germany 163, 173, 193, 301, 321, 324, 364
Germany: Frankfurt 383; Hamburg 301
Gibbons, Cedric 212
Gibson, Russ 45 – 46, 48 – 49
Gilbert, John 124
Gilbert, Roland 400
Gilmore Field 146
Golden Globe Awards, The 320, 376, 408
Goldwyn, Samuel 123, 139 – 140, 142, 222, 406; Samuel Goldwyn Studio 70

Goodman, Richard 189- 190
Gorbachev, Mikhail xv
Gorgeous Hussy, The 117 – 118
Grace, Dr. Geoffrey 143
Graham, Sheilah 106, 283, 376 – 377, 407 – 408
Granger, Stewart 271 – 272, 331, 407
Grauman's Chinese Theater 179
Gray, Professor Herbert 26 – 29, 41, 55 – 56
Great Caruso, The 299
Grunwald, Bernice 36

Halsey, Colonel Edward 114
Hamilton, Gertrude 21, 36
Handy Andy 83
Hanhisalo, Judith 9 – 10, 41, 84, 142, 151, 239, 351, 360, 363, 379, 383, 399
Harlow, Jean 69, 87, 104 – 107, 111, 114 – 115, 338, 407; aka Harlean Carpenter 104
Harmon, Delores 36, 90
Harmony Boys, The 46, 48
Hart, Moss 154
Hart, William S. 20
Hawaii: Honolulu 383
Hawks, Howard 180
Hay, Harry x, 136
Hays Office, The 202
Department of Health, Education, and Welfare, United State Government 363
Heffelfinger, Catherine "Kate" 35
Heflin, Emmett Evan, Jr.; aka Van 194, 399
Herald-Times 298
Hervey, Irene 119 – 121, 124
Hinsdell, Oliver 68 – 69, 71, 74, 82
His Brother's Wife 88 – 89
Hitler, Adolph 182, 301
Hoover Dam 370
Hoover, Herbert 81
Hoover, Herbert, Jr. 81
Hoover, J. Edgar 143, 214, 217, 226, 254 – 256, 338
Holiday Inn 385
Hollywood Baseball Association 147
Hollywood Free World Association 214 – 215

Hopper, Hedda 234
Horse Soldiers, The 349
Hotel Statler 45
Houdini, Harry 45
House Un-American Activities Committee (HUAC) 9 – 10, 190, 215, 227, 231, 238 – 239, 244, 247, 255
Howard, Kathleen 180
Howard, Mary 179
Hughes, Howard 303 – 304, 321

I Dream of Jeannie 361
Idaho 153, 183
Idaho: Payette Lake 153
Illinois: Chicago 27, 98, 112, 384; Creve Coeur 189; Evanston 40; Mattoon 298; Pekin 188; Springfield 188 – 189
Indiana Jones and Raiders of the Lost Ark 320
Indio/Palm Springs Odlum Ranch 168
Inglis, Mary Ellen 41, 44, 55
Iowa 34, 54
Iowa: Webster City 333
Iron Glove, The 327
Italy 153, 276, 278, 281, 283, 287 – 289, 306
Italy: Rome 271, 276, 278 – 279, 282, 319, 383
Ivanhoe 293, 296 – 297, 312
Izvestia 233

Jackson, President Andrew 117
Jackson, Peggy 10
Johnny Eager 163, 175 – 177, 367
Johnny Tiger 20, 371 – 374
Jolis, James 10, 17
Jones, Allan 122, 124, 407
Jones, Indiana 320

Kansas: Colby 370, 377
Kaufman, George S. 154
Keller, Beth Naden 10, 52, 405
Kelly, Gene 269
Kerr, Deborah 271, 275
Kilgallen, Dorothy 311, 409
Kilpatrick, Rosana 36

King Solomon's Mines 299
Kitchen Cabinet 376
Kiwanis 256
Kleveland, Jeanelle 10
KMMJ 48, 54, 369
Knapp, Evalyn 74
Knights of the Round Table 311
Knox, Secretary of the Navy Frank 195 – 196, 237
Korda, Alex 100
Koverman, Ida 80 – 81, 150
Kral, E. A. 10, 405

Ladd, Alan 320
Lady of the Tropics 147, 152 – 153
Lamarr, Hedy 147, 151 – 152, 237
Last Hunt, The 330 – 331
Lawson, John Howard 213 – 214
Legate, Esther 35, 53
Leigh, Janet 10, 405
Leigh, Vivien 171 – 173, 338, 407
Lenhart, Frank 28
Leonard, Meredith 10
LeRoy, Mervyn 271
Life magazine 89
Lombard, Carole 121, 213
London Film Productions 100
Loomis, Don 82
Loren, Sophia 277
Los Angeles Examiner 212
Los Angeles Times 212, 215, 406
Love, Joe 10, 206
Loy, Myrna 148
Luce, Clare Booth 302
Luce, Henry L. 89
Lucky Night 147 – 148
Lucky Strike Cigarettes 118, 387
Lyles, A.C. 390

MacDonald, Jeanette 144
Magnificent Obsession 85 – 86, 90, 205
Mann, Anthony 283
Mannix, Eddie 297, 300, 380

Many Rivers to Cross 316 – 317, 327
March of Dimes 112, 338
Maree, A. Morgan 191, 290, 313, 400
Martin, Bill 10, 369 – 370
Martin, Tony 123
Marvin, Bob 344
Marwyck Ranch 154, 156
Marx Brothers 232
Marx, Harpo 140
Marx, Marion 127, 149, 154, 157
Marx, Zeppo 127, 149, 154
Maryland 114
Maryland: Annapolis 112
Maxwell House Coffee 100
Mayer, Louis B. vii, xix, 62, 67, 69, 75 – 76, 80 – 81, 87, 90 – 91, 100 – 101, 109 – 112, 115, 122 – 124, 135, 137, 145 – 146, 149 – 150, 154, 165, 167, 170, 172, 178, 183, 185 – 187, 191 – 195, 198, 201 – 203, 207, 212, 219 – 222, 224 – 227, 229 – 230, 235 – 237, 245 – 246, 250 – 251, 253, 261 – 262, 264 – 265, 271, 274, 331 – 332, 338, 348, 407
Mayhew, Robert 11, 407
McCall, George 66
McCrea, Joel 139 – 140
McDermott, Tom 364
McDowell, John 227, 251 – 252
McGuiness, Jim 212
McOstrich, Darrell 369 – 370
Meet John Doe 179
Mellett, Lowell 185, 191 – 192, 194 – 195, 198, 229 – 230, 235, 246 – 247
Menjou, Adolphe 213, 218, 234, 255
Meroney, John 11
Metro-Goldwyn-Mayer (MGM) viii – ix, 8, 62, 67 – 68, 70 – 71, 73 – 76, 79 – 82, 84, 87 – 90, 92 – 94, 96, 100, 107 – 108, 112, 117, 120 – 125, 146, 153, 165, 169 – 170, 173, 184, 187, 190 – 194, 199, 201, 203, 207 – 208, 212 – 213, 219, 225, 229 – 230, 233, 237, 251, 259 – 262, 272, 285, 295, 297, 299 – 300,

310, 320, 322, 331 – 333, 337 – 342, 344, 348 ; MGM-British 100
Michigan: Detroit 45, 408
Millikan, Dr. Robert 144
Missouri: Kansas City 65, 104; Kirksville 4, 6, 9, 56
Mix, Tom 20, 72
Monsoon 320 – 321
Montana: Billings 147, 378
Montgomery, George 358, 399
Montgomery, Robert 198
Moratz, Ralph 11
Moore, Bill 10, 369
Moore, Harold 101 – 103
Moore, United States Commissioner W. H. 189
Mooring, Ivy Pearson 9, 268 – 270, 286 – 287, 290, 292 – 293, 295 – 297, 304, 306 – 307, 310 – 315, 317 – 320, 323, 325 – 326, 345 – 347, 361, 380, 386, 394, 405
Morgan, United States Commissioner Robert W. 188
Morley, Karen 244 – 245
Morris, Chester 84
Motion Picture Alliance for the Preservation of American Ideals (MPA) 211 – 221, 227, 234, 242, 255 – 256, 260
Multi-Vue TV 369 – 370, 377, 381
Mulvey, Kay 81
Mumford, Kathleen 36
Muni, Paul 144
Murder In The Fleet 85
Murphy, Audie 359
Murphy, Senator George 213, 283, 378
Murray McMurray Hatchery 333

Nachtwache 304
Naval Academy, United States 112
Navy Hour, The 204 – 205
Nebraska 10, 17, 22, 28, 54, 57, 65, 70, 75, 83, 86, 95 – 97, 102, 107, 114, 135, 158, 150, 164, 257, 337, 344 – 345, 364, 369, 382, 385

Index

Nebraska: Beatrice 10 – 12, 17, 19 – 21, 26, 29, 31 – 33, 35, 39, 41, 58, 65, 72 – 75, 77, 96 – 97, 109, 164, 344 – 345, 370, 378, 383, 385; Beatrice Junior High School 25, 27, 29; Beatrice Senior High School 20 – 21, 31 – 32, 39; Beatrice Public Schools 26; Clay Center 48 – 49, 52; Crete 29, 39, 41 – 42, 48; Filley 1 – 3, 5 – 6, 17 – 18, 385; Fremont 9 – 10; Grand Island 369 – 370, 377, 381; Kearney 370; Lincoln 21, 26 – 27, 29, 45, 51, 54, 65, 370; Nebraska City 83; Omaha 147, 370, 385
Nebraska Association of Osteopaths 11
Nebraska State Journal 9, 408
Nebraska State Penitentiary 28
Nebraska Wesleyan University 21
Neuhauser, Auntie 12 – 13
New Jersey 235: Trenton 154;
New York 27, 84, 88, 98, 104: New York City 88, 93
New York American 107
The New York Times 238, 285, 398, 406
Night Walker, The 361
Ninotchka 237
Niven, David 268 – 269
Nixon, Richard 251 – 253
Northwestern University 40 – 41, 43

O'Brien, Margaret 232
O'Brien, Pat 144, 234
Odlum, Floyd 168
Odlum, Jackie Cochran 169
Office of War Information, United States Government (OWI) 184 – 187, 191, 194, 196, 198 – 199, 202 – 203, 247
Oklahoma: Muskogee 6
Olivier, Laurence 172
Osborn, B. P. 26 – 27
O'Sullivan, Maureen 99
Other Love, The 224

Paddock Hotel 344 – 345

Paget, Debra 330
Palladium, The 148
Palomar, The 132
Paramount Pictures 169
Parker, Dorothy 154
Parker, Eleanor 315 – 316
Parmerter, Robert 10 – 11, 405
Parry Lodge 10
Parsons, Louella 137, 153, 287 – 288, 409
Party Girl 340 – 341
Pasadena Playhouse 71, 136
Pearson, Drew 231, 409
Pearson, Leonard 268 – 269
Pearson, Mike 269, 347
Peck, Gregory 271
Pellegrini-Stieda Disease 317
Pennsylvania 115
Pennsylvania: Bucks County 134; Holicong 154
Pennsylvania Dutch 2
Personal Property 105 – 106, 111 – 12, 114
Personality Parade 365, 409
Peters, Susan 194, 196, 200, 202, 246
Piazza, Ben 62
Pickford, Mary 179
Pidgeon, Walter 194, 399
Pomona College 57 – 58
Powell, Dick 269, 283, 351
Powell, Eleanor 98
Powell, William 104
Power, Tyrone 268
Poynter, Nelson 185 – 186, 194
Price of Peace, The 348
Procter & Gamble Company 348
Purchase Price, The 139

Queen Elizabeth 79, 87
Quentin Durward 330, 367
Quincy Work House 189
Quo Vadis 272, 274 – 277, 280, 299

RKO Studios 169, 304, 306
Radcliffe, Senator George L. 114

Radio City Music Hall 173
Ralph, Jessie 94
Rand, Ayn 198, 201, 407
Random House Publishers 54
Rathbone, Basil 156
Rathbone, Ouida 156
Ray the Pooh 312
Reagan, Nancy 15, 334 – 335, 378, 286, 397, 399, 407
Reagan, Patti 397
Reagan, Ronald 15, 156, 20, 213, 234, 251, 334 – 335, 358, 375 – 376, 378 – 379, 381, 398 – 399, 407
Red Salute 216
Reeves, Art 9, 18, 349 – 350, 355, 358, 393, 398, 405
Reeves, Barbara 10
Reid, Mr. and Mrs. 298
Reid, Tom 43 – 44, 46
Remember? 90, 153, 155
Return of the Gunfighter 379
Reynolds, Senator Robert R. 114
Riddle, Randy 10, 405
Ride, Vaquero 307
Riedesel, Laureen 10
Rippe, Rosemary 11, 405
Rivoli Theater 20, 28, 385
Robert Taylor Show, The 363
Robert Taylor's The Detectives 348
Robinson, Edward G. 144
Robinson, Justice of the Peace Russell 325
Rogers, Ginger 140, 201, 214, 218
Rogers, Howard Emmett 212, 234
Rogers, Lela 201, 215, 255
Rogers, Will 83
Roland, Gilbert 400
Rollo, Primula "Primmie" 268
Romeo and Juliet 367
Romero, Cesar 121
Rooney, Mickey 123, 136 – 137
Roosevelt, Eleanor 114
Roosevelt, President Franklin D. 112 – 113, 147, 183 – 186, 198, 214, 219, 222, 225, 234

Rorke, Hayden 361
Ross, Robert 59 – 61
Rotter, Robert 10
Rubin, J. Walter 124
Rush, Helen 30
Russia 182, 187, 193, 195, 225, 229, 237, 245, 254, 259
Russia aka *Scorched Earth* 191 – 196, 198 – 200, 202
Ruttenburg, Joseph 171

Santa Monica Airport 208
Schary, Dore 225, 260 – 266, 331 – 332
Schenk, Nicholas 184
Schmidt-Hut, Ursula 301 – 302
Scott, Brenda 373
Scott, Joseph 144
Scott, Walter 365, 409
Screen Actors Guild (SAG) 195, 243
Screen Writers Guild 217, 242
Sebree, Linda 10
Selznick, Daniel 11
Schumann-Henk, Ernestine 30
Shearer, Norma 79, 87, 89, 173, 367
Sherry, Bert 65
Shimerda, Anthony 17 – 18
Shimerda, Rose 17 – 18
Shirley, Anne 140
Show Boat 299
Sinatra, Nancy 297
Sindlar, Sue 10
Small Town Girl 90
Smith, Judge Phil 149
Society Doctor 84, 124
Sokolsky, George 201
Song of Russia 193, 198, 200, 202, 204, 216, 225, 227 – 230, 233, 235 – 238, 242, 245 – 247, 249, 251, 253, 264, 407
South Dakota: Black Hills 330; Custer State Park 331
St. John's Medical Center/Hospital 10, 356, 388, 391 – 391, 397
Stack, Robert 10, 327, 358, 400, 405

Index

Stalin, Joseph 182 – 183, 210
Standley, Admiral 237
Stanhope, Ethel 2
Stanhope, Father 2, 4
Stanhope and Brugh 2
Stanwyck, Barbara viii, xix, 8, 77, 88 – 89, 102 – 103, 127 – 162, 165, 167 – 170, 172, 174 – 175, 178 – 182, 190 – 192, 196, 199, 205, 208, 215 – 216, 218, 223 – 224, 234, 256 – 258, 269, 274, 278 – 279, 282, 285 – 291, 293, 297, 304 – 306, 310, 316, 320, 324, 327, 339, 343, 361 – 363, 389, 398, 400, 407; aka Stevens, Ruby 190; aka Mrs. Robert Taylor 146, 151, 190, 269
Stewart, James 82, 123, 406
Strickling, Howard 79, 87, 93, 95, 108, 122
Stripling, Robert 240 – 244, 246 – 251, 254
Summers, Debra 10

Taylor, Elizabeth 175, 258 – 260, 271, 407
Taylor, Ramsey 82
Taylor, Robert iii, vii, viii, ix, x, xv, xxi, xxii, 1, 5 – 7, 10, 19, 25, 27, 36, 40, 46, 60, 65, 67, 76 – 77, 79 – 93, 95 – 99, 101 – 102, 104 – 105, 107 – 108, 110, 112 – 113, 117 – 119, 121 – 122, 125, 127, 129, 132, 135, 138, 141, 143, 145 – 146, 148, 151, 155, 159, 163, 165 – 167, 170 – 172, 175 – 176, 179, 181, 187, 190, 192, 196, 201, 204, 206 – 207, 209, 213, 223, 229, 231, 233, 235, 238, 240, 242, 256, 258, 262, 264, 266, 268 – 269, 274 – 276, 279 – 280, 282, 285, 294, 300 – 303, 307, 310 – 311, 314, 317, 323 – 324, 326, 329, 331 – 332, 337, 339, 341 – 342, 344 – 348, 350, 354, 363, 365 – 367, 369, 378, 380, 388, 391, 395, 397 – 398, 401, 403; aka Bob Taylor 10, 13 – 14, 19, 87 – 88, 121 – 122, 134, 140, 142, 158, 181, 183, 198, 223 – 224, 226, 237 – 238, 257, 264, 266, 270, 272, 276, 278, 299, 306, 308, 311, 349, 368, 376; Robert Taylor Productions 339
Taylor, Terry 9, 14 – 15, 328, 343, 347, 352, 361, 366, 381, 389 – 390, 393 – 394, 399, 405
Taylor, Tessa 9, 14, 346 – 347, 352, 361, 366, 381 – 382, 389 – 392, 399, 405
Tcherina, Ludmila 308 – 311
Telesis Corporation of Indiana 369
Temple, Shirley 144
Texas 197; Corpus Christie 197; Dallas 130, 203, 383; San Antonio 383
Thailand: Bangkok 383
Thiess, George 301, 365
Thiess, Manuela 9, 20 – 21, 199, 227, 301, 322 – 325, 329, 343, 346 – 347, 357, 361, 365, 375, 377, 382, 389 – 390, 396, 398 – 399, 405
Thiess, Michael 301, 328, 343, 347, 364 – 365, 377, 389 – 390, 395 – 396
Thiess, Ursula ix, xv, xviii, xix – xxii, 301 – 304, 306 – 311, 314 – 316, 318 – 329, 333 – 335, 342 – 344, 346 – 347, 351 – 353, 357 – 362, 364 – 366, 368, 370, 375 – 376, 378 – 379, 381, 383 – 386, 388 – 389, 391, 393 – 401, 405; aka Mrs. Robert Taylor 326, 347
Thin Man, The 347
This Is My Affair 133
Thomas, J. Parnell 224, 228 – 229, 231, 234 – 235, 238 – 239
Thorpe, Richard 398
Times Square Lady 85
Today Show 385
Tracy, Spencer 137
Trocadero Nightclub 119, 338
Trojan Horse in America, The 210, 407
Truman, Harry 169
Turner, Lana 163, 175 – 177, 308, 406 – 407
Tuttle, Holmes P. 376
TV-Radio News 355
Twentieth Century Fox Studios 285

U. S. Borax and Chemical Corporation 380
University of Nebraska School of Music
    26 – 27, 29
Ursulor Productions 351
Ustinov, Peter 277
Utah 295: Kanab 307
VFW 256
Vail, Richard 251
Valentino, Rudolph 130, 205
Valley Fever 357, 386
Valley of the Kings 313 – 314, 316, 320
Van Dyke, Woody 107, 111 – 112
Vaudeville Kiddie Review 98
Victor Hugo's 150
Virginia: Alexandria 112;
    Mount Vernon 112

Wade Air Service 332, 338
Walpole, Hugh S. 1
Warner, Jack 222, 235 – 236
Warnock, Nancy 11
Washington Star 235
Waterloo Bridge 170 – 173
Wayne, Jane Ellen 11, 407
Wayne, Jeff 11
Wayne, John 210, 218, 251, 255, 349, 358,
Weinhardt, Beth 10
Welles, Orson 310
Wellington, Mr. and Mrs. 298
Wenkos, Paul 373
West Point of the Air 85
Western Air Express 81
Westerville Library 10

Westward the Women 295
Wexley, John 201 – 203
Whelan, Mr. and Mrs. Thomas 150
When Ladies Meet 179
Whitney, Eleanor 133
Wiebe, Gerhart "Garry" 26 – 28, 40 – 43,
    45 – 46, 53, 77 – 78, 95
Wilson, Kent 10
Winchester Rifles 383
Winnie-Poo 312
Winters, Shelley 398
Wolfe, Shirleen 11
Wood, Sam 211, 215, 234 – 236, 255, 260,
    266 – 267
Woods, Congressman John. S. 222
Wort, Jess 325
Wort, John 325
Wrigley Field 147
Writer's Guild of America 213
Wyler, William 139
Wyman, Jane 156
Wynn, Keenan 399
Wyoming 325, 342 – 343, 361, 364, 369 – 370
Wyoming: Big Horn Mountain 360; Cheyenne 97, 343; Jackson 11, 297; Jackson Lake 325; Laramie 58; Newcastle 343; Sheridan 332; Teton Mountains 325

Yates, Maurice 343
You and I 126
Young, Robert 216

Zimbalist, Sam 275 – 276

www.ingramcontent.com/pod-product-compliance
Lightning Source LLC
Chambersburg PA
CBHW050326230426
43663CB00010B/1751